Advance Praise for The Deposition Tutorial

The Deposition Tutorial is a superb, innovative, and much-needed contribution to the library of materials available to those teaching and learning the vital skills of deposition-taking and defending. Its particular strengths that distinguish it from all other primers on the topic include:

- The authors recognize, and adapt their tutorial methods to, the reality that almost no civil cases are taken to trial. Litigation is now "trial by deposition," which significantly affects the skills, methods, and strategies the modern deposition-taker must master.
- By use of a representative fictional case file threaded through the book, with a variety of illustrative examples of transcript excerpts, the tutorial takes the reader through an actual deposition. The result places the reader in a "real life" deposition setting.
- The format is equally useful as a self-taught tutorial for newer lawyers / refresher for experienced litigators as for a more traditional training program where instructors lead participants through exercises using the case file.
- The book is short and to the point—eminently as usable as a quick reference tool as for a complete deposition course of study.

Thomas Jay Leach & Cary A. Bricker,
Pacific McGeorge School of Law

Bocchino and Sonenshein continue their mastery of the importance of deposition use and strategy in this new and insightful book. In addition to asking and answering the questions that new (and sometimes not-so-new) lawyers and law students ask about traditional deposition practice, they have recognized that depositions have become the "new trial" experience, important for the purpose of persuading opposing clients, their attorneys and "neutrals" that pretrial disposition is an alternative that is better than a trial to a jury or an ADR panel. This should be required reading for all "litigators" not just trial lawyers.

Laurence M. Rose
Professor Emeritus and Director of the Litigation Skills Program
University of Miami
President of NITA (2006-2010)

Depositions aren't what they used to be, as the very nature of litigation has been transformed in the age of the "vanishing trial." Bocchino and Sonenshein have perfectly captured the ways that deposition practice must be adapted for the new environment, making The Deposition Tutorial a must-read for every twenty-first century lawyer.

Steven Lubet
Williams Memorial Professor
Director, Bartlit Center for Trial Advocacy
Northwestern Pritzker School of Law

The modern deposition is not one destined for use at trial; the odds are it will be the tool for summary judgment or some form of alternative dispute resolution process. Lawyers must rethink deposition practice to accommodate this reality. In THE DEPOSITION TUTORIAL, David Sonenshein and Tony Bocchino—masters of the law of Evidence, of Civil Procedure, of civil litigation, and of trial advocacy—teach the art and skill of the modern deposition, supplementing insight and analysis with examples derived from a model case file. What at first seems counterintuitive—e.g., disclosing your case when you "defend" a deposition—is just one of the invaluable insights this text offers.

Professor Jules Epstein
Director of Advocacy Programs
Temple Beasley School of Law

Tony Bocchino and David Sonenshein have written a wonderfully accessible book. It's perfect for a law school class, in-house training, or a lawyer wanting to learn to take depositions as they should be taken in a world where almost every case resolves before trial. I will be recommending it to every early career litigator I know—and to more than a few older ones.

Donald Beskind
Professor of Law
Duke University

Seldom does there come along a book that can help you transform the way you take and defend depositions. THE DEPOSITION TUTORIAL is such a book.

The authors incorporate insights from modern practice into a more efficient and effective strategy that can help you pin down your opposing deponent, test your theories, and produce damning admissions. They show you how to mine electronic discovery and social media to prepare yourself for the most important points of discovery and attack. They give real world and specific examples of the most effective questioning techniques for setting up dispositive motions in your favor.

This book will also help you prepare your witnesses to present their best facts, see your opponents' attacks before they are sprung and avoid the mistakes and falling victim to "gotchas" that your opponent might have at their disposal. Again the authors provide specific and real world techniques for witness preparation that will help your witnesses stay in control and best manage their telling of their good facts, and at the same time, will provide them the means for avoiding their volunteering of bad facts that the opponent likely has yet to discover.

The authors' expertise in evidence and civil procedure, remind you and explain the important legal provisions to help you deal both with difficult opponents, but also prepare you for any legal issues that arises from your depositions that make their way to the court.

Paul Zwier
Professor of Law
Emory University School of Law

The Deposition Tutorial: Questions, Answers, Tactics, Demonstrations

The Deposition Tutorial: Questions, Answers, Tactics, Demonstrations

Anthony J. Bocchino

Feinberg Professor of Litigation Emeritus
Temple University Beasley School of Law

David A. Sonenshein

Feinberg Professor of Litigation Emeritus
Temple University Beasley School of Law

NITA®

Address inquiries to:
Reprint Permission
National Institute for Trial Advocacy
1685 38th Street, Suite 200
Boulder, CO 80301-2735
Phone: (800) 225-6482
Fax: (720) 890-7069
Email: permissions@nita.org

ISBN 978-1-60156-791-8
eISBN 978-1-60156-792-5
FBA1791

Library of Congress Cataloging-in-Publication Data

Names: Bocchino, Anthony J., author. | Sonenshein, David A., author.
Title: The deposition tutorial : questions, answers, tactics, demonstrations / Anthony J. Bocchino, Feinberg Professor of Litigation Emeritus, Temple University Beasley School of Law; David A. Sonenshein, Feinberg Professor of Litigation Emeritus, Temple University Beasley School of Law.
Description: Boulder, CO : National Institute for Trial Advocacy, [2018].
Identifiers: LCCN 2018033322 (print) | LCCN 2018034014 (ebook) | ISBN 9781601567925 (ebook) | ISBN 9781601567918
Subjects: LCSH: Depositions--United States--Miscellanea. | Evidence (Law)--United States--Miscellanea. | Trial practice--United States--Miscellanea.
Classification: LCC KF8900 (ebook) | LCC KF8900 .B579 2018 (print) | DDC 347.73/6--dc23
LC record available at https://lccn.loc.gov/2018033322

ASPEN PUBLISHING

Official co-publisher of NITA.
aspenpublishing.com/NITA

Dedication

To Lynn, my life's love, Chrissy and Mike and Jennica and Jacob
Anthony Bocchino

To Jennifer, Emily, and Peter
David Sonenshein

Contents

Foreword

Of all the skills of the civil litigator, the first undertaken outside legal research and away from the computer is taking and defending depositions. The authors have been working in their own practices since 1972 and teaching and writing about those skills since the early 1980s. As young lawyers, we learned and developed our skills the old-fashioned way. At that time, law schools maintained that skills could not be taught—that their acquisition was for the practice of law. So, we watched some senior lawyers, we read transcripts of others, and we learned through trial and error in our representation of clients—what we describe as our craft.

Our experience was typical of our generation. But as law schools ventured into the world of skills training and embraced simulation pedagogy—first in appellate advocacy (through moot court), followed by trial advocacy, interviewing, counseling and negotiation—the obvious conclusion was that skills could be taught, and the "no harm" simulation methodology was designed to provide skills training outside the practice of law, where no one went to jail and no dollars were exchanged.

In the early 1970s, the National Institute for Trial Advocacy was formed with the express purpose of teaching trial advocacy skills to young lawyers by utilizing learning pedagogy (simulation). Eventually, we adapted these skills for use in deposition training. We benefited from being part of that revolution in lawyer education. In some 1,000 programs for practicing lawyers in public, private, and institutional practice we developed—initially on our own[1] and then in conjunction with the greatest and most talented assembly of advocacy instructors, the faculty of the National Institute for Trial Advocacy—discrete programs focusing on the nuances of deposition practice.

We gained insight into what young lawyers think they know about depositions, what they admit to not knowing, what they don't know but won't admit to, and what never occurred to them but is necessary for competent deposition representation. This volume will identify those questions, provide specific responses, and then use simulated deposition transcripts[2] to show how to execute the skill set necessary for modern practice.

1. In programs, utilizing materials designed for the Washington, DC, law firm of Steptoe and Johnson.

2. All of the examples will be based on a trial simulation, Bocchino & Sonenshein, *Williams v. Simonson, et al.*, 2nd Ed. (National Institute for Trial Advocacy, 2017). We use one file so that the interrelationships of depositions from one section to another and from one witness to another can easily be understood. The case involves a claim of gender discrimination, but the demonstrations are in no way apply solely to that practice. They are generic in that the plaintiff claims injury and the defendants deny responsibility.

This is not a treatise, nor a text. Such volumes exist, and we recommend them.[3] This is a volume for quick answers to typical questions and easy-to-follow demonstrations. Read cover to cover, it provides a functional overview of current deposition practice and can support a deposition skills program or course, but that is not its specific design. It will, however, be very helpful in demonstrating how to implement the questioning strategies advised by the text book writers, and it is with that limited, but significant purpose that we offer this volume.

3. The oldest and most comprehensive text on the topic is Malone, Hoffman, and Bocchino (contributing author), The Effective Deposition: Techniques and Strategies That Work, 4th Ed. (NITA 2012). The newest entrant to the genre is Bocchino & Sonenshein, The Modern Deposition, Amazon, 2017.

Acknowledgments

Professors Bocchino and Sonenshein acknowledge former Dean (now University Provost) JoAnne Epps and current Dean Gregory Mandel of the Temple University Beasley School of Law for research grants and other support provided for this project. We are also grateful to the generations of law students and lawyers who asked the questions and informed the answers that appear in this volume. The authors are extremely grateful to Virginia Judd, JD, of NITA for her editorial and substantive improvements to our product. Her work was superbly performed with great humor and patience. We believe she has helped us to reach a new audience.

INTRODUCTION

THE MODERN DEPOSITION PARADIGM

In the 21st Century, there are virtually no civil jury trials. Despite that fact, we still execute depositions as if the case was going to trial. The reality is that the vast majority civil cases are disposed of in motion practice, negotiations, or some other alternative dispute resolution (ADR). It is time to adopt a new paradigm for deposition practice, designed to fulfill modern case disposition needs. We wrote this book is to describe that paradigm and explain how to execute it.

We have chosen a question and answer format, assuming the authors are senior and experienced litigators speaking to fourth- and fifth-year lawyers who are about to be assigned cases for which they will have the responsibility of taking and defending deposition. But why should you accept our assertion you should conceptualize and execute deposition practice in a different way? Consider our description of modern litigation and the resulting vanishing jury trial, and see if it doesn't match yours.

VANISHING JURY TRIALS

To begin, it's a matter of numbers. The courts are not staffed at a level sufficient to handle modern civil litigation through the trial process. More and more modern, technology-enabled courtrooms are needed. And there aren't enough judges.[4] A "speedy" civil trial is unlikely. And yet, conflicts have not decreased. There are more people, and more people mean more lawsuits.

We also live in an increasingly technical and regulated world. Complex and technical systems are difficult to explain and understand. Lawyers rely more on expert witnesses, with their attendant costs, not only for describing and explaining the things about which they litigate, but also to create case theories on which their clients can prevail. Adding to the costs, the courts must scrutinize these experts and their testimony to assure sufficient reliability for juror consumption and consideration.[5]

Our complex and technical world has the ability and the inclination to create abundant records. It seems for every action, decision, or conversation there is a record someplace. And we are no longer just talking about the formal record; we also need to examine references to the topic in email, text, or on Facebook or some

4. The political process exacerbates this shortfall, and the number of open judicial positions unfilled for some reason other than merit is huge.

5. *Daubert* hearings are so commonplace that many pretrial orders provide for them in the sequence of litigation leading to case disposal.

other social media. The hours of trial time and cost to present those records is daunting, if not overwhelming.

Even popular opinion is against civil jury trials. Some claim, without empirical evidence, that jurors are unreliable. Often-sued organizations invoke the specter of the runaway jury so frequently that many people believe them to be the norm. They also claim that jurors are called on to make decisions about the technical topics beyond their ken.[6] People assume that removing jurors, inexperienced in litigation, from the process will result in lower judgments.[7]

Finally, jury trials are expensive. Experts (often billing portal to portal), computer animations and graphics, and attorney's fees all contribute to the economics of even staging a trial.

As should be apparent, proceeding to and through a trial by jury is time consuming, viewed as risky, and expensive. No wonder there are so few; in fact, jurors hear less than 2–3 percent of filed civil cases.

Modern Case Disposition

Nonetheless, civil disputes occur, civil litigation ensues, and resolutions are reached. How does that occur?

Many cases do not reach the point where trial can even be contemplated, but depositions are critical in all but the first of the following disposition devices.

- Many cases do not survive the increased fact pleading requirements in the federal courts.[8]
- Discovery makes it clear that the plaintiff cannot prevail, and cases are voluntarily dismissed.
- Discovery makes it clear that the defendant has no legitimate defense to plaintiff's claims, and the case is settled.
- In cases where expert witness testimony is necessary for a party to prevail, a court either excludes or approves the expert testimony, and the case settles.

---

6. We believe this argument is overbroad. The ken of jurors in a trial depends on the skill of the trial lawyer in translating and teaching the technical (through expert witnesses, computer-generated exhibits, just plain speaking, etc.). Every day, jurors correctly decide about medical, legal, and economic matters both in determining professional liability and evaluating the costs and value of damages.

7. As one might surmise, we reject the notion of jury unreliability, but necessarily accept that that the belief in the unpredictability of juries has dramatically increased the number of cases resolved by means other than trial by jury.

8. Ashcroft v. Iqbal, 556 U.S. 662 (2009), Bell Atlantic Corp. v. Twombly, 550 U.S. 544 (2007).

- In response to motions in limine, critical evidence for either party is ruled admissible or inadmissible, and the case is dismissed or settled.
- Once discovery is complete, the parties file motions for summary judgment, and the ruling fully or partially dismisses a claim or defense; based on that ruling, the case is dismissed or settled.

In the new millennia's second decade, most cases are disposed through some form of ADR. The most typical, negotiation between or among the parties, has already been mentioned. Many parties who are not amenable to settlement based on counsel's negotiations are more likely to settle when their cases face ADR involving the intercession of a neutral third party: a mediator or arbitrator.

Mediators and arbitrators are also less likely (or so the argument goes) to be impacted by emotional responses to matters raised by lawsuits (e.g., bias for or prejudice against any party)—the "runaway arbitrator" is not a known phenomenon. They are certainly more efficient. ADR providers typically come from one of two backgrounds: the retired judiciary or experienced litigators.[9] They bring with them their experience, which may work for good or ill. In other words, *you*—and your peers—are these so-called neutral ADR providers.

Former lawyer ADR providers bring with them biases from their previous profession. Few former litigator did not specialize predominantly as either a plaintiff or defendant representative. Former judge ADR providers also bring their experience, and as a result, they are more likely to view each individual matter for disposition "just like the hundreds I tried as a judge," making it more difficult you to make the judge ADR provider appreciate the nuances of your client's cause. Finally, ADR service providers are growing in number and becoming more competitive. Anecdotal evidence suggests that if a party is likely to create more business for the ADR provider, that party's cause may be viewed more favorably.

The Modern Deposition Paradigm

View the modern deposition through the lens of its ultimate use. Unlike in the past—where every deposition was taken assuming that the case would be decided by jurors and depositions were conducted with that end alone in mind—there is no single method for conducting the modern deposition. Different case-dispositive devices require different information in different forms. That being said, because ADR (including negotiation) is the most likely way in which your case will be decided, your deposition is not complete unless and until you have developed the information necessary for that ADR result to be in your client's favor.

9. There are no hard demographics published about ADR providers generally. Anecdotal evidence from numerous sources suggests that ADR providers are older, more male, and more Caucasian, which may bring its own set of preconceptions.

What are the characteristics of your next deposition?

- It will typically be shorter (because information is available from other sources)[10] and more focused, especially where the end game is case-dispositive motion practice; in all cases your clients are interested in reducing litigation expense.
- It will likely be the only time (because there will be no trial) that you have to reveal the facts that damage your opponent's case theory—and benefit your client's—*and* show that the opposing party and witnesses are not credible.
- It will likely be the only time (because there will be no trial) that you will be able to present your witnesses (who are being deposed) in their most persuasive manner, even as they provide all the information that supports your case theory and does damage to the opposing party.
- It will be audio or video recorded and available for use by parties in case evaluation, courts in legal decision making and case disposition, and—eventually and most likely—by ADR (to persuade a mediator or arbitrator or even the party decision maker in the negotiation).

The modern deposition paradigm requires new strategies and skills. As we look at those, we will remind you about the skills and tactics you already possess and have practiced for many years. The modern deposition assumes those classic deposition skills are already in the litigator's arsenal. But the paradigm has changed based on the reality that there will be no trial, and depositions must move from discovery to persuasion.[11]

The Design of this Book

Abstract theory is always clearer when demonstrated with concrete example. Therefore, we will explore all the potential uses of deposition in litigation through examples from a single simulated case file, *Williams v. Simonson, et al.*[12] A brief

10. Internet and increased documentation.

11. Throughout this volume, when referring to a lawyer we will use the feminine pronoun (except for Williams and Jefferson in our hypothetical case for examples); all other actors will be referred to using the masculine pronoun. This is for ease of writing and by no means suggests that all lawyers must be women and all witnesses and judges must be men. Nonetheless, we expect most people will not read this footnotes, and someone will write to complain that there are no male lawyers and no female expert witnesses in our book. We apologize in advance for any ruffled sensibilities.

12. This case file was written by the authors of this book and is published by NITA. It is available in various formats to use in litigation skills practice, including trial advocacy, depositions, and motion.

description of the facts at issue in that file follows to provide context for those examples. We set them up in this separate introduction so you can easily refer back to the facts as you read this book.

In *Williams,* Mary Anne Williams has sued Professor David Simonson; Nita University and its School of Public Policy; the school's dean, Christine Jefferson; and the Patterson Institute of Public Policy. She alleges gender discrimination. Ms. Williams claims that despite having met all the requirements set out in university regulations, she was denied tenure at the Nita University School of Public Policy. She claims this denial was in retaliation for ending a consensual sexual relationship with Professor Simonson of the School of Public Policy, who also was her supervisor at the Patterson Institute. She also claims that Nita University created and tolerated a hostile work environment at the School of Public Policy and that the university discriminated generally against women in tenure and promotion decisions by granting tenure to men who were less qualified than women applicants for tenured faculty positions.

Ms. Williams (then, Associate Professor Williams) received a split, but positive, vote for tenure from the School of Public Policy's tenured faculty. She was nonetheless denied tenure by Dean Jefferson. The university claims that Williams was not qualified for tenure and that Dean Jefferson determined that her tenure was not "in the long-term best interests of the university." The dean claims that her decision to deny tenure was required by university regulations because she determined that the plaintiff was not collegial in her dealings with members of the Public Policy School and other members of the university community.

Ms. Williams also claims that after her tenure denial, she was defamed by Professor Simonson and Dean Jefferson when they were asked for recommendations by various universities to which Ms. Williams applied for teaching positions. Simonson and Jefferson deny those claims, saying the representations made by them concerning the plaintiff's qualifications were true.

Professor Simonson counterclaims against Ms. Williams for slander, based on statements Simonson made to university community members and others.

It is not necessary to purchase that case file for use with this book, unless this book is being used in a law school or CLE course where course members are assigned to perform the skills described herein.

Chapter One

The Multiple Uses of Depositions in Litigation

1. I know that the primary purpose for taking depositions is to gather information, but what are the other typical deposition uses in the litigation process?

That's a great first question, which unfortunately requires a lengthy response. In modern civil practice, most civil litigations never reach trial. Instead, the parties engage in alternate dispute resolution, reach a settlement, or come to some other pretrial disposition, such as summary judgment; although there remains a small potential that there will actually be a trial, depositions are no longer focused primarily on the courtroom. Whatever the eventual case disposition, you are right—when taking and defending depositions, counsel must perform the basic discovery tasks of information gathering to protect the client from surprise at a later proceeding. At the same time, recognize the deposition as a persuasive tool for other forms of case disposition. Understanding those uses is an excellent starting point for properly understanding and developing the necessary skills for taking and defending the deposition. By reverse engineering from the deposition's end use, we will learn about their scope and content and how to prepare for their taking, defending, and execution.

Depositions must be understood in context. They inform the facts and law of the case and provide bases for other steps to be taken in litigation. Those steps include:

1) terminating the litigation by settlement or otherwise;
2) conducting further discovery;
3) case dispositive or case limiting motions;
4) filing pretrial motions regarding admissibility of evidence;
5) preparing for the examination of witnesses at trial; and
6) using the deposition as evidence in trial or other proceeding.

2. How can a deposition be used to modify or terminate litigation?

In some cases, taking depositions—together with other discovery—can spell the end of the litigation. After all, it may be that the facts necessary to support a winning case theory simply do not exist. In that instance, the proper next step is to terminate the case by taking voluntary dismissal, thereby saving your time and your client's money.

Example: In our hypothetical case, deposition testimony might make it clear that the defendant's counterclaim for slander has no factual support because there are no witnesses who believed the statements allegedly made by the plaintiff about Professor Simonson. As a result, there was no damage to his reputation or otherwise that supports continuing his counterclaim. The counterclaim should be the subject of a voluntary dismissal.

Similarly, deposition testimony may support going forward on some potential claims or defenses while discarding others, resulting in streamlining the remaining litigation.

Example: Again, from our hypothetical, the deposition testimony may contradict the plaintiff's assertion that men less qualified than the plaintiff were granted tenure; that is, the testimony may show that the men tenured after the plaintiff was denied tenure all had credentials at least as meritorious as the plaintiff. In that circumstance, the plaintiff should dismiss her general discrimination claim while keeping alive her quid pro quo discrimination claim based on retaliation for ending her relationship with Simonson as well as the discrimination claim based on hostile work environment.

And finally, the information obtained in depositions may cause the litigator to amend pleadings to add claims or defenses.

Example: Deposition testimony may develop facts that suggest that Ms. Williams was denied tenure based on the exercise of her First Amendment rights to free speech, which were characterized by Dean Jefferson as "lack of collegiality." In that case, the plaintiff's complaint can be amended to reflect that claim.

Effective discovery depositions (taken together with all other discovery), often result in parties envisioning a fair outcome of the case and thus pursuing meaningful alternatives to litigation. Once all parties understand the facts, settling is much more likely—the best result of the proceedings. In more contentious circumstances, especially when the client does not see, with the clarity of counsel, the appropriate resolution of the case, the parties may decide to use ADR resolve the case.

3. You said that many cases are disposed of through ADR—how are depositions used in ADR?

There are four typical forms of ADR. Let's consider them one at a time and how depositions affect their operation:

a. Minitrials

This ADR incorporates many aspects of trial without the full-blown procedure. The parties jointly retain a former judge, a panel of former judges,[1] or a former judge and mock jurors drawn from a panel similar to the one that would decide the case at trial. These factfinders hear a truncated trial. Typically, both parties present opening statements, examine and cross-examine a limited number of witnesses (usually the main factual witness for each party and a summary expert witness for each party, with a narrowed scope of relevant evidence), and present closing arguments. In addition, deposition testimony can be published to the factfinder, either by reading selected transcripts or by showing selected portions of recorded depositions. Parties can present these either as independent offers of information or as part of the opening statements, witness examinations, and closing arguments.

In addition to the hired judge, panel of judges, or judge/jurors, these proceedings are usually observed by the decision makers for each party.[2] This allows the decision makers to fully appreciate the case—including the relative strengths and weaknesses of the parties' positions—as it would play out to a jury. They then hear feedback from the judge, judges, or jurors on their perception of the case and an appropriate resolution of the issues. The parties use this information and feedback to decide how to resolve the case.[3] Actual deposition testimony about the facts, as opposed to mere argument by counsel, conveys a nuanced view of the case, making the

1. We are speaking here about trial-level decision making. Businesses exist aside from all-purpose ADR firms that offer the exclusive view of judges on a particular matter. These entities will frequently be retained when the matter under consideration involves an issue of appellate law. In that case, the parties can obtain an unofficial, but well-educated view of the likely appellate outcome and make appropriate decisions on how to resolve a matter without the necessity of appeal. These "judicial" ADR panels work well in a case where the litigation has been conducted with an eye toward summary judgment as the end-game. Summary judgment has been ruled on and the matter is on appeal.

2. This is very common in commercial litigation, where often the decision maker was not actually involved in the conflict underlying the case. For such a person, frequently the president of a company or a member of a board of directors, the mini-trail is often their first view of the real contentions of the opposing parties in such a proceeding. This frequently makes a resolution without further proceedings more likely.

3. The alternative exists, of course, that despite the added information of the mini-trial, the parties still cannot agree on an outcome and the matter can go to another form of ADR or to trial.

process as realistic—and useful—as possible as well as leading to more effective and persuasive presentation.

A minitrial is the most expensive form of ADR, however. Instead, developing a case in discovery can provide the necessary information to help a mediator guide the parties to settlement or for arbitrator(s) to reach a fair conclusion in the case.

b. Binding Arbitration[4]

This ADR device can take several forms. The parties can agree on one arbitrator to decide the case. Alternatively, the parties can each select an arbitrator and then agree on a third arbitrator; another scenario allows the two party-selected arbitrators to select that third person.

Most arbitrations begin with written or video submissions of the case facts followed by conclusions proposed by the parties. Those facts should include significant information gleaned from well-conducted depositions. The arbitrator(s) then hear the respective positions from both parties and ask questions to clarify the issues. The process can provide an opportunity to present some live testimony, but in general the number of witnesses and duration of testimony is limited. Following the factual presentation, the parties usually present summations. The panel then decides the case from the information presented and counsel's arguments. The resolution is final.

This form of resolution, although final, is an even less formal and more truncated version of actual trial than the minitrial. Depositions are a primary information source in both, filtered

4. There is some confusion about the title of these decision makers. Some define mediators as people who assist the parties to come to a conclusion (they are facilitators), while arbitrators are decision makers. In other jurisdictions, these same people are called nonbinding versus binding mediators. What is intended in this description is a person or group of people who will make decisions that conclude the case. These professional decision makers may be individuals who make their availability commercially known or work for an entity formed to provide mediators and arbitrators to litigants. For our purposes, we will denominate the facilitators as mediators and the decision makers as arbitrators.

through written submissions (settlement memoranda) and the presentation of testimony and exhibits to the arbitrator(s). Video recorded depositions are of particular value—both in prehearing submissions and at the arbitration session—because they convey not only the facts, but also the witness's demeanor, which has additional persuasive value. As a result, counsel possesses a richer factual information set for the arbitrator, significantly impacting the case outcome.

c. Mediation[5]

Mediation is nonbinding and helps resolve lawsuits by using a neutral mediator to act as the go-between for the parties. This mediator helps the parties resolve a dispute. He explores the case's strengths and weaknesses, informing the parties of all the facts and law and making the client more comfortable with settlement. In this form of ADR, the parties typically agree on a person (usually a retired judge or experienced litigator) to act as the mediator.[6] The parties then provide written or video submissions of the case facts, informed in large part by deposition testimony. This testimony can take the form of deposition transcripts in written or audio-visual form; a video presentation with testimony (created from depositions or solely for presentation purposes); and other material, including graphic displays and exhibits. The mediator, after having reviewed the premediation submissions, usually meets with all the parties to get a sense of where they are on the road to resolution. He then separates the parties, speaks with the parties privately, and then acts as a go-between, helping the parties reach a conclusion to the case.

5. Again, nomenclature can vary from place to place. The ADR person used may be called either a mediator or an arbitrator, but in mediation, as we define it, the mediator is facilitator of settlement, not the decision maker.

6. These people are either individual entrepreneurs or aggregated in larger businesses. Although the mediator is usually a former lawyer or judge, there are very successful mediators who do not have a law degree, but rather are professionals from another discipline, typically psychology.

During this process, the mediator will frequently express opinions on the case's strengths and weaknesses and will often suggest an appropriate settlement amount. At the least, the mediation session provides parties neutral information and closes the settlement gap between the parties. At best, the mediator, using the facts presented from the depositions and other discovery materials in the case, brokers a final resolution.

Mediation is the ADR likely to be used in our hypothetical case. The mediator, after viewing the party submissions, can make frank observations about the facts and their delivery. He can also talk about nonmonetary factors, like public relations issues for the university and privacy issues for the plaintiff, to help the parties reach a conclusion to the case.

d. Party Negotiation

In this, the least formal, most typical, and first to be utilized ADR, the parties exchange offers and demands through counsel to settle the case. Deposition testimony lends perspective to decision-making parties and may lead them to be less strident in their relative positions. For example, a fact that a party thought was significant and unimpeachable before discovery may have been shown to be either insignificant when contextualized or simply untrue during depositions. After viewing the demeanor of a primary witness for a party, the case decision maker (e.g., business owner, insurance adjuster) may change the valuation of the case (either higher or lower). Depositions also provide ammunition for a lawyer—who should have a more dispassionate view about the case merits than the client—to persuade her client that settlement is the proper resolution, rather than paying for the expense of trial and subjecting the resolution to the uncertainty of the jurors' verdict. Negotiations occur throughout the lawsuit, and settlement is not uncommon after party depositions—where not only the opponent's version of the facts, but their manner and credibility in delivering those facts can be influential in reaching an appropriate accord.

Example: in our hypothetical case, if the plaintiff, Williams, appears and testifies in too strident and argumentative a manner, and/or the defendant, Simonson, appears arrogant and unable to relate to the ordinary people who serve as jurors, such information, as a portent of trial (particularly if captured by a videographer) can facilitate resolution of the lawsuit.

So you see, then, deposition testimony is at the heart of all ADR and serves two main functions. First, the facts learned at deposition—and the parties' reactions to those facts—suggest not only the appropriate litigation resolution, but also the proper nonjudicial decision making or settlement-assisting techniques. Second, mediators and arbitrators use deposition testimony to learn and understand not only the case facts, but often the way jurors would likely view the demeanor of the witnesses. In virtually all ADR, deposition testimony, along with documents identified and authenticated during depositions, form the factual predicate for the position of the parties as presented to the ADR facilitators. Depositions are frequently read (or preferably viewed) in toto, but most certainly are quoted and made reference to in the submissions made by the parties. In this regard, video depositions of parties and expert witnesses effectively convey the case facts. And because of their visual nature, they also help the ADR facilitators judge the credibility of these witnesses, based on the witnesses' demeanor not available from a written transcript.

4. Do depositions impact litigation, other than in ultimate decision making?

Of course. Deposing a principal party may lead to further discovery. The deposition may disclose additional people with information relevant to the litigation, identify documents, and describe physical evidence. This new information can lead to informal discovery, such as witness interviews and agreed-upon exchanges of information. It may also lead the parties to take further depositions; make additional document requests;[7] make requests for production, inspection, and/or testing of physical evidence;[8] file interrogatories;[9] or make requests for stipulations or admissions.[10]

Example: Several examples using our hypothetical gender discrimination case may be helpful. During the plaintiff's deposition—and in response to questioning regarding her defamation claim—she might list professors at other universities who told her about

7. Fed. R. Civ. P. 34.

8. Fed. R. Civ. P. 34, 35.

9. Fed. R. Civ. P. 33.

10. Fed. R. Civ. P. 36.

the content of letters sent to those universities by the defendants Jefferson and Simonson as well as the effect those letters had on hiring committee decisions. As a result, counsel for the defendant may want to seek the names, addresses, and phone numbers of those potential witnesses as supplemental mandatory disclosures under Fed. R. Civ. P. 26. Having obtained that information, the defendant may then depose those other professors.

By way of further example, defendant Dean Jefferson may state during her deposition that she kept notes of the comments the faculty made during the meeting about Professor Williams's tenure. Plaintiff's counsel would request those notes during the deposition, but to ensure the right to receive them, she should file a motion for document production.[11]

Finally, in the plaintiff's deposition and in response to questioning concerning her damages, Professor Williams might state that she has ongoing depression problems for which she is being treated by a psychiatrist. That testimony would lead to a request to produce the medical records of the psychiatric treatment as well as a request that the plaintiff undergo a defense psychiatric examination.[12]

In fact, it would be an unusual deposition that did not lead to some additional discovery practice. In addition, during discovery—and after its completion—significant motion practice will have important effects on the litigation. Deposition testimony is crucial to that motion practice

5. You mentioned earlier that a typical conclusion for a litigation a case-dispositive motion; how do depositions figure into that motion practice?

The information gathering process may reveal that the parties do not differ on the existence of significant facts. The case, then, may well be ripe for a Rule 56 summary judgment motion.[13] Increasingly, summary judgment is the end game of the litigation. The parties use discovery, especially deposition testimony (the form of which we discuss later) to demonstrate the lack (or existence) of a material issue of fact. If summary judgment is denied, settlement is often the next step.

Example: Our hypothetical case is one such case. If the plaintiff's claim (or defendant Simonson's counterclaim) survive summary judgment, it is in the best interests of both parties to dispose of the case without trial. More important than the trial expense, the university must preserve whatever good reputation it has for promoting and encouraging women on its faculty. Williams would prefer no further publicity of her claims, as in the real world being labeled (albeit questionable legally) as one who challenges her academic

11. Fed. R. Civ. P. 34.
12. Fed. R. Civ. P. 35.
13. Fed. R. Civ. P. 56.

employers will not be an asset in obtaining future academic positions. Some sort of ADR with reciprocal confidentiality agreements would seem the likely end game.

If summary judgment is granted and the losing party seeks appellate review, whether an issue of material fact exists is front and center. Determining whether a material issue of fact exists for jurors to decide will rely, in the main, on deposition testimony and exhibits produced during discovery.

As every modern litigator knows, summary judgment is an increasingly successful way to dispose of cases without trial. As the law of summary judgment has developed, deposition testimony has taken on new importance. Beginning with the U.S. Supreme Court trilogy of *Celotex Corp. v. Catrett,*[14] *Anderson v. Liberty Lobby,*[15] and *Matsushita Elec. Indus. Co v. Zenith Radio Corp.*,[16] district judges were encouraged to consider summary judgment as the proper conclusion of a case.

Celotex made it easier for federal courts to find the absence of issues of material fact by clarifying earlier cases that had been taken to suggest that it was incumbent on the defendant to anticipate legal claims of the plaintiff and disprove them before summary judgment should be granted. Instead, *Celotex* ruled that the defendant need only address the theories presented by the plaintiff, and not any unstated but anticipated theories.[17] *Anderson* required that when determining whether there existed a genuine issue of material fact, the court must determine whether a reasonable juror, applying the burden of proof incumbent on the plaintiff, would be able to find for the nonmoving party.[18] And in *Matsushita*, the Court ruled that courts must consider the plausibility of the nonmoving party's claim, as compared to position of the moving party on the same issue, when determining whether a genuine issue of material fact exists for jurors to decide.[19]

The net effect of the 1986 summary judgment trilogy of cases, and the later pleading cases *Iqbal*[20] and *Twombly,*[21] has been that district courts must do more than just view the facts in the light most favorable to the nonmoving party. The courts are now called on to consider the weight of the evidence when making such determinations as the nonmovant's ability to meet a required burden of proof and the plausibility of

14. Celotex Corp. v. Catrett, 477 U.S. 477 (1986).

15. Anderson v. Liberty Lobby, Inc., 477 U.S. 242 (1986).

16. Matsushita Elec. Indus. Co. v. Zenith Radio Corp., 475 U.S. 754 (1986).

17. Celtotex, 477 U.S. 477 (1986).

18. In *Anderson*, a libel case, the burden of proof on the public figure plaintiff on the issue of actual malice was plain clear and convincing evidence. *Anderson,* 477 U.S. 242 (1986).

19. In *Matsushita*, the Supreme Court determined that the district court must find the plaintiff's economic theory plausible in light of the economic theory of the defendant and required that if the plaintiff's theory was less plausible, that greater proof of its viability is required to avoid summary judgment. *Matsushita,* 475 U.S. 754 (1986). For recent application of this principle, see Anderson News LLC v. American Media, 2nd Cir. DKT. # 15-2714, August 6, 2018.

20. Ashcroft v. Iqbal, 556 U.S. 662 (2009).

21. Bell Atlantic Corp. v. Twombly, 550 U.S. 544 (2007).

its claim.[21a] In modern deposition practice, then, if you anticipate facing a motion for summary judgment, be certain that the depositions you defend reveal enough favorable information to overcome the heightened burden of showing facts in dispute—particularly where the deponent may not be available to later supply a counter-affidavit. With summary judgment decisions now being made on the weight of the evidence on relevant issues, the credibility of the information providers becomes part of the equation.

In a complicated case, summary judgment can be an excellent tool for streamlining the issues in dispute. Particular claims may be disposed of on summary judgment even if others remain for trial.[22]

Example: With respect to the plaintiff's defamation claim in our hypothetical case, the evidence might show that the defendants' only statements made about Williams and her professional qualifications were in response to inquiries from prospective employers. In that circumstance, the defendants could seek summary judgment of the plaintiff's defamation claim based on a qualified privilege and an allegation that there is no evidence of actual malice on the part of the defendants. In making that determination, the depositions of both the defendants would be critical, as their state of mind in making the recommendations would be critical in determining whether they intended to harm the plaintiff—as opposed to providing information regarding potential employment, which is covered by the qualified privilege. In determining whether a genuine issue of fact regarding the defendants' motives (i.e., state of mind) exists, it would be critical for the defendants' counsel to question their clients during the deposition to place evidence of their lack of malice in making the recommendations at issue on record.

Assuming issues of fact remain for trial, the next step after summary judgment practice might be to try and limit the evidence that will be admissible at that trial.

6. Tell me how deposition testimony is used in evidentiary motions.

If summary judgment has not eliminated all claims for trial, use the depositions to limit or exclude various items of evidence from the litigation. Deposition practice both identifies the facts as understood by the parties and witnesses and determines the source of those facts and the basis for parties and witnesses to believe their existence. One witness may believe that a fact exists because he was told about the fact by someone else. That witness's evidence is hearsay and should be excluded. Another witness may have reached a conclusion about the meaning of certain facts. His conclusion may be excluded as an inadmissible opinion. Documents that are proposed trial exhibits may be objectionable on relevance, privilege, authentication, original

---

21a. Indeed, in a number of cases, courts have said that though courts are not ordinarily permitted to weigh the relative credibility of witnesses on summary judgment, in some extraordinary cases where the moving party is heavily impeached, a court is correct in discrediting an affidavit or deposition and granting summary judgment. Rojas v. The Roman Catholic Diocese of Rochester, 660 F.3d 98 (2d.Cir 2011); Gill v. Teva Respiratory LLC., 2017 WL 6614228, (D. Conn, 2017).

22. We will discuss this issue in greater detail in later chapters regarding the preparation for and the content of depositions and their manner of recording.

documents rule, and hearsay bases. Even if a proposed piece of evidence meets the necessary requirements for admissibility, counsel may seek to exclude it because whatever probative value the evidence provides is overwhelmed by unfair prejudice.

All these evidentiary issues will be raised at the final pretrial conference[23] or before, in a motion in limine. In limine motions seek to exclude evidence. Counsel can also bring a pretrial motion requesting the judge to admit evidence. If the judge's pretrial determinations regarding admissibility of evidence are definitive, they are preserved for appeal.[24] This will obviate the necessity of making objections at trial and enduring the tactical disadvantage of having an objection overruled in front of jurors or remain a source of argument in ADR proceedings.

7. Can I use the deposition to establish that a piece of evidence is either admissible or inadmissible, in anticipation of the pretrial hearing or motion you just mentioned?

Definitely. Although a deposition does not require laying the formal evidentiary foundation necessary to introduce exhibits at trial (unless the deponent is expected to be unavailable at the trial), trial judges with crowded dockets prefer to avoid expending time laying evidentiary foundations at trial. For that reason, laying the foundation at deposition positions the parties and the court to handle evidentiary objections via motions in limine, at the pretrial conference, or the agreement of the parties.

At the same time, when there are objections to exhibits, those objections are informed by the recorded deposition testimony. That is, just as counsel may seek to lay the foundation for the introduction of an exhibit during a deposition, so too may counsel seek to show through deposition testimony that a potential exhibit is inadmissible, thereby laying what we will call a "negative foundation." Further, the judge will decide about nonstipulated exhibits based on proof established in deposition testimony. Absent the positive or negative foundation (more on this later) in the deposition record, the court has little on which to base its ruling on admissibility.

Example: In our hypothetical case, a tenure report's admissibility relies on that report being made by a person with knowledge of its contents, at or near the time of Professor Williams's evaluation, and that the report was both made and kept by the university as part of their routine practice. Whether the tenure report meets the requirements for the hearsay exception for records of regularly conducted activity will be determined in the deposition of one or several of the witnesses to the case: Dean Jefferson's deposition testimony, in words or substance; the plaintiff's counsel as a matter of discovery; or the defendant's counsel as a matter of demonstrating the admissibility of the report, for example. If at the pretrial conference the defendant objected to the tenure report as hearsay, the judge would reference Dean Jefferson's deposition testimony to overrule because

23. Fed. R. Civ. P. 16(e).

24. Fed. R. Evid. 103.

the report qualifies as an exception to hearsay[25] *and have the exhibit be marked and admitted as a trial exhibit.*

Conversely, deposition testimony can also provide the factual predicate for a motion to exclude evidence. If you can show that a witness does not have firsthand knowledge of the events about which testimony is proposed, or that a document fails to meet the requirements for admissibility on any legitimate grounds, the judge can exclude the proposed testimony or document at the pretrial conference.

Example: In our hypothetical case, suppose the university proposed to introduce a memorandum from Simonson to Jefferson and the deposition of those two parties, taken together, appear to lay the foundation for a record of regularly conducted activity. Skillful deposition questioning by the opponent could demonstrate that the memo was prepared in anticipation of litigation. This would lead the court to exclude the proposed exhibit offered by the defendants[26] *because its preparation purpose "indicate(d) a lack of trustworthiness" and therefore fits the exclusionary clause of Rule 803(6).*

8. One of the biggest pretrial issues is the admissibility of expert testimony. Do depositions have a role in *Daubert/Kumho Tire* motion practice?

One of the most frequent uses of deposition testimony in pretrial motion practice appears in a *Daubert*/Rule 702 motion regarding the admissibility of expert testimony. In this hearing, the judge serves as the gatekeeper to determine the admissibility of expert testimony and to rule on whether the proposed expert testimony is admissible. At one time, it was common for a trial judge to hold an evidentiary hearing to determine the admissibility of expert testimony, employing the standards now encompassed in Rule 702. Those standards require that the theory or methodology supporting the expert testimony is reliable; that the theory and/or methodology was reliably performed and "fit" an issue at trial; that the opinions provided are based on sufficient facts and data; and that the person proposed as an expert is qualified to provide such opinions. These hearings incurred enormous costs in time and energy.

The admissibility of expert testimony in a modern federal court is often decided without resort to a full-blown evidentiary hearing,[27] based instead on the expert's reports, expert depositions, and the written arguments of counsel. In many cases, when a motion to exclude expert testimony is filed, the judge provides a limited time for discovery, during which he may order the depositions of expert witnesses on the admissibility issue alone, in addition to previously completed expert discovery.[28]

---

25. Fed. R. Evid. 803(6).

26. If offered by the plaintiff (the opposing party), the report would be a nonhearsay opposing party statement admissible pursuant to Fed. R. Evid. 901(d)(2).

27. If a hearing is held, it will almost certainly be limited to argument of counsel and not be evidentiary in nature.

28. We fully discuss the issues regarding expert depositions in chapter twelve.

Example: In our hypothetical case, the plaintiff's expert witness may have provided a Rule 26 report in which she opines about the economic value of hedonic damages.[29] *The defendants should move to exclude the opinion as unreliable and therefore not helpful to finding any fact in issue. In that instance, a court may order depositions on the issue be taken and submitted, especially if the reliability of "hedonic" damages calculations are not adequately addressed in the Rule 26 reports of both parties' experts.*

Motion practice on pretrial admissibility could not be efficiently handled without careful and precise deposition practice. This use of depositions dictates the scope, depth, and manner of lawyer preparation for, and execution of, deposition practice. Of course, evidentiary motions are ancillary to the main purpose for taking depositions—learning the facts as known by the witnesses to the case—and in some cases the deposition itself, or portions thereof, will be admissible in evidence.[30]

9. Are there other uses for the deposition that don't involve introducing it in evidence?

Preparing a witness's trial or other sworn testimony[31] begins with that witness's deposition testimony. Before calling a witness on direct examination, carefully review the witness's deposition testimony—and have the witness review it as well. The witness's deposition testimony both guides and limits trial testimony. First, the deposition guides the witness's testimony by refreshing memory about the important case facts and reminding the witness of important issues raised by the litigation. Second, if the deposition is well done, it limits the witness's testimony to the facts reflected in the deposition because expanding on those facts in trial or other testimony risks impeachment by inconsistent statement by omission.

Example: In our hypothetical case, if counsel at deposition has Dean Jefferson list all her reasons for not recommending Williams for tenure and further have her state that those were indeed all her reasons, that deposition will limit her testimony at trial. Likewise, a well-conducted deposition will make Jefferson accountable for all her testified reasons for not recommending Williams. Her direct examination must account for all of those reasons; failure to do so will result in plaintiff's counsel using her deposition testimony to impeach her trial/ADR testimony by showing her failure to testify to a complete list of reasons for her actions.

---

29. Hedonic damages are damages sought for the loss of the enjoyment of life. It is not in controversy that in our gender discrimination case, and in all tort cases involving personal injury (physical or emotional), jurors may award damages for the loss of the enjoyment of life. What is controversial is whether an economist can opine on the value of that loss in dollar terms. Some jurisdictions allow such opinion testimony, others do not, and the question is an open one in many courts.

30. As we have described above, witness testimony may be given not only at trial, but in various forms of ADR. In addition, witness testimony may be taken during motion practice, most typically that of experts in a *Daubert*/Rule 702 hearing regarding the admissibility of expert testimony.

31. For purposes of this section, assume that preparation for trial testimony also refers to preparation for other venues, e.g., arbitration, motion practice.

10. Can I also use the deposition in cross-examining a deponent?

The deposition also provides common ammunition for cross-examination. It is often said that a lawyer should not ask a question on cross-examination unless she knows the answer.[32] The well-executed deposition provides the factual predicate for that informed cross-examination. When a witness fails to acknowledge in testimony a fact that he admitted in deposition, his deposition provides impeachment fodder for cross-examination questions. You use the deposition as impeachment in one of a number of ways. With a traditionally transcribed deposition, note the page and line that supports each cross-examination question before witness cross-examination.[33] With electronically transcribed depositions, bar-code each supportive deposition segment for easy access and electronic display in the courtroom. Do the same for depositions taken by digital recording. If a witness should vary from deposition testimony, access the video deposition by bar code for replay in the courtroom—literally impeaching the witness by inconsistent statement out of the witness's own mouth.

Example: In our hypothetical case, if Williams denies that she made negative statements about Simonson's academic honesty during cross-examination, counsel can read or display her deposition testimony to the contrary to the factfinders as an inconsistent statement, admissible not only for impeachment, but for the truth of the content of the deposition as an opposing party statement.[34]

11. What are the formal uses of depositions at trial?

There are five basic ways in which a deposition can be used at trial or ADR:[35]

1) to refresh recollection;
2) as prior testimony;
3) for an offer of proof;
4) as a source of opposing party statements; and
5) for impeachment by inconsistent statement.

32. This is not so much a rule, but a suggestion for the inexperienced cross-examiner as the safe path to tread on cross-examination.

33. This used to be done by tabbing testimony or using a "post-it" type note. In modern depositions, where transcription is digital, you can easily create an electronic notation of the source of information for cross-examination.

34. Pursuant to Rule 613, the inconsistent statement impeaches merely because two different statements are given about the same fact. In addition, because the statement was one made by a party, it is admissible as nonhearsay and for the truth of its content pursuant to Rule 801(d)(2)(A), and because it was under oath, it is also admissible for the truth of its content pursuant to Rule 801(d)(1)(A).

35. The examples provided in this section assume that the matter is being heard at a jury trial. Changes in the form and manner of the uses described should be modified for different fora such as a bench trial, an ADR minitrial or arbitration.

a. How is the deposition used to refresh memory?

A most common occurrence at trial (or other presentation of testimony) is for a witness to have a failure of memory. This is especially true for nonparty witnesses, because the events that underlie the litigation may have occurred several years before trial and are not personally important to the witness—they just slip from memory. When that occurs, and the witness's deposition has been taken, use the deposition to refresh memory pursuant to Rule 612.

Example: In our hypothetical case, consider the following exchange at trial with Williams testifying on direct examination.

<u>Direct Examination of Mary Anne Williams</u>

Q: *How many credits were you assigned to teach in your first year on the faculty of the School of Public Policy?*
A: *Fourteen.*
Q: *What were those courses?*
A: *I taught two sections of Public Policy 101, which is a survey course; they were three credits each. I taught a course on public institutions, another three credit course. I taught a course called Legislation for Policy Planners, a three credit course. And I taught a seminar on public school funding, which was a two credit course.*
Q: *Did that course assignment change in your second year?*
A *No, it remained the same in my second year.*
Q: *At some point were you assigned to teach an overload?*
A: *Yes, I was assigned to teach sixteen credits in either my third or fourth year and every succeeding year after that until I was forced to leave the university.*
Q: *Let me show you what has been marked as Exhibit 32. Do you recognize Exhibit 32?*
A: *Yes, that's a copy of my deposition.*
Q: *Please turn to page 104 of Exhibit 32 and read lines 10–22 to yourself. Please tell me when you have finished reading.*
A: *I've finished.*
Q: *After reading that portion of your deposition, do you now remember the year in which you began teaching an overload?*
A: *I do.*
Q: *Taking from you Exhibit 32. Please tell the jurors the year in which you began teaching overload?*
A: *It was in my fourth year.*

b. How and under what circumstances is the deposition used as "former testimony"?

If a witness is unavailable to testify at trial for any reason, Rule 804(b)(1) allows the deposition can be used as former testimony . In ADR proceedings, depositions normally takes the place of live witness testimony.

Example: In our hypothetical case, suppose Dean Jefferson has changed positions and is on sabbatical in Australia at the time of trial. Her deposition testimony can be read to the jurors, usually with the questioning counsel from the deposition reading the questions asked and someone sitting in the witness chair reading Dean Jefferson's answers. Of course, if the deposition was audio or video recorded, it can be played for the jurors.

Former testimony may also be useful when a witness is testifying at trial and has a failure of recollection.

Example: Consider the following from the testimony of Professor Taylor in our hypothetical case.

Direct Examination of Professor Marvin Taylor by the Plaintiff

Q: Professor Taylor, were you the Chair of the Tenurial Faculty of the Nita University School of Public Policy in the year in which Ms. Williams was considered for tenure?
A: Yes, I was.
Q: Was it part of your duties to appoint tenure review panels?
A: Yes, it was.
Q: Did you appoint a tenure review panel for a Professor Vasquez, who eventually received tenure that year?
A: I did; the panel consisted of Professors Esposito, Graham, and Brownstein.
Q: Was there a particular reason why you chose that panel for Professor Vasquez?
A: I'm sure there was, but as I sit here I can't recall. I've appointed many such panels over the years.
Q: Let me show you Exhibit 33. Do you recognize that document?
A: Yes, that's my deposition in this case.
Q: Directing your attention to page 84, Lines 4–20. Please read that to yourself and let me know when you are done.
A: I've finished.
Q: Do you now remember why you selected that particular panel for Professor Vasquez?
A: I know what it says here, but honestly, I can't say that those were the reasons. It was a while ago, and I just don't recall if those were the reasons. The deposition was closer in time to the appointment, and I had some notes I used to get prepared for the deposition, so it's probably accurate, but I just can't recall.
Plaintiff's Counsel: I move the admission of page 84, Lines 4–20, of Professor Taylor's deposition and ask permission to publish that portion of Professor Taylor's deposition to the jurors.
Defense Counsel: Objection, hearsay.

Plaintiff's Counsel: Your Honor, Professor Taylor has testified to an incomplete memory as to the reasons he chose the review panel for Professor Vasquez, which makes him unavailable pursuant to Rule 804(a)(3). The proffered evidence is therefore former testimony pursuant to Rule 804(b)(1).
By the Court: The exhibit will be received, and it may be read to the jurors.

The plaintiff's lawyer reads the questions asked at the deposition and Professor Taylor reads his responses. Again, an audio or video recorded deposition can just be played for the jurors.

c. Can you describe how the deposition could be used as the basis for an offer of proof?

For every question asked at trial or in ADR proceedings, counsel must have a good-faith basis. When opposing counsel objects to a question, the trial judge will frequently request an offer of proof from questioning counsel to show the legitimacy of the question.

Example: In our hypothetical case, consider the following from the cross-examination of Simonson.

<u>Cross-examination of David Simonson by Plaintiff's Counsel</u>

Q: Ms. Williams is not the first woman in the Nita University community with whom you have had sexual relations, is she?
A: That's correct.
Q: And there were other women with whom you attempted to have a sexual relationship, where the relationship never occurred?
A: What do you mean? I never forced myself on anyone.
Q: I understand your position sir, but there were women in the university community to whom you suggested a sexual relationship, who declined your suggestion, correct?
A: I'm sure that's accurate.
Q: And Ms. Williams is not the first women at the School of Public Policy with whom you have had a sexual relationship, is that right?
A: That, too, is correct.
Q: It is a fact, Professor, that in both the cases where a sexual relationship was proposed and declined and where the sexual relationship was consummated, the women involved are no longer in the employ of Nita University?
Defense Counsel: Objection. The question is argumentative, vague, and calls for irrelevant information.
Plaintiff's Counsel: If I may be heard, your Honor.
By the Court: Approach the bench.
(At side bar)

Plaintiff's Counsel: It is our position, your Honor, that Professor Simonson was involved in numerous sexual relationships with women in the university community and attempted others. When those relationships either ended or were declined, the woman involved was out of employment with the university in a matter of months, and that evidence goes to both our retaliation and hostile work environment claims.

The Court: What is the basis for those factual allegations?

Plaintiff's Counsel: I would refer to Exhibit 34 of the deposition of Professor Simonson and Exhibit 35 of the deposition of then-Dean Jefferson. First in Exhibit 34, please refer to Pages 111–117 . . . .

Assuming the deposition transcripts show the facts as claimed by the plaintiff's counsel and the judge concurs with the proposed relevant use, the examination of Simonson would continue.

d. If opposing counsel offers a party's deposition, it would be a statement of an opposing party. What are the mechanics for introducing the deposition of a party at trial or in ADR?

The parties' depositions (as well as the depositions of witnesses who provide information that is attributable to a party) are admissible substantively as opposing party's statements[36] and may be published to the jurors at any time.

Example: Consider this excerpt from Taylor's testimony in our hypothetical case.

Direct Examination of Marvin Taylor by the Plaintiff

Q: *Were you present at the meeting where the tenure of Ms. Williams was considered?*

A: *Yes, I chaired the meeting.*

Q: *Were there negative votes on her tenure?*

A: *Yes. She received fifteen favorable votes and eleven negative votes.*

Q: *What were the bases for the negative votes?*

A: *I'm sure different people had different reasons.*

Q: *Was one consideration whether Professor Simonson would be comfortable with having Ms. Williams on the faculty, given their relationship and the aftermath of the ending of that relationship?*

A: *There was no articulation of that consideration, but some people raised the issue of Ms. Williams's collegiality, which I believe to be code for the fact that Professor Simonson was upset about some things that Ms. Williams said about him after their breakup.*

Defense Counsel: Move to strike. The answer is pure conjecture.

36. *See* FED. R. EVID. 801(d)(2).

Plaintiff's Counsel: May I offer an exhibit, your Honor, that will shed light on this issue?

By the Court: Approach the bench.

(At side bar)

Plaintiff's Counsel: Your Honor, I offer in evidence a portion of Dean Jefferson's deposition, Exhibit 35, Page 124, Lines 6–22 in which she testified to the following:

> *DEPOSITION OF JEFFERSON:*
>
> *Answer by Dean Jefferson: Professor Simonson was and is an important and respected member of our faculty and is responsible for bringing both public and private funding to the university. Although he never openly complained about the attacks by Ms. Williams on his personal and professional character, I am sure that those attacks made him uncomfortable; anyone would feel that way. I am also sure that his discomfort was a cause for concern on the part of his colleagues and adversely affected their view of Ms. Williams's collegiality within the school and the university.*

Plaintiff's Counsel: Your Honor, I withdraw my last question and agree to the motion to strike. I instead offer Exhibit 35, Page 124, Line 6–22, and request that I be allowed to publish that exhibit to the jurors. The Deposition of Dean Jefferson—a named defendant—is an opposing party's statement pursuant to Rule 801(d)(2)(A).

Defense Counsel: May we have a limiting instruction that the exhibit is admissible against Dean Jefferson, but not against Professor Simonson, the university, the Public Policy School, or the Patterson Institute?

Plaintiff's Counsel: I agree to the limiting instruction with regard to Professor Simonson and the Patterson Institute, but the statement is admissible against the Public Policy School as it was a statement by their employee, Dean Jefferson, during the course of her employment, about matters within the scope of her employment. It is, therefore, a vicarious opposing party statement pursuant to Rule 801(d)(2)(D).

By the Court: The exhibit will be received, but its admissibility is limited only to the defendants Jefferson, Nita University, and the Public Policy School, and I will so instruct the jurors.

e. Can you demonstrate using a deposition at trial to impeach a witness by a prior inconsistent statement?

Perhaps the most typical and common use of depositions during cross-examination at trial or in ADR is for prior inconsistent statement impeachment. As noted earlier, this impeachment can be direct or by omission.

Example: Consider the following excerpt from the cross-examination of Williams in our hypothetical case.

<u>*Cross-examination of Ms. Williams*</u>

Q: *You ended your relationship with Professor Simonson, didn't you?*
A: *Yes.*
Q: *You were upset about ending the relationship?*
A: *Yes, I was. I felt betrayed.*
Q: *And you were upset?*
A: *Yes, I said that.*
Q: *Your mental state affected your teaching?*
A: *A little, perhaps, but not substantially so.*
Q: *Wouldn't you say your teaching for the spring term in which you sought tenure was subpar?*
A: *I was an effective teacher.*
Q: *Have you ever said that your teaching for that semester was subpar?*
A: *I don't believe so.*
Q: *This isn't the first time you've given testimony under oath in this lawsuit, is it?*
A: *That's right, my deposition was taken.*
Q: *You were under oath?*
A: *Yes.*
Q: *Your lawyer was there?*
A: *Yes.*
Q: *There was a court reporter there taking down your testimony?*
A: *Yes.*
Q: *And of course you told the truth?*
A: *Of course.*
Q: *I asked you a series of questions?*
A: *Yes.*
Q: *And you answered those questions?*
A: *I did.*
Q: *You received a written transcript of your deposition?*
A: *I did.*
Q: *And you were asked to make any additions or corrections to the transcript?*
A: *I was.*
Q: *And you made no additions or corrections, did you?*
A: *I did not.*
Q: *And then you signed the deposition, swearing that it was a true and accurate transcription of your deposition testimony, right?*
A: *Yes, that's right.*
Q: *Showing you Exhibit 32. That's your signed deposition, isn't it?*
A: *Yes.*

Q: *Now let me ask you again, Ms. Williams: your teaching for the semester in which you applied for tenure was subpar wasn't it?*

A: *No, it was effective.*

Q: *Directing your attention to page 142 of Exhibit 32, your deposition, and looking at lines 4–10, please tell me if I am reading your deposition correctly?*

> *Question: In light of your mental state after the ending of your relationship, your teaching in the semester you applied for tenure was not your best was it?*

Have I read that question correctly?

A: *You have.*

Q: *And your answer to that question under oath at your deposition was, "It was not my best; it was a subpar teaching performance for me." Have I read your answer correctly?*

A: *You have.*

Q: *You also missed some deadlines at the Patterson Institute, didn't you?*

A: *Yes, Professor Simonson was not as available to me as he had been, so I was late on some assignments.*

Q: *So today you claim that your lateness had something to do with Professor Simonson's availability?*

A: *It's true.*

Q: *We discussed the lateness of your assignments at your deposition didn't we?*

A: *We did.*

Q: *And at the beginning of the deposition, I told you we were interested in obtaining your full, complete, and accurate answers to my questions, didn't I?*

A: *You did.*

Q: *And I also asked you that if during the deposition you remembered more information about a topic we had previously discussed, that you tell me so that you could complete your answer?*

A: *You did ask that.*

Q: *And you agreed?*

A: *Yes.*

Q: *And after every break in the deposition didn't I ask you if there were any of your previous answers that you would like to complete?*

A: *You did.*

Q: *And you never provided additional information to any of your answers, did you?*

A: *That's right.*

Q: *And I also asked that when you reviewed you deposition transcript that you provide the information necessary to complete any of your deposition answers, didn't I?*

A: *You did.*

Q: *And you made no such additions, did you?*

A: *No, I didn't.*[37]
Q: *Let's return to the reasons why you missed deadlines at the Patterson Institute. You have told these jurors that Professor Simonson was unavailable to you and that was a cause of your missed deadlines, correct?*
A: *That's right.*
Q: *Let me again direct your attention to your deposition, Exhibit 32, beginning on Page 167, at the top of the page. I'm going again to read to you from your deposition and please correct me if I do not read it correctly. Will you do that?*
A: *Yes.*
Q: *All right, beginning on the top of page 167.*

> *Q: Did you miss some deadlines on your work at the Patterson Institute?*
>
> *A: I did.*
>
> *Q: Why was that?*
>
> *A: I was under a lot of stress after the breakup, given the way Simonson treated me.*
>
> *Q: Why else?*
>
> *A: I was trying without much success to finish an article.*
>
> *Q: Why else?*
>
> *A: That was a semester when I was teaching an overload.*
>
> *Q: Why else?*
>
> *A: Those are the reasons.*
>
> *Q: Those are all the reasons why you were late on some of your work at the Patterson Institute?*
>
> *A: Yes, but I eventually finished all of my work.*
>
> *Q: But my question is whether you have told us all the reasons for the lateness of your work?*
>
> *A: I have.*

Q: *Did I read those questions and your answers under oath correctly?*
A: *You have.*

37. The previous questions about making additions to answers is part of the beginning portion of depositions that we suggest. Those questions are covered in chapter seven.

Q: And in your deposition you made no reference to the availability of Professor Simonson to you as a reason for the lateness of your work, did you?
A: I guess not.

12. What conclusions about the form and content of depositions can we draw from the functions they can perform in modern litigation?

The above-stated potential uses for depositions as a litigation tool inform the skill of taking and defending depositions. They also demonstrate the characteristics of a professional deposition. To be effective and fulfill all its potential uses, every deposition must be **complete, comprehensive, accurate, understandable, and fair.** We define these characteristics as follows.

- A **complete** deposition must cover all potentially relevant topics in the lawsuit.
- A **comprehensive** deposition must secure all potentially relevant facts about each topic.
- An **accurate** deposition must demonstrate that the deponent was be given every opportunity to testify about everything they know about any given topic.
- An **understandable** deposition is one in which questions and answers avoid legalese and have language that will be easily understood by any person who later reads, hears, or watches it.
- And, finally, a **fair** deposition is one where the deponent is shown all courtesies and given the opportunity to complete and/or correct the answers provided.

These goals, and how to implement them, will be explored in the rest of this book. First, however, it is helpful to review the law as it relates to the typical deposition and is reflected in the Federal Rules of Civil Procedure, the Federal Rules of Evidence, and typical discovery.

CHAPTER TWO

LEGAL CONSIDERATIONS

In chapter one, we talked about using depositions in the litigation process. We now turn to typical questions about the law that applies to deposition practice. We will make particular reference to the Federal Rules of Civil Procedure[1] (which we will refer to as Civil Procedure Rules) to provide the legal framework found predominantly in Civil Procedure Rules 26, 27, 29, 30, 31, 32, and 37.

1. How is a witness compelled to give deposition testimony?

You may take the deposition of any person who potentially has information about the subject matter of a lawsuit, either orally[2] or by written questions.[3] The depositions of parties are taken pursuant to notice.[4] You may take the deposition of a nonparty by serving the witness with a subpoena[5] and providing notice to the parties.[6] You may also include a subpoena duces tecum, designating what materials the witness must produce at the deposition.[7] In addition, special rules cover deposing party representatives[8] and expert witnesses.[9] Although the rules allow the deposing party to decide who, when, where, and by what method (oral or written questions) a

1. We have chosen the Federal Rules of Civil Procedure as our model for obvious reasons: the federal courts exist in all jurisdictions, and most state civil procedure rules are modeled, at least in part, on the federal rules. Obviously, you must consult your local federal court's variations on the rules as well as your state rules when preparing for and taking or defending depositions.

2. FED. R. CIV. P. 30. Deposition by oral examination is the predominant method of taking the pretrial testimony of a witness and will be the primary topic of this chapter and of this book.

3. FED. R. CIV. P. 31. Depositions by written question are predominantly used to cover technical matters in discovery. Typical of such a deposition is that of a records keeper for an institution to verify the method of making and keeping relevant records to determine their admissibility against legal requirements such as authentication, compliance with the original documents rule, and to show an exception to the hearsay rule—e.g., that the record is one of a regularly conducted activity (business record) and meets the requirement of Fed R. Evid. 803(6).

4. FED. R. CIV. P. 30(a)(1).

5. FED. R. CIV. P. 30(b)(1).

6. *Id.* If the noticing party fails to proceed with the deposition or fails to serve a subpoena on a nonparty witness, who fails to attend, then a party or the party's representative who expected the deposition to occur is entitled to reasonable expenses, including attorney's fees.

7. FED. R. CIV. P. 30(b)(2). In the case of a party, the notice may be accompanied by a Rule 34 request for production of documents and tangible things, also to be produced at or before the time of the deposition.

8. FED. R. CIV. P. 30(b)(6). To be discussed more fully in chapter twelve.

9. FED. R. CIV. P. 26(b)(4)(a). To be discussed more fully in chapter thirteen.

deposition will be taken, that decision is not without legal limitations—and tactical and professional considerations.

1. What are the legal limitations on taking a deposition?

The party taking the deposition must provide notice to all parties involved in the lawsuit.[10] The procedural rules also limit the number of depositions—either oral or by written questions or in combination—to ten per party.[11] Each deposition is limited to one seven-hour day, although the judge may allow additional time, if needed, to fairly examine the deponent.[12] The party noticing the deposition controls the place that the deposition is conducted. As a practical matter, the deposition must be noticed for a place within the district court's subpoena authority.[13] In multiparty litigation, each party has the right to question any deponent, including (in every case) the party's own counsel.[14] In multiparty cases, however, one lawyer is usually designated as the lead counsel for both the plaintiff(s) and defendant(s), respectively.

Leave of the court is required whenever more than ten depositions per party are sought, the witness has already been deposed, the deposition is sought before the time prescribed by Rule 26(d)(1), or the deponent is confined in prison.[15] These requirements, as all procedures governing or limiting all forms of discovery, may be altered by stipulation as long as the stipulation does not interfere with time set for completing discovery, holding a hearing, deciding a motion, or trial.[16]

---

10. Fed. R. Civ. P. 30(b)(1) (oral); Fed. R. Civ. P. 31(a)(3) (written questions).

11. Fed. R. Civ. P. 30(a)(2)(A)(i). Fed. R. Civ. P. 29 allows the number of depositions in a matter to be varied by the parties as long as it does not interfere with the authority of the district judge to control the litigation. Should the parties decide to vary the number of depositions, they should file a stipulation with the court. In addition, the court may order, on good cause shown, that more than ten depositions be allowed by either oral (Fed. R. Civ. P. 30(a)(2)(A)(i)) or written (Fed. R. Civ. P. 31(a)(2)(A)(i)) examination.

12. Fed. R. Civ. P. 30(d)(1). Again, the parties may agree to vary the length and duration of a deposition (Fed. R. Civ. P. 29). Most courts have read the rule to provide that each party has the right to a deposition of seven hours, although the cases where such a duration is necessary are few. In addition, the seven-hour rule applies specifically to the questions and answers of deposing counsel. In places or particular cases where defending counsel, or counsel for other parties, interrupt the deposition, many court reporters have resorted to using a time clock akin to that used in a chess match. In most cases, however, digital time records can be kept, along with the recording of the deposition, should a length issue arise.

13. Fed. R. Civ. P. 45(b)(2).

14. Obviously, with a nonparty witness, all parties will have an interest in developing the facts available from that witness during the deposition. We will make the case throughout this book that in the modern deposition, defending counsel should take the opportunity to question her own witness at the time the party is deposed by opposing counsel. This position is consistent with the presumption that in modern litigation, there will be no trial and that the deposition will be the last time for a party to personally present the facts favorable to their position in the litigation.

15. Fed. R. Civ. P. 30(a)(2).

16. Fed. R. Civ. P. 29.

2. What are the tactical and professional considerations in compelling deposition testimony?

Although the date, time, and place of a deposition is controlled by the party who notices the deposition—or subpoenas the witness for deposition—professional courtesy requires that you consult with opposing counsel to choose a convenient time and place for all counsel and the deponent. In addition, consult subpoenaed witnesses to determine a convenient deposition time.

These courtesies avoid objections over schedule conflicts—opposing counsel will not have to file protective orders to prevent scheduling conflicts or motions to move the deposition to a convenient time;[17] furthermore, you'll avoid irritating the judge, who has to take time resolving such matters. Moreover, consulting with opposing counsel can facilitate scheduling multiple parties and/or witnesses for the same day and place, saving time and money for everyone. For example, in our hypothetical case, a number of witnesses from the School of Public Policy will be deposed. To the extent that they can be scheduled for the same and/or consecutive days, depositions can proceed efficiently, avoiding waits between witnesses and lawyers needing to come back up to speed on the case facts on multiple occasions. Finally, providing deposition testimony is an inconvenience, at best for nonparty witnesses; avoid further impediments to gathering information by being as flexible and courteous as possible.

Most lawyers will, as a matter of tactics and convenience, schedule depositions at their own offices, where they have easy access to paralegal and other administrative assistance. In reality, the best place to take a deposition should be the place that facilitates the purpose of the deposition.

If the purpose of the deposition is primarily to obtain information,[18] it makes sense to depose the witness in a place where he is comfortable and at ease and has access to documents that may have not been disclosed before the deposition. In such a case, notice an information-gathering deposition for the deponent's office or workplace. In our hypothetical case, the individual defendants are a chaired professor, who is also the director of an important institute, and the dean of the School of Public Policy. Depose these parties at their offices, where they will feel comfortable. This can lead to them being more open and giving more complete responses to questions. If, however, the deposition is noticed to obtain opposing party's statements, notice it for a place where the deponent is not used to being in control; he will be more susceptible to leading or directive questions that form the precursor for later uses, such as request for admissions[19] or a motion for summary judgment.[20]

---

17. Fed. R. Civ. P. 26(c).

18. All depositions will contain an effort to obtain opposing party's statements and test case theory to some extent. We are speaking here, however, where the deposing counsel needs to obtain information.

19. Fed. R. Civ. P. 36.

20. Fed. R. Civ. P. 56.

3. Are there choices to be made regarding how to record deposition testimony?

The method of recording the deposition must be stated in the notice. The rule assumes that audio, video, or stenographic recording methods are always acceptable and that the costs of the recording are to be paid by the party noticing the deposition.[21] All of the parties are entitled to receive copies of the recorded deposition (in whatever form) at their own expense.

Any party can use additional methods of recording as long as the deponent and other parties are provided with notice and the costs of that recoding method is borne by that party.[22]

Example: Suppose, in our hypothetical case, that the defendant deposes the chair of the tenurial faculty, to be recorded by a stenographer. The plaintiff—on notice to the witness, the noticing defendant, and any other parties—may arrange to video record the deposition. The plaintiff's attorney may do this because the witness is particularly well spoken and forceful in his demeanor, and video could be of great persuasive force in a later arbitration. In that case, the noticing defendant is responsible for the costs of the stenographer, and the plaintiff would be responsible for the costs of the videographer.

In a related topic, the parties can stipulate—or the court can order—a remote deposition, through telephone calls, teleconferencing, or other methods.[23] Every party has the prerogative to be present during the taking of a deposition. For example, the party defending a telephonic deposition may choose to go to the place where the deponent is situated.[24] In a remote deposition, counsel will stipulate to the location of the court reporter; if this is in controversy, the court will issue an order.

4. What are the tactical considerations for recording testimony?

Virtually every deposition will be transcribed digitally. If the case is of sufficient value to support the additional cost, include video recording.[25] In that case, the end product will be a digital video and a digital transcript. Digital recording, be it stenographic, audio, or video, provides enormous time savings. A digitally transcribed deposition makes searching and accessing information contained in the deposition

21. Fed. R. Civ. P. 30(b)(3)(A).

22. Fed. R. Civ. P. 30(b)(3)(B).

23. Fed. R. Civ. P. 30(b)(4). It seems modern communication technologies open new methods of taking deposition testimony on a daily basis. Presumably, the only requirement for using these new technologies will be that the court has sufficient evidence that the method of communication and/or recording is reliable.

24. Fed. R. Civ. P. 30(b)(3)(A) and (B).

25. The cost of an audio-visual deposition varies, of course, but typically, the extra cost for an audio-visual recording of the deposition over that of a stenographic recording is $1,000–$1,250.

relatively easy and efficient. In most jurisdictions, deposition transcripts are available in "miniscript," which contains four pages of transcript per page and a word index to page and line at the end of the transcript. The ability to perform digital word searches makes gathering information about a particular topic—for motion practice, ADR, or otherwise—much more efficient.

The value and impact of video depositions has many implications that we will address in response to later questions. As a basic matter, digital video depositions have the added discovery value of portraying two types of information: 1) the content provided by the deponent, and 2) the deponent's demeanor (and, thus, credibility). Nervousness, evasiveness, attitude towards testimony, and the tone of the testimony are not fully revealed—or revealed at all—by a written transcript. This additional information from the video recording is valuable in ADR decision making, motion practice, and trial.

5. What legal formalities must be observed in beginning, recording, and ending depositions?

A deposition must be taken before an officer who is authorized—by federal law or local law, or appointed specifically for the case at hand—to administer oaths.[26] Before the deposition, the officer must state on the record the officer's name and business address; the date, time, and place of the deposition; the deponent's name; the administration by the officer of the oath or affirmation to tell the truth; and the identity of all persons present at the deposition.[27]

During the typical video deposition, the officer must repeat his name and business address; the date, time and place of the deposition; and the name of the deponent at the beginning of each unit of the recording medium. For example, if a deposition was recorded using audio or video tape, the tape would have to be changed periodically. At the beginning of each tape, the officer would have to state the basic identifying information for each tape of testimony. Digital audio-visual transcripts obviate the need for this rule, as the recording is contained in one digital file.

Additionally, in the video recorded deposition, the officer must assure that no recording techniques distort the deponent's or attorney's appearance or demeanor.[28] For this reason, most judicial districts have local rules that include standing orders for the manner in which audio-visual depositions are to be recorded. The typical order requires that the camera be situated over the shoulder of the questioning counsel, with the view of the deponent a "head and shoulders" shot. These two requirements allow the deponent to speak into the camera when addressing questioning counsel,

26. Fed. R. Civ. P. 28(a)(1) and (2). The witness must either swear or affirm that the testimony that they are about to give will be truthful.

27. Fed. R. Civ. P. 30(b)(5)(B).

28. Fed. R. Civ. P. 30(b)(5)(B).

avoiding the video of the deposition appearing as if the deponent was unwilling to make eye contact with the decision maker (judge, jurors, ADR officer). It also avoids distractions from hand movements or other gestures that would be visible with a wider video shot displaying more of the torso of the deponent. In most jurisdictions, local rules provide that the camera will remain on the deponent at all times.[29] The typical order will also provide that when questioning counsel changes, the new questioning counsel move to the position from which the initial questioning was accomplished. Further, in most circumstances, the camera will not be focused on opposing counsel when objections are stated, although all counsel will be provided with a microphone. Finally, the local rule may contain—or counsel might seek stipulation and failing that, a court order for—specifications for the technical equipment and recording media to be used in the deposition.

At the end of the deposition, the officer must state on the record that the deposition is complete; the officer must further state the agreements of counsel regarding such matters as custody of the exhibits and the original recording of the deposition, and the preservation of issues raised by the deposition.

Example: In our hypothetical case, counsel for the university might have instructed Dean Jefferson not to answer a question concerning her conversation with university counsel about tenure regulations on the grounds of attorney-client privilege. Assuming the plaintiff had some basis to challenge either the existence or waiver privilege, the parties would likely stipulate to continue the deposition until the privilege issues is resolved by stipulation or court order. Should it be determined that the plaintiff was entitled to the information about which Dean Jefferson was instructed not to answer, counsel would reconvene her deposition for the limited purpose of inquiring into this matter.

6. Are there also tactical and professionalism issues involved in beginning, recording, and ending depositions?

Court reporters and, where applicable, videographers are key players in beginning, recording, and ending depositions. Develop professional relationships with specific court reporters. Court reporters and videographers are normally employed by services; within each such service there is a court reporter for every lawyer—that is, a court reporter who easily and efficiently understands the lawyer's style and demeanor and those things that make depositions a less cumbersome enterprise. Depositions require is a good deal of coordination between the court reporter, videographer, and the lawyer. Over time, court reporters, lawyers, and other professionals working in the recording of deposition testimony will develop a rhythm

29. As we will discuss more fully in considering dealing with obstreperous opposing counsel, the existence of audiovisual recording has a calming effect on their interfering tactics. But because the camera typically remains on the witness, if the distractions of opposing counsel are accomplished physically, mention these tactics while taking the deposition.

and flow that enhances information gat hering from the witness and helps the lawyer obtain full and complete information.[30] On the other hand, there are court reporters and lawyers who are like oil and water; once you've had a difficult deposition session, don't repeat the mistake.

Most court reporters prefer to situate themselves at the end of a conference table, with deposing counsel on one side of the table and the deponent and defending counsel on the other. In that way, the court reporter is closest to the people who are doing the talking during the deposition. Deposing counsel typically prefers that seating plan as well, so counsel can engage the witness without opposing counsel's eye contact interfering.

Nothing is more troublesome to a court reporter than the spelling of unusual names[31] (or usual names spelled unusually).[32] For that reason, provide the court reporter with a business card, the name of the client you represent, the case caption, the names of the witnesses to be deposed, the names of opposing counsel, and a glossary of terms that will be used during the deposition.[33] As a matter of professional courtesy, offer the same information to all counsel, although most counsel will be familiar with the names of the parties and places relevant to the case as well as the technical terms that are in issue at the deposition. This information will help make the deposition efficient and accurate, even in the most technical of cases.

Dealing with exhibits is another typical deposition activity that might interfere with its smooth running. We will speak at greater length about this issue in chapters seven and eight, but as a basic matter, premarking exhibits will make collecting information smoother as well as the court reporter's life much easier. Provide the court reporter with the exhibits you expect to use so that they may be premarked.[34]

---

30. For many lawyers—including one of the coauthors of this book, who still maintains an Of Counsel practice—scheduling depositions will include, as a major consideration, the availability of a particular court reporter. In that case, the court reporter, with years of experience, not only performs her professional duties at the highest of levels, but acts as an excellent evaluator of the credibility of witnesses and the common-sense evaluation of the story each witness has to tell. This is not unusual. Court reporters spend their professional lives listening to lawyers question and witnesses answer, and some become excellent evaluators of the abilities of both. Young or inexperienced lawyers would be wise to seek the opinion of the seasoned court reporter regarding the state of the case, given the testimony of the witness. A more enlightened young or inexperienced lawyer will seek the reporter's opinion of the ability of the lawyer in taking depositions and how that skill might be improved.

31. E.g., Bocchino and Sonenshein.

32. Smythe pronounced as Smith.

33. The glossary of terms is especially important in depositions where scientific terminology will be part of the deposition, as in patent, professional negligence, and commercial cases involving products and/or transactions outside the ken of the reasonably intelligent person.

34. *See* chapter five regarding preparing to use exhibits and chapter nine on use of exhibits at deposition.

Provide opposing counsel with copies of the premarked exhibits, either in a bundle or as they are referred to during the deposition.[35]

Finally, video recording depositions raises numerous potential issues regarding the manner in which recording will be accomplished. The videographer can be of great assistance in resolving any such issues. First, this professional will be familiar with the local rules' technical requirements for audio-visual recording (e.g., positioning of camera, number of microphones, nature of the visual recording). Second, in the absence of a court rule, the videographer can suggest stipulations for the technical aspects of the recording, which in the absence of agreement can provide support for a court order. Work with opposing counsel to ensure the fair audio-visual recording of testimony.[36] In the absence of a contrary local rule, the videographer will typically provide a backdrop screen for the witness and record the deponent from the shoulders up and from a position that facilitates the witness looking into the camera while providing testimony, usually over the shoulder of questioning counsel.[37]

f. What are the legal limitations in taking deposition testimony?

Depose witnesses in the same manner as the Federal Rules of Evidence allow at trial, with the exception of Rule 103 (dealing with the preservation of objections for appeal[38]) and Rule 615 (dealing with sequestration of witnesses[39]). We will discuss in detail the interface of the law of evidence, particularly Rule 611, and deposition practice as it arises throughout this volume. This rule is not intended to govern the substantive law of evidence, but rather provides that the parties can examine the deponent using nonleading questions on direct examination and leading questions on cross-examination. There are a number of exceptions to Rule 611—allowing, for example, the leading questions on direct examination for adverse parties and

35. There is, of course, the possibility that a premarked exhibit is not used during the deposition. In that case, it is simply not part of the record. There is no requirement in any rule known to the authors that there necessarily be an Exhibit 8 if there is an Exhibit 9, despite the custom of marking exhibits in the order in which they are used in the deposition. Further, as we will suggest in chapter nine, for ease of litigation, the exhibit numbers should be the same for all witnesses in a particular matter, doing away with the arcane necessity of concordance charts.

36. Some videographers may suggest certain technical aspects of the recording that are designed to undermine the deponent's credibility. Putting aside, but remembering, the professional responsibility issues raised by such tactics, any tactical advantage or disadvantage can be overcome by requiring the same technical requirements for all audiovisual recordings. This way, no one recording contains enhancements or distractions.

37. If the videographer does not provide a background, ensure that the witness is seated with a neutral wall behind him—a window or framed art may not appear to be a problem, but reflections of the videographer or others in the room can be distracting on later viewing.

38. Preserving objections to deposition testimony for trial is covered by Fed. R. Civ. P. 30(c)(2) and 32 (d)(3)(B).

39. Fed. R. Civ. P. 30(c)(1). In the typical deposition, the only people present are counsel for the parties and the deponent. While the parties—or in the case of an entity party, a representative—are entitled to be present, they typically are not.

deponents associated with the adverse party. Civil Procedure Rule 30(c)(1) also makes clear that all parties may examine the witness, no matter which party caused the deposition to be taken.

Example: In our hypothetical case, when the defendant university notices Ms. Williams's deposition, the defendant university may examine her, using leading questions if desired, and the defendant Public Policy Institute may also examine her, using leading question if desired. Plaintiff's counsel may examine her only with nonleading questions.

The rules also anticipate that you will use exhibits in depositions. We will speak in greater detail about the use of exhibits in chapters five and eight. As a matter of formality, however, documents or other exhibits used during the deposition are marked for identification and attached to the deposition. The party making such use of exhibits may arrange to retain the original exhibit, but in that case, the party must provide copies to all other parties and allow ample opportunity for them to verify the accuracy of those copies.[40] The originals documents used in the deposition are normally made part of the deposition record.[41]

Finally, a party may participate in an oral deposition by submitting written interrogatories to the party noticing the deposition. Counsel must in turn deliver them to the court reporter, who must ask the questions verbatim and record the witness's answers.[42]

g. What are the rules for making objections during deposition testimony?

When defending the deposition, make objections to form and foundation as at trial, but the deposition continues. State objections concisely, in a nonargumentative and nonsuggestive manner, such as: "Objection, assumes a fact not in evidence" (a concise, nonargumentative, nonsuggestive objection), followed by an instruction: "You may answer." The objection preserves the legal point until the deposition is offered in evidence in any proceeding. The witness must still answer the question that has been posed and to which an objection has been raised.[43] The only time that a witness will not answer a question is on instruction of defending counsel and only where necessary to preserve a privilege (or trial preparation materials protection), honor a

40. FED. R. CIV. P. 30(f)(2)(A)(i) and (ii) also provides that the parties be given a fair opportunity to make their own inspection and copies of the original exhibits after they have been marked.

41. It is impossible, of course, for the original of a document to be made part of the record of the numerous depositions in a case in which it is used. This problem is rectified by a number of electronic means discussed more fully in chapters five, eight, and nine.

42. FED. R. CIV. P. 30(c)(3). This procedure is usually saved for those occasions where the deponent had nothing to do with the party who submits the written questions and the questions are limited to demonstrating that fact or the relevance of the witness to the position of that party.

43. FED. R. CIV. P. 30(c)(2). Local Court Rules and agreements of counsel can vary the way objections are stated. (More on this later).

protective order granted by the court, or seek a protective order.[44] When defending counsel claims a privilege or trial preparations material protection (work product),[45] questioning counsel has the right to have the privilege or work product protection expressly claimed, together with the nature of the privileged item (or testimony) not to be produced and other information necessary to assess the claim of privilege.[46]

Objections to competence, relevance, and materiality generally need not be made during the deposition to preserve them for when the deposition may be offered in evidence.[47] The only time such objection must be made, or waived, is when the grounds for the objection might have been corrected at the time. The relevance standard applied is, of course, the same as for all discovery: the information sought need not be admissible at trial as long as it appears reasonably calculated to lead to the discovery of admissible evidence.[48] The most typical example of an objection that must be made or waived is an objection to the competence of the witness to testify as a general matter; it can easily be shown whether a deponent is able to recall and relate information and understands the nature and quality of the oath or affirmation to tell the truth.

Other objections that must be made in a timely manner at the deposition or waived when the deposition is offered in evidence at trial or in another proceeding are those relating to the manner of taking the deposition, the form of a question or answer, the deponent's oath or affirmation to tell the truth, the conduct of a party, or any other matter that could have been corrected at the time.[49] The difficulty with

---

44. Fed. R. Civ. P. 30(c)(2). Although not expressly stated in the rule, claims of trial preparation materials protection can also be the subject of an instruction not to answer.

45. In the Federal Rules of Civil Procedure, the work product doctrine, as delineated by the U.S. Supreme Court in *Hickman v. Taylor*, is referred to as a protection of trial preparation materials (Fed. R. Civ. P. 26(b)(3)). Trial preparation materials are of two sorts. Materials discovered in preparation of litigation or trial are protected from disclosure unless they are otherwise discoverable *and* there is a showing of substantial need and the inability of obtaining the materials, or their equivalents, without undue hardship. Trial preparation materials that consist of the mental impressions, opinions, or legal theories of an attorney are subject to strict protection that is invaded in only the most unique of circumstances. There are also special rules regarding trial preparations materials when dealing with expert witnesses (*see* Fed. R. Civ. P. 26(b)(4), to be discussed in greater detail in chapter thirteen).

46. *See* Fed. R. Civ. P. 26(c)(5). By the terms of the rule, questioning counsel is entitled to the same information regarding a claim of trial preparations material protection as she would with a claim of privilege. In the case of a claim of attorney-client privilege, questioning counsel would be entitled to the same sort of information provided in a privilege log submitted in response to a request for document production. That information would include the date, time, place, and parties to the privileged communication, the nature of the communication generally (e.g., to obtain information necessary to provide legal advice), any writing or other recording reflecting the communication, and the distribution list for that writing or recording that provides information as to the validity of the claim of privilege and potential waiver.

47. Fed. R. Civ. P. 32(c)(3)(A).

48. Fed. R. Civ. P. 26(b)(1).

49. Fed. R. Civ. P. 32(d)(b). We will speak in much greater detail about the application of the law of evidence to the taking and defending of depositions in chapters eight through eleven. This rule is also the genesis for a typical stipulation to reserve all objections except as to the form of the question until such time as the deposition is offered in a trial or other proceeding. This topic will be discussed more fully in chapters seven and eleven.

determining the nature of the objections that must be made or waived at the time of deposition is the lack of precision of the phrase "matter that could have been corrected at the time."

7. Are there tactical issues for formulating questions?

The manner of examining a witness should be governed by the purpose for which the examination is conducted. As we will discuss more fully in chapter eight, if the purpose of the deposition is information gathering, the questions should be open-ended to encourage the witness to provide more, rather than less, information. Questions that draw one word answers are better suited to obtaining admissions rather than information gathering.

Example: In our hypothetical case, if the defendant wanted to find out about the educational background of Ms. Williams (who we know to be a lawyer), it is preferable to ask, "Tell about your educational background beginning with high school," to which Ms. Williams must respond in paragraphs, or at least sentences, as opposed to asking a series of interrogatories such as:

Did you attend high school?
When did you graduate from high school?
Did you go to college?
Where did you go to college?
What was your major?
Did you graduate?
When?
Where did you go to law school?
When did you receive your law degree?

All of these questions can be answered by simple, less-than-three-word answers, which have the disadvantage of limiting the information gathered to topics specifically asked about by deposing counsel. This manner of questioning is counterproductive to the goal of information gathering. Once a witness learns to provide short, specific answers, the tone is set for the entirety of the examination—one that is not conducive to broad answers and volunteered information.

If, however, you want to obtain information in a concise and clear manner for use in motion practice or in a request for admission, make the deposition should be more formal and the questions more directive. The basic tactical rule is that the form of the question used should match the goal of the question: information gathering = open-ended questions; obtaining admissions = leading questions.

Example: In our hypothetical case, defendant Simonson has an enormous amount of information about the nature and quality of the plaintiff's work at the Patterson Institute. The goal of information gathering on the topic is best executed by using open-ended inquiries like, "Tell me about your professional relationship with Ms. Williams." After following up on that answer to get complete information on the topic, counsel can focus on particular issues and obtain clear and precise answers. To be culpable for damages pursuant to a gender discrimination allegation, Simonson and the Patterson Institute must be the plaintiff's employer. For purposes of a request for admission or to prove the employment relationship, a series of leading questions such as the following could be much more easily used for their intended purpose, such as motion practice.

You are the Director of the Patterson Institute for Public Policy, aren't you?
You make decisions on whether to hire or fire Institute employees?
You decided on her work assignments?
You evaluated her work?
You controlled her employment at the Patterson Institute?
All hiring, firing, work load, work evaluation, and compensation decisions for research fellows are yours and yours alone?
You were the director of the Patterson Institute when Ms. Williams worked there as a research fellow, weren't you?
And while you were the director and she was a research fellow, you had a sexual relationship with her?
And you were still in that director/research fellow relationship when your sexual relationship ended, correct?

These questions and answers are readily accessible on the employer/employee issue and can easily be appended to a Rule 36 Request for Admission or made part of a motion about which the nature of the professional relationship between Simonson and Williams is relevant.

8. What are the professionalism issues in making objections and instructing a witness not to answer a question?

The current federal rules regarding objections that instruct witnesses not to answer are the result of concerns voiced openly and vehemently by the organized bar and the judiciary about the conduct of lawyers during depositions. During the 1980s and before, the custom in many parts of the country was to treat the discovery process as warfare,[50] where the sole objective was to prevent opposing counsel from discovering information.[51] Deposition practice became a visible battlefield in

50. The litigation as war metaphor is most frequently attributed to lawyers in large cities, primarily in the northeast region of the country. Interference with the orderly and easy access to information in a deposition, however, was a time-honored tradition in all parts of the country, although accomplished in less outwardly aggressive ways. Author experience in the southeast was that in reading deposition transcripts, it became apparent the commentary, cajoling, and speaking of objections of opposing counsel, although quite cordial, resulted in the deposing counsel receiving no information other than what defending counsel wanted received.

51. As we have and will continue to assert, in modern litigation it is often a tactical advantage to disclose information, at least that favorable to a client's position, on any given issue. As such, obfuscation tactics are less prevalent today than as short as three decades ago. Litigation as war still exists in the nation's courts, but the practice seems to be on the wane.

that warfare. In fact, the tactics of defending counsel were sometimes so intrusive in depositions that they gave rise to the phenomena known as "Rambo depositions."

In the "Rambo Deposition" the following occurred.

1) Deposition testimony was incessantly interrupted by objections, frequently with no basis whatsoever. For example, a lawyer might object to every question posed by saying, "Objection as to form, you may answer," solely for the purpose of irritating opposing counsel and interfering with the flow of information.
2) Objections were frequently accompanied by comments by objecting counsel about the question, the potential answer, the case, and the questioning counsel.
   For example, during the plaintiff's deposition in our hypothetical case, in response to the question, "Please describe your scholarly production in the year before you were denied tenure?" defending counsel might have objected by saying: "What kind of question is that? What's scholarly is a matter of opinion; production can include having thought through a thesis for an article or only writing an article; or production could require publication. The period of your inquiry is so broad that it is virtually impossible to answer with any precision. But if it is possible as posed to answer the question, you may do so, Ms. Williams." The objection suggested various ways in which the answer could be given, while really merely giving a series of reasons that would underlie an objection simply that the question was "vague or ambiguous."[52]
3) Witnesses were instructed not to answer on the whim of defending counsel, or at least when opposing counsel did not want information responsive to deposing counsel's question to be disclosed. The following exchange would not be uncommon:

Questioning Counsel: Tell me, Dean, on what basis did you refuse to recommend the plaintiff for tenure to the University Board of Trustees?

Opposing Counsel: Don't answer that question.

Questioning Counsel: Are you claiming privilege, that you have a protective order, or are you intending to seek a protective order?

Opposing Counsel: I'm instructing the witness not to answer.

Questioning Counsel: On what basis?

Opposing Counsel: Because I said so.[53]

52. Although this example may seem somewhat extreme (there are recorded exchanges that are more heated), the genre of objection is often referred to as a "speaking objection"—that is, argumentative, suggestive of an answer, or merely an instruction to the witness not to answer the question without directly doing so.

53. While cast in the circumstances of our hypothetical case, this exchange actually occurred in the first deposition conducted by one of the authors in the Philadelphia.

The problems, of course, with these tactics were not only that they interfered with the fair receipt of information during the depositions by either distracting questioning counsel or the witness, but they could also have the effect of instructing the witness how to answer a question or how to avoid answering a question. When it came to baseless instructions not to answer, the net effect was to increase litigation time and expense. As a result of such behavior and similarly obstructive behavior in all manner of discovery, the organized bar and finally the drafters of the Civil Procedure Rules amended the rules to provide:

> An objection . . . must be stated concisely in a nonargumentative and nonsuggestive manner. A person may instruct a deponent not to answer only when necessary to preserve a privilege, to enforce a limitation ordered by the court, or to present a motion under Rule 30(d)(3).[54]

Opposing counsel is thereby limited to stating the word, "objection," and then the grounds in as short a manner necessary to provide notice to the questioning counsel with sufficient information to cure the objection—e.g., "Objection; calls for conjecture."[55] With regard to instructions not to answer, the rule merely states the law that existed pre-rule: that instructions not to answer are limited to matters of privilege,[56] information that is protected by some sort of protective order, or that the instruction not to answer is made to allow counsel to file for a protective order on Civil Procedure Rule 30(d)(3) grounds. Those grounds are that the discovery is being sought in "bad faith or in a manner that unreasonably annoys, embarrasses, or oppresses the deponent or party." When such an instruction occurs, counsel can demand that the deposition be suspended, but usually the deposition will continue, the motion for court intervention will be made, and if denied, the deposition will reconvene, with cost normally borne by the party making the motion under Procedural Rule 30(d)(3).

Chapter nine will provide specific examples and suggested ways of dealing with such tactics.

---

54. Fed. R. Civ. P. 30(c) (2).

55. Some judges in their discovery orders and some local rules further restrict the form of objections during depositions by limiting counsel to stating the word, "Objection" or the phrase "Objection to form." The problem with such rules is that the word objection does not provide any information to questioning counsel about the defect in the question so that it can be cured. Additionally, if the only objection available is to the form of the question, such a rule is inconsistent with the requirement of Rule 32(d)(3) to make an effort to correct an objection at the time of its making.

56. The instruction not to answer on grounds of privilege is then litigated through either a motion for protective order by the party claiming the privilege or a motion to compel testimony by the party seeking the information. Local practice varies on which party must raise the issue, although most courts have taken the position that when a party is instructed not to answer, the burden to protect the information from discovery falls on the party that instructs a witness not to provide information. Such a procedure is mandatory if the instruction not to answer is made to seek Rule 30(d)(3) relief.

9. What are the legal requirements for ending the deposition?

In the normal course, depositions are terminated once all parties have had the opportunity to question the witness, and except for circumstances where the deposition is continued or suspended by the parties in anticipation of some further, legal event,[57] the witness cannot be noticed or subpoenaed for another deposition absent a court order.[58]

The deposition will then be transcribed or recordings produced,[59] and on request of either party or the deponent—made before the deposition is completed—the deponent is provided with an opportunity to review the recording[60] and make any changes in form or substance. The deponent makes a list of those changes, along with the reasons why the changes have been made.[61] The witness must then sign that list of changes.[62]

The deposition officer then certifies that the witness was duly sworn and that the record is accurate testimony of the witness; seals the deposition in a package marked with the title of the action and a statement of what the package contains (e.g., "Deposition of Mary Jones"); and sends the deposition recording to the attorney who arranged for the deposition and recording.[63]

Finally, the deposition officer must maintain a copy of the recording of the deposition and provide copies to any party or deponent, on payment of a reasonable charge.[64]

10. Are there any tactical decisions that need be made about ending the deposition?

The primary tactical move for ending the deposition is typically made and executed at the beginning of the deposition, when counsel discuss stipulations for the deposition.[65] The deposition will be read and corrected only if a request to do so is

---

57. Such as where a party has been instructed not to answer pursuant to Rule 30(d)(3), which anticipates motion practice before the deposition can be completed or in a circumstance where a party appears pursuant to a subpoena duces tecum and fails to provide certain documents about which questioning will be required.

58. Fed. R. Civ. P. 30 (a)(2)(ii).

59. For ease of writing transcriptions, audio recordings, video recordings and any other manner of taking down the testimony of a witness at the deposition will be referred to as a "recording."

60. Fed. R. Civ. P. 30(e)(10)(A).

61. This review previously took place days or weeks later, when the transcript became available. Now it can be accomplished on the same day, though defending counsel can reserve the right to review over a day or two.

62. Fed. R. Civ. P. 30(e)(1)(B).

63. Fed. R. Civ. P. 30(f)(1). The attorney who arranged for the deposition is then responsible for protecting it from loss, destruction, tampering, or deterioration.

64. Fed. R. Civ. P. 30(f)(3).

65. The topic of stipulations will be discussed more fully in chapters seven and eleven.

made by a party or the deponent.[66] It is in the interest of all parties and the deponent to have the deposition read and corrected. Further, even if corrections are not made, the deponent should sign the deposition transcript to affirm its accuracy.[67] The times when a court reporter makes an error in transcription are rare and then usually only with spelling names or places, but a deposition that has been read, corrected, and signed has greater reliability. For deposing counsel, should the deponent testify inconsistently at a later proceeding, the impeachment by inconsistent statement has much greater tactical value if the transcript has been read, with an opportunity to correct, by the deponent. Otherwise, during such an impeachment, the now-witness can protest that the recording is inaccurate or that he did not intend to communicate what is contained in the transcript. If the witness has had the opportunity to read, correct, and sign the transcript, such protestations are unavailing.[68] For defending counsel, in the unusual circumstance where the recording is inaccurate, it can be corrected. In addition, the substance can be changed to reflect accurate testimony as long as those changes are explained. Defending counsel is better off having a corrected transcript that contains an explanation than waiting for trial to make the correction, where that correction can look nefarious.

In litigation concerning technical processes and equipment, parties frequently seek protective orders to prevent the disclosure of trade secrets. Such requests are normally stipulated and granted. Protective orders for other matters can also be granted, considering the context of the litigation.

11. Can you give a quick review of the legal issues that arise in the uses of depositions that you described in chapter one?

The Federal Rules of Civil Procedure provide specific guidance for using depositions in a court proceeding.[69] These rules generally run in tandem with the Federal Rules of Evidence and its provisions regarding hearsay and relevance. Assuming that a party or counsel was present at the time of a deposition in a matter,[70] an opposing party's deposition, including that of a party representative,[71] is generally

66. Although Rule 30(e)(1)(B) only requires signing if there is a list of changes or corrections, it is the custom in most jurisdictions for the deponent to sign the deposition (usually under oath) even if no corrections are made.

67. If the recording is other than by transcription, the deponent should be requested to sign a certificate stating that he has read the deposition and had an opportunity to make corrections, that none were made, and that he certifies that the deposition recording is an accurate record of his deposition testimony.

68. To this end, the authors recommend that during the deposition, usually at the outset and perhaps repeated at the end, instruct the witness to read and correct the deposition before signing. Remind the witness that when correcting, finish incomplete answers and correct inaccurate answers.

69. Fed. R. Civ. P. 32. It is fair to assume, however, that uses allowed in court proceedings would also be permissible in ADR proceedings and provide guidance for negotiated settlements.

70. Or had reasonable notice and failed to attend or have a lawyer present. Fed. R. Civ. P. 32(a)(1)(A).

71. Fed. R. Civ. P. 32(a)(3).

admissible, both substantively and for impeachment purposes, to the same extent as the testimony contained therein would be if the deponent was present.[72]

Nonparty witness depositions are admissible, if the witness is unavailable,[73] through a combination of the broad view of unavailability contained in Rule 804(a), taken with the hearsay exception for former testimony in Rule 804(b)(1). It includes depositions taken in other cases, if the parties in the present litigation were present and the same or similar motive for the development of the witness's testimony existed.[74] Properly preserved objections may be interposed and ruled on before the deposition evidence is presented.[75] If one party enters a portion of a deposition, the opposing party has the right to enter other portions of the deposition that should, in fairness, be considered at the same time.[76]

The last issue the rules raise for the use of depositions in a court (or other) proceeding is how they are presented to the factfinder.[77] The rules express a preference for publication to the factfinder by some means other than the factfinder reading the transcript. If the deposition was video recorded, that recording can be played for the factfinder. If the deposition record is a written transcript, the normal manner of presentation is to have a person sit in the witness chair; counsel will read the deposition questions and the person in the witness chair will read the deponent's responses. In a jury trial, the trial judge will instruct the jurors that what they are hearing is previously recorded testimony and that the person reading the deposition responses is doing so in lieu of the actual deponent, who is unavailable.

72. This use of party depositions is consistent with the Fed R. Evid. 801(d)(2) hearsay exception for opposing party's statements.

73. FED. R. CIV. P. 32(a)(4).

74. FED. R. CIV. P. 32(a)(8). *See also* Fed R. Evid. 804(b)(1). Note that the motive for the development of testimony must have been the same at the time of the deposition as it is at trial. Motive is read broadly by the courts, so much so that in some cases, the mere fact that the deponent and deposing party both had an interest in a particular version of a fact, as opposed to another, has been considered as a "similar" motive for purposes of Fed R. Evid. 804(b)(1). *See* BOCCHINO, A., SONENSHINE, D., A PRACTICAL GUIDE TO FEDERAL EVIDENCE, 12th Ed., NITA, 2017.

75. FED. R. CIV. P. 32(b), referencing Rule 28(b) and Rule 32(d)(3) discussed above at note 105.

76. FED. R. CIV. P. 32(a)(6). Fed R. Evid. 106 would allow admissibility of any portion of any writing (not limited to the deposition) that meet the criteria that it ought to be considered in fairness at the same time as the proffered evidence.

77. FED. R. CIV. P.32(c).

Chapter Three

Case Theory for Depositions

In chapter one, we set out the many uses of deposition testimony in litigation and posited that accommodating those uses requires the deposition to be complete, comprehensive, accurate, understandable, and fair. In the days of scorched-earth deposition practice, that goal was accomplished by depositions that seemed to begin with asking the witness "to the best of your knowledge, when were you conceived?" and followed chronologically to end with "when you leave this earth, how would you like to be remembered?" Put more realistically, every question having any potential to have anything to do with any possible view of the case from any witness (and about the witness) was posed. Depositions could, and did, last for days. There was little direction or skill used, except amazing stamina and persistence. Every possible fact was sought, without any real focus on an identified goal. And at the end of the day, someplace in the morass of information was a usable legal, factual, and persuasive case theory.[1]

Those days and tactics are, for the most part, gone. Forced by the rules of civil procedure to a limitation on the number of depositions (ten) and their length (one seven-hour day each) and made less necessary by more extensively available digitally maintained records, Civil Procedure Rule 26 disclosures, and the internet, law firms can no longer rely on the tactic of allowing depositions to proceed "day to day until completion."[2] Just as important, clients demand efficiency. They are unwilling to pay for wandering litigation; they demand a lot of "bang for the buck" without any loss of quality of representation.

In part, the demand for efficiency is economic. Depositions are expensive. Aside from the direct costs for recording (likely via digital audio-visual technology) and transcribing the deposition, there are the obvious attendant costs of counsel fees and the deponent's lost production time, who is away from work to prepare for and testify at the deposition. Commercial litigants are no longer interested in scorched-earth litigation tactics involving enormous attorney's fees and other litigation costs. Individual plaintiffs cannot afford either the lawyer time involved

1. In the early 1980s, Professor Bocchino was hired by a large firm that routinely conducted depositions of the sort described. They asked him to help senior and partner-potential associates learn how to locate and construct case theory from the mass of unfiltered information available to them. This helped them avoid the necessity of senior partners, who billed at a much higher rate, from having to do so.

2. The classic deposition notice regarding the duration of the deposition.

or delayed resolution of their cases.[3] Institutional clients that pay their lawyers on an hourly basis have monthly bills to remind them of this cost of litigation. The luxury of exploring all possible claims and defenses for both liability and damages, in deposition or otherwise, no longer exists. Clients still demand first-rate representation, but at reduced costs.

1. That sounds at the same time both unfair and unworkable. I understand the need for efficiency, but how can a lawyer be efficient (meaning spending less time) and at the same time maintain the high quality of representation the client deserves?

The best way to obtain economic efficiencies in litigation—while at the same time effectively discovering and successfully concluding a case—is to develop potential case theories early, thus guiding discovery and its attendant costs. There exists at the same time, of course, the hazard that case theory will be narrowed so early that it fails to identify the *best* case theory to reach the client's goals. So you must strike a balance between pursing every fact for every potential case theory and limiting case theory exploration too early and too narrowly. Let's talk about narrowing the appropriate potential case theories for development throughout discovery, but most particularly in deposition practice.

2. What do you mean by the term "case theory"?

In every litigation, case theory exists at three levels: **legal theory**, **factual theory,** and **persuasive theory**. A successful litigation must account for successful case theory at all three levels.

Stated in the most basic terms, **legal theory** demonstrates why the law supports a finding for or against a party; **factual theory** identifies the facts that explain and prove what events that precipitated the case really occurred and why they occurred; and **persuasive theory**[4] identifies a view of the case facts that explains why, as a matter of fairness or equity, a party should prevail. The persuasive theory is usually suggested once you have developed all the potential factual theories are developed and have decided the final legal and factual theories of the case. Only then will you determine the best persuasive theory or theme. For that reason, we will discuss persuasive theory in another volume on case disposition.

---

3. It is true that personal injury cases are handled on a contingent fee basis so that no fees are paid by the client during the litigation process and costs are properly advanced by their counsel. But for the truly injured plaintiff, the time spent without resolution of their case has economic effects: attendant medical bills and loss of income. And, of course, at the end of the day, contingent fee lawyers are paid their fees, and their clients must reimburse costs.

4. Often referred to as a theme for the case.

3. There are a lot of legal theories that can be pursued in a case—how do I account for that and prioritize them?

Legal theory provides the basis in the law for a party to prevail.[5] Put in practical terms, the legal case theory is successful if, after achieving the juror's verdict, that verdict has a legal basis to be upheld on appeal. For a plaintiff, the facts in the record much be sufficient enough that an appellate court will find that reasonable jurors had a basis in law and fact to determine that the plaintiff has proved both liability and damages. For a defendant, the legal theory must support an appellate finding that the facts presented by the plaintiff, as considered by reasonable jurors, were insufficient to legally support a verdict for the plaintiff or that despite the fact that the plaintiff has proved a legally sufficient case for liability, there existed a factual predicate for a legal defense that absolved the defendant of liability and/or damages.

The sources of legal theory are obvious. Legal rights are established by either statute or by common law.[6] In either case, the plaintiff must prove all elements of his claims to prevail, and the defendant is responsible for demonstrating either the failure of the plaintiff's proof or all the elements of a recognized defense defeating the plaintiff's claims.

Most legal claims and defenses are well established. A party may, however, offer at trial—and have affirmed on appeal—a new theory of claim or defense.[7] As a general matter, because new claims or defenses cannot be established until there is an appeal, a legal theory based on creating new law is an expensive—and therefore unattractive—prospect for most parties.[8] Ordinarily, then, counsel can readily

5. We begin with a discussion of legal theory, but of course the legal theory of a case is fact driven, depending on the facts available at any given time in the litigation.

6. If faced with an unfamiliar legal issue, a good starting source (perhaps even before legal research) will be to speak with a lawyer experienced with the sort of claims and potential defenses your fact pattern presents. More experienced lawyers will have a good idea of the likely legal theories of claim and defense. And, of course, if the matter is outside your ken and cannot efficiently be learned, refer to more expert counsel.

7. Even if a trial judge allows a party to pursue a new legal claim, and even if that party prevails on that new theory, there always exists the losing party's tactical judgment (typically an institutional defendant or its insurance company) of whether the case at hand is the "best" vehicle to decide the new legal theory and should therefore be appealed. Institutional clients, who run the possibility of facing the "new" theory is future cases, will much rather pursue the legality of the claim in the most "attractive" case (for them) possible. That is, an insurance company would rather not have the viability of a new legal theory of liability decided (thereby making it available in the future) in a case where the plaintiff is a sixty-five-year-old handicapped widower who cares for orphans and habitually does other good deeds. They would prefer the plaintiff injured in the commission of a crime or other distasteful act. Appellate judges, although ostensibly making dispassionate "legal" decisions, are human—and, the authors suspect, motivated by the same emotions as the rest of the world.

8. That being said, new claims and defenses are urged by parties on a regular basis. Although few reach the ultimate test of viability at the appellate level, the specter of the new claim or defense can encourage settlement on well-established principles to avoid the creation of new law for claims or defenses. In fact, most settlement agreements uniformly disclaim liability, or any inference thereof, as grounds for the settlement. In addition, there are parties for whom the establishing of new claims and

identify legal claims and defenses—and their requisite elements of proof—in the statute books and relevant case law.[9] The lawyer must then determine whether there are sufficient facts to prove any particular legal position, and if not, whether there is a reasonable expectation that depositions will reveal such a factual basis. Once you have identified potential legal case theories, you can decide on tactical and practical grounds (including the economics of the case) whether to pursue any given legal course.

Example: Our hypothetical case has a number of potential theories for both parties. Examining the case from the plaintiff's point of view illustrates a typical process of legal theory selection.

The plaintiff claims that she was denied tenure on the basis of her gender. She can proceed in several ways. She can attempt to prove gender discrimination by showing that she was qualified for the tenured professorship, that she was denied that position, that it remained available, and that it was filled by a male of lesser qualification. She can attempt to prove that the university, School of Public Policy, and/or the Patterson Institute discriminated as a matter of policy, or effective policy demonstrated by performance. She could claim that the entity parties maintained a work environment hostile to women. She could attempt to show that she was denied tenure in retaliation for her ending a voluntary sexual relationship with her supervisor, Simonson. Plaintiff also claims that when she searched for other teaching job, she was slandered in less-than-accurate and unflattering reference letters by Simonson (her supervisor at the Patterson Institute) and Jefferson (the dean and her supervisor at the School of Public Policy).

Given these and other potential legal theories, the plaintiff must decide how to proceed. The damages for gender discrimination are available on proving any of the four theories of discrimination noted above. To make out the general case of discrimination, the plaintiff must take on the Public Policy School faculty, the majority of whom voted for her, and claim they discriminated against her when they promoted a male colleague. In that theory, she attacks many of the same people on whom she relies to prove her qualifications to be tenured. The claim would require depositions of many faculty members and would also require some expert statistical testimony, both of which add expense to the case. In the alternative, she can show, through facts about the university and statistical analysis, a pattern of gender discrimination.

The hostile work environment theory does not have much in the way of support from the facts as known (there are tenured women on the faculty, and the dean of the faculty is a woman), and the only real hostile work claim would have to be based on a showing

---

defenses is part of their goals and they will pursue that case, assuming there is a good-faith basis for asserting the new claim or defense, in the hope of creating favorable precedent.

9. An easy and obvious source for the elements of claims and defenses are court-approved pattern jury instructions that exist in every jurisdiction. At a minimum, these instructions will guide more in-depth research on the applicability of a claim or defense in any given case.

that Simonson was a sexual predator (of which there is rumor, given Simonson's history of relationships with colleagues in the past); but that theory has the problem that the plaintiff's sexual relationship with Simonson was consensual.

The retaliation theory requires plaintiff to show either that Simonson campaigned against her tenure (of which there is no evidence, although he also did not support her tenure and publicly abstained from voting) or that it was understood that Simonson (a powerful and revenue-producing faculty member) would consider leaving the university (taking grants and other funding personal to him to another university) rather than deal with regular encounters with the plaintiff.

The slander cases requires plaintiff to deal with the nuance of a equating letter that "damns with faint praise" with libel and further requires showing damages to plaintiff's reputation. This would likely involve testimony of friends from other universities, who brought the "less than glowing" reference letters to plaintiff's attention. In addition, there is a qualified immunity for employment references that must be overcome by actual malice, making the libel claim, at the least, difficult to prove.

All the plaintiff's claims require divulging information about and exploration into her private life. And given that plaintiff has been able to obtain alternate (although less well-paying) employment, her out-of-pocket economic damages are not great.

In light of all the above, at least at this juncture of fact gathering, the most promising, least expensive, and tactically most advisable legal theory appears to be the gender discrimination based on retaliation. Without precluding openness to information, document collection, and at least cursory discovery of other legal theories, full discovery on all but the retaliation claims would not proceed unless discovery on the retaliation claim revealed real problems with the claim, requiring the pursuit of one of the alternatives.

Note that potential legal theories may be inconsistent and claimed in the alternative. This is certainly true at the pleading and discovery phases of litigation. By the time the litigation has progressed to the point of trial or ADR disposition, however, one coherent case theory—or multiple factually consistent case theories—must, as a matter of tactics, be chosen.[10]

Legal theory often changes over the course of litigation. Discovery can suggest new viable theories of claim or defense, while at the same time excluding legal theories that are not supported by the discovered facts in the case. Amend complaints and answers so they are consistent with the available facts as discovered. In the end, legal case theory is reasonably easy to pinpoint with a great deal of certainty, and in most cases will be quite obvious.

10. Inconsistent theories, based on differing views of the facts, show a party's uncertainty of the viability of any particular claim and often undercut one another.

Once potential legal theories have been identified based on the facts known to a party, you must develop potential factual theories sufficient to inform those theories.

4. **Are there any devices to help seek information that supports chosen legal theories?**

You can make the process of informing factual theory easier by creating a legal theory chart. This will later be incorporated into and made part of the primary deposition preparation tool, the chronological storyline chart, which will be discussed in full in chapters five and eight.

The legal theory chart displays the elements of each claim and defense, matched with the factual sources for those elements. As a matter of mechanics, write the elements of each claim and defense across the top of the chart. List the potential sources of information (witnesses, documents, interrogatory answers, admissions, stipulations, etc.) for those elements vertically along the left margin. Draw lines and create a graph depicting the potential confluence of element and source. Complete the graph by highlighting each match of claim and source. If all elements have factual matches, all you need to assure—during the discovery process—is that the source provides that information in an admissible form. For elements lacking factual support, seek potential sources through depositions and otherwise. Part of the purpose of the chronological storyline chart, which you will create later in preparation, will be to help you evaluate the facts available on each element to determine whether they are **known** (agreed on by both parties) **believed** (provided only by sources from deposing counsel's client), **disputed** (the parties disagree as to the existence of a fact), or **hoped for** (facts, yet undiscovered, that fill in gaps in legal and factual theory).

5. **Legal theory seems pretty straightforward, but that's all available in the law library—how do I go about identifying potential factual case theories? In the past, I have identified a factual theory pretty early, based on what my client had to say; later the facts didn't pan out, and we got a less than desirable result.**

This problem is a typical one. Let's talk about the basics of case theory and then tackle the more difficult issues.

The obvious first step in developing factual case theory for deposition practice is identifying the facts that underlie the lawsuit. Because depositions can be taken at any phase of discovery, the volume of facts available for developing factual theory vary, consistent with whatever informal and formal factual investigation has occurred.

Whatever the litigation stage, the deposing party's factual theories and the opposing party's potential factual theories should drive the deposition. The basic tools we will discuss are timelines, relationship charts, focus groups, and storylines. What follows are methods that can help you with these tools.

a. Tell me about using timelines.

Timelines may be the best way of identifying what really happened in any particular case. Build them from the very outset of fact gathering, the initial client interview. The sequence of facts reveals a lot about the reliability of any version of an event. The timeline begins with the first event potentially relevant to the case outcome[11] and continues to include every other fact in the case. For each fact on the timeline, note the date and source(s).[12] The timeline will identify not only facts, but their relative strengths. From this you can develop potential factual theory.

With regard to the strength of facts in a potential theory, we identify four categories of facts: facts that are **known** to be true; facts that are **believed** to be true; facts whose truth is **disputed**; and facts that are **hoped** to be true.

Looking at the timeline, sources from both parties may agree about a certain fact. Or the fact may be corroborated by an undisputed, accurate document. This makes that fact, for the purposes of the litigation, a *known* fact. If the timeline shows that the only source for a fact is the client, at best it can be characterized as a fact *believed* to be true and in need of corroboration. Further, if the timeline shows that opposing parties allege a different version of a fact or there is disagreement between a party and a document,[13] that fact's truth is *disputed,* and the factual theory must resolve the dispute in the favor of your client.

Finally, examining the timeline might (and frequently does, in its earliest stage) reveal non sequiturs. That is, Fact 17 on the timeline does not follow from Fact 16. With that assessment, several realities may be true. Fact 16 did not occur; Fact 17 did not occur; or there is a gap in the timeline and something happened between Fact 16 and Fact 17 that erases the apparent non sequitur. It is the function of case theory to suggest and develop facts that do so—these are facts *hoped* to be true.

Finally, with regard to "believed," "disputed," and "hoped-for" facts, in seeking resolution of "truth" for any of these category facts, a critical question is: if the believed, disputed, or hoped-for fact is true, what else must be true? That is, what other facts would one expect to find that would support the truth of the client's position? For a party's position on any particular fact, you should be able to discover other testimony, documents, lack of evidence, or just use plain common sense to support it.

11. This starting point can and usually does change, either expanding or reducing the time over which facts necessary to the resolution of a case occurred.

12. Many facts will be agreed on by more than one witness or contained in the evidence available from a witness, a document, or other factual source in the case.

13. It is the author's experience that when there is a dispute between the testimony of a witness and an authentic document, the accuracy of the fact will be determined to be consistent with the document version.

EXAMPLE: Consider the following abridged time line:

Date	***Fact***	***Source***
6/1/YR-3	*Williams qualified for promotion*[*]	*Client, Taylor, Promotion Letter*
6/30/YR-3	*Williams promoted to Assoc. Prof.*	*Unanimous Vote, letter from Univ.*
6/30/YR-3–2/1/YR-2	*Relationship between Williams & Simonson continues*	*Client*
11/1/YR-3	*Williams offered Assoc. Director, Patterson Institute (eff. 7/1/YR-2), conditioned on tenure*	*Letter from Simonson to Williams*[†]
2/5/YR-2	*Williams ends relationship with Simonson because he refused to seek promised divorce from wife*	*Client—Simonson denies promise*
2/8/YR-2	*Simonson seeks reconciliation; Williams refuses. Simonson threatens—Williams in "precarious position," "will regret decision."*	*Client—D denies in pleading*
2/8/–5/10/YR-2	*Williams makes public statements critical of Simonson's character*	*Client, Taylor*
4/1/ YR-2	*Tenure committee report: split 2–1 for tenure*[‡]	*University report*
6/1/YR-2	*Faculty votes 16–12–1 for tenure*[§]	*University letter Taylor to Williams, Taylor*
6/10/YR-2	*Dean denies Williams tenure—notes reduced teaching evaluations; missed deadline; lack of collegiality*[**]	*Jefferson letter*

[*] Promotion requires consideration of three categories: teaching, scholarship, and service. Teaching rated at 8.5 by students and faculty; number and quality of scholarship offerings meet university regulations for tenure. Promotion letter suggests Williams met standards for tenure; should be forthcoming in the next year.

[†] Letter states that offer is contingent on tenure in June YR-2 and states Simonson's belief that tenure, based on Williams's performance "presents no difficulty."

[‡] Report notes drop in teaching evaluations to 7.5 students, 7.2 faculty. Williams missed deadline for article. No comment on collegiality.

[§] Faculty vote has never been rejected by dean when making independent recommendation on tenure.

[**] Collegiality not a required factor for tenure in university regulations.

The timeline shows a number of things.

The following are known facts: 6/1/YR-3 (promotion vote); 6/30/YR-3 (promotion); 6/30/YR-3–2/YR-2 (relationship between Williams and Simonson continues); 11/1/YR-3 (offer of associate director position at the Patterson Institute); 2/8–5/10/YR-3 (negative statements of Simonson's character by Williams); 4/1/YR-2 (tenure report); 6/1/YR-2 (tenure vote); and 6/15/YR-2 (tenure denial by Jefferson). They are proved not only by the testimony of Williams—and in some places corroborated by Taylor—but are agreed to in documents created by the defendants.

The facts of 2/5/YR-2 (Williams breaks up with Simonson) and 2/8/YR-2 (Simonson seeks reconciliation—threatens Williams) are facts "believed" to be true. That is, they are from the recollection of Williams alone, and corroboration must be found if the fact is necessary for a successful factual theory. Simonson denied making threats in his answer. As such, the claimed threat to Williams by Simonson is a "disputed" fact.

The timeline also points out that while the faculty was unanimous in their vote for Williams's promotion—for which they used the same factors considered for tenure—their favorable vote on tenure was 16–12–1. Several questions arise.

Williams was the same teacher (albeit with lower evaluations), and the same scholar, and had performed the same service at both junctures—so what happened? Whether the one semester drop in class evaluations and/or a missed article deadline are legitimately fatal for tenure is a matter for further exploration—has either event ever occurred in the past? Has tenure been granted to a faculty member with a 7.5 teacher evaluation? Have candidates with similar scholarship to that of Williams (as characterized by defendant documents) been granted tenure in the past?

Dean Jefferson bases her denial of tenure, at least in significant part, on Williams's alleged lack collegiality. Has that ever happened before? Is lack of collegiality a legitimate basis for tenure denial? If so, how does Jefferson know? What was the "lack of collegiality"? Was Jefferson's decision influenced by other factors? Did Simonson weigh in with Jefferson on Jefferson's decision?

The timeline does show, of course, that the evaluation of Williams's professional performance was significantly different before and after she ended the relationship Simonson. If Simonson in fact threatened her, was the denial of tenure the culmination of that threat? The threat is at once ***believed***, ***disputed***, *and* ***hoped*** *to be true. For this theory to be proved, counsel must find support, the source of which is informed by research, experience, and focused thought. That is, a potential factual theory is that Williams was denied tenure either at the behest of or to accommodate Simonson, who was displeased with Williams for ending their relationship. This should be the topic of the depositions of any number of witnesses associated with the defendants, both within and outside the Public Policy School. The plaintiff will be seeking evidence showing that theory, such as* *statements from Simonson to faculty members, statements by faculty to other faculty, and statements to and from Jefferson. In all of this questioning, counsel will* ***hope*** *to find facts to prove that Simonson was the motivating factor in the denial of tenure for Williams.*

Finally, the timeline suggests a potential case theory for the defendants. They can claim that Williams was not qualified for tenure. If so, given what they have written in ***known*** *documents will make the theory problematic. Given the timeline, the more probable defense—in the terms of the university regulations—is "in the long-term best interests of the university."*

The timeline will of course evolve, as the conflict among the parties is joined. The factual theory will demonstrate the true facts by showing the reasons why the facts as claimed by one party are more likely true than those by the opposing party.

b. How is a relationship chart created, and how is it used to develop potential case theory?

The key to understanding any event is understanding the relationships between the various people and entities involved. Factual theory requires you to determine not only what really happened, but why. Relationships between and among people and entities often provide that answer by explaining why one fact on the timeline followed from another. Relationships add nuance to the meaning of facts discovered and offer the possible motivation for a person or institution to act. Examining relationships, with or without the chart, is valuable. The chart itself adds significantly to the utility of motivation to explain action.

There is no orthodoxy as to the shape of the chart. Its content, however, is well settled. To begin, place the names of the primary actors in the lawsuit in the center of the page (which could be a whiteboard, poster-board, or digital visual aid. Draw lines of connection between the actors, and describe the relationship on the line. Add additional people and entities, with coinciding lines of connection that show the nature of the relationship.

Add people or entities to the chart as potential actors in the lawsuit, and draw descriptive connection lines, including relationships between newly added actors and relationships between the newly added actors to those you initially placed on the chart. You will need to reorganize over time as it becomes clear that certain relationships between actors are the same for a grouping of actors—if the entity is an employer, each employee has at least one descriptive connection in common with the entity and it might make sense to group them accordingly on the chart. A look at potential entries on the relationship chart in *Williams v. Simonson* should illustrate the value and use of the charting process.

Example: At the center of the chart are Williams, Simonson, and Jefferson. At the outset, the line of connection between Williams and Simonson shows their relationship has multiple levels: S hired W and, as her dean, was her employer for a few months; S offered early critique of W's teaching and scholarship at W's request; S hired W as a researcher at the Patterson Institute and again became her employer; S and W had a consensual, intimate relationship for almost two years; S evaluated W's work at a high level; S offered W the associate director position at the Patterson Institute; S and W split up when S refused to divorce his wife, as W claims he promised to do; W made disparaging remarks re S; W applied for tenure, about which S abstained; W sues, claiming sexual discrimination by S as reason for her failure to receive tenure. S denies allegation. Note that the lines of connection are listed chronologically, using the timeline previously prepared.

Turn then to the relationship between Jefferson and Simonson. S supported J for tenure—the first woman to achieve that rank; J replaced S as Dean when S went to direct the Patterson Institute; S supported J's deanship candidacy; J was aware of S's previous sexual relationships with women employed by Nita Univ.; J was aware of S's importance in prestige and fund-raising for the PPS and the university; J frequently consulted S about decisions she made as Dean; J was aware of and approved by silence the relationship between S and W; J was aware of the S–W breakup and disparaging remarks by W re S; J consulted with S about her decision to veto tenure application of W despite favorable faculty vote.

Finally, consider the relationship of Williams and Jefferson. Although J was the senior woman of PPS faculty, she made no offer or attempt to mentor W; J's review of W were in the main positive; during pendency of S–W relationship, J reviewed W's performance, and those reviews were more positive after S–W relationship began; in a yearly review, J characterized W complaint of sexual harassment by the dean of the business school as "a serious question of collegiality;" in YR-3 J predicts in yearly evaluation that W will easily meet tenure requirements in the next year (YR-2); J warns W of drop in performance in semester (lower teaching evaluations, publication deadline missed) in semester before YR-2 tenure vote—offers to put off decision until YR-1—W declines; J was first dean of PPS not to support a positive faculty vote for tenure; J states her failure to recommend tenure for W was lack of collegiality, a standard not articulated in university regulations.

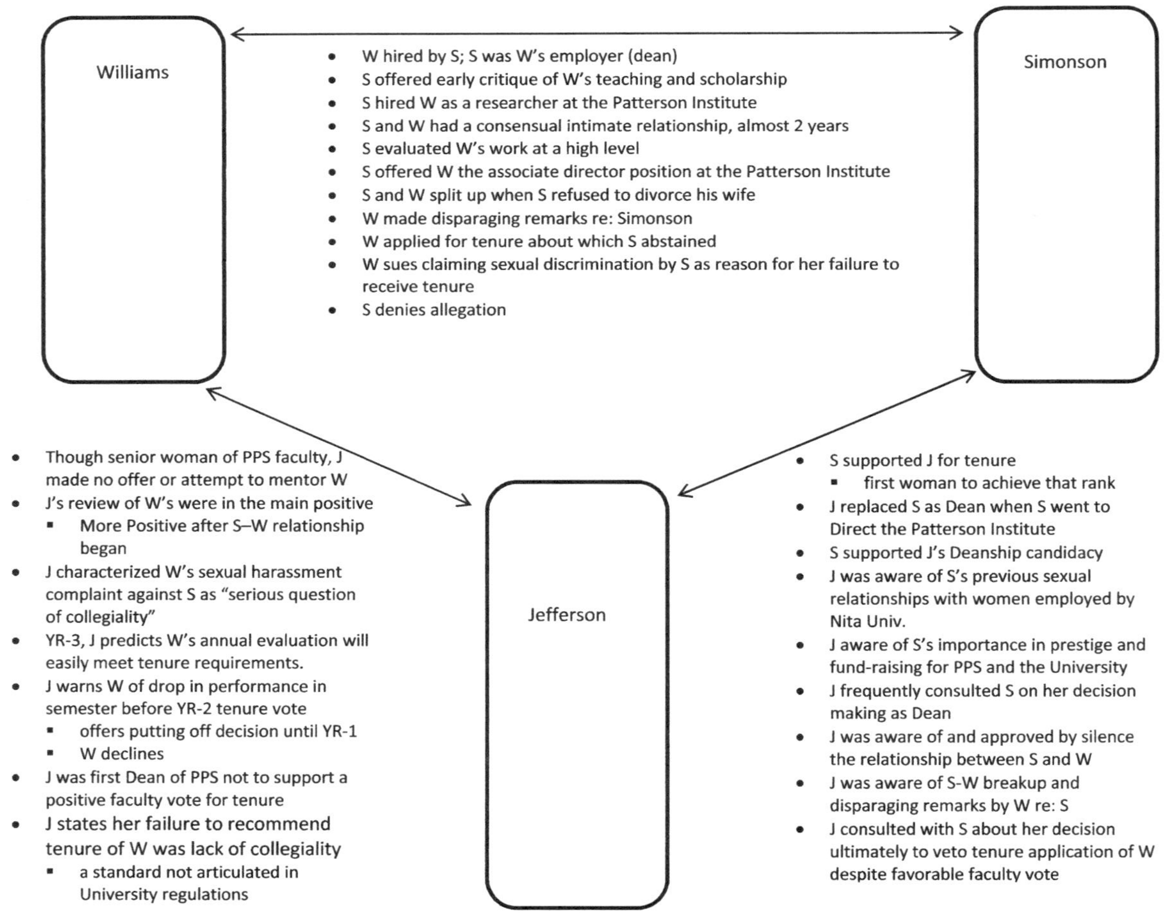
Williams
Simonson
Jefferson
• W hired by S; S was W's employer (dean)
• S offered early critique of W's teaching and scholarship
• S hired W as a researcher at the Patterson Institute
• S and W had a consensual intimate relationship, almost 2 years
• S evaluated W's work at a high level
• S offered W the associate director position at the Patterson Institute
• S and W split up when S refused to divorce his wife
• W made disparaging remarks re: Simonson
• W applied for tenure about which S abstained
• W sues claiming sexual discrimination by S as reason for her failure to receive tenure
• S denies allegation
• Though senior woman of PPS faculty, J made no offer or attempt to mentor W
• J's review of W's were in the main positive
▪ More Positive after S–W relationship began
• J characterized W's sexual harassment complaint against S as "serious question of collegiality"
• YR-3, J predicts W's annual evaluation will easily meet tenure requirements.
• J warns W of drop in performance in semester before YR-2 tenure vote
▪ offers putting off decision until YR-1
▪ W declines
• J was first Dean of PPS not to support a positive faculty vote for tenure
• J states her failure to recommend tenure of W was lack of collegiality
▪ a standard not articulated in University regulations
• S supported J for tenure
▪ first woman to achieve that rank
• J replaced S as Dean when S went to Direct the Patterson Institute
• S supported J's Deanship candidacy
• J was aware of S's previous sexual relationships with women employed by Nita Univ.
• J aware of S's importance in prestige and fund-raising for PPS and the University
• J frequently consulted S on her decision making as Dean
• J was aware of and approved by silence the relationship between S and W
• J was aware of S-W breakup and disparaging remarks by W re: S
• J consulted with S about her decision ultimately to veto tenure application of W despite favorable faculty vote

When the relationship chart, as created at the outset, is considered in conjunction with the overarching relationships between Williams and Simonson, Simonson and Jefferson, and Jefferson and Williams, several factual theories are suggested.

For the Plaintiff: *Williams was qualified for tenure; her evaluations and recommendations from Jefferson and Simonson said so. She was only denied tenure after she broke off her relationship with Simonson, with whom Jefferson consulted, and only after that consultation did Jefferson veto Williams's tenure based on "collegiality," a consideration for tenure not articulated in university regulations. Jefferson did so out of loyalty to Simonson, knowing his importance to the school, and under the odd belief that rejecting sexual advances by a male colleague is demonstrating a lack of "collegiality."*

For the Defendant: *Williams voluntarily consented to a sexual relationship with Simonson, which she ended the semester of her tenure consideration. In that semester, her teaching evaluations were significantly lower, she missed a publication deadline, and she openly made disparaging personal and professional remarks both in and outside the university about an important faculty member. She was given an opportunity (by delaying her tenure consideration) to stop her disparaging comments and repair her teaching and scholarship evaluations, but she declined. As a result, the faculty barely approved her tenure. In all of these circumstances, Jefferson did her job and made a decision to deny tenure based on the standard required in university regulations: "the long-term interests of the university."*

As discovery continues and more relationships are noted, the lines of connection expanding the relationship chart may support the above articulated factual theories or some other, not yet revealed.

Once you've gotten a robust relationship chart, put that information into the case's timeline to develop further factual theory.

6. I've heard about using focus groups for trial—how are they helpful during deposition preparation and execution, and can I afford them?

Lawyers have long recognized the value of focus groups in developing case theory. Given modern practice, where trial is unlikely, using focus groups during the litigation process has become more commonplace. Properly used before the depositions, focus groups can help you hone in on case theories that have the best likelihood of success. That is not to say that focus groups are not without cost. Focus groups as described below, conducted by a qualified psychologist, cost an average of $20,000. They can, however, help you exclude potential factual case theories that are likely to involve retaining multiple expert witnesses, along with their attendant high costs. The amount involved in the lawsuit will, of course, govern whether the expense of a focus group is appropriate. Do not forget that lawyers, experienced in participating in focus groups led by professionals, can learn to perform the analysis themselves, without hiring outside consultants.[14]

The goals of conducting focus groups are to identify areas for factual inquiry; alert lawyers to facts and witnesses about and from whom a decision maker would want to hear; and identify psychological hot spots in any potential case theory. We suggest three focus group methodologies to help you develop your factual theory. Each require a minimum of ten members in the focus group, selected from a fair cross-section of the community,[15] and each would benefit by replicating the process with a second ten-person focus group.[16]

a. Timeline-building focus

In the first methodology, the focus group members fill out a form that asks for general demographics (to insure diversity of opinion).The form also poses questions about their ethical values and, perhaps most importantly, their basic world view of how and why events occur.[17] Each focus group member is assigned a number by which they will be referred for the entirety of the process. The entire session is video-recorded, usually with two cameras, showing in split screen the person speaking to the focus group and the focus group members.

The session begins with a "focus group leader" presenting as neutral a statement of the case facts as counsel knows at this stage of the litigation. After this presentation, the group is asked the following question:

> Based on what you heard, is the plaintiff or defendant right? Please vote with a show of hands.

Then each focus group member should be asked to respond to the following statements and questions.

a) Explain why you believe the plaintiff/defendant is right.

b) What did you assume was true when you made your decision?

14. *See* How to Do Your Own Focus Groups: A Guide for Trial Attorneys, David Ball, 2000.

15. Good sources for potential focus group members are community groups, old juror lists, and voter lists. Focus group members are usually paid a reasonable amount for their assistance, typically $100 for each session. Finally, the focus group members are not told which party is conducting the session, as people tend to want to please the person who conducts the session.

16. The replication can be conducted at the same time, in two separate rooms, or a second run-through after completing the first. The latter sequence is usually preferable, as lesson learned in the first session can be used to make the second session more valuable.

17. In this regard, there are two predominant views, known as locus of control. About half of the people believe that things happen randomly and outside the control of any individual. The other half believes that events can be controlled by the people who participate in the event.

c) Do you have any questions about what happened? (If the leader knows the answer, she should provide it. If not, the leader should so respond.)

d) If what you think is true, what else would you expect to be true?

e) What fact would you like to hear to make you confident in your opinion about who is right?

f) What new fact would change your opinion?

g) Based on everything you have heard, vote again whether you think the plaintiff or defendant is right.

h) If you changed your mind from your initial vote, why did you do so?

All of these responses are video-recorded for later reference, but some things are revealed instantly.

The response to the first question provides the basic view of which party, given the neutral statement, has the strongest position. Individual explanations in support of the response to the first question reveal the strongest facts for each party. Seek the "new" facts identified by group members voting in favor of your party from multiple sources. During deposition, minimize or impeach on the facts identified as favorable to the opposing party.

The question on assumptions helps you identify biases and prejudices that the parties' positions might generate. Use deposition practice to obtain information that corroborates favorable assumptions and negates unfavorable assumptions.

The questions asked by focus group members suggest facts they believe should exist in the fact pattern as described. Explore those facts in depositions. If you can't find them, explain their absence if you believe a factfinder will think any factual theory without that information is insufficient.

The question that asks "what else must be true" identifies facts that the holder of a particular belief—in favor or opposed to a party—expects to be presented in a persuasive factual theory. Find those facts, and if they are unavailable, account for them.

In response to questions (f) and (g), focus group members identify those facts that solidify their belief. In a deposition, you need to discover facts that make the position of your client either stronger or weaker to properly evaluate the case for disposition. **Do not make the egregious error of not pursuing the discovery of "negative" facts**. These facts, if they exist, will not go away, and you must account for them to have an effective factual theory.

Finally, facts that have the ability to change the mind of focus group members are absolute necessities for discovery. Most people like to remain consistent in their opinions, which will harden over time. If certain facts move the focus group members to change their minds, those facts will be powerful for later decision makers as well—they need your special attention to create a winning factual theory.

After the session, examine the parallels between the focus group members' ethical positions and beliefs about locus of control and their belief in the correctness of either party. This will identify how decision makers might match up in regard to ethical systems, locus of control beliefs, and disposition toward one party over another. A factual theory that works best for characteristics typical of likely decision makers is, of course, much stronger than a factual theory that appeals mainly to people who are not likely to share the characteristics of likely decision makers.

b. Unpacking the case

The second focus group methodology is called "unpacking the case." It is particularly helpful when you are using a predeposition focus group to identify persuasive factual theory. The makeup of the focus group, their number, the collection of pre-session information, and the video-recording of the session is the same as with the previous methodology. The unpacking begins with the statement of the basic case facts as it exists predeposition. In our hypothetical case, for example, the leader might say, "a woman faculty member consents to a sexual relationship with a powerful senior faculty member; she ends the relationship," then ask the focus group some questions like, "what happens to her," "how does the senior faculty member feel about the breakup," and "what does the senior faculty member do?" From the responses to these questions, you will learn about the focus group's assumptions about workplace sexual relations—who bears the brunt of the breakup of the relationship, how men take rejection, and how they respond.

The leader then continues to unpack the case. She might add, "the senior faculty member is married, the junior faculty member is not," "the woman says the man promised to divorce his wife, and he did not," and "the junior faculty member loses her job." She may then ask further questions, such as, "what do you think about the senior faculty member," "what do you think about the woman faculty member," "do you think the man really intended to divorce his wife, "was the woman naïve to believe the man about the divorce," "did the senior faculty member have anything to do with the woman losing her job?" The answers will reveal the focus group's attitudes about sexual relationships, now with the overlay that the man was married and the woman believed that he would divorce his wife for her. The focus group members might say that the man was lying all the time; that the woman was foolish to think he would get a divorce; or blame the woman for trying to break up a marriage.

As the facts are unpacked, record the ebb and flow of group reaction to the case to show the impact of certain facts. Ask questions after each cluster of facts—which party is right, which party is at fault, etc. Also ask what facts would help sway the group one way or another. You will learn a lot about hidden attitudes that might affect the resolution of the matter as well as the direction and focus of deposition discovery.

c. Reverse engineering the jury verdict

The final focus group methodology is one that is particularly helpful in cases where adjudicators must make specific factual findings to prove particular legal elements of a cause of action. In such cases, jurors might, if left to their own devices, do what jurors do and hone in on fault, fairness, and responsibility rather than the specific elements required by law.[18] This focus group methodology is called "reverse engineering the jury verdict."

This methodology uses the same focus group membership, their collected background information, and the video-recordings of all sessions. The leader lists the elements of the claims and defenses in the lawsuit in the same manner that a judge might instruct jurors at a trial. In the alternative, provide the focus group with the set of special interrogatories contained in a "Special Verdict Form" that would be provided to jurors to guide their deliberations. Then ask focus group members to explain their understanding of what findings the instructions required them to make and, importantly, whether the group members felt that requiring such findings is fair and appropriate. The answers to these questions show the likelihood of jurors ignoring the law and making their own determination of the fairness and responsibility required to apportion liability for a plaintiff's injuries.

After these questions, present the focus group with a neutral statement of the case facts, as you understand them from the available information. Ask whether, based on those facts, they could decide that there is sufficient evidence to meet the requirements of the law from the instructions or Special Verdict Form. From that juncture, follow the process of inquiring as described in the first focus group methodology. This provides information about facts that each party should seek in favor of and opposition to their positions. In addition, this process provides material for crafting different or better jury instructions, usually by simplifying the language.

7. What are storylines, and how do they help case theory identification and verification?

We have given you several tools with which to evaluate information: legal theory charts, timelines, relationship charts, and focus groups. From these—and a careful analysis of the available facts, against the strongest backdrop of common sense—identify, create, and write potential storylines that encapsulate the factual theory

18. For example, in many jurisdictions, responsibility for a defective product applies to all entities in the chain of commerce and does so even if the party that designed and manufactured the product did not realize, despite good intentions, that the product was defective. In those jurisdictions, the law of product liability is designed so that irrespective of fault, liability for injuries to a consumer caused by a defective product is placed on parties who make money on the sale of the product instead of the innocent consumer. And this is so even if the defendant in the chain of commerce is a wholesale dealer of the product who had nothing to do with the product's design, manufacture, or even sale to the ultimate consumer.

in a persuasive narrative. Each storyline must present a narrative, including already identified facts, that emphasizes the favorable facts, recognizes and deals with the unfavorable, and suggests facts—yet undiscovered—that complete the persuasive narrative.

Each case will be susceptible to a range of storylines, each with a different emphasis and each pointing to a different legal theory. Each storyline depends on the facts you discover in deposition practice. These will confirm **known** facts, find support for **believed** facts, resolve opposing versions of **disputed** facts (or leave them in dispute), and disclose facts **hoped** to exist. The workable storyline will account for all of the identified facts in the case—positive, negative, and yet to be found,

Once you reduce the potential factual case theories, stated in a storyline narrative, to writing, perform an evidence check. Each storyline must account for all the required elements of each claim or defense. Because the storyline is a marriage of legal and factual theory, you can determine the admissibility of each fact supporting your factual theory—each relevant fact in a storyline must also be admissible for the storyline to support the legal theory. If you determine that your storyline is based on inadmissible evidence you must either discard it or identify some admissible purpose for the evidence. The deposition process will help you identify a range of admissible purposes. For example, use deposition testimony to find a nonhearsay purpose or an exception to the hearsay rule, for hearsay statements—or have the witness adopt it as a party statement, thereby overcoming the hearsay issue.

As we will describe in chapter four, each storyline, when set out fact by fact in chronological order, creates a chronological story outline. This outline serves as a guideline for taking deposition testimony. Chapter Seven discusses the benefits and potential detriments of using the chronological storyline as an organizing device for depositions. Suffice it to say that ultimately, the effective litigation of any lawsuit, including—and most importantly, taking and defending—depositions, will be driven by following your factual theory/storyline chronology throughout discovery and by matching that chronology to the facts.

Chapter Four

Deposition Preparation

Preparation is, of course, the key to a successful deposition. The areas of concern for preparation are the timing of the deposition, topics for consideration, factual sources, and the method for creating the end-use preparation document, the **Chronological Storyline Chart**, which will encapsulate the potential legal and factual case theories and identify the necessary facts and their sources.

1. What is the significance of the timing of the deposition in the litigation process?

A deposition's timing in the litigation is one of the primary drivers of preparation. There are as many opinions as to when in the litigation process a particular deposition will take place as there are lawyers.[1] Some lawyers prefer to depose opposing parties and witnesses as early in the process as possible. These lawyers, usually representing plaintiffs,[2] want to get information from key witnesses before counterclaims and defenses are fully developed and while events are fresh in the minds of parties and witnesses. They are mindful of the fact that as time passes, "memory" about an event will be reconstructed and hardened consistent with the witness's basic point of view. That is, if a person believes that an incident occurred in a certain way (e.g., the plaintiff was driving too fast), over time, that belief will become hardened. When questioned about that belief and its bases, the witness will report her recollection in a way that is consistent with her basic point of view. Witnesses will not lie. They will, however, reconstruct and confabulate (fill in the gaps in actual memory) consistent with their basic point of view. One of the goals of a deposition is to effectively end the witness's reconstruction process; if you conduct the deposition properly,[3] any testimony at trial that exceeds the deposition testimony will be subject to impeachment by omission.

Other lawyers like to take important depositions late in the litigation process, when they developed facts more fully through other means. At this point, witnesses

1. Use Rule 30 party representative depositions to obtain background information about parties—especially entities and how, and by whom, they operate. This topic will be fully discussed in chapter ten.

2. Plaintiff lawyers overpopulate this grouping; they have the luxury and advantage of fully developing their case theory before pleading. As a result, their knowledge of the facts of the case early in the litigation make them better prepared, and less likely to miss discovery opportunities.

3. Chapters Seven through Eleven demonstrate the process of obtaining reliable information in a deposition by making the deponent agree that he has exhausted his memory on a topic and provided complete information on questioning topics.

can more likely be made to conform their deposition testimony to the discovery already completed (and attendant case theory). Defense attorneys overpopulate this group.[4] They believe that taking a deposition before the facts are more fully developed might preclude fruitful inquiry into case theories, both legal and factual, that become apparent after full discovery. They then depose key witnesses, who can be confronted by—and perhaps guided to testify consistent with—the discovery revealed before the deposition.

No one method fits all cases. Lawyers who prefer early depositions may choose to postpone a deposition or group of depositions (usually related to the same legal theory) until later in the process. Lawyers who prefer later depositions (usually defendants) may take early depositions when they believe that a case can be disposed of with relatively narrow discovery on a particular topic. The timing of depositions, like everything else in litigation, must be purposeful and based on your best calculations of the legal and tactical advantages.

2. Can you give me an overview of the process of deposition preparation?

The deposition will likely occur after you have gathered many facts—client and witness statements, internet research, and document collection—and begun testing your initial legal theories.[5] In addition, in the federal courts, the mandatory disclosures requirements of Rule 26 will identify the witnesses and documents that support the claims of each party. The further along in the litigation process a deposition occurs, the more information is available: from document discovery, investigation into the parties' claims and defenses, formal document and other evidence production, and—in all but the first deposition in the case—the previous sworn testimony of other witnesses.

Following from the above, when you prepare for a deposition, be sure to include at least the following.

a) Review all the available materials in the litigation to check the current state of your legal and factual case theories, then consider the information the witness to be deposed may add to those theories.

---

4. This is in part true because the goal of defendants is frequently to dispose of the case through summary judgment or other case dispositive motion practice. Late in litigation depositions can focus on the important issues for such motion practice.

5. Given the fact pleading requirements of *Twombly*, *Iqbal*, and their progeny, the plaintiff will have laid out a relatively complete factual position that support legal claims she made to overcome a motion to dismiss. Although it is not required to do so, in the opinion of the authors, good practice dictates that the defendant, too, will state factual bases in the answer—and especially in affirmative defenses and counterclaims. *Ashcroft v. Iqbal*, 556 U.S. 662 (2009), *Bell Atlantic Corp. v. Twombly*, 550 U.S. 544 (2007).

b) Review the elements of each claim and defense in light of your legal theories to assure that your proof of those elements is sufficient to survive appellate scrutiny.

c) Examine the available discovery to determine the current state of factual development for each element.

d) Where there is little or no proof of a required element of a claim or defense, consider whether the witness to be deposed can repair that legal theory weakness.

e) Review the deponent's place in factual theory, and determine how the deponent helps demonstrate the persuasive theory.[6]

f) The deponent's demeanor, as reflected in the video recording of testimony, will often impact the persuasive theory; the video recording will also reflect the style, tone and attitude you choose to use when taking the deposition.

Example: One of the plaintiff's claims is that the university, and in particular the Public Policy School, maintained a hostile work environment. One element of such a claim is not only that the environment existed, but that there was institutional knowledge of the environment, usually with a failure to correct. Assume that Professor Taylor is to be deposed. Although he has knowledge of facts relevant to all aspects of the case, he is an excellent witness for the plaintiff to pursue with regard to the hostile work environment claim.[7] Taylor has been at the Public Policy School for over thirty years; he served as its dean for fifteen of them, during which Simonson joined the faculty and rose to the position of dean. As such, if the hostile work environment claim is based on the Public Policy School and the university tolerating Professor Simonson's conduct with women members of the university community, Taylor, as the Dean of the Public Policy School for fifteen years, is an excellent source of "institutional" knowledge. Williams says that Taylor warned her that Simonson had a reputation for, and did, take advantage of women over whom he had some university-recognized control. Taylor can corroborate what he told Williams about Simonson's history of sexual relationships with women within the university community—and additionally, that when those relationships ended, so too did the woman's employment at the university. Importantly, if that activity occurred during Taylor's deanship, as believed, his knowledge of Simonson's pattern of behavior can be attributed to the Public Policy School and university, thus breathing life into the hostile work environment claim.

6. Why, in fairness, equity and common sense a party deserves a favorable juror consideration.

7. As the case sets out, Taylor is likely a witness for the plaintiff, whose deposition will be sought by the defendants. We will suggest in chapter nine that you should consider taking the depositions of favorable witnesses. At any rate, many witnesses typically have facts helpful to opposing parties, so even if the defendants subpoena Taylor, the plaintiff should develop those facts needed for plaintiff's case theory during his deposition.

For Williams to prevail, she must prove that she was qualified for tenure. Dean Taylor has the advantage of thirty years perspective of what makes a person qualified for tenure and can demonstrate that Williams had those qualities.

Finally, a persuasive theory in the case for the plaintiff is that the faculty, and especially Dean Jefferson, had a self-interest in keeping Simonson, with his academic reputation and the millions of grant dollars he brought to the university, from leaving. Taylor can verify Simonson's importance as well as the negative impact his leaving would have on the university—and the evaluation of the success of Jefferson's deanship. Given Simonson's embarrassment at Williams's statements about him (both personally and professionally), even without his asking, his colleagues—and especially his dean—might have considered Simonson's future with the university when voting on Williams's tenure. Simonson, after all, had many other options in academia. As a result, the plaintiff may argue that she was denied tenure, even though qualified, because she displeased an important faculty member by ending a sexual relationship and that the faculty and Jefferson were driven by their perceived need to keep Simonson happy.

3. What sources should I review?

a. Collect all the information available about this deponent.

This includes everything from Google and social media searches to what the client or anyone else might have said about the witness in formal or informal discovery. The deponent may also be referred to in pleadings, motion practice, or Rule 26 disclosures.[8] All of this background information will help you determine the topics, tone, and scope of the deposition.

Example: Internet research has shown that defendant Simonson is, in fact, a legitimate superstar in the field of public policy. With multiple highly regarded publications, professional awards, government service on highly regarded commissions, congressional testimony, grants that bring money to the university, and the ability to raise significant amounts of money (in his short tenure as dean he brought a $10 million grant to the university that resulted in the creation of the Patterson Institute of Public Policy), Simonson's professional excellence, and his importance to the university, is unassailable. His résumé raises the question of why he remains at Nita University, when his qualifications and accomplishments are the equal of faculty members at the most prestigious public policy schools in the country. He appears to be the proverbial "big fish in a small pond." There must be reasons for his choice, and those reasons need be explored.

8. Fed. R. Civ. P. 26 requires mandatory disclosure of the witnesses each party intends to call to testify in support of their claims or defenses in the case. If the deponent is a person who obviously knows something about the facts of the case, and a party is aware of that fact, the failure to list that person in Rule 26 disclosures would suggest that something about the witness—and his testimony—concerns that party.

In addition, witnesses have suggested that Simonson's accomplishments come with an attitude of superiority that can be off-putting. He is, according to these witnesses, used to being listened to—while not himself an attentive listener—and arrogant. Avoid the natural tendency to meet arrogance with arrogance and the desire to put Simonson in his place; although satisfying, it would be contrary to complete and easy fact gathering. While there may be a time for this tone and tactic at some point in the deposition, Simonson's status and attitude suggests using a tone and tactics that recognize his importance and encourages him to talk about his accomplishments—and more importantly, the facts of this case. As a result, consider noticing this deposition for the conference room at the Patterson Institute, which Simonson directs. He will be comfortable, at ease, in charge, and forthcoming, all of which are consistent with complete fact gathering.

b. Collect all documents that you believe the deponent knows—or should know—that reference the deponent; also include documents about topics you believe to be within the ken of the deponent.

Each document will provide topics for your questions to the deponent, even if limited to their proper use in the litigation. Consider each document's admissibility, and then consider what information you need from the witness to build a foundation for admissibility or, conversely, to make the document inadmissible.[9]

Example: Assume that the defendant is taking Williams's deposition. The defendant possesses five years of documents assessing Williams's performance, created by Dean Jefferson as part of the evaluation process. Although Williams would not, as a matter of course, receive these documents, it is reasonable to assume that in her oral reviews with Dean Jefferson the content of those documents would have been revealed. This is the information that defense counsel has from Jefferson. In Williams's deposition, each of these evaluations should be shown to her. After she states, as assumed, that she did not see the document except during the course of the litigation, question her about facts contained in the document to confirm both their accuracy and that the facts had been communicated to her. In addition, ask about oral communications Williams believes Jefferson made to her that are either inconsistent with or more expansive than what is shown in the evaluation record document.

The defendants also have in their possession a document that appears to be a letter from Professor Taylor, acting as the chair of the tenurial faculty, to Williams. The letter offers Williams the opportunity to delay her tenure decision for a year so that any weaknesses in her previous year's performance could be repaired. Further, the letter states that should she

9. The use and tactics of exhibits is discussed in chapter nine. Generally, if the document is one which you want to use substantively, question the deponent to show that substantive admissibility. Likewise, if the document is one that you would like to exclude substantively, develop deponent testimony that shows that inadmissibility.

choose to go forward in YR-2, the tenure decision made would be final. Question Williams to prove that she received not only the letter (making it relevant to the case, and overcoming any hearsay objection as it is offered to show notice to Williams as a precursor to admissibility), but also the advice and the repercussions of not postponing the decision.

Finally, the defense has in its possession a letter that appears to be from Williams to Taylor, in which Williams declines Taylor's offer to put off tenure consideration for a year and insists on a YR-2 tenure decision. This letter was produced by Professor Taylor, but not by Williams. Williams should be asked to verify that she wrote the letter. Question her to confirm that she understood that she was acting contrary to Professor Taylor's advice in failing to take the extension and that she understood that a decision to go forward in YR-2 meant the result of that process was final. In so doing, defense counsel will insure that Williams's letter is admissible, showing not only its relevance, but its authenticity, establishing an exception to the hearsay rule as an opposing party's statement.

c. Review the case timeline.[10]

Determine which facts are assumed as known to be true because of some act, knowledge, or attribution of the deponent. Then determine which facts are believed to be true, which the deponent can either corroborate or dispute. Finally, determine what facts you hope to be true that the deponent may have, which can help you fill gaps in the timeline. Each and every fact on the timeline that refers to the deponent as a source—or a document or statement made by the deponent as a source—must be memorialized and confirmed as such for the rest of the litigation. Referring to the timeline advances the goals of obtaining complete, comprehensive, and accurate information from the witness.

Example: Consider the deposition of Simonson, who is at the heart of the case for both parties. It is a known fact (one corroborated by witnesses for plaintiff and undisputed by defendants) that Simonson was the director of the Patterson Institute and hired Williams as a researcher. Simonson's legal status at the institute is not clearly known. To make a claim of gender discrimination against Simonson and the institute, Simonson must be an "employer." Simonson can confirm his authority over all things at the institute, including hiring and firing, thereby making a Rule 36 admission that Simonson was "an agent of the Patterson Institute" (the deeper pocket for damages) and Williams's employer. This fulfills an element of her gender discrimination claim against Simonson and the institute. In addition, Simonson will likely willingly admit his importance to the university (a key to several of plaintiff's legal and factual theories).

10. By the time of depositions, the case timeline will contain many entries showing the facts identified by their source(s). In addition, the timeline will show gaps in information that might exist, and those gaps will be filled in by potential facts from your case theory that are consistent with the timeline and the position of the client. Facts on the timeline can then be further characterized as known, believed, disputed, or hoped.

A requirement for tenure at the university is "service," which includes attracting grants and donations to the university. Although Williams has not attracted new grant money, it is her position that she did virtually all the work necessary to obtain a renewal of a federal grant awarded to Simonson and the institute. This is a fact the plaintiff believes to be true. Simonson can corroborate the fact that Williams worked on the grant as well as the fact that although she was not the grantee on the grant, her work was incorporated, in full, in the renewal application, which was awarded in the amount of $350,000.

Williams says that she ended the sexual relationship with Simonson because he refused to leave his wife, as promised, and that at their final break-up Simonson was quite angry and said, "Think about who you're talking to; you're in a precarious position; and you will regret this, I promise you." These are facts that Williams believes to be true, but Defendant's Answer to Plaintiff's Complaint denied the allegation that Simonson threatened Williams's position in the university. During Simonson's deposition, explore that general denial. First, question Simonson about whether, to induce Williams to continue the relationship, he ever stated or alluded to divorcing his wife. If he denies this, it remains a disputed fact; probe why, absent such a promise, Williams would continue a long-term relationship with a married man. Similarly, explore Simonson's other relationships with university employees and whether he ever made such a promise to those women. In addition, try to establish that Simonson did not want the relationship to end; it is likely that Williams ending it induced anger. Against that backdrop, make Simonson relate the exchange of words between him and Williams; after exhausting his recollection, confront him with what Williams alleges he said.

Finally, all of plaintiff's gender discrimination claims depend on her demonstrating that she was qualified for tenure pursuant to university regulations. Confront Simonson with all the facts on the timeline showing his opinion of Williams's qualifications,[11] *seeking an inference of her meeting the qualifications for tenure.*[12]

d. Review the relationship charts prepared at the outset of the case and amplified through litigation—they show the interactions between and among the parties.

Although not required in most litigation, the motivation of the parties is always relevant to the case, and important to final determination. The relationship of a party with the other actors in the case often shows potential motivation for what

11. Simonson hired her on to the faculty, hired her as a researcher at the Patterson Institute, and later offered her the Associate Director position there, in both cases over more senior applicants. He also wrote in several places that he considered Williams an excellent candidate for tenure.

12. Counsel may go so far as to amalgamate all the positive things Simonson has said about Williams's qualifications and seek affirmation that on the specific requirements of teaching, scholarship, and service, Williams met the qualifications for tenure.

really happened and explains the key question of why those events occurred. As a result, identify the deponent's relationships with and among people and entities in preparation for his deposition.

Example: The ultimate decision maker in this case was Dean Jefferson. Even in the face of a positive faculty vote on tenure, she exercised what was essentially a veto of Williams's tenure application. This decision is remarkable: no other dean had ever refused to support the faculty decision on tenure; Williams's demonstrated teaching, scholarship, and service matches well with a male tenure candidate who was granted tenure; and there is no mention of "collegiality" as a tenure requirement in university regulations. Jefferson's letter to Williams stated that she exercised her nonreviewable discretion to deny tenure to Williams as (in the terms of university regulations) not in the long-term best interests to the university, citing lack of collegiality, with specific reference to negative statements Williams admitted to making about Simonson.

Look for potential motivations for Jefferson to act as she did by referencing the relationship charts. Portions of those relationship charts reveal the following.

Jefferson/Simonson—Simonson was Jefferson's successor as dean, and he championed her candidacy; Jefferson was aware of Simonson's status in the university; Jefferson knew of Simonson's relationship with Williams and condoned it by silence; and Jefferson frequently consulted with Simonson when making decisions and in fact consulted with Simonson regarding her required review of Williams's tenure.

Jefferson/Williams—Jefferson had a mostly cordial relationship with Williams, but was not her professional mentor, nor as the senior woman faculty member did she counsel Williams about potential gender issues at the school;[13] *Jefferson's praise of Williams only began after Simonson took on Williams as a researcher at the Patterson Institute and Simonson made positive comments about Williams's abilities; and Jefferson made a negative comment about Williams's collegiality in her evaluation of Williams in YR-5 referring to Williams's work with other university community members on a fundraising committee.*

Williams/Dressler—In January of YR-5, Williams made a complaint to the University Committee on Discrimination, accusing Dean Richard Dressler of the Nita University Business School of sexual harassment. In addition to being dean of the business school, Dressler was the chair of a university fundraising committee on which Williams served. Williams claimed that Dressler made sexual advances towards her, including touching her inappropriately and asking her to join him on trips out of town. Williams objected to this conduct and expressed the same to

13. On the basis of sheer numbers of faculty—twenty-seven men to six women—there would seem to be at least some history of women faculty members being either not sought or not promoted. It would be natural for Jefferson, as the senior woman on the faculty, to relate that history to Williams and at least assure her that it was a "new day" at the public policy school.

Dressler; Dressler's activity persisted, and Williams complained to the University Disciplinary Committee about Dressler's conduct in YR-4. The complaint was dropped when Dressler left the university for a position as president at another university later in YR-4.

Jefferson/Dressler—Jefferson and Dressler were longtime friends; Dressler became the president of another university, and after Williams filed this lawsuit, Dressler offered Jefferson a position at his new university.

You can draw several inferences from this abridged relationship chart. Most notably, Jefferson appears to condone senior men seeking sexual relations with women over whom they have some authority, equating complaints about such conduct as demonstrating lack of collegiality on the part of the junior woman faculty member. The coincidence of Williams's complaint against Dressler, Jefferson's friend, and Jefferson's notation of Williams's lack of collegiality (without expansion or explanation) while serving on a university committee, needs to be explored. It may be that Jefferson regards sexual advances by senior men directed at junior women (at least when the men involved are friends of Jefferson) as acceptable conduct; or at least she appears to regard complaining about those advances demonstrates a lack of collegiality, this view impacting the tenure of the woman involved. Such an attitude shows motive, beyond that officially stated, for Jefferson's declination of Williams's tenure—or at least debunks "collegiality" or lack thereof as a relevant factor in a tenure decision.

e. Review the results of any focus group research performed in the case.

In particular, review the focus groups that considered the case facts and tentative case theories and answered critical questions such as the following.

- Given the case facts as presented, which party did the focus group members believe should prevail?
- Given the case facts as presented, what other facts did they expect to have occurred?
- What facts would they have to hear to decide the case in favor of either party?
- Given the facts presented, what did the focus group members think really happened in the fact pattern presented and why did they hold that belief?

The answers to these questions will, of course, be reflected in potential storylines for all parties. Facts the focus group identified as helpful in finding for your party are the facts **hoped** to be true in your factual theory. And of course, the reverse is true: facts identified by the focus group as being helpful in reaching a decision for the opposing party will be contained in potential storylines for the opponent, and you will identify as those as facts hoped **not** to be true. The deponents' testimony will provide most facts identified by focus groups as important in deciding the case in either direction, so be sure to use the focus group feedback as a fruitful source for focusing questions.

Example: A focus group conducted by the plaintiff might reveal that for the focus group members to find for the plaintiff on the theory that she was denied tenure in retaliation for her ending a sexual relationship with Simonson, they would need the following facts: 1) Simonson did not want the sexual relationship to end; 2) Simonson was a vindictive person; 3) there is evidence other than from the plaintiff that Simonson threatened her tenure when she ended their relationship; 4) Simonson had done the same thing in the past to other faculty members; 5) Simonson lobbied his colleagues to vote against tenure for Williams; and 6) Jefferson's denial of tenure was done at the behest of Simonson.

Simonson would be the source for much of this information, if true, and counsel should focus the questioning to gain those facts. Simonson, of course, won't agree that he threatened Williams, but you could like get him to agree that he didn't want the relationship to end; that he was upset when Williams ended the relationship; that he was hurt and surprised by her decision; and that he reacted verbally in a manner consistent with those feelings. You could ask Jefferson about the ultimate fact, but again, she won't agree that she was carrying Simonson's retaliation water when she decided against tenure for Williams. She could, however be made to agree about Simonson's status in the university; that he was more important to the well-being of the Public Policy School than Williams; that Williams's lack of collegiality took the form of saying negative things about Simonson; and that no one likes to have negative things said about him and would prefer not to have such a person around them.

By following the focus groups' suggestions of information that would help or harm the position of a party, you can develop facts that will necessarily lead to a fair conclusion of the case. If you (or the other party) can discover facts from a witness consistent with what the focus group believed to be helpful to either you or the other party, you or the other party have enhanced your case disposition position.

f. As you frame questions for the deponent, review the storylines developed from the facts as they exist at the time of the deposition.

Note in particular facts contained in the storyline that only your party supports (believed facts) or that have no factual support at all (hoped for facts).[14] The storyline review, of course, will also include potential storylines the opponent either might have identified (based on the direction of their discovery—as early as the

14. These are facts that fill in timeline gaps, provide more information about relationships, or tighten and verify storylines, usually envisioned from a common-sense view of what happened—or just an intuition that such facts must occur for the known facts of the case to be true.

identification of witnesses)[15] or might develop based on facts that you know or believe to be true that have not yet been discovered by the opponent.

Example: A key portion of Williams's storyline is that Simonson had induced her to remain in their sexual relationship by promises to leave his wife. That is, she believed that her relationship with Simonson went well beyond a sexual relationship and that absent promises or assurances from Simonson that he would divorce his wife, she was uninterested in maintaining that relationship. There is no known evidence of this believed fact other than the plaintiff's statement. In his deposition, Simonson won't corroborate plaintiff's claim. That does not end the inquiry. Ask Simonson about acts he took that showed more than a casual sexual relationship, such as keeping clothes, academic materials, personal items, etc. at Williams's condominium. Ask him why he believed Williams remained with him, if not for the prospect of a long-term relationship. Ask him about other extra-marital relationships, whether he ever told any of those women he would leave his wife and whether at the time he made the statements they were true or merely made to induce the continuance of the relationship in question.[16] *It may be that all of this ends up with the question of whether promises to seek a divorce were made remaining a disputed fact likely resolved by resort to credibility of the witnesses and their demeanor as revealed on the video transcript and common sense.*

On this same issue, Simonson's storyline may be that Williams did, in fact, continue the relationship—not because of any promise of Simonson of permanence, but because Williams, in fact, loved Simonson, enjoyed his company; in addition to these personal benefits, her relationship with Simonson was good for her professionally. Counsel should ask Williams not only how she felt about Simonson, but also whether because the closeness of their relationship allowed him to know her and her professional abilities so well, he had opened doors to her professionally. Much of this storyline can be gleaned from the facts on the timeline. Williams's relationship with Simonson was consensual, arising out of a close working relationship. Their personal relationship furthered her professional development, providing access to work not otherwise available, opportunities for professional activities—grant writing at a high level, reports on important issues of public policy, attendance at professional gatherings—and the offer to serve as the Associate Director of the Patterson Institute, with its attendant honorific and financial benefits. Williams can be expected to testify that she earned all of her academic successes based on hard work and talent. Again, the resolution of this storyline will be based

15. The plaintiff may list, as potential witnesses, women with whom Simonson had previous sexual relationships that ended, followed shortly thereafter with the woman leaving the University. She may also list the university officials overseeing the departments in which those women were employed. If she does, it becomes obvious that the plaintiff will seek character evidence about Simonson, potentially admissible to show his intent with regard to the ending of his relationship with Williams (a permissible Rule 404(b) proffer) or evidence that the repeated course of those relationships provided notice to the university of a potential hostile work environment created by tolerance for Simonson's proclivities.

16. The other women can be deposed for their recollection of what Simonson said to them as inducement to remain in a relationship with a married man, a relationship that seemed to have no future.

on credibility, demeanor as revealed on the video transcript of the deposition, and the evaluation of others of Williams's academic and professional bona fides.

g. Identify potential topics on which you can impeach the deponent.

Find these by reviewing the statements made by the deponent, either written or oral, for inconsistencies already apparent or that might result from deposition testimony; documents that reveal bias or interest or conduct inconsistent with deponent's previous statements; relationship charts; the statements of others about the deponent that point to facts attributable to the deponent; and documents or statements made by others as compared to those of the deponent.[17]

This impeachment of a deponent highlights a breach between the classic deposition, which would save impeachment for trial or other confrontational testimony (e.g., arbitration), and the modern deposition, which assumes that the deposition is the last opportunity to examine any witness before disposition of the matter—thus making it imperative that you effectively impeach the deponent's credibility at the deposition.[18]

Example: Dean Jefferson, while ultimately relying on a failure of collegiality to deny Williams's tenure, also claims that Williams failed to fulfil university requirements for teaching, scholarship, and service. Jefferson authored progress reports for Williams that were inconsistent with those stated failures. In addition, as a basis for either her retaliation claim or a claim of defamation, Williams points to a series of letters Jefferson wrote to other potential university employers to which Williams had applied. The inconsistency between those letters and Jefferson's progress reports and oral statements also impact Jefferson's credibility. All the above should be topics in Jefferson's deposition. The timing and tone of that impeachment is, of course, a matter of tactics that we will discuss in chapter nine.

4. What are the preparation materials for use at the deposition?

Assemble the documents you will use in the order in which you intend to use them. Make a preliminary decision about how you will use each document. If you intend use a document for substantive purposes, make sure there is a sufficient foundation for the document to be admitted. Make note of the facts you believe the deponent possesses that are necessary to show that foundation. Likewise, if you want to exclude the document from future substantive use, make note of the facts

17. With mandatory disclosure of witness names and addresses and interrogatories seeking more biographical information such as date of birth, you can run a public records search that might reveal such things as prior involvement in similar lawsuits, prior acts that might reveal admissible character for impeachment, and even criminal records. In this day and age of commercial and financial regulation, a deponent may very well have a criminal or administrative record that provides fodder for potential impeachment for dishonest acts (Rule 608(b)).

18. We will discuss this issue in more detail in chapter nine.

you believe the deponent has that make the document inadmissible. This is referred to as a "negative" foundation.

a. Paper Documents

Once you have identified the document, make sufficient copies for all parties and the deponent, with the original going to the court reporter to become part of the deposition record. If the documents are premarked as exhibits for the deposition, provide those markings to the court reporter for verification on the record during the deposition.[19] All counsel and the deponent can be provided premarked copies of the paper document exhibits, either as they are used or in an exhibit book prepared for the deposition. If the court reporter marks documents, in sequence, as they are used, the copies of documents are provided as they are used.

The classic manner of marking exhibits at a deposition was to mark each exhibit with a unique number for each deposition in which it was used. The same exhibit was marked with as many different numbers as depositions in which the exhibit was used. For later use in the litigation, a "Concordance Chart" was created, which showed all of the different markings a single exhibit had received. Then, an exhibit number was assigned to each document for use throughout the rest of the litigation.

Example: In the Williams deposition, assume the first exhibit shown to her was the University Regulations Regarding Tenure and Promotion. This exhibit would be marked by the court reporter as "Williams Exhibit 1." In the deposition of Dean Jefferson, however, assume those same regulations are the fifteenth exhibit shown to her. For the Jefferson deposition, the marking on the university tenure regulations would be "Jefferson Exhibit 15." When those regulations are used as an exhibit in the resolution of the litigation by motion or trial, a "Concordance Chart" will show that the University Tenure Regulations (Williams Exhibit 1 and Jefferson Exhibit 15) are marked for further use as Concordance Exhibit 3, or merely Exhibit 3.

In many depositions, especially those involving commercial litigation, the documents drive the deposition, and their culling and ordering will be the primary organizational tool for the deposition. Little else will be necessary to bring to the deposition. In all depositions, however, it is the rare case where documents and their interpretation by the parties will not be critical to the lawsuit's outcome.

b. Digital Exhibits

The modern deposition, and the litigation it informs, is likely to be accompanied by a large volume of documents, many of which are electronic. The sheer volume of exhibits suggests a different manner for presenting those exhibits to deponents.

19. This is merely a routine process of counsel—on use of the exhibit, state "Mr. _____, I am handing you what we have premarked as Exhibit 22 and providing a copy of the same to the court reporter and opposing counsel."

In many litigations based on document exchange, most—if not all—of the potential document exhibits will be identified before depositions begin.[20] Once these documents are identified, counsel can agree on all potential documents they will use during the litigation. These documents are preserved in digital form, a copy of which is provided to the court reporter and all parties.[21] At the time of the deposition, rather than counsel handing a deponent a piece of paper, the digital document is called up on computer monitors in front of the court reporter, all counsel, and the deponent and referred to by whatever exhibit number it has been given in the digital amalgamation.

c. Topical Outlines

Collect the topics of information relevant to a lawsuit on a topical outline. You will find that important topics arise at many junctures throughout the litigation. Topical outlines evolve with the litigation, but they are usually most appropriate when you have a good understanding—through other discovery, including documents and earlier depositions—of the universe of relevant facts and topics. In the modern deposition, you will most likely employ the topical outline successfully when you focus on dispositive information early. Once you have identified a topic as an important one, you can address it over time, providing better opportunities to highlight changes, consistencies, or inconsistencies; and by revisiting it over time, you can craft completing information on the topic.

Example: For the plaintiff to be successful in her discrimination lawsuit, no matter what theory of discrimination she employs, she must prove that she was qualified for tenure. The regulations for tenure have three categories of qualification: teaching, scholarship, and service. Each category of qualification is a topic for a topical outline. So in Jefferson's deposition, the topic of teaching qualifications generally, and in Williams's qualifications in particular, can be visited at numerous times—e.g., the general requirement for quality teaching, how categorized, how shown, how evaluated:

- *The expectation for Williams's teaching*
    - *how she was informed of requirements*
    - *her understanding*
    - *any questions posed.*

---

20. This, of course, assumes competent and ethical counsel.

21. This process is so common that many judges, and some local rules, provide for the creation of this kind of document collection in their pretrial order. The order makes clear the electronic format to be used so that these same exhibits are readily available for the judge to use when ruling on motions and, in the most unusual case, at trial. It is of no matter that most of the documents digitally collected will not be used in motion practice, hearings, trial, or ADR. Only those documents actually used will be presented in such proceedings.

- *Williams's quality of teaching each year, as evaluated by Jefferson*
  - *how evaluated, at what level*
  - *what was good, what needed improvement*
  - *how communicated*
  - *how understood*
  - *how to address improvement needs, consistent with expected performance (above or below norm)*
  - *how relates to quality of teaching necessary for teaching, whether advice for progress heeded, did progress occur.*
- *Records of Williams's teaching*
  - *how made*
  - *how maintained.*
- *Quality of Williams teaching at tenure review*
  - *how evaluated, by whom,*
  - *how measured*
  - *rank relative to standards*
    - *other tenured professors*
    - *as against university standards.*
- *Quality of teaching's impact on Jefferson's tenure decision.*
- *Quality of teaching as reflected in letters of recommendation for Williams to other universities.*

Counsel can make the same sort of outline and resulting inquiry for other topics relevant to tenure, in the end providing an excellent picture of Williams's performance to compare with the tenure requirements in the relevant qualification categories.

Prepare an outline for each topic in chronological order, then incorporate these topics into timelines and legal theory charts (discussed in chapter three) to produce a chronological outline.

d. Chronological Outlines

Assuming that a primary objective of any deposition is gathering complete information, the best way to question the deponent about events is in the chronological order in which the events of the lawsuit occurred. For reasons explored more fully in chapter eight, it is much easier and more accurate to remember things in sequence than it is with any other organization. A chronological outline should contain the facts necessary to prove the legal theory; it should also address the charting described in chapter four regarding facts necessary to support the legal theory and potential storylines. The outline provides you with a complete understanding of the case facts as they exist at the time you are preparing for depositions.

To be clear, we suggest a chronological outline, not a list of questions. Written questions can limit the information-gathering process because they elicit only the information sought in the written question. And you can get so focused on getting the answer to the specific question that you don't engage in active listening—you may be looking to the next question and miss the hint of further information in a deponent's answer. The outline is much more flexible and less limiting.

Use all of the above organizational devices to prepare the ultimate reflection of deposition preparation: the chronological storyline chart.

5. Can all preparation materials be collected into an easy to refer to device?

Absolutely. **The chronological storyline chart** includes all facts necessary to prove the client's potential legal and factual theories,[22] which you glean from a review of timelines, relationship charts, legal theory charts, focus group information, and the facts gathered through the formal and informal discovery that has occurred up to the time of the deposition.

Create the chart with the facts necessary for the storyline listed in chronological order across the top of the chart (the horizontal axis), producing a row of facts. All facts of the storyline are put on the chart in the chronological order in which they are believed or hoped (based on current information, and inferences) to have occurred. They include what we have previously described as known, believed, disputed, and hoped for facts. The sources of the facts are listed along the left side of the chart (the vertical axis), producing a column of factual sources. The chart is created with as many columns on the chart as there are facts in the storyline, and as many rows on the chart as there are the sources of information. You then mark the chart to show where a fact on the storyline is available from a known source. By viewing the chart, the nature of the fact (known, believed, disputed, hoped) is apparent. Known facts will be corroborated by sources associated with the opposing parties; believed facts will be those charted as available only from sources associated with your client; believed facts that are contradicted by opposing parties are disputed facts; and hoped for facts will have no current factual source, but for some reason (common sense and the drawing of reasonable inferences) you suspect are available.

22. Usually, you will have not yet determined the persuasive theory of the case during the discovery process. It is only after full discovery in the case that you can articulate a persuasive way of thinking about the client's position, such that the client's point of view makes common sense and has persuasive equitable force.

Place the deponent on the chart in the source column, producing his own row of potential facts from the chronological storyline. Before the deposition, note any facts on the storyline that you can already attribute to the deponent. In addition, because of what you know about the defendant, you can note potential areas where the deponent can corroborate believed facts, or weigh in on disputed facts (to help resolve the dispute), or provide hoped for facts. At a minimum, you not only must ask the deponent about those facts noted on the chart, you must also remain open to complete fact gathering using the techniques articulated in chapters seven, eight, and nine.

Check off each topic on the outline as it is addressed and completed before moving to the next chronological event on the outline. If the deponent's response to a question divulges information that you did not know and therefore did not include within any preparation materials, choose whether to withhold inquiry until the place in the chronology where the information belongs or make further inquiry immediately.[23] When following the new information immediately, use some system of marking (circling, underlining, arrows) or place your pen to note your current place in the chronology. After you have completed the examination of the new information, pick up the pen and get back into the chronology. Similarly, if using a digital outline created on a computer, make a mark on the digital outline to return to when you have exhausted the information on the unforeseen matter raised by the deponent. If you choose to stay with the chronological order, take a moment to mark a reference to the new information in its proper place on the chronology so that you do not forget to return to the topic when the time is right.[24]

B. In addition to the chronological storyline chart, are there other materials that I should have at the deposition?

For many years, lawyers have relied on what is called a deposition notebook, which contains all the information—both legal and factual—that we have discussed as well as other information counsel might need during the deposition. Although in many depositions, the notebook itself will not be referred to, it should include:

a) the notice of deposition or subpoena for deposition testimony;[25]

b) the Pretrial Discovery Order;

23. We refer to this phenomena as "chasing rabbits" and discuss the tactics of how and when to chase the rabbit in detail in chapter nine.

24. Professor Bocchino, after preparing the chronological storyline chart, advocates converting that document into information goals for actual deposition use, preferring to concentrate on communication with the deponent, both verbal and nonverbal. To insure completeness, however, he also brings a paralegal with him to the deposition, who carefully follows the chronological storyline chart to insure his failures of chronological inquiry are minimal—before moving on in the chronology, he consults with the paralegal to make sure he hasn't missed a topic missed or the topic needs further questioning.

25. Provide a copy of the notice to the court reporter.

c) a copy of at the least Civil Procedure Rules 26 and 30 (or comparable state rules);[26]

d) a memorandum covering the Federal Rules of Civil Procedure as might arise in the deposition;[27]

e) all interrogatories answered by the deponent (if a party);

f) any statement prepared by or taken of the deponent;

g) a copy of the Federal Rules of Evidence (or relevant state evidentiary rules);[28]

h) a copy of relevant statutes enabling the claims and defenses at issue in this lawsuit;

i) a statement of the elements of claims and defenses enabled by case law relevant to this lawsuit;

j) a thumb drive containing all pleadings, discovery produced and received, motions, and rulings;

k) hard copies of the documents to be used (even if you are using digital documents in the deposition);[29]

l) a copy of any stipulations you wish to adopt regarding the taking, recording, signing, making, and preserving of objections;[30] and

m) the chronological storyline chart.

6. Are there any final factors that must be accounted for before going to the deposition?

There are a number of housekeeping matters that you must address before the deposition. Most of these matters are taken care of efficiently and professionally by support staff. They include:

---

26. Most lawyers will carry with them a pocket copy of the Federal Rules of Civil Procedure for easy reference. The authors have found it helpful to have at least all of the rules regarding discovery (Rules 26–37) for easy reference.

27. Chapter three of this volume is one such memorandum.

28. The authors have also written a lawyer's quick reference for use at trial and deposition entitled THE FEDERAL RULES OF EVIDENCE WITH OBJECTIONS, 12th Ed, NITA, 2017. This book contains the Federal Rules of Evidence, the form of objection, the form of response to objection, and foundational questions necessary to overcome or avoid objections. It is published in a 5×8-inch spiral bound format that opens flat on a table. A more complete explication of the Federal Rules of Evidence is contained in another volume by the authors entitled A PRACTICAL GUIDE TO FEDERAL EVIDENCE, 12th Ed., NITA, 2017, which provides a lawyer's guide to the rules of evidence and how they are understood, applied, and enforced by judges and lawyer.

29. Just in case of technical failure.

30. *See* chapter seven.

1) checking notice or subpoena for date, time, place of deposition, manner of recording;
2) sending notice to the court-reporting service you intend to use;[31]
3) confirming the reservation of room for deposition;[32]
4) notifying paralegal or other support staff who will attend the deposition;[33]
5) arranging for water, coffee, tea, etc.; and
6) reviewing preparation materials to assure readiness.

As in everything a lawyer does, properly preparing for deposition is the key to outstanding performance. Substantive knowledge and the skills of examination, cross-examination, and presentation of facts are no guarantee of competence absent properly preparing to use that knowledge in the taking and defending of depositions.

31. Most lawyers have a favorite court reporter who they will use in every deposition as well as a backup to account for emergencies and conflicts.

32. Most lawyers have a conference room in their offices they like to use for taking depositions. That room might differ, if, as we suggest, the deposition is recorded by digital video.

33. Most lawyers will work with a paralegal or junior lawyer on all of the preparation, but typically good paralegals and associates will be very much in demand, and if you require them to assist at deposition, you must schedule their time.

Chapter Five

Preparing the Deponent for Testimony

1. We now assume that depositions will be a key factor in resolving civil litigation. What effect does that have on the deponent preparation process?

Preparing the deponent has always been key to a successful deposition. As a general matter, the common wisdom at least into the 1980s was that a party, or any witness, should be prepared to reveal as little as possible when he is deposed by opposing counsel; in most cases, this is no longer true. Given the new uses of depositions—occasioned by the fact that a jury trial (or even another opportunity to present sworn testimony) is not in the offing—the better advice is that a party (or any witness who is willing to be prepared) should reveal all the information favorable to the preparing party for the uses to which the deposition will be put. Given the presumption from which we now proceed—that there will be no trial, but rather some other form of dispute resolution—there are many conventions about witness preparation that must be reconsidered and, in some cases, abandoned. We will consider the questions that this new paradigm raises, while at the same time discussing those issues that arise in the increasingly unusual circumstances where there will be sworn testimony in a litigation after the deposition. But let's begin with some background questions.

2. Who should be prepared for deposition?

Prepare every witness who is willing to be prepared. Parties, and people controlled by parties, will always be prepared for their depositions. Also prepare witnesses who are not parties, but who have information favorable to your client or take a position consistent with your client.

Example: In our hypothetical case, counsel will prepare each individual defendant (Professor Simonson and Dean Jefferson). In the case of the entity defendants (Nita University, the School of Public Policy, and the Patterson Institute), representatives of the entities will also be prepared. Nonparty witnesses who are generally favorable to the party's position should also be prepared. On the plaintiff's side, in addition to the plaintiff, herself, a former woman faculty member of the School of Public Policy who had a sexual relationship with the Simonson and who was fired or denied tenure after ending that relationship, as well as faculty members who voted for Ms. Williams's tenure will also likely be amenable to being prepared by plaintiff's counsel.

3. What attorney-client privilege issues arise when preparing a deponent?

Remember that the attorney-client privilege protects the conversations that occur between preparing counsel and a party.[1] The communications between a lawyer and a witness (not associated in a legal way with a party) are not privileged and may be inquired about at the deposition.

Example: When, in our hypothetical case, preparing the former professor with the history of sexual relations with Simonson, take care not to reveal confidential information during prep sessions with that witness—defendants' counsel may inquire about any information plaintiff's counsel revealed to that witness.

Although such an inquiry is permissible as a general matter as against a claim of privilege, the local custom and notions of professionalism may frown on such an inquiry. The unstated agreement between counsel is often "I won't ask what you tell a witness, and you won't ask what I tell a witness."[2]

In some jurisdictions, some lawyers claim that in the case of a witness deposition, the lawyer represents the witness "for the purpose of the deposition." By so doing, preparing counsel seeks not only to have the benefit of the attorney-client privilege, but also to acquire the right to instruct the witness not to answer the deposing counsel's questions.[3] The legal viability of such a position is tenuous at best. No traditional aspects of an attorney-client relationship exist between the lawyer for a party and the typical witness who has favorable information. The witness has not sought legal advice, the witness has no legal issue for which resolution is sought, the lawyer provides no legal advice to the witness as a potential party to a lawsuit, and, of course, there exists no contract of representation nor are fees paid to the lawyer by the witness. Moreover, the authors believe that if preparing counsel reveals privileged information from her actual client or divulges trial preparation materials to such a witness, that revelation would act as a waiver of either attorney-client privilege or trial preparation material protection for the information revealed.[4]

---

1. The extent of the protection depends on the state law of attorney-client privilege. Some jurisdictions protect only statements made *by the client* to a legal representative (or her agents) for the purpose of obtaining legal advice, not the statements of the lawyer, unless the lawyer's statements reveal what had been said by the client. Other jurisdictions protect all statements made by the client and the lawyer (subject to waiver and exceptions) that are made during the course of and for the purpose of legal representation. In any event, the professional custom in most jurisdictions is that even if there is a hole in the law of privilege that allows inquiry into what is said to a client by her lawyer during a preparation session, such inquiry is not made, and that custom is reciprocal.

2. This so-called agreement is, of course, unstated; in a case where there is a good reason for deposing counsel to believe that the statements of opposing counsel to the witness has impacted the substance of that testimony, the unwritten agreement will be broken.

3. Subject to the limitations of Fed. R. Civ. P. 30(c)(2).

4. This circumstance, of course, is distinguishable from the situation where counsel discloses client or trial preparations material to a witness with whom the lawyer's party has a joint defense agreement.

4. When should the preparation session occur?

Prepare witnesses close in time to the deposition. With important witnesses, especially clients, it is often wise to schedule two sessions: one several days before the deposition and one the day before the deposition. The length of the preparation session depends on a variety of factors.

a. How much information does the witness have?

In a simple tort case, the plaintiff will know about his life before his injury, the facts leading up to his injury, the nature of the injury, the treatment received, and any continuing problems resulting from the injury. In such a case, the typical preparation will take no more than several hours. A witness to an automobile accident has little information except the nature of the collision. You can prepare such a witness in less than an hour.

In our hypothetical gender discrimination case, however, the events leading to the denial of tenure occurred over a several-year period, and the merits of tenure are determined on the quality of teaching, scholarship, and service to the university, factors that involve professional judgment and subjective consideration. In addition, there is the sensitive matter of a sexual relationship between the plaintiff and her supervisor, Professor Simonson, that must be discussed. Expect this preparation session to take several days.

b. How important is the witness to the case?

The more important the witness is to the case, the longer the preparation session. An important witness will face questioning that is probing and expansive, so the preparation session must match in breadth and depth.

Example: In our hypothetical case, Professor Taylor supported tenure for the plaintiff and criticized not only the decision of Dean Jefferson not to recommend tenure on Williams's merits, but also how the decision was made, as a matter of policy, given that Jefferson's action was a de facto veto of the majority of the public policy faculty that had voted in favor of Williams's tenure. Because of his position as the chair of the Tenurial Faculty Committee and his position as a former dean of the Public Policy School, his testimony has a great deal of weight and potentially case-changing information. His deposition will be lengthy, perhaps confrontational, and contain an enormous amount of critical information. As a result, expect his preparation session to take close to the same time as that of the plaintiff or the individual defendants.

c. How many documents are involved?

In a commercial case, where there has been the exchange of hard copy and electronic communication over a period of years, examine each of those communications with care during preparation. Asking the witness about the time, place, and circumstance of each communication can be time consuming. Familiarize the witness with any document that he has or should have seen in the past, as well as documents authored by others and communicated to others about topics in the scope of the witness's knowledge. Prepare him to be examined about documents (no matter the authorship) that relate to information about which he claims to have knowledge. In most cases, the documents about which the witness has information have been identified long before the deposition was scheduled.[5] In that case, as a precursor to the preparation session, show the documents relevant to the potential questioning by deposing counsel as well as the documents defending counsel has identified as those the deposing counsel needs to provide information to flesh out her chronological storyline chart.

d. What is the method of recording the deposition?

Digital video recording has had an enormous impact on witness preparation. Although the demeanor of a deponent has always been important,[6] video has made it even more so. In the classic deposition, normal stenographic transcription limited the testimony's audience to the transcription itself—a series of written questions and answers; deposing counsel could later try to communicate what she observed.[7] Pauses, facial expressions, nervous habits, reflected attitude, etc., were irrelevant. Video recording puts all these issues in play as it records the witness's demeanor, attitude towards testimony, apparent nervousness, etc.—in other words, all of those factors evaluated by jurors. With a video-recorded deposition, all later considerations of what the deponent had to say will be impacted by *how* he said it—and those impressions will be available to the lawyers, judges, arbitrators, mediators, and party decision makers. As a result, the preparation for a video deposition is much more akin to the traditional preparation of a witness for trial testimony, except more difficult because the witness must become comfortable speaking while looking into a camera.

e. What are the witness's communication skills?

Most witnesses are not used to being a witness, being the center of attention, being forced to answer questions—some of which may be embarrassing—and having every word they say recorded, either on paper or video. In fact, most people are not used to being the center of attention of a group of strangers. These factors

---

5. In the normal case, depositions will occur after discovery of documents and other physical evidence has been completed. This is so because the document production commonly leads to deposition inquiry, and in fairness, a witness may be re-called to testify about documents and other evidence produced after the completion of an early deposition.

6. Deposing counsel, in addition to obtaining information about the case, always served the additional function of evaluating the demeanor of the deponent as would be viewed by the trier of fact at a later trial. Deposing counsel's evaluation of the deponent, as a witness, particularly in the case of parties, has always been a significant factor in the calculus of the strength of opposing counsel's case.

7. The impact on deposing counsel, however, was difficult to concretely communicate to decision makers in the case, who had only written transcript as a basis for decision making.

can create tension and nervousness, which might come across on a video recording as lack of certainty or veracity. In addition, many people have distracting nervous habits, like tapping their fingers or playing with their hair. Still other witnesses have verbal tics, or use words oddly, or have difficulty expressing what they mean. Take note of these factors in your interactions with the witness, so you can adjust the planned preparation time to remedy any communication failings before the video deposition.

5. Where should the preparation session take place?

Prepare the witness in a setting that is as much like the place where the deposition will occur as possible. Obviously, if the deposition is scheduled for your office, then the session should occur there. In the more typical situation, the deposition will occur in the law offices of deposing counsel. In either situation, depositions occur in law office conference rooms, which are relatively generic—so any conference room will do. For tactical and other reasons, however, depositions are increasingly taken in places other than the conference room of a law firm. For example, to avoid paying hourly fees for the portal to portal travel, the deposition of an expert witness can be taken in the expert's office. And an increasing number of lawyers advocate taking discovery depositions[8] in a place where the witness feels comfortable and in control—that setting will be more conducive to the witness giving expansive answers to deposition questions, which enhances the fact-gathering process. Witness preparation should match the locale of the deposition.

Example: In our hypothetical case, the plaintiff might notice the deposition of Simonson for a conference room at the Patterson Institute, of which Simonson is the director. This tactic would put Simonson in a place where he is used to being in charge. Simonson would be comfortable and forthcoming with information. In addition, if as reported, Simonson tends towards arrogance and high-handed dealings with those in his ambit of influence, that arrogance and high-handedness might be displayed on Simonson's home turf.

6. What attire is proper for the preparation session?

As part of preparation, both the preparing lawyer and the witness should consider the clothing they will wear to the deposition. For the lawyer, that will depend on the local customs in their jurisdiction. In some law firms, suits and ties for men and courtroom attire for women is customary—in many cases men will remove their jackets and loosen their ties. In other law firms, business casual attire is worn for all but courtroom proceedings.

8. We have made the distinction between discovery depositions, which are for the purpose of information gathering, and depositions taken for the purpose of obtaining admissions or for theory testing. Consider the purpose of the deposition when deciding where it should occur.

For witnesses, their clothing should be neat, but comfortable. If the witness's employment is relevant to the case, attire should also be consistent with the person's work environment. For example, medical doctors should be encouraged to dress in their white hospital jackets. A school teacher should dress in clothes that are appropriate for a classroom. For nonprofessionals, the best suggestion is the clothes they would wear to a social engagement[9] or a religious service. That being said, jeans and t-shirts are never advisable as they do not comport with the seriousness of the deposition event.

Attire becomes more of an issue if the deposition is video recorded.[10] Given the use of depositions (in a court proceeding, ADR session, transcript appended to motion practice), the deponent's attire should be appropriate for the setting in which the video will be viewed. Sometimes, that venue is uncertain. As a default, the easiest solution is to have the witness dress for the most formal use to which the deposition might be put (e.g., courtroom attire).

7. What specific preparation must counsel complete before the preparation session?

a. Begin witness preparation planning by determining where the witness fits in the case theory of both the taking and defending lawyers.[11]

That determination helps you focus on the expected area of questioning by deposing counsel and the necessary facts the witness divulges either in response to questions from both deposing counsel and defending counsel. For the parties, identifying facts that support or oppose their legal theory is relatively straightforward and more inclusive of the universe of facts known to the witness.

b. Review all documents (both paper and electronic) that are relevant to the witness's testimony.

These include documents the witness created, sent, and received. They will also include documents that are relevant to the topics about which the witness has information.

Example: Dean Jefferson may not have seen a memorandum shared among University Board of Trustees members regarding her refusal to recommend Williams for tenure. The information contained in that communication must still be the topic of preparation, as

9. What we have in mind is dinner at a person's in-laws-to-be, not the clothes a person would wear on a date at a bar or what the authors used to call a disco.

10. The videographer will advise you how attire is likely to record on the video. Most videographers use a gray back-screen to minimize distractions and provide a neutral color background. Even then, some colors may not record well (for example, white clothing could create a glare on the recording; stripes may appear to ripple). The best source for such advice is, of course, the videographer.

11. Although the deposing lawyer preparation for the deposition was the focus of chapter five, a brief restatement is helpful here.

plaintiff's counsel possesses the document and its topic is Jefferson's action, as viewed by the Board of Trustees. Dean Jefferson can be confronted with the document, or at least its contents, by plaintiff's counsel; she must be prepared on its contents before her deposition.

Another obvious source of documentation to review before witness preparation is all written or oral statements made by or attributed to the witness regarding the events underlying the lawsuit.

Example: In our hypothetical case these documents can include direct communications, like a memorandum by Dean Jefferson to the Public Policy School faculty notifying them of her decision not to recommend Williams for tenure and her reasons. Further, if her decision was announced in a faculty meeting, the meeting minutes, although not created by the dean, reflect the dean's statements and should be known by counsel before deposition preparation begins.

In addition, counsel needs to review statements provided by other witnesses, including previous deposition testimony, that attribute actions or words to the deponent are sources of information.

Example: Professor Simonson denies meeting with the dean before the tenure decision was made, whereas the dean recalls that such a meeting occurred—the inconsistency will be a topic of the dean's deposition and therefore a matter for preparation.

Also review statements given by others about the same event, including previous depositions by other witnesses who may or may not agree with this witness's version of the events. Finally, review discovery already completed in the case. Counsel must review answers to interrogatories by opposing parties and co-parties to see if they are consistent with the deponent's. If completed, review expert witness reports, information provided by consulting experts, and any notes about the opinions of testifying experts—not yet reduced to a report—that are relevant to the facts and issues of the questioning of the deponent.

Example: In preparing for Professor Simonson's deposition, defendants' lawyer would review Simonson's statement, Dean Jefferson's statement, the plaintiff's answers to interrogatories, documents produced by the plaintiff, the depositions of any witnesses (for all parties) that have been completed, all job performance records of the plaintiff, documents in the plaintiff's employee file, and paper and electronic correspondence regarding the plaintiff's job performance and progress along the tenure track. She would also review any records of previous claims made against Simonson, including statements made by those women with whom he either had or attempted a sexual relationship; answers to any interrogatories; interrogatories that have yet to be answered, as they are probable deposition topics; the pleadings; and all relevant law.

Review potential case theories, to the extent that they have been reduced to writing. In most cases, you will not have settled the legal, factual, and persuasive case theories and will not do so until discovery is complete. Nonetheless, consult the multiple theories regarding the law, the facts, and the equities of the lawsuit to insure you explore all case issues during deposition preparation.

Once you have concluded that review and considered potential case theories (for both parties), you are ready to begin the preparation session.

8. After reviewing all this information, what should I show to the deponent before the preparation session?

Many lawyers begin the process by welcoming the client and then providing him with any written information (like previous statements or authored documents) to review before the session begins. Remember that anything the witness reviews that refreshes memory of testimony given[12] is discoverable on request by the opposing party, so consider whether the documents or other information you provide for review consist of information the opposing counsel already has. At the very least, never include information you do not want to provide to the opponent. And never show the deponent any sort of attorney work product, such as memoranda hypothesizing about case theory or memoranda you prepared to memorialize information you or your staff obtained.

Once that review is finished, ask the witness to review all documents you think will be relevant to the deposition testimony. This is important because for all but the parties—and even for some of them—the events at issue in the lawsuit may have long faded from memory; reviewing documents can bring those memories to the fore. Once the deponent has reviewed the documents and other material you provided, the interaction between you and the witness can begin.

9. How should the prep session begin?

Most witnesses come to the preparation session with questions and concerns about the deposition and its process. Once you deal with those questions or concerns, the actual preparation can begin.

Example: Although Professor Simonson is used to being the center of attention as a university professor teaching classes, he still might have some things he needs to get off his chest before being able to fully concentrate on the task at hand. As the preparation session begins, the following conversation addresses this issue.

Lawyer: Good morning Professor, thanks for coming in. It's been a while since we've talked in person, but as you know the case has been proceeding and we've gotten to the point where your deposition testimony will be taken next week.

Simonson: Not a problem. Your legal assistant told me when the deposition was scheduled and that we would be talking before, so I was expecting to hear from you.

12. Fed. R. Evid. 612, Berkey Photo, Inc. v. Eastman Kodak Co., 444 U.S. 1093 (1980); Sporck v. Piel, 759 F.2d 312 (3d Cir. 1985).

L: *All right, Professor, before we get started, do you have any questions or concerns about the deposition?*

S: *Not so much a concern, but will Ms. Williams be there?*

L: *Well, she has a right to be there, but it is very unusual for the opposing party to attend the deposition. Would her presence present a problem for you?*

S: *Not really, but it wouldn't be the most comfortable situation, what with all the allegations she's made against me. Will anyone else be there?*

L: *Just the lawyer for the other side, the court reporter, and the videographer. Only one lawyer will question you, but she might have an associate or a paralegal with her. I've spoken with the university counsel, and no one else from the university will be there, including Mr. Patterson, who is out of the country. There will be lawyers for the other defendants, and they might ask you some questions, but from what they've told me, I doubt they will ask you questions. As you know, we have taken a unified case defense, but we can talk more about that later. What other concerns questions or concerns do you have?*

S: *How graphic will the questions be about my relationship with Ms. Williams?*

L: *I'm sure that you'll be asked about the nature of the affair, but it is unlikely that any questions about the details of intimate acts will be asked. You will have to answer questions about whether you had sexual relations at all, however. The same would be true regarding other relationships you have had with other university employees.*

S: *Can they ask about relationships with people outside the university?*

L: *They can ask, but if they do, I'll instruct you not to answer and seek a protective order from the court. I don't see how relationships outside the realm of university employees (including students) are relevant.*[13]

S: *I've never had a relationship with a student. That is against university regulations.*

L: *Any other questions or concerns?*

S: *Not that come to mind. If something does come up, I'll ask.*

L. *Be sure you do. There is no such thing as a silly question when preparing for a deposition.*

The above exchange clears the air so that the session can focus on developing the facts as they will be revealed during the deposition. As is typical, counsel has learned that the witness is less comfortable in the witness chair than he would be in a professional setting of his own choosing and experience. She will need to pay attention to how Simonson displays that discomfort while testifying. Counsel also knows that Simonson feels uncomfortable talking about certain matters in his past that may be the subject of inquiry. She will need to emphasize those matters during the substantive preparation so that the witness gets more comfortable speaking about matters that he prefers remain private.

13. Such a statement about whether questioning on a topic will be allowed is not without danger. If, in fact, the judge did not grant the protective order, the deposition will have to be reconvened, no doubt to Simonson's consternation. At a minimum, counsel should ask about the relationships outside the university (if not already known) and Simonson's concerns about an inquiry into them.

10. Are there any other preliminary matters with the deponent before actual preparation begins?

A significant amount of time has probably passed since you last spoke to the witness, so it is important to insure that both of you are on the same page regarding the case—most importantly that you have the same understanding of the facts. The factual flow goes both ways: the witness may have new information about the case or a change of recollection, and you may have received some information that you believe the witness should know. To set a cooperative tone, begin the preparation session with this information exchange.

Example: The preparation session between defense counsel and Professor Simonson might continue as follows:

L: *Has anything happened since we last spoke that might be relevant to the case or that you just think I should know so I can best represent your interests?*

S: *As you know, Dean Jefferson left Nita University for another position. Randy Cates is the new dean. He's been here six months and is doing a good job. We have a good relationship, but we aren't close. I think he has some trepidation about this lawsuit and its potential effect on the school.*

L: *What else?*

S: *I've received several communications from Mr. Patterson about the progress with the case. He is a bit worried that his namesake institute might be tarnished by Ms. Williams's allegations.*

L: *What have the tone of the communications with Mr. Patterson been?*

S. *Oh, we remain friendly, and he's happy about the work we're producing at the institute. He just wants to close the door on this episode and move along with our important work.*

L: *Anything else?*

S: *No, that's it.*

L: *As you know, we took Professor Taylor's deposition and sent a copy to your office. Have you read it?*

S: *Yes, I did.*

L: *Any surprises?*

S: *Well, Marvin and I have some different recollections about some events in the past, but I wasn't surprised by what he had to say or how he said it. Ms. Williams was a favorite of his, and they remain close friends. I didn't expect him to mince his words in being critical of either me or Dean Jefferson.*

L: *Let's talk about the differences you have with Professor Taylor's recollection. What was the first disagreement you had with what he had to say?*

S: *Well, I made a list, like you asked when you sent over the deposition, so let me go down the list.*

L: *Very good, and if you think of anything else, feel free to fill me in.*

S: *Absolutely. This first real disagreement was . . . .*

The opening exchange of information gets the session focused on the task at hand and addresses the case facts as they will be revealed in the deposition. It also assumes a good practice has occurred: counsel provided Simonson a copy of the deposition of a key witness for the opposing party, who has testified at length about him. In addition—and also consistent with good practice—counsel asked the witness to review that deposition and note the points of conflict between the deposition of the opposing witness and his own recollection of events. The list prepared by a party witness to his counsel is, of course, privileged.

11. What does the deponent need to know about the deposition process?

For most witnesses, providing a deposition is a once in a lifetime event, and one that is much different than legal proceedings depicted on television and in the movies. As a result, you need to explain how depositions proceed. Cover the following items:

a) The location of the deposition—usually it is best to have the witness meet you at your law firm and go to the deposition together.

b) What the witness should wear—for Simonson, normal business attire (jacket and tie) would be appropriate, especially if the deposition will be video-recorded.

c) The setup of the deposition room—where the court reporter, the videographer, opposing counsel, and the two of you will sit.

d) The witness takes an oath or affirms to tell the truth before testifying.

e) Breaks are allowed for any reason unless there is a question pending. The only real limitation on breaks is that in some discovery orders, the judge will not permit the witness and counsel to discuss the deposition's content once it has begun. If that is the case, explain the rule to the witness; also explain that those orders do allow consultation to decide whether to assert a privilege or for counsel to help the witness correct any misstatements the witness may have made.

f) The witness has the opportunity to read, correct, and sign the deposition—and should take that opportunity.[14]

12. How do I assure that the deponent and I are on the same page about the facts the deponent possesses?

The first substantive order of business in the preparation session is to confirm what information from other sources the witness recalls and believes to be true.

14. Some lawyers/law firms have produced (or purchased) videos explaining depositions to deposition witnesses. The better practice is for the lawyer who will defend the deposition to cover these matters with each witness. Counsel can expand on important matters, provide examples, and clear up any misunderstandings. This process also confirms for the witness the importance of the witness's preparation session.

Ask the witness about the topics you anticipate will be the subject of deposition testimony. This is nothing more than a witness interview, conducted predominantly through the use of open-ended questions. Show the witness documents or other exhibits you expect opposing counsel to ask about—you should have provided most of the documents to the witness for review before the beginning of the preparation session.

13. What do I do when a witness provides either new information or information that's different from my understanding of the facts?

The witness may share new information or different (or more) information. New information may result from refreshed memory, speaking to others with knowledge, or discovering new information. Be aware that, in thinking about the events that make up the basis for the claims and defenses of the lawsuit, the witness may have reconstructed events in his mind, and that changed or enhanced his recollection. As mentioned before, testimony is not so much recalling events and speaking from memory as reconstructing events based on everything the witness has learned about the case from all sources, including other witnesses and documents. That is not to suggest that witnesses intentionally make up information that is helpful to them. Remember that a witness has a core belief about an event in the case. As he is thinking about that event—certain that his version is true—he is also reconstructing the event in his mind. Witnesses often include information consistent with their core belief that never occurred. This reconstructed testimony is not a "lie;" the witness believes the facts as stated and believes that he knows them from his own first-hand knowledge. If there was a reliable lie detector, the witness would pass the test about the reconstructed fact.

When this phenomenon occurs, and you believe that what the witness now trusts is true is a reconstruction, ask about the information's source. This forces the witness to reveal how he "knows" a certain fact. In most cases, if the event did not occur—and the witness's belief in it is based on reconstruction—you can point to evidence that counters the reconstruction. The evidence that contradicts the reconstruction may exist in the form of documents, previous statements by the witness (where a reconstructed fact is contradicted or omitted in a place where inclusion would have been likely), or statements and/or testimony of other witnesses. You may need to lead the witness through the evidence to help him come to the realization that the reconstruction, in addition to being inconsistent (either directly or by inference) with other case facts, is just not the way that things usually happen (the way of the world) and therefore rings false. Present the witness with those contrary facts to test his current belief of the case facts. If the witness persists in his beliefs, you may need to persuade him that his current belief about the facts is inaccurate. Try to do this delicately. A witness who believes his version of the story may become hostile if he thinks you are calling him a liar.

Example: Assume the following exchange in the preparation of Simonson by his counsel:

L: *While your sexual affair was ongoing, how often would you spend the night with Ms. Williams?*

S: *Not that frequently. I'd say I spent most nights at my family home. My wife knew of my relationship with Ms. Williams (she was in a relationship herself). Although my wife and I were not sexually intimate at the time, we still slept at home most nights.*

L: *You know, Professor, that Ms. Williams said in her deposition that you spent on average of five nights a week at her condominium.*

S: *I believe that's an overstatement. That's not accurate. I know she claims that our relationship was leading to a permanent status, but despite our intimacy, we did maintain separate lives.*

L: *You did have a dresser and a closet that you used for your clothes at her condo, right?*

S: *That's true.*

L: *And at least at some point, you and Ms. Williams considered marriage, didn't you?*

S: *We talked about the possibility.*

L: *Didn't you also have some luggage at her condo?*

S: *Yes. We traveled to conferences together with some frequency.*

L: *And a computer.*

S: *That's right.*

L: *I don't know if her lawyers have talked to the doorman at the condo, but I suspect they have. He told our investigator that it seemed that you were there every night, like you lived there.*

S: *Well, I'd disagree with that.*

L: *Could it be that when your relationship began, that your overnight stays were once or twice a week, but as your relationship got more serious you spent more nights with Ms. Williams? That's how I had it in my notes from an earlier interview with you.*

S: *You know, that's probably true. I do recall spending every night for several weeks when my wife was out of town. Ms. Williams and I never stayed at my family home; that was an understanding that my wife and I had. Other relationships that we both had were outside the home.*

L: *So if asked about the frequency of your overnight stays, how would you answer?*

S: *I did stay there frequently. Like you said, the more serious our relationship became, the more frequently I stayed overnight. Although it varied, I can't argue that there weren't weeks when I stayed every night.*

L: *And we're not denying the relationship and its seriousness, so that sounds like a reasonable answer. So your answer to the frequency of overnight stays?*

S: *It varied, but there were weeks when I would spend every night there.*

L: *OK, that sounds good. Let's talk about something else.*

As the preceding exchange with the witness demonstrates, refer to other facts and witnesses to help the witness correct a fact reconstruction so that the witness's testimony becomes consistent with otherwise agreed-on facts.

Take the time and use your skill to correct the reconstruction; otherwise a factfinder could believe that the witness is intentionally fabricating evidence. Once a factfinder believes that a witness has lied about one fact, that belief will impact the witness's credibility generally.[15] In the above, suppose the factfinder, having heard testimony from other witnesses (including an unbiased doorman), believed that Simonson was lying about the frequency of his overnight stays to minimize the seriousness of his relationship with Williams. That belief would likely influence the factfinder to believe that Simonson might be lying about other, more important, matters in the case—like his influence on Dean Jefferson's decision to veto Williams's application for tenure.

While some lawyers might object to the ethics of counsel "assisting" the memory of a witness, in reality, the failure to correct (or at least attempt to correct) a client's inaccurate recollections is a failure of professionalism. The fact of reconstruction is well known by every litigator. It is also well known that when a witness reconstructs the facts in a way that is inconsistent with the weight of the credible evidence, a factfinder often disbelieves not just the reconstructed fact, but more generally the witness.

If, however, a witness persists in an unrealistic reconstruction of a fact, your only choice is to accept the fact as true, present it to a factfinder, and argue the fact for whatever worth it has, while advising the client of the likely downside effect of his testimony. This is only the case if you believe that the witness actually believes his reconstruction. In most, but not all, jurisdictions, if the deponent testifies falsely at the deposition, you have an obligation to not only counsel the deponent to correct false testimony, but actually reveal such falsity to the court and opponent.[16] The standard, however, is a high one. Only when you believe that the witness has *intentionally* falsified evidence must you communicate this to the court and counsel.

14. How much of my client's case theory should I divulge and explain to the deponent?

This is an important tactical decision. A client informed of the potential legal, factual, and persuasive case theories you seek to confirm or develop will naturally use that knowledge when reconstructing facts, as discussed in the previous section. That is, if the party knows the factual case theory and believes it to be true, it makes

15. At trial, many jurisdictions provide for a jury instruction that states, "If you find that a witness has told a falsehood in any part of his or her testimony, you are entitled to infer that the witness's testimony has been false in any other or all parts of his or her testimony." Commonly referred to as "false in one, false in all" instructions.

16. *See* Model Rules of Prof'l Conduct rr. 3.3(a)(3), 3.4(b) (Am. Bar Ass'n, 2013); RTC v. Bright, 157 F.R.D. 397, 399–400 (N.D. Tex.1994).

it likely that the party will reconstruct his "memory" of the case facts to conform to that factual theory. Be vigilant in limiting the testimony of parties to facts that they actually know, as opposed to facts that you hope to be true. Ultimately, you will have to develop those other facts from other witnesses and discovery material in the case; any reasonable inferences from those facts should be made by you, not by an eager client.

Most nonparty witnesses have—and only need—a limited knowledge of the facts. If the witness generally believes a party deserves a favorable litigation outcome, knowing the factual theory of that party might spur reconstructions beyond actual first-hand knowledge.[17] It is usually best, therefore, to limit what you tell the witness about the purpose of his information in the lawsuit.

Example: Williams's working theory might be that when she ended her relationship with Simonson, Simonson retaliated by using his influence on the faculty, with the dean, and with the university to prevent her from receiving tenure for which she was qualified. As part of that theory, Williams needs to show the seriousness of the relationship between her and Simonson, and as evidence, she would like to show that Simonson was essentially living at her condo. The doorman at Williams's condo could be told, as a precursor to his deposition preparation, the following:

L: We have identified you to the attorneys for the defense as someone who can testify how frequently Professor Simonson visited Ms. Williams. Our position is that they had a close and intimate relationship. What you can tell us about the frequency of Simonson's visits, and what you can tell us about how you saw them interact, can help us prove that it was a serious relationship. We expect that Professor Simonson's attorney will want to hear what you have to say about that in your own words. That's why you have been called to give deposition testimony.

Narrow explanations of the scope and purpose of a witness to his place in the lawsuit's theory. Do not fully explain case theory. To do so might encourage the witness to overstate or expand reconstruction of his testimony into areas about which he has little knowledge, making the witness an apparent advocate for a party. Once a factfinder views a witness as an advocate, his testimony is devalued by that perceived bias. For most witnesses, their testimony is much more persuasive if they are viewed as a neutral person who happens to have relevant information favorable to a particular party about an issue in the lawsuit.

15. What tone should I adopt for the preparation session?

Since deposing counsel conducts a deposition for the primary purpose of gathering and confirming information, it follows that the more comfortable a wit-

17. We assume, of course, that a witness willing to be prepared by the counsel for a party has a favorable view of that party and would like that party to prevail.

ness is with the deposition process, the easier your task is as defending counsel. For that purpose, although a witness has nothing really to fear in a deposition, make it clear that the only reason the deposition is being taken is to collect information that is helpful to the deposing party's position in the lawsuit.

Example: The lawyer for the university might explain to Dean Jefferson the following:

L: *Now Dean, let me tell you that the lawyer for the plaintiff is a very good one. She is smart and articulate. As such, she knows that the more relaxed she makes you, the more likely it is that you will provide information that she can use to draw inferences that are contrary to your interests in the lawsuit. So I suspect that for the most of the deposition, she will be quite friendly and conversational. What you need to understand is that the only reason she is doing that is in the hopes that she can get information from you that will cost the university millions of dollars.*

J: *Is she likely to try to twist my words?*

L: *I wouldn't say that. What she will be doing is trying to get any information she can from you that will help her client's case. Our purpose today is to make sure you are comfortable with answering questions and confident in the accuracy of your testimony. Just remember, the other lawyer, no matter how she acts, is not your friend.*

J: *But you'll be there to protect me from any unfair questions, won't you?*

L: *Of course, but remember that she has the right to ask any question that can lead to admissible evidence, and that's a broad range of information. Unless I instruct you not to answer a question, you should answer it, even if you think that it's unfair. Just be sure to listen carefully to the question, make sure you understand it, and answer it fairly.*

A witness so warned is likely to appreciate the seriousness of the proceeding and therefore better able to provide information in a confident but careful way. Do not frighten the witness; a frightened witness will likely appear less than credible. Instead, put the witness on guard, and make sure that he is mindful to keep his testimony truthful and accurate, limited to facts as opposed to inferences.

16. What does the deponent need to know about answering questions to which I've objected?

As to the making of objections, Rule 30(c)(2) provides:

> An objection at the time of the examination . . . must be noted on the record, but the examination still proceeds; the testimony is taken subject to any objection. An objection must be stated concisely in a nonargumentative and nonsuggestive manner.

> A person may instruct a deponent not to answer only when necessary to preserve a privilege, to enforce a limitation ordered by the court, or to present a motion under Rule 30(d)(3).

The rule allows defending counsel little control over deposition testimony. Gone are the days of speaking objections, where the lawyer would essentially instruct her witness how to answer questions. As we discuss in chapter seven, in many circumstances counsel will stipulate to reserve all objections, except as to the form of the question, until the witness's deposition testimony is offered as evidence in any trial or other proceeding. That does not mean, however, that you should not cover the topic of objections with the witness during preparation, with particular attention to instructions not to answer a question.

17. What does the deponent need to know about the purposes of objections and how to respond to them?

The process of making objections is not in concert with what the witness is likely to have seen on television or in the movies. In media, the setting is normally a trial and a judge is present, ruling on objections. That, of course, is not the case at a deposition. Inform the witness that any objections will be ruled on later, if at all. Also inform him that when you object, he should stop answering the question until you have fully stated the objection, at which time you will tell him to go ahead and answer the question. This process, while well known to lawyers, is off-putting for most witnesses, who believe that when an objection is made, something should happen other than merely responding to the question.

That does not mean, however, that the witness should not listen carefully to the objection. Objections to the form of a question exist because some questions raise the possibility that unreliable, or at least confusing, responses will follow. Prepare the witness for objections to the form of the question by telling him the following about each objection, using examples of how the objection might be made. Explain the danger that lurks in responding to a question posed in an objectionable form.

a) **Argumentative**—A lawyer does not ask an argumentative question to elicit information from a witness, but rather to get the witness to agree with her conclusion or inference regarding a particular set of facts. Inform the deponent that if you object to the question as argumentative, he should carefully consider the question and the conclusion or inference it seeks to reach from other facts. If he disagrees with the conclusion (argument), he should say so. If—after considering the conclusion sought by the question—the witness agrees with the conclusion, he should feel free to so testify. Provide an example of an argumentative question and discuss with the deponent how he can handle it during the deposition.

Example: In our hypothetical case, after discussing the nature of his relationship with the plaintiff as well as the facts of that relationship, counsel can engage in the following exchange.

L: *Now, Professor, assume that you have answered all of counsel's questions about the facts of your relationship with the plaintiff. The lawyer might then ask, "In light of your intimacy with Ms. Williams, the closeness of your relationship, the time you spent together, and the discussions you had with Ms. Williams about the problems in your marriage and your dissatisfaction with the marriage, wasn't it fair for Ms. Williams to believe that you were considering a divorce and a more permanent relationship with her?" I would object that the question was argumentative. If that happened, I would want you to consider the inference of counsel about the "fairness of Ms. Williams's belief" and decide whether you agree or disagree with the inference and answer appropriately.*

C: *I know you would prefer that I say that I disagree with the inference, but my real answer is that I don't know what Ms. Williams was thinking, only that I didn't ever consider marrying her and didn't try to make her believe that I did.*

L: *Let's be clear, Professor, this isn't about what I want or don't want. I want you to provide accurate answers, and if in this case your accurate answer is that you didn't know what Ms. Williams was thinking, but that you never intended to marry her and never tried to make her believe that you did, then that should be your answer. When I object on argumentative grounds, I want you to appreciate that the question calls for an inference and then answer honestly. The honest answer you just gave would be exactly how you should answer.*

The preceding exchange is an important one. Clients often believe that defending lawyers want them to shade (or even invent) testimony. That, of course, is not the case. Make this clear as many times as necessary in the course of a representation, including in the deposition preparation session. In fact, as in the above example, the answer provided by the witness is usually much better than his saying he disagrees with the inference in counsel's question.

b) **Assuming a Fact Not in Evidence**—This is a question that assumes in its first clause a fact that may not be provable while asking in the second clause a question with which the deponent will likely agree.

Example: During the preparation of Williams, you could say:

L: *You might be asked, "After Professor Taylor strongly recommended that you put off your tenure request for a year, you nonetheless decided to go forward with your tenure application after your sixth year on faculty, is that right?" If that question was asked, I would object because I believe the question assumes a fact not in evidence. When I make such an objection, carefully consider the question to be sure the fact assumed is both known by you and that you agree with it. In the example I just gave, the question assumed that Professor Taylor strongly recommended postponing your tenure application. If you agree that Professor Taylor's recommendation was indeed a strong one, feel free to respond to the question. If you believe that the so-called recommendation was instead a suggestion and/or that it was not strongly made, say so before answering the question about deciding not to postpone your tenure application.*

C: *How do I do that?*

L: *You can just tell the lawyer that Professor Taylor just suggested putting off the vote, and that you didn't consider it a strong suggestion. Then answer the question by explaining why you chose to go forward despite what Professor Taylor had to say.*

This exchange emphasizes the importance of accuracy when providing responses and gives a concrete example from the case being litigated on how listening to an objection and carefully considering a question can avoid communicating unintended meanings. It also empowers the witness to disagree with deposing counsel's assertions about the facts if they do not comport with the witness's understanding of those facts.

c) **Asked and Answered**—This objection, sometimes stated as "cumulative," is made to a question that the current deposing lawyer has previously asked and that the witness has already answered. Some lawyers will ask a question several times, hoping for or believing that the previous answer was inaccurate. Be sure to tell the witness that merely because a lawyer asks a question several times, there is no reason to change the answer—unless, of course, it was inaccurate. (Some legal authority holds that this is an improper objection at a deposition.)

d) **Compound**—A compound question is really a question that asks for more than one fact; if the witness answers "yes." it is unclear that the answer is "yes" to part one, or "yes" to part two, or "yes" to both. Inform the witness that when the compound objection is made, he should take care to make clear which portion of the question he is answering.

Example: During the preparation of Dean Jefferson, you might say:

L: *Plaintiff's counsel might ask you a question like this: "Professor Simonson was a top-rated teacher and scholar on the faculty whose value in bringing funding to the university was well known, and he was well respected by you despite his well-known unconventional marriage, which allowed for sexual activity outside the marriage, correct?" At that point, I would object that the question was compound because the question asked about Simonson's teaching, scholarship, fund raising, philandering and your respect. Would you say you respected the professor for his unconventional marriage?*

J: *No, not at all.*

L: *Then you should make that clear in your answer and separate out those things you respected and those things that you do not.*

J: *What happens if there are so many facts loaded into the question that I can't remember them all?*

L: *Just tell the lawyer that you both agree and disagree with her question, and I'll ask that the question be read back in pieces so you can respond to each part of the question. What's important is that you listen carefully to the question to be sure you appreciate all that is being asked. When I object that a question is compound, it just means it has more than one moving part, and you should be sure to appreciate that. If you do not understand what makes the particular question compound, simply ask that the question be read back to you so you can answer completely. If you agree with the whole of the question, you can say so, of course, but it's usually better to take it one fact at a time.*

This exchange between you and the witness empowers the witness to take some control over the deposition flow and at the same time reminds him that as the defending lawyer, when you see the possibility that unintended or confusing meaning can come from an answer because of the form of the question, you will make that possibility known by objecting. The exchange also lets the witness know that he can have the court reporter read back questions when necessary.

e) **Misquoting the witness**—This objection is made to questions in which a deposing lawyer misquotes or mischaracterizes the witness's previous testimony. Tell the witness that when you make such an objection, he should carefully consider whether he agrees first with the characterization or quotation of the previous answer and then whether he agrees or disagrees that the quote or characterization is consistent with his truthful testimony.

Example: During the preparation of Dean Jefferson, the following exchange might occur after she is told about the "misquoting" objection.

L: *Let me give you an example. Ms. Williams's lawyer might ask you a question like, "Given that Professor Simonson was the face of the Public Policy School, did the school or the university use him in promoting both institutions?" At which point I would object that the question misquotes your testimony. That's because as you just told me, Professor Simonson was one of the most influential and well-known members of your faculty and a face of the Public Policy School, not* ***the*** *face of the university. After I objected, it would be for you to either correct counsel or accept her version of your testimony. The objection is only intended for you to focus on the question and make sure it accurately reflects your testimony.*

Such an exchange not only provides specific information about the "misquoting" objection, but also reminds the witness that the opposing counsel is not his friend and that the witness should be vigilant in listening carefully to every question and objection and respond with appropriate testimony.

f) **Vague**—A vague question is one where the question's form does not clearly identify what information it seeks; answering this question may lead to inaccurate testimony. Tell the witness that when you object to the question as vague or ambiguous, he should either seek clarification or include in his answer his understanding of the information the question seeks. Failing to specify a time frame is frequent example of a vague question.

Example: The university's tenure polices may have been subjected to a relevant official interpretation by university counsel after the decision was made regarding the plaintiff. A question to a Rule 30(b)(6) witness that asks for the tenure policies during a YR-0 deposition can naturally receive an answer about the policies in YR-0, even though the relevant policies for the lawsuit are those of YR-2.

g) **Speculative**—Finally, although most lawyers will preserve all objections except as to the form of the question until the deposition testimony is offered, there is nothing that precludes the making of other objections. One of the most common areas for such objections are those that a question "calls for speculation or opinion;" in other words, the witness is merely being asked to guess about the facts.

Example: In preparing Williams, you might say to her that university counsel might ask, "Why did Dean Jefferson believe your performance at the Public Policy School to be noncollegial?"

L: *I would object that the question calls for speculation. To answer the question, you would only be speculating about what was in the mind of Dean Jefferson, and you can tell the lawyer just that. But you can also to feel free to share your belief that Jefferson was merely trying to appease Simonson.*

Not every witness should be encouraged to state their own opinion on important matters in the case. Williams, of course, is very smart and sophisticated. Most lawyers, however, would counsel that when they object to a question as "calling for speculation" the witness should say that she would prefer not to guess.

18. What does the deponent need to know about instructions not to answer a question and how to respond to the instruction?

Few objections will be accompanied by an instruction to a witness not to answer. Explain to the witness that you will only make that instruction when, at least in your opinion, answering the question will waive a privilege or provide information that is covered by a protective order—or sometimes because the question is being asked "in bad faith or in a manner that unreasonably annoys, embarrasses, or oppress the deponent"[18] such that it would be appropriate to seek a protective order. At a minimum, before responding to a question in the face of an instruction not to answer, the witness should seek a recess to discuss whether she should provide an answer.

18. Fed. R. Civ. P. 30(d)(A).

19. Are there rules for the deponent on how to answer questions?

There are no real rules other than to answer honestly, but there can be an issue regarding the form of those answers. We have mentioned that there are depositions taken in anticipation of a jury trial and those taken when the likely case resolution will be some sort of ADR or motion practice.

a. Assuming a jury trial, the classic proscription regarding the form of a deponent's response is known as "The Seven Answers."

In a perfect world, answering deposition questions would be a process of carefully listening to a question; thinking about the information being sought; thinking about the answer; formulating the answer in the witness's mind; and finally answering the question. Lawyers typically advise witnesses of that as the perfect formulation of an answer to any question—and virtually no witness is able to heed it for any significant period of time. In fact, in the modern, digital video deposition, the time to do all of that would make the witness appear hesitant, lacking knowledge or truthfulness—or both. The best one can really expect is that the witness listens carefully to the question, understands what is being asked, and answers it fairly and honestly.

Proceeding from the perfect world of answering depositions questions, and assuming that there was going to be a trial, lawyers practicing the classic deposition mode have devised a set of rules for implementing that perfect world. As a result, lawyers limited witnesses to only seven possible answers to a question at a deposition, and during preparation sought to impose that limitation.[19] The seven answers are:

1) Yes.
2) No.
3) Green (the shortest possible answer to a question).
4) I don't know.
5) I can't remember.
6) I don't understand your question.
7) (If all else fails) I need a break.

The seven answer approach has several premises:

1) that there will be a trial, and if the opposing counsel does not find out about information that is harmful to her case, her client will have to deal with that harmful information without the opportunity to prepare a response;
2) that the least amount of information provided to an opponent, the better;

19. The origin of the seven answers is unknown to the authors. They have been in the lexicon of legions of lawyers and reprinted in countless articles and books, so frequently in fact, that they are probably in the public domain for which no attribution is necessary. We do not claim these "answers" as our work product; what we provide is our understanding of their use, their purpose, and ultimately their lack of value for the modern deposition.

3) that no information should be volunteered;
4) that the deposing lawyer should have to work to receive any information from the witness;
5) that the deposition would be transcribed stenographically; and
6) that no case can be won at a deposition.

The problem with the seven answer advice is that it, too, cannot be followed for any appreciable period of time. Moreover, when and if the deposition is read—or more likely, shown on video—to a decision maker, a mediator, or an arbitrator, or reviewed by a judge in deciding motions or in deciding appropriate recommendations to the parties for settlement at the final pretrial conference, or even shown to jurors, it appears stilted and false.

The reality of modern civil litigation is that, absent a trial, the only real opportunity to present evidence from the parties and their witnesses will be through the depositions.[20] The depositions—and, even more, any video recordings of them—will show the credibility of parties and witnesses. These recordings will ultimately decide the case. Moreover, if a witness does get to testify at a trial and does provide information not disclosed during deposition because of the seven answers, opposing counsel will conduct an impeachment by omission, making the "new" or "surprise" information look like last-minute fabrication.

b. Assuming that motion practice or ADR is the probable case disposition mechanism in a case, does the "seven answer" advice on form of responses still apply?

There is some question whether the seven answers were ever a good idea because they did not allow a party or a witness to put their best factual and credibility foot forward. The seven answers advice was nonetheless routinely given, and some lawyers continue to follow the routine, holding to the belief—in the face of all evidence to the contrary—that it is always advantageous to avoid disclosing information to the opposing party that undermines that party's claim or defense.

We have already pointed out the statistical rarity of civil jury trials. Given the ubiquity of nontrial civil dispute resolution, hiding the ball—particularly with respect to the deponent's strong points—may not be the best approach.

Example: Compare the following deposition transcripts of Ms. Williams. First is the deposition of Ms. Williams, following the seven answers rule.

L: Did you attend college?

20. While it is true that in summary judgment, affidavits can be submitted, or in ADR, statements of fact attributed to parties and witnesses can be provided by lawyers, they are, at most, second-best information. Moreover, every federal circuit has decided that a party is not allowed to contradict testimony in her deposition for purposes of summary judgment.

W: *Yes.*
L: *What college did you attend?*
W: *I don't understand your question.*
L: *What don't you understand?*
W: *I attended two universities.*
L: *What was the first university you attended?*
W: *Northwestern.*
L: *In Chicago?*
W: *No.*
L: *Where is the Northwestern you attended?*
W: *Evanston.*
L: *North of Chicago?*
W: *Yes.*
L: *Did you receive a degree?*
W: *Yes.*
L: *What degree did you receive?*
W: *A Bachelor of Arts.*
L: *What was your major?*
W: *Public Policy.*
L: *When was that?*
W: *Ten years ago.*
L: *Did you receive any honors?*
W: *Yes.*
L: *More than one?*
W: *Yes.*
L: *What were those honors?*
W: *I was elected to Phi Beta Kappa, graduated summa cum laude, and was elected to the Public Policy Honorary Society.*

****

Consider now, the same information in the deposition of Ms. Williams after she is freed from the shackles of the seven answers rule.

L: *Did you attend college?*
W: *Yes, I graduated ten years ago from Northwestern University with a degree in BA Public Policy and seven years ago with a PhD in Public Policy from Duke University.*
L: *Did you receive any honors?*
W: *At Northwestern I was elected to Phi Beta Kappa and the National Public Policy Honors society and I graduated summa cum laude. At Duke I also graduated summa cum laude.*

When Ms. Williams follows the seven answers rule she appears evasive and annoying, demonstrating an unwillingness to come forward with even the most basic background information and requiring thirteen questions and answers to find out about her Northwestern and Duke degrees. In the second example, she was able to provide the same information and more in two answers, and most importantly, she provided that information in a natural and forthcoming way.

c. What advice should I give when the likely resolution is motion practice or ADR?

We suggest that there now is only one rule about answering questions. Assuming the witness understands the question, has the information from his own firsthand knowledge, remembers it, and doesn't need a break,[21] the witness should provide ***the shortest, persuasive, fair answer to the question*** from the point of view of the party defending the deposition.[22] The benefits of this one-rule approach are that not only is it a natural way for a person to answer a question, it is also the natural way a person listening to a conversation receives information from that conversation. Of course, the problem with the one-rule approach is that it requires the witness to exercise judgment—and the only way to learn how to exercise judgment on what a short, fair, and persuasive answer would look like to have the witness practice answering anticipated questions.

A simple "yes" answer to the question "Did you attend college?" is short, but neither fair nor expected. The answer "Yes, I graduated from Bucknell University in 1969 with a BA in Political Science"[23] is both short and fair. If in response to the question during preparation, the witness answered, "Yes, I graduated from Bucknell University in 1969 with a BA degree in Political Science. It was the sixties, so I did a lot of drug experimentation, frequently inhaling. There was nothing to the alleged plagiarism charge, and I absolutely deny any claims of stealing exams from my political science instructor,"[24] you need to work on the witness's judgment.

The modern approach comes with some considerable cost in terms of preparation time. The witness needs to practice answering questions to develop the art of the shortest fair and persuasive answer. The more important the witness is to the case, the more topics there will be to cover and the more practice time you need to allot.

d. Should I prepare the deponent to volunteer information?

It is here that the persuasive nature of answering deposition question comes most into play. You may know particular information that is helpful to your client's

21. There is nothing wrong with a witness answering truthfully that he doesn't know, or doesn't remember, or doesn't understand.

22. The shortest fair answer may be "yes," "no," "I don't know," "I don't remember," or "I don't understand." Although it is usually true that the "yes" or "no" answer deserves some explanation, a witness may not know the answer to a question or may have known the answer at one time, but has a failure of memory. A witness should never answer a question that he does not understand.

23. The answer refers to truth about Professor Bocchino.

24. As to this answer, Professor Bocchino refuses to comment.

position that opposing counsel does not know. Prepare the witness to provide that information when a pertinent question arises. This will make the answer to the question not just short and fair, but persuasive. This information, if it comes in response to questioning, will gain significant importance to deposing counsel because it came unencumbered from the witness. In the alternative, if there is no opportunity for the witness to volunteer this favorable information in response to questioning, you will have an opportunity at the end of deposing counsel's examination. Be prepared to ask questions that reveal that positive information so it will be available to all decision makers when determining the appropriate nontrial case resolution.

The key to understanding the modern deposition is appreciating that where trial is unlikely, the deposition must place your client in the best position to succeed in mediation, arbitration, summary judgment, or negotiated settlement. "Hiding the ball" with respect to positive information is counterproductive where you do not anticipate trial (and the advantage of surprise).

20. Does the deponent get a chance to practice all of this preparation advice before the deposition itself?

Once you have gathered and confirmed all the information that the witness possesses and have gone through the topics discussed above, take a significant break. During the fact-gathering and confirmation process and the one-on-one preparing process described above, you have been in a fact-seeking, advice-providing mode. This exchange of facts is different from the interaction of a deposition. Without the break, the witness may remain in interview mode, which is not suited for preparing actual deposition testimony.

While it is possible to provide the necessary practice of answering questions with the defending lawyers assuming the role of the deposing lawyer, the process can be confusing. You might start out well playing the role of the deposing lawyer, but there comes a time when that the witness needs some help in forming that short, fair and persuasive answer. Changing hats takes the witness and you out of one role (deposing lawyer and deponent) and into another (advisor and client). This is a line you don't want to blur. It may also take time to get back into the practice mode.

a. Roleplaying in the Practice Session

It is therefore far better to enlist the aid of another lawyer in the firm to play the role of deposing counsel during the practice session. That will avoid the above-noted confusion of roles and message. If possible, choose someone whose style of questioning is as close as possible to that of the lawyer who will take the deposition. You assume the role that you will occupy in the real deposition, leaving you free to perform the additional function of advisor on how to respond to particular questions. To be clear, you can never tell the witness what the facts are, but you can and should help the witness articulate those facts.

In addition, consider whether you should video record the practice session, especially if the actual deposition will be recorded that way. At a minimum, you should set up the rehearsal so that the deponent and questioning counsel are seated in the same position vis-à-vis a video camera as will occur at deposition.

You should always record the practice session on digital video when you notice that the witness has certain things about his demeanor that do not reflect positively on his credibility. Telling the witness about such demeanor flaws (e.g., averting eyes, qualifying answers, verbal tics, facial expressions) helps— showing them has much more impact.

Example: Consider the following from the roleplaying preparation session of Professor Simonson.

L: [By person playing role of deposing counsel.] *When did the personal relationship between you and Ms. Williams begin?*
S: *Well, during her first year at the university, she asked me to sit in on her class and provide her a critique of her teaching, which I was happy to do.*
L: *Were you sexually attracted to her at the time?*
S: *I found her attractive—she's always been an attractive woman, but there was nothing sexual about our meeting. We talked about her class, which is very common in professional relationships.*
L: *So during the first year of her teaching, there wasn't a personal relationship?*
S: *It was person-to-person, but I suppose you could characterize it as professional, with personal interaction.*
L: *So was the relationship personal or professional?*
Defending Counsel: Objection; asked and answered.
L: *Please answer the question, Professor.*
S: *I already have. It was in a professional setting, and we had personal interaction, mainly about professional matters.*
Defending Counsel: Let's take a short break and talk about the last set of questions and answers. Professor, that was an example of how the deposing lawyer was trying to get you to go along with her characterization of what constituted a personal versus professional relationship. I think you did a good job of answering the questions in a short and fair way, and you paid attention to our preparation and stuck to your guns; but then you qualified that the interaction was mainly about professional matters. What did you mean by that?
S: *At faculty meetings or in the hallway, we would exchange pleasantries, chat about the weather, that sort of thing.*
Defending Counsel: Then I think to be complete, your answer should be phrased that way; that other than the exchange of pleasantries or chatting about things like

the weather, the relationship was person-to-person about professional matters. Okay, let's try that again.

Deposing Counsel: So was the relationship between you and Ms. William in her first year at the university, personal or profession?

S: Well, we would say hello if we saw each other in the hall or sometimes have a brief conversation about things like the weather, but I would characterize our interaction as person-to-person about professional matters.

Defending Counsel: That was much better because it was as complete as it needed to be and accurate about the relationship.

[Later in the practice session.]

L: [By person playing role of deposing counsel.] *You were Ms. Williams's direct supervisor in her role as a researcher at the Patterson Institute where you were the Director, is that right?*

S: She reported to the Associate Director, Judith Harriman, as well, but I was one of her supervisors.

L: How did your sexual relationship with Ms. Williams begin?

S: We had been working night and day on a grant application, and when we got it done, we went to dinner to celebrate. There was some wine with dinner, and when I took her home, she invited me in for a cup of coffee. I accepted, and one thing led to another, and we had sex that evening. The relationship grew from there and became more intimate over time.

L: Did you frequently stay overnight as her condo?

S: I wouldn't say frequently, but I did spend the night from time to time.

L: Did you talk with Ms. Williams about your relationship with your wife?

S: Not often.

L: Did you ever tell Ms. Williams that you were going to divorce your wife?

S: I know that's what she wanted to hear, but I did not ever say that to her.

L: Did you speak with Ms. Williams about having a long-term relationship?

S: I think that was understood. I was very much in love with her, and she with me.

L: And you believed that Ms. Williams would be happy with a long-term relationship with a married man?

S: Yes, she did not seem to object.

L: But you said that you believed she wanted you to divorce your wife?

S: Yes.

L: Did she raise the possibility of your getting a divorce directly?

S: A couple of times, but I would put her off. I had no intention of divorcing my wife.

L: Did you ever say that to Ms. Williams?

S: No. I would change the subject by saying things like, this isn't the right time, and that would seem to satisfy her.

L: So you intentionally misled her?

S: Listen, she knew the score. She was not the first person I had an affair with; there had been many others. I never divorced my wife for any of them and had no intention of doing so to please Ms. Williams. She's a smart woman. I'm sure she understood that divorce was not on the table. If she didn't, she was misleading herself; there was no misleading on my part.

Defending Counsel: All right Professor, let's look at the video of that last exchange. First, as we predicted, there was a question of how often you spent the night at the condo. Your answer was from time to time. Didn't we agree this morning that as the relationship got more serious, you stayed over more frequently? Remember, they have information that there were times that you spent weeks at a time at the condo.

S: That's right. If she asks me about the frequency of my spending the night, I'll say infrequently—once, maybe twice, a week at first, but as our relationship progressed, there would be times that I would live there for weeks at a time; especially when my wife and kids were out of town.

Defending Counsel: That's good, and more importantly, it's accurate. The less we have to quarrel with the other side about the accuracy of facts, the better off we are. Now let's look at the last exchange. Obviously, that line of questioning bothered you. You see, you were much more adamant and argumentative. Your voice is raised, and the last bit where you blamed Ms. Williams for your not wanting to get a divorce is over the line. The lawyer asked, "So you intentionally misled her?" From what you told me in the past, you knew that Ms. Williams wanted you to get a divorce, but you always avoided the topic and never gave her any indication that you intended to divorce your wife. Is that accurate?

S: Yes.

Defending Counsel: We'll practice that answer in a minute, but see what you did here. You lost your temper and then volunteered that there had been a lot of other relationships and you never divorced then. I think the way you answered the question, especially in an angry tone, would be taken by jurors as an admission that in addition to being unfaithful to your wife, you would allow women to believe that you would be leaving your wife for them with no intention of doing so. So if you find yourself getting angry, take a deep breath and answer directly and carefully, and if you still find yourself angry, then ask to take a break, and we will.

S: I understand.

Defending Counsel: One additional thing. You were asked about who supervised Ms. Williams at the Patterson Institute and spoke of Ms. Harriman as having the day-to-day supervision as her responsibility. Didn't you tell me earlier that Professor Harriman had to write to Ms. Williams in her last semester—before she was denied tenure—about being behind in her work?

S: Yes, that's true.

Defending Counsel: Well, when you were asked about supervision, that would be a good time to volunteer the fact of her work being late. So you might answer, "The Associate Director had the day-to-day supervision of Ms. Williams in her portfolio. For example, when Ms. Williams was late with her assignments in her last semester with us, it was Professor Harriman who spoke to her about that problem."

S: *I see. Can we go over that line of questioning again?*

The preceding vignette demonstrates how important the practice session is as well as the benefits of using video to prepare, especially when the deposition will be recorded. The witness, after having been prepared on the frequency of overnight stays question and answer, reverted to a less than accurate answer that can now be corrected. Second, the video lets the witness see how he testified and appeared in response to aggressive questioning and suggests that the witness should engage in more preparation on demeanor. Third, counsel helped the witness draw the line between a short and fair answer and one that volunteered information in a way that could be detrimental to his position in the case. And finally, counsel gave the witness an example of how he could volunteer helpful information when questioning counsel provides the opportunity.

21. Is there ever a time in a deposition when the defending counsel asks the deponent questions?

It is possible, even likely, that opposing counsel will not ask about information that is helpful to your client's case, and that information (for reasons discussed earlier) should be known by a decision maker. There are other ways to get this information to the decision maker: summary judgment motions allow you to submit affidavits on the issue of whether a genuine issue of material fact exists sufficient to have a trial in the matter; settlement negotiations counsel can state that a particular witness will provide helpful information that was not developed during depositions; and most forms of ADR allow you to provide information not disclosed during discovery. But each of those proffers of facts are less forceful than deposition testimony. Depositions most resemble trial testimony: they are taken under oath, all parties are represented, and all parties are allowed to question a witness.

In light of the above, we suggest another break with the tradition of depositions. If, at the end of questioning by deposing counsel, you know of undisclosed information that is important to the fair evaluation of the case and is in the interest of your client, request a break, and then prepare and execute a direct examination of the deponent (including your own client) that discloses the information missed by deposing counsel. The length of the break is the time necessary to prepare the direct examination. By so doing, later decision makers—parties, counsel, mediators, arbitrators, judges, etc.—will benefit from this helpful sworn testimony provided while the witness was available for cross-examination.

Deposing counsel often fails to ask about information provided in interrogatories; in other situations, previous depositions of other witnesses have not gone into a vital factual area; or the facts are known only to the witness now being deposed. Presume that this "defending counsel examination" will be the only way to disclose these facts. Be sure to formulate and practice your questions during the witness's deposition preparation session.

22. How does the preparation session end?

At the end of the session, you should cover the following with the witness.

1) Arrange to meet the witness at your office so you can go to the deposition together.
2) Agree on the witness's attire.
3) Tell the witness not to bring anything with them—especially notes or documents or anything else that might become fair game for discovery.
4) Tell the witness that if he has any questions or concerns before the deposition, he should feel free and encouraged to call you.
5) Instruct the witness **not to review any further information** unless he feels it absolutely necessary, and not to do so without first discussing it with you.
6) Finally, encourage the witness to get a good night's sleep.

Chapter Six

Beginning the Information Gathering Deposition

In addition to the primary goal of complete information gathering, a secondary goal of the deposition is to demonstrate that it is a fair proceeding. This is important if the deposition is used for either substantive or impeachment purposes. In either case, the user of the deposition should feel confident that the deposition gave the deponent the opportunity to testify to all known information, that the deponent was not intimidated, and that the deponent was provided with every reasonable opportunity to ensure that his testimony was complete and accurate. These goals continue throughout the deposition, and their predicate is set at the outset of the deposition.

1. Is there a preferred positioning at the deposition table to foster the fairness goal?

The deposition begins with the seating of the participants. Foster fairness by positioning the participants in a way that does not interfere with either communication or the appearance of credibility. In the typical setting, the deposition officer[1] sits at the end of a conference table, the deposing counsel and any assistants are on one side of the table, and the deponent and defending counsel are on the other side of the table, with deponent next to the reporter. If the deposition is being video recorded, situate the camera over the shoulder of questioning counsel[2] and provide microphones for counsel, the witness, and the court reporter.

This arrangement makes it easy for the court reporter to hear and record the questions and answers accurately, makes eye contact between the deponent and questioning counsel natural, and makes it easy for defending counsel to object in a timely and effective way, without being in a position to interfere with or signal the witness. As a matter of fairness, when an objection is interposed, testimony should cease. From her position next to the deponent, defending counsel speaks the word "objection" and holds her hand in front of the deponent, stopping testimony while the objection (or instruction not to answer) is made. This avoids objecting counsel and the deponent speaking over each other and promotes a clear record. Once counsel has stated the objection, absent an instruction not to answer, the deponent can answer the question unimpeded.

1. In most cases, a court reporter.

2. When questioning counsel changes, the lawyer, not the camera, is moved.

In video-recorded depositions, the positioning of the camera (over the shoulder of questioning counsel) insures that the deponent's head and shoulders face into the camera, thereby making recorded "eye contact" between the deponent and the viewer of the testimony. This "eye contact" presents the deponent in the most credible way.[3]

Finally, all parties are entitled to have a legal representative (in addition to counsel) present at all depositions, though such practice is unusual.[4] In the case of multiple parties on either side of the case, it is the norm that a primary questioner or defender takes the lead at the deposition, although all parties are usually present to represent the rights of their clients, and they may object. Secondary counsel frequently ask follow-up or clarifying questions. When that occurs, and the questioning includes more than a few questions, the secondary counsel will assume the primary questioner's position, thereby maintaining the proper camera aspect between the witness and the recording camera.

2. Are there any formalities that should occur before the deponent's examination begins?

There are several preliminary matters that typically occur before questioning begins.

a) All counsel provide business cards to the deposition officer and identify their clients to the reporter. Deposing counsel also provides to the court reporter the case name and caption, the names and addresses of all deponents for the day, the spelling of names and addresses of people to whom reference will be made during the deposition, and a glossary of terms the deponents and questioning counsel will use.

b) The deposition officer begins the deposition by identifying the case by name and docket number as well as the identity of the person to be deposed. In addition, the videographer identifies himself and his function. Counsel for the parties then introduce themselves on the record and state on which party's behalf they appear. Any additional people present are identified as well. Any objection to the presence of any person present is then made, the most typical being to a person whose deposition will also be taken in the case.[5] The deposition officer then

3. Social science and generations of parental instruction teaches that if a person wants to be believed, he must make eye contact with the person with whom his is communicating.

4. The usual custom will typically vary when the key witness for the opposing party is being deposed. In these circumstances, a settlement decision maker may choose to attend to get a feel for the main opposing evidence to help value the case for settlement.

5. In most cases, the parties will agree to exclude from the deposition any witnesses yet to be called except parties, who have a right to be present. If there is no such agreement, the objection will be noted, the person will be allowed to remain, and the deposition will proceed with the objected-to person present unless and until objecting counsel can obtain a court order to the contrary. In the modern deposition situation, where transcripts/videos of the deposition are available quickly, later deponents will see the transcript (written or video) before their deposition, so their presence is less of a tactical problem.

states the date, time, and place of the deposition, and the witness is administered the oath or affirmation to tell the truth.

3. **In every deposition I've participated in, either opposing counsel or the court reporter asks if the deposition is going to proceed with the "usual stipulations." What are the "usual stipulations?"**

The reality is that agreement to the "usual stipulations" means agreement to what the deposition officer believes to be the "usual stipulations." These "usual stipulations" then appear on the record not in those terms, but as specific agreements as to the manner in which the deposition will be taken, recorded, transcribed, etc., that govern the deposition for the rest of the case. Most deposition officers will state the stipulations in accordance with the prevailing rules of civil procedure.

The better practice is for counsel who notices the deposition to provide a list of proposed stipulations to the deposition officer and opposing counsel. Then, in the absence of any opposition by counsel, these stipulations are adopted for the deposition. Pay attention to stipulations offered by opposing counsel—the stipulations that govern the deposition can have significant consequences.

As the rules of civil procedure have been modernized over time, the need for many of what were the "usual stipulations" has evaporated. Typical formalities regarding the filing, certification, and the signing and swearing of the deposition transcript before the deposition officer have been marginalized by rule changes. There do remain, however, certain stipulations—sometimes considered as "usual"—that have a substantive impact on the manner of deposition and the usefulness of its recording.

4. **Should the reading, correcting and signing of the deposition be waived?**

In chapter two, we discussed the tactics of reading and signing, but a brief recap in this context is helpful. The deponent has the opportunity to read and correct the deposition. In the Federal Rules of Civil Procedure and most state civil procedure rules, "correction" includes not only transcription errors, but substantive corrections as well. The opportunity to correct is a significant one. As to reading, correcting, and signing, the *default position* in the Civil Procedure Rules is that if either party or the deponent make no reservation to read, correct, and sign, *there is waiver*. Waiving the reading, correction, and signing of the deposition is a bad idea.

The deposition's value (reliability) is enhanced by the deponent reading, correcting, and signing. Deposing counsel wants that enhancement—if the deponent provides testimony that is inconsistent with the deposition recording or transcript (either directly or by omission), the impeachment value of the recorded deposition is higher if the deponent reviewed the deposition transcript; had the opportunity to correct it, but didn't, then signed the deposition. Otherwise, when you confront a witness on cross-examination with an inconsistency from the deposition recording and he responds that the recording is inaccurate or the meaning unintended, your impeachment is blunted, despite the effect of the waiver.

At the same time, defending counsel wants the witness to read, correct, and sign the deposition transcript so the witness can correct errors in recording and misimpressions left by testimony. And of course, the deponent (putting aside the inconvenience of the process) wants the opportunity to read, correct, and sign so that his sworn testimony is accurate.

As a result, counsel for all parties should want the following stipulation:

1) the witness will have the opportunity to read the deposition;
2) the witness will make all corrections (including those of substance)[6] on a correction (errata) sheet, note the reason for the correction, and sign the correction sheet; and
3) The witness will sign the deposition recording on the transcript, if prepared in writing, or by certification of an audio or visual recording, whether corrected or not, verifying its accuracy.[7]

5. What objections must I make to preserve them for a later trial or other proceeding?

Most lawyers seem to believe that the only objections waived if not made at the time of the deposition are those to the form of the question.[8] In reality, the civil procedure rules require that objections to questions or answers (both as to form and substantive) must be made (or waived) if making the objection can provide the opportunity to correct the evidentiary infirmity at the time of the deposition.[9] For example, strict compliance with Rule 32(d)(3)(A) could arguably require hearsay objections at the deposition because the hearsay problem could be obviated by an objection and the consequent laying of a hearsay exception foundation.

We agree with the vast majority of litigators who reject this extreme reading of Rule 32(d)(3)(A), believing that strict compliance with the words of the rule could lead to the waiver of many evidentiary objections that would ordinarily be made to a deposition recording at the time it was offered as evidence in another proceeding.[10]

6. Some lawyers (enough to make this explanatory note worthwhile) believe that the deponent may only make corrections in spelling and other errors in transcription. The Federal Rules of Civil Procedure directly provide that the deponent has the right to make substantive corrections (Rule 30(e)(1)). It is to the tactical advantage of deposing counsel to have the deponent make substantive corrections to the recording. First, it increases the reliability of the deposition for purposes of case decision-making, and second, the rules require that any substantive correction be explained, thereby lessening the likelihood of a dishonest substantive change being effective.

7. Most lawyers believe that signing the deposition is part of the civil procedure rules review process. The rules do not so provide. Hence, the above-suggested stipulation.

8. We base this statement on the experience of the authors, questions put to colleagues, and observation of opposing counsel at depositions.

9. Fed. R. Civ. P. 32(d)(3)(A).

10. To be clear, the federal rules regarding objections at the time of the deposition apply only when the substance of the deposition (as contained in the deposition) is offered in a later proceeding. There is no waiver to an objection to an inadmissible opinion offered at the time of trial merely because that objection was not made at the time of deposition.

Were the civil procedure rules so interpreted at a deposition,[11] counsel would be required to make many more objections than are typical, and the requirement to do so would be to the disadvantage of counsel both taking and defending the deposition. Deposing counsel, seeking the smooth flow of information from the witness, would be constantly interrupted by objections. Defending counsel would be burdened by having to make objections to testimony at a time when case theory is not fully developed and the substantive correctness—and tactical advisability—of objecting is not known. For that reason the authors propose the following "usual" stipulation.

> Counsel agree that all objections, except as to the form of the question, are reserved until such time as the deposition recording is offered in any proceeding or designated as an exhibit.[12]

Finally, any given case might call for stipulations outside the realm of the "usual;" such stipulations are useful devices to streamline the process of taking and providing deposition testimony. For example, in our hypothetical case where there is a claim of gender discrimination, counsel might inquire about past claims of gender discrimination made by the entity parties' current or former employees that are recorded in personnel files. In such a case, the parties should stipulate that those personnel records be sealed and that all counsel agree that the information be held in confidence, available only for use during the litigation of the case, after which the parties agree that on case disposition, the stipulation becomes a part of a post-litigation confidentiality agreement.[13]

6. Once the witness swears or affirms to tell the truth, what preliminary matters do I need to cover to help fulfill the goals of a complete, accurate, and fair deposition?

The goal of the pure discovery deposition, at least at the outset,[14] is to gather all potentially useful information (full, complete, and accurate)[15] in a useful and reliable

---

11. *See* chapter ten, which contains a more complete discussion of the impact of the rules of evidence on defending a deposition. *See* chapter seven for a discussion on the need to conform some information discovered during the questioning of a witness to insure admissibility or inadmissibility of evidence at some other proceeding.

12. This "usual" stipulation is common in many jurisdictions, unheard of in others, but in the opinion of the authors, wise. The vagueness about the proceeding at which potential objections must be considered is intentional. Potential venues when depositions will be offered in evidence, in addition to trial, are during evidentiary motions in limine (including *Daubert*/Rule 702 motions regarding admissibility of expert testimony); motions for summary judgment or partial summary judgment; and ADR proceedings, such as arbitration.

13. The post-trial confidentiality agreement is necessary because the stipulation (or even judicial protective order) lasts only until the conclusion of the litigation.

14. At the conclusion of the discovery phase of every deposition, deposing counsel may attempt to obtain admissions or party statements regarding certain facts and the legal, factual, and persuasive theories of her client.

15. The tactics and other considerations regarding gathering information are discussed in chapters eight through eleven.

form to accommodate all of its potential uses as identified in chapter one. As a result, the beginning of the discovery deposition serves the multiple functions of:

1) establishing the fairness of the deposition process;
2) establishing the expectation of full, complete, and accurate information;
3) setting out the formula for asking and answering questions to anticipate and obviate impediments to understanding and clarity;
4) putting the witness at ease; and
5) setting a conversational tone so that questions are asked and answers given using language that will be easily understood by any reader or listener.

We will explore these issues by presenting and commenting on the following "transcript" of the beginning of plaintiff's deposition in our hypothetical case, first in annotated pieces, and then as a whole to demonstrate how we suggest you establish the above objectives and set the most effective tone for taking deposition testimony. We are assuming for the purposes of this example that this is a modern deposition, using digital video recording and providing real-time digital transcription.

THE SCENE

The case caption has been stated; the court officer, videographer, and the parties to the deposition have been identified; and the witness has affirmed that she will tell the truth.

a. How do I make a record of putting the deponent at ease with the deposition process?

Defense Counsel: Good morning, Ms. Williams. My name Jerome Smith, and I represent your former employer, Nita University.
Plaintiff: Good morning.
Q: We know that you hold a PhD degree. Do you prefer to be addressed as Dr. Williams?
A: That's not necessary, Ms. Williams will do.
Q: As you can see, there is a video camera set up right behind me, which will be recording my questions and your answers. Mr. Jon Desjardins is the videographer. He will focus the camera on your head and shoulders; in other words, you are the star of this deposition. The camera is situated where it is so that when answering my questions, you will be also answering to the camera. Do you have any questions about the video recording of your deposition?
A: No, I understand.
Q: Are you comfortable with the camera recording your deposition?
A: It is a bit unusual for me, but I'm OK with it.

Q: *Our experience is that within a few minutes, as you and I begin to talk with each other, it's like the camera doesn't exist.*

All right then, Ms. Williams, we have asked you to be here today to provide testimony in a case in which you have sued my client, Nita University, the Public Policy School, the Patterson Institute, Dean Jefferson, and Professor Simonson for gender discrimination of various forms resulting in the denial to you of tenure. Is that your understanding?

A: *Yes.*

Q: *I will be asking questions on behalf of Nita University, but all the parties you have sued have agreed, in the interests of time, that I will also be making inquiry on their behalf. Counsel for each of those defendants might also have some follow-up questions. Is that acceptable to you?*

A: *Yes.*

Q: *Because of the nature of your allegations, it will be necessary for me to ask you about some intimate details of your life. You understand that I do so not out of curiosity or to embarrass you, but because of your allegations?*

A: *I do.*

In this introductory exchange, you have established how the witness prefers to be addressed, dealt directly with the fact of video recording, and pointed out that Ms. Williams initiated the lawsuit that necessitated this deposition. Explaining the video recording is designed to put on the record that its use is accomplished in a fair way and designed to be as unthreatening as possible.

By stating that the deposition is occasioned by Ms. Williams's lawsuit, you put on the record that questions about the bases of her claim are perfectly reasonable; that given the nature of her claim, it is fair for the university to question her about the case, and some of those questions may be personal in nature. You further establish that those personal questions are not to pry or out of lurid curiosity, but because of claims Williams chose to assert. There is also a subtext: that Williams can avoid a more public airing of her personal life by resolving the case before trial.

b. How can I encourage the witness's full and complete testimony and prevent the deponent from later claiming that there was something about the manner or form of my questions that provides an excuse to change an answer?

BACK TO THE TRANSCRIPT

Q: *Very well. We are interested in exploring everything that you know about the facts that underlie this lawsuit. Therefore, I am going to ask you to provide full, complete, and accurate answers to my questions, as you understand them. Will you do that?*

A: *Yes.*

Q: *Now, of course, for you to provide full and complete answers, I need to ask understandable questions. If there comes a time that my question is not clear—and I'll try to keep that to a minimum—or you are not sure about what I am asking, will you tell me so that I can ask a better question, and we can get an accurate answer on the record?*

A: *I will.*

Q: *So if I speak too fast, as I've sometimes been accused of, or mangle the English language such that my question is unclear, or I'm unclear in any other way, will you tell me so that we can be sure that my question was understandable so we can have a clear exchange of information?*

A: *Yes, I will.*

Through this next set of questions, you establish the need for full, complete answers in an unintimidating way. The witness agrees to answer the questions as she understands them (which she would do anyhow) and takes some responsibility for addressing other potential problems occasioned by counsel either speaking too fast or misspeaking. When you take responsibility for potential clarity problems and allow the witness to profess lack of understanding, you establish the deposition testimony's reliability while making the process appear as an apparently easy and fair one for the witness. You have also made it difficult for the deponent to say later that the deposition recording was unreliable because he did not understand the question, given that he did not say so during deposition.

Some lawyers add an additional question to this portion of the deposition and ask, *"So can I assume if you answer a question that you understood it?"* The authors counsel against such a question as it allows defending counsel to fairly interject, *"Ms. Williams will of course answer the questions as she understands them, not necessarily as you intend them."* The problem with allowing room for such an interjection is that it interferes with the relationship of fairness between you and the witness you are trying to build (and show)—with the interjection, opposing counsel is implying that you are already trying to "trick" the deponent. This reminds the witness that he is facing opposing counsel, not his friend, and that he should be wary.

c. There is a lot of nonverbal communication that isn't necessarily captured in a written transcript. How do I guard against such an unclear transcript?

BACK TO THE TRANSCRIPT

Q *Of course, full and complete testimony doesn't do us any good if we don't get an accurate transcript. Ms. Robinson is an excellent court reporter, but there are a couple of things that can happen that will get in the way of her doing her job. And even though Mr. Desjardins is video recording what you say, the recording, too, can be impacted by many of the same issues I'm going to raise. The first thing is that we have to keep our voices up. Since you teach, you shouldn't have any trouble with that, but will you be mindful to keep your voice up?*

A: *I will.*

Q: *Second, Ms. Robinson can't take down head nods, so will you answer out loud and not shake your head "yes" or "no"?*

A: *Yes.*

Q: *Third, in that vein, while we're talking, it's clear that "u-huh" means "yes," and "uh-uh" means "no," but that doesn't translate well, so will you use full word answers like "yes" or "no"?*

A: *Of course.*

Q: *And finally, to help Ms. Robinson, she can only take down one person talking at a time, so even when you know where my question is going, can you wait until I finish my question before you start your answer?*

A: *I will.*

Q: *And even more important, if I make a mistake and start a new question before you finish your answer to my previous question, will you be sure to tell me so you have a chance to give your full answer?*

A: *I will.*

The previous portion of the transcript merely covers some housekeeping matters that are important to the deposition transcript's accuracy. In reality, most experienced court reporters do take down head nods with the transcript reading "witness nods 'yes'" or "witness shakes head 'no'," and nonverbal utterances become "yes" and "no" in the transcript. And of course, the video recording cures most iterations of those problems. The lawyer starting a question before a witness finishes his answer is more problematic. This agreement between counsel and the witness—that the witness will insist on completing his answer in the face of an interrupting question by counsel—is more important to full, complete, and accurate testimony. It also serves to prevent a witness later claiming that he wasn't allowed to finish his answer during the deposition.

d. Are there any devices that help to insure that the deponent's testimony is complete—or at least that it is fair for me to rely on the answers provided as being complete?

BACK TO THE TRANSCRIPT

Q: *Now Ms. Williams, there are two circumstances that occur with enough frequency that I would like to bring them to your attention to avoid interfering with our learning about all the information you have regarding your claim. The first is this. Let's say, for example, later this morning we'll be talking about your job duties at the Public Policy School in your first year on faculty and I will ask you for a list of all of those duties as you remembered them. Then, over lunch you remember that were some things that you did in your job that you had not told me about. That's a pretty typical thing. If that happens to you, about any topic, will you tell me if you remember something more about a particular area in which you provided an answer and tell me that you need to complete your answer?*

A: *I will.*

Q: *Does that sound fair to you? You get to give your full testimony, and we get to know your complete information.*

A: *It does.*

Q: *There's another situation, and it doesn't happen as often, but enough to talk about. It sometimes happens that a witness will provide some testimony about an event and describe that event in a certain way. And later, while testifying or during a break, it occurs to the witness that the testimony may have left an incorrect impression about the event. If that happens to you, will you tell me so your testimony will be accurate?*

A: *Certainly.*

Q: *And because accuracy is critical to a fair case determination, I'm going to ask you that if you, for any reason, believe that your testimony will be understood inaccurately, you go ahead and tell me. In fairness to both of us, will you make corrections if those uncertainties arise?*

A: *I will.*

Q: *Thank you, I appreciate that. In fact, during the deposition, we will take regular breaks, and after each break, I will give you an opportunity to either complete or correct any previous testimony that you might have given—so you know that opportunity will always be there for you.*

A: *I understand.*

The above exchange is an important one because the most typical reasons witnesses give when changing or amplifying testimony are that they didn't remember the new fact at the time of the deposition or they said what the transcript shows, but did not mean to convey what their answer appears to convey. These phenomena will still occur, but with the above questioning and agreements, changes in testimony—either by adding information or by changing meaning—will be less credible. And just as important, the witness's testimony will be reliably known for all purposes in the litigation.

When speaking of adding or changing testimony, raise the topic as if it typically occurred at depositions. That will make it easier for the witness to make corrections—and thus more likely to do so—thereby providing a reliable record. It will also make it easier to blame the witness for the failing to make those corrections.

e. How do I close off the preliminary matters with the witness before getting into the substance of the deposition?

BACK TO THE TRANSCRIPT

Q: *Speaking of breaks, it's my habit to take a break every ninety minutes or so, for about fifteen minutes. That gives us all, especially the court reporter who's doing all the work, and the videographer, a chance to stretch, take a restroom break, or take care of any issues that need attention. Is that acceptable to you?*

A: *Yes, that's fine.*

Q: *If there comes a time that you need a break earlier, for whatever reason, please tell me, and we'll make every effort to accommodate you as long as a question is not pending. Will you do that?*

A: *I will.*

Q: *According to the discovery order entered by the judge in this case, you are allowed, in a few limited circumstances, to ask for advice from your counsel even after the deposition has begun.*[16] *If that need arises while there is a question pending, we ask that you answer the pending question, and then we can take a break.*[17] *Will you do that?*

A: *Yes.*

Q: *We want you to be comfortable, so if you want coffee, tea, or water, just let us know.*

A: *OK.*

Q: *Finally, is there any reason that you know of why you cannot give full, complete, and accurate testimony at this deposition?*

A: *No, I'm fine.*

Q: *Do you have any questions before we begin?*

A: *No, I'm ready.*

This last section is designed to give fair notice of the deposition session's duration and allows the witness to express concern about going so long without a break, in which case he can be accommodated. It is designed to put the deponent at ease. Consultation or a ban on the same with defending counsel during the deposition is a matter for the discovery order (or local rule) governing the case.

The final question is asked in lieu of questions about medical or mental condition, legal and illegal drug or alcohol use, and any other human circumstance that might interfere with a full, complete, and accurate deposition. The authors recommend the generic question for three reasons. First, witnesses may be understandably offended by personal questions about such things as medical and mental condition and the use of medications or intoxicants, thereby destroying the good will you attempted to establish. Second, even if such a condition or drug use exists, straightforward responses are unlikely. Finally, there is no way to anticipate every-

16. Increasingly, discovery orders preclude counsel from discussing the client's testimony with the client once the deposition has begun. (The preclusion of speaking with a nonparty witness during the pendency of a deposition is virtually universally recognized.) There are obvious exceptions when consultation is necessary to decide whether to assert a privilege (Fed. R. Civ. P. 26). Exceptions are also made for the need to correct testimony when a witness may have misspoken and whether to seek a protective order (Fed. R. Civ. P. 30).

17. Answering a pending question is commonly understood as being part of discovery orders allowing consultation between the lawyer and client.

thing that might interfere with full, complete, and accurate testimony,[18] thereby making the generic question not only the broadest possible inquiry, but also the best and most efficient. Finally, to be sure that there are no lingering ambiguities in the deponent's mind about the deposition process, you should ask if they have any questions. This both demonstrates fairness and makes the deponent's later claim of ambiguity less credible.

f. Do I need to repeat any of these preliminary questions after a break in the deposition?

It is not necessary to repeat these preliminary admonitions/agreements after each break in the deposition. We do suggest, however, that after every recess, you ask the witness the following questions.

1) It there any answer that you have given that you would like to complete by providing more information?
2) Is there any answer you have given that you would like to correct to make it more accurate?
3) Is there anything that happened over the break that will prevent you from giving full, complete, and accurate testimony?

There is nothing magical about the precise language of these questions. You will eventually come to a set of questions you can deliver naturally, in a conversational tone, that convey the intended information and set the intended tone for the deposition. To reach that goal, even though the introduction to the deposition contains rules, do not deliver them as such. They are not so much directives to the witness as agreements between deposing counsel and the deponent.

Many inexperienced lawyers will state the agreements as one long rule that contains all the information covered above. Because only the lawyer is speaking, there is no way to know whether the witness understands what the lawyer is saying. More importantly, the witness makes no commitment to comply with what the lawyer is saying. In addition, giving a list of rules does not set a tone for the deposition that is conducive to easily obtaining information. It is better, then, to engage the witness in a conversation in which the witness has the opportunity to express any confusion with what counsel is saying, and must agree to do as requested and provide assurances that he understands and intends to comply.

---

18. The experience of one of the co-authors is instructive. During trial, a witness provided testimony that was inconsistent with his deposition. During impeachment, when the witness was asked about his testimony at the time of deposition, the witness responded, "I remember talking about this in my deposition—it was in the afternoon. Over lunch I got a phone call from my mom that my brother was involved in a serious car accident, and I really can't say whether anything I talked about that afternoon was accurate." The generic question, if repeated after each significant break, would have eased the pain of this answer.

Chapter Seven

The Basics of Taking the Information Gathering Deposition

The most basic function of a deposition is, of course, gathering information. To be clear, however, once you have finished information gathering, you will often perform other functions: amalgamating facts from the witness for a particular purpose (e.g., defending a summary judgment motion, supporting or opposing anticipated in limine motions, etc.); obtaining party statements and admissions; and testing factual theory. We will discuss those functions later in chapters eight and eleven, but no matter what the deposition's purpose, it cannot be achieved without thoroughly exploring the case facts in the fact-gathering portion of the deposition.

The goal of fact gathering from any deponent is to obtain complete, comprehensive, accurate, and reliable information about the facts of a lawsuit. Put another way, the deposition must explore every topic about which the deponent has knowledge, every fact or occurrence within that topic, and insure that the information the deponent provides about each topic is exhaustive. It is by exhausting the facts known by the deponent for each and every topic within his knowledge—coupled with the deponent's assurance or agreement that the same has occurred—and a complete understanding of the deponent's basis for his knowledge that makes the deposition reliable for use in the rest of the litigation.

1. How do I use the chronological storylines that we talked about earlier in information gathering?

In chapter five, we discussed how you should prepare for taking a deposition: come to the deposition armed with the potential case storylines that encapsulate potential legal and factual theories.[1] Set those storylines out chronologically on a graph that shows the storyline facts across the top and lists the witnesses and other sources of information (predominantly documents) that provide the facts in the storyline along the left side of the page. Complete the graph (matching fact with source) to show which information source provides which facts in the case and what you must explore with the current deponent.

1. As discussed in chapter five, the storylines are created from legal theory charts, timelines, relationship charts, documents, witness statements, and the then-existing facts revealed in litigation (i.e., from pleadings, interrogatories, document production, Rule 36 admissions, etc.) Review the chronological storyline example, *infra* at page 76).

Some facts in the chronological storyline are, as we have previously characterized, *known* facts. These are facts your client provides and the opposing party corroborates in pleadings, interrogatories, documents, previous statements made or adopted by the opposing party (including the deponent), or previous depositions by opposing parties or their witness. You can easily see the known character of the fact on the chart by locating the fact and then following the column down to see which row of fact informants provide the fact.[2]

The potential storyline will also contain facts previously characterized as those that are *believed* or *disputed*. Believed facts are those your party provides in some form, typically in statements or internal documents. A believed fact will not, as of yet, be corroborated or agreed on by the opposing party (by witness, document, or otherwise). Looking down the column of a believed fact reveals that only your client provides the fact, and so it must be explored in the current deposition. A fact is disputed if the storyline chart shows the fact as one provided by the deposing counsel's party, but contradicted by the opposing party. In the column for the fact, deposing counsel's party will provide one version, while the opposing party will provide controverting sources. The current deponent, if he has information about the disputed fact, can help resolve the believed/disputed fact in favor or opposed to your client.

Finally, the chronological storyline will contain facts *hoped* to be true. These are facts for which no evidence has been obtained in the litigation. However, your analysis and common sense—perhaps informed by focus group results—point to these facts as potential explanations for gaps in the chronological storyline, which need to be filled to make its narrative complete and believable. On the storyline chart, the column underneath the hoped fact will be blank—that is, neither known nor believed nor disputed. The deponent's testimony is always a potential source of such facts; use the deposition to explore your theories about the hoped-for fact.

Compare the deponent's potential as an information source by referring to the chronological storyline—what information do you expect this deponent will be able to provide? Before the deposition, you will have already checked off some facts in the deponent's row of facts. These are facts contained or referred to either in documents or in the testimony of others where the deponent is identified as a participant in the topic area of inquiry. At a minimum, ask about all facts you have already identified on the chronological storyline chart, hopefully guaranteeing that they are known facts.

Be aware of the danger that the storyline chart can limit the scope of your inquiry. It should not and must not. The storyline chart guarantees that you won't miss areas of inquiry already identified; only careful questioning and attention to the answers

2. Many lawyers provide a color scheme that identifies the category to which the fact belongs—e.g., "known" facts are printed in black letters, "believed" in green, "disputed" in red, and "hoped for" in blue.

will reveal new avenues of information you should follow. Be open to and attempt to find every fact known by the deponent.

2. What is the tone and sequence of the fact-gathering deposition?

Fact gathering is easiest when the deponent is at ease and comfortable. In the main, then, the fact-gathering deposition should have the feel and the tone of a conversation, not an interrogation. Further, because its purpose is to learn all that the deponent knows, let the deponent dominate the conversation. Your questioning style should be a species of what psychologists call the "cognitive interview," during which the interviewee does most of the talking. It is of no matter, and often an impediment, that you believe you know the case facts. That belief might lead you to make assumptions about how the deponent would answer a particular question, and thus fail to ask the question. It also might lead you skip asking the deponent about a particular topic because you do not believe the deponent has any knowledge about the topic. Neither is acceptable.

In the interest of completeness, the deposition conversation should proceed chronologically as, essentially, the deponent's narrative. The chronological narrative is the way that most people relate events they know about, so chronology eases the deponent's memory retrieval process.[3] With the prepared chronological storyline chart for all potential storylines, you can discern where the deponent's statements agree with, dispute, add to, or are silent about the facts represented on the chronological storyline.

Generally, be friendly, professional, and inquisitive, with the goal of having a relaxed, unintimidated deponent. Keep questions short, simple, noncolloquial, and nonconfrontational. You are seeking complete information, as known by the deponent. Your initial questions should identify the topics of information the deponent knows, and then the facts within those topics; keep your questions as open-ended (nonlimiting) as possible. Open-ended questions encourage the deponent to dominate the conversation. Be respectful, but not formal.

3. Are there any studies about how to best encourage the deponent to provide full and complete testimony?

Experience conversing is the most valuable experience you can have. There is a large body of research and scholarship about conversational situations that is similar to the taking of depositions—which could also be understood as the art and science

3. We have spoken about memory actually being reconstruction—that witnesses reconstruct events in their minds and adopt the reconstruction as memory. A well-executed deposition becomes reliable only when it effectively ends the reconstruction process by getting assurances from the deponent that the information provided on every topic of significance is complete.

of interviewing—from which we should learn.[4] Scholars of interviewing suggest there are basic inhibitors and facilitators to a free flow of information. Those relevant to the taking of a deposition follow.

a. What are the known inhibitors to obtaining full information from a deponent?

As identified in Fact Investigation, and from our experience, inhibitors to obtaining full information from a deponent include the following.

1) **The Setting:** For most deponents, testifying under oath—with a court reporter, videographer, opposing counsel, and a lawyer by their side—is an unusual and off-putting experience. For that reason, prepare your witness by familiarizing him with the setting and the deposition process, as described in chapter five. Similarly, as deposing counsel, use the run-up to the deposition, when you are setting the deposition parameters and rules, to ease the deponent's mind about the deposition's purpose and goals. While doing so, assure the deponent that the process will be fair: answers can be amended or corrected, and defending counsel is available (at least in some circumstances) for consultation, as described in chapter six.[5]
2) **Ego Threat:** Deponents, like most people, have difficulty talking about matters that negatively impact their self-esteem. To overcome that ego threat, you must remain nonjudgmental in manner, facial expression, tone, and questioning—you want to encourage the deponent, making it acceptable for her to discuss such matters.
3) **Case Threat:** Parties, and those witnesses closely tied to a party, will be reluctant to provide information they believe will harm the party's chances of prevailing. So, again, deposing counsel must make the process as encouraging and nonthreatening as possible.

Example: Professor Simonson must be asked about previous relationships outside of his marriage. Encourage him to answer freely.

---

4. For those who seek first-hand consideration of interviewing, the authors suggest reference to Binder, Bergman, and Price, Lawyers as Counselors: A Client Centered Approach, (1991) and Zwier and Bocchino, Fact Investigation, A Practical Guide to Interviewing, Counseling, and Case Theory Development, 2d ed. (NITA 2015). We borrow from the Fact Investigation book in this section, with the permission of the authors of that volume. Professor Bocchino acknowledges that both he and Professor Zwier learned much of what they know about interviewing from their mentor, Dean Emeritus Joseph D. Harbaugh of the Nova Law School, amplified by decades of experience in teaching about fact-gathering.

5. Although conversation between the deponent and his counsel about testimony (except when discussing potential instructions not to answer) is prohibited, you can modify this order by stipulation. Normally, both counsel will agree that it is appropriate for a lawyer to discuss testimony with her client during the deposition as part of an appropriate, ethical representation; ethical lawyers will not abuse this stipulation.

Q: *In open marriages, such as yours and your wife's, it's normal for relationships to occur with people in the workplace because of close professional contact—did that ever happen with you?*

When you make the behavior sound normal, it becomes easier for the witness to speak about it. When a deponent provides information helpful to the deposing counsel's client—and contrary to the deponent party's position—and the deposing counsel in tone, style, and attitude communicates "Ah ha" or "Gotcha," etc., further information on that point is not forthcoming.

4) **Role Expectations:** Most people have never been to a deposition, or even a trial, their only reference being TV and other media. As such, they might expect that if deposing counsel wants to know about something, she will ask directly. Frequently, in fact, deposing counsel does not know that the deponent knows a particular fact. As we will discuss later, using open-ended questions and nonverbal facilitators will help overcome this potential impediment.
5) **Etiquette Barrier:** Lawsuits such as our hypothetical case involving gender discrimination often involve topics of the sort that are not politely discussed among strangers (much less on camera). Your nonprurient tone when asking some questions will help overcome this inhibitor, as will explaining why such questioning is necessary.

Example: Deposing counsel is questioning Professor Taylor.

Q: *There has been an allegation that you have a prejudice against Professor Simonson because of comments he made about your sexual preference, so I need to ask you some questions about that topic. If this embarrasses you, I apologize in advance.*

7) **Trauma:** We use the word trauma to describe the request for a deponent to talk about, and thereby relive, an unpleasant event. To avoid reliving the trauma of an unpleasant occurrence, a witness might provide less complete information than they possess. Deposing counsel should be mindful of this particular barrier.

Example: Ms. Williams claims emotional distress as a ground for recovery. As such, deposing counsel must ask about that distress.

Q: *Ms. Williams, you claim to have experienced emotional distress as a result of the university's tenure decision. I need to ask you about your experience, your treatment, and your current condition. I know that these are difficult topics, but these questions are necessary to evaluate the claims you are making. Since these questions will deal with your psychiatric treatment, we will not oppose a motion from your attorney to seal the deposition, except as necessary for litigation purposes, nor to having the deposition and records relating to this claim permanently sealed at the end of this case.*

8) **Perceived Irrelevance:** The deponent may not believe that information he possesses, although responsive to a question, has anything to do with the lawsuit and as a result will not volunteer the information.

Example: At the deposition of a member of the Public Policy School faculty, counsel might ask something like the following.

Q: *When you learned that Professors Williams and Simonson were involved in a relationship, how did that make you feel?*
A: *It was none of my business.*

Even if the witness means his answer, it not responsive and in effect avoided the question. Deposing counsel must listen to the deponent's answer, identify the avoidance and inquire further about the faculty member's feelings about the relationship, using, if necessary, more pointed questions.

9) **Forgetting/reconstructing:** Memories fade, are reconstructed, and change over time. As we have noted earlier, a deposition goal is to end the reconstruction process. When seeking to revive memory, suggest what another witness has said or show the deponent a document. When seeking to show the witness that he is reconstructing memory, use a document or a previous statement that gives a version of the events different than the deponent's answer. This difference can either be a direct contradiction or, more likely, a less complete recollection than the deponent's current testimony.
10) **Perception Characterization:** People characterize the same facts in different ways. What is fast to one person is not to another; short to one, not another; large to one, not another, etc. Each of these perceptions is value laden. The best way to control for these variations in perception description is to ask for specific, nonevaluative factual information. If a deponent says another person was tall, your follow-up question is how tall in feet and inches. If the witness says fast, the follow-up is how fast in mph or in reference to some other nonevaluative occurrence, such as speed compared to the other traffic. Of course, some perceptions cannot be broken down into component parts; if that's the case, accept the perception for whatever force it has.
11) **Chronological Confusion:** This is a typical problem when reciting events, especially a nonparty witness testifying about matters that occurred perhaps years before the deposition and/or topics that have not been of any particular concern to them. Although chronological order is a reliable way of getting an accurate recitation of the sequence of things, sometimes a witness is confused. This will often be apparent when a chronological storyline of the case reports a fact from most witnesses on one date or in one sequence, and the deponent reports the same fact on a different date or in a different sequence. Point out that others—or other documents—agree on a different timeframe, and that in light of those facts, might the

witness be confused; given that, the witness will frequently concede that his memory of the order of things might by inaccurate.

b. What are the known facilitators for obtaining full information from a deponent?

Relevant communication facilitators to deposition information gathering, as identified in FACT INVESTIGATION and from our experience, include the following.

1) **Exploding Expectations:** Most deponents come to the process with little experience and expect aggressive and hostile counsel. Merely by being civil and friendly, you can encourage information. Delivering the run-up to the deposition as described in chapter six, in a calm, friendly, self-deprecating way[6] in informal, everyday simple language, can go a long way to disabuse the deponent of his concerns about the process and what he is about to experience.
2) **Open, Nonjudgmental Questions:** While we will consider forms of questions in greater detail later, it is obvious that the less limiting a question is, the more likely it will produce information. So we suggest that at the beginning of information gathering, you use open-ended nonjudgmental questions that start with words like "tell me," "describe," and "explain."
3) **Empathetic Understanding:** You can induce deponents to provide information by communicating that you are listening. The best way to communicate listening is through eye contact. Because narrative responses are sought in every deposition, encourage that narrative by responding to answers with prompts such as "I see," "tell me more," and "go on." This helps expand the deponent's narrative, and the longer a deponent speaks, the more free-flowing and complete the information will be. Don't fall into a robotic repetition of these vocal cues, however; you can prompt deponents to continue their narrative with head nods . . . or just silence. Whenever there is a pause in conversation, *someone* will jump in. Unfortunately, most lawyers abhor silence and will jump in with another question or comment to fill the silence—fight that impulse. Instead, when a witness stops an answer and you believe he has more to offer, meet him with silence; that should encourage him to dig deeper.
4) **Recognition:** When a deponent is talking about a topic that presents some difficulty for the deponent, encourage such information with comments such as "I appreciate your telling me that, what more can you

6. For example, when insuring the witness understands the questions put to him, deposing counsel might say: "Now Professor Taylor, one of the things that can interfere with our developing full and complete information from you is my not asking an understandable question, and I'm sure this will happen. So if, and more likely when, I ask an unclear question, will you just tell me, and I'll try to clear up any confusion I have created." Put this way, the witness will be disabused of an expectation of officiousness on the part of the lawyer and at the same time take responsibility for understanding the question before answering.

tell me?" or "I understand that was difficult for you to talk about, thank you; now, let me ask you this . . . ."

5) **Extrinsic Reward:** It is axiomatic that very few deponents want to be participating in the process. Especially for nonparties, deponents have much better ways to spend their time. Because every deponent wants the process over ASAP, respond to a complete narrative answer by saying: "That's exactly the kind of expansive answer we are looking for. Answering that way will get us out of here early today." It then becomes in the deponent's self-interest to provide narrative, fact-inclusive responses.
6) **Catharsis:** Some deponents, especially parties, come to their depositions seeking to resolve a disagreement in which the deponent believes he is in the right. Deposing counsel, of course, wants to hear everything the opposing party believes entitles it to prevail. Asking the party deponent an open-ended question like, "Why do you believe you were the victim of discrimination?" provides him with an outlet to do exactly that—and in the process reveal both case theory and the lawsuit's real goal (e.g., an apology) that might help settle the matter early.

We will amplify and comment further on these inhibitors and facilitators when exploring questioning systems and techniques.

4. Are there any assumptions that deposing counsel should make in information gathering, and how are those assumptions best reflected in the tone of questioning?

Despite the fact that there are court reporters, videographers, cameras, and a number of lawyers present, if someone were to listen in on the deposition, it should sound like a conversation between two people who have just met, where one of those people (the deponent) knows a lot about something that the other person (deposing counsel) would like to know. The questions asked should serve as a conduit for the deponent to tell his story of the case.

Your working assumption and mindset should be that the witness has information not yet revealed in the litigation; for information already revealed, assume the deponent is a source of potential conflicting information or reinterpretation. That is not to suggest that you treat the deponent as hostile toward your client or cause—such a deponent could be a witness favorable to your client. Therefore, practice complete and absolute neutrality when posing questions.

5. What is the first topic I should explore in a fact-gathering deposition, and what are the goals of that first topic?

Although you can begin questioning the witness with any topic, typically it is tactically advisable to find out about the deponent's relevant personal, educational, and professional background. Conversations proceed more easily when you know something about the parties to the conversation.

In the modern deposition, you will already know much about any deponent. A simple Google search will reveal the deponent's basic demographics: his education, and his professional history. Although you have all of this information, a later reader or viewer of the deposition record will not. For that reason, every deposition should provide that background. In addition, given the goal of putting the deponent at ease, questions about a person's background are, in the main, comfortable—neither controversial nor off-putting. Most fact-gathering depositions should provide every deponent the opportunity to talk about himself.

For most deponents, this is an easy goal for you to reach—most people like talking about themselves. This part of the deposition conversation gets the deponent used to answering questions, giving him a painless experience of answering questions, and reinforces the goal of getting the deponent to do most the talking. Finally, background information can reveal much about the deponent's general demeanor and attitude about the lawsuit and the deposition process

Example: Plaintiff is taking Simonson's deposition. Deposing counsel identifies herself and explains why she is there and what she is interested in finding out from the deponent—which is, of course, everything.

Q: *Good morning Mr. Simonson. My name is Amanda Jenkins, and I represent Mary Anne Williams in this lawsuit. I know you are a distinguished academic and carry many titles. Do you prefer to be addressed as Professor? Doctor?*
S: *Most people call me Professor Simonson.*
Q: *Then Professor Simonson it is. As you know, Professor, you have been named as a defendant in this lawsuit, and as such, we are interested in finding out everything that you know that you believe is necessary to come to a fair resolution of this matter. So, to begin, I would like to go through some preliminary matters to be sure we are all on the same page in this session.*

Counsel then asks the questions as reflected in chapter six.

Q: *Do you have any questions about what we have just covered?*
S: *No.*
Q: *All right, let's begin, then. Professor, tell me about your personal background, where you grew up, family, that sort of thing?*
S: *I was born in Wallingford, Connecticut, the home of the Choate/Rosemary Hall School, which I attended, as did my brother and sister. I was the oldest. Even though the school was in our hometown, we boarded at the school, as did most of the students, who came from all over the world. After I graduated from Choate, where I was the valedictorian, I went on to Harvard University, where I graduated summa cum laude with a degree in public policy, and then I was the only Harvard undergrad to be admitted to the Harvard Public Policy School, where I obtained a Masters and PhD degree, both with highest honors—they didn't have a class rank.*

L: *And then?*

S: *I met my wife while at Harvard. She was in medical school, and she matched with Nita University for her surgical residence. It was her first choice and her home town. So I accepted an offer to join the faculty of the Nita University School of Public Policy, even though of the five academic appointments I was offered, Nita University was the least prestigious school. The rest as they say is history.*

This small bit of testimony reveals quite a lot. First Simonson does not need much prodding to talk. He is articulate, even glib. He picked up the chronology of his academic and professional history after education with the most benign suggestion of counsel, "And then?" Second, he likes to talk about his professional accomplishments, being sure to note schools, degrees, honors, etc. Third, he views himself primarily as a professional person with many accomplishments. Although asked where he grew up, after naming the town, he used it as a vehicle to speak about his attending a prestigious and elite prep school. And even though asked about family, he did not mention his parents, the names of his siblings, the name of his wife, or their children; they were contained within "the rest is history." He knows all of this information, but chose, probably out of habit, to talk only about himself and his own accomplishments.

6. Are there additional substantive goals that I can accomplish in the introductory examination?

Very much so, including learning how the deponent would be received by jurors. Decide whether to take the witness back to particular topics within the personal, educational, and profession background at this juncture or wait until they arise in the case narrative. For example, Simonson mentioned his wife, but other than her medical training and some connection with Nita City, we know little else about her. We know that the marital relationship between Simonson and his spouse will be relevant in light of Simonson's claim—to Williams and others—that they have an open marriage and that Williams claims she ended her relationship with Simonson when he refused to divorce his wife, so it must be discussed.

Purely as a matter of background, however, explore Simonson's spouse—her personal background and her family's connection with Nita City. This is not to say that most lawsuits necessitate a great deal of information about the family background of a party's spouse. But when the party or the party's spouse has long-time connections to the place where the lawsuit will be litigated, that history gains some degree of importance.[7] Decision makers (mediators, arbitrators, other ADR participants, and obviously jurors), as well as witnesses, will come from the community where

7. Deposing counsel, of course, will know all about Dr. Simonson, MD, and her family from Google-style searches that will have been conducted before the deposition. She must still inquire into these matters because the end-users (like mediators and arbitrators) of the deposition may not already know this information.

Dr. Simonson, MD, grew up; her grandfather was a former President of Nita University. Most participants in the litigation process will have an opinion about the Simonson family that may have an impact on the lawsuit.

7. Can you provide another example of how substantive matters are fleshed out in the introductory phase?

Case theory will often revolve around relationships between and among the parties and witnesses. Our hypothetical case is one such matter. A prominent case theory for the plaintiff is that her denial of tenure, if not done at the behest of Simonson, was done because Jefferson and others were concerned that Williams's tenure would be uncomfortable for Simonson in light of negative comments Williams made about him. Simonson's status made him an important asset to the university, so much so that if he left for other opportunities, it would be a blow to the university, both as a matter of academic prestige and, of at least equal importance, fundraising. This topic will be raised with a number of deponents from the university. Use Simonson's willingness to speak glowingly about his successes to develop a substantive set of facts that favor the plaintiff's case theory in the guise of obtaining background information.

Example: The deposition of Simonson proceeds.

Plaintiff's Counsel: All right Professor, I'd like to explore that history with you. Have you told us everything about your impressive academic record? For example, what other awards did you receive either in undergraduate or graduate school, other than graduating from both with highest honors?

S: At Harvard undergrad, I was elected to the Public Policy Honorary Fraternity; received an award for Outstanding Student Publication; and was elected to Phi Beta Kappa, the national academic honorary society. At graduate school, I again received the award for Outstanding Student Publication; received notations in six of my classes for Distinguished Classroom Performance; and was editor-in-chief of the Harvard Public Policy Quarterly, the graduate school's scholarly publication.

Q: What other awards did you receive in undergraduate or graduate school?

A: There were others—they are on my résumé.

Q: We are conducting this deposition here at the Patterson Institute—do you have a copy of your résumé in your office here?

A: I do.

Q: During our first break, can you provide your counsel with a copy of that resume so we can mark it as an exhibit?

A: I will.

Q: Let's turn then to your appointment to the Nita University Public Policy School. You mentioned you had other offers at more prestigious schools. What were those schools?

A: There were four others: the University of Pennsylvania, Northwestern, Duke, and the University of North Carolina.

Q: *If you chose to, do you believe you could receive lateral offers from those schools today?*

A: *Assuming they had a slot for a senior tenurial faculty member and an open chaired professorship, I am confident I could. I have received numerous offers from other public policy schools over the years, but my family has kept me in Nita. But with the kids all out of the house, and Ann, my wife, being a well-regarded thoracic surgeon, we might be more amendable to a move today. It would depend on offers made to both of us.*

Q: *So you would consider a lateral move now?*

A: *Yes, as I said, depending on what was offered to me and Ann.*

Q: *Tell me about your career at Nita University.*

Assume that through this question and follow-up the witness has described his career at the Public Policy School. The deposition now continues.

Q: *I'd like to turn now, Professor, to a particular aspect of your career at Nita University. I understand that faculty members are expected, to the extent possible, to attract money to the university. Please describe your accomplishments in bringing funding to the university.*

A: *My most important fundraising effort resulted in the building in which we are sitting, the Patterson Institute. Bob Patterson is an old and dear friend, who has a history of philanthropy. I persuaded him to make a donation to the university in the amount of $10 million, which resulted in the building of the Patterson Institute for Public Policy and the creation of the Patterson Professorship in Public Policy, which I am honored to hold. That was in YR-6, when I was the school's dean—I left the deanship to become the Director of the Patterson Institute. Both before and after the creation of the Patterson Institute, I attracted government and foundation grants and other funding over the years that brought over $25 million to the university, in addition to the Patterson money.*

Q: *How do you compare to other faculty members in the university?*

A: *Other than the medical school, the law school, and the business school, I am told I am the top fundraiser for academic pursuits.*

Q: *I'm sure that gives you some notoriety in the university?*

A: *I believe that's correct.*

Q: *Do you continue to attract government and foundation grant money?*

A: *Of course, every year.*

Q: *And if, as you mentioned earlier, you moved to another institution, would that grant and foundation money follow you?*

A: *I can't say for sure, but most of it would. Foundation grants—that is, large grants dedicated to a particular school or scholarship—would remain with the university. But most funds are given on a renewable basis, meaning that they require new grant applications every year or two. Those grants are given largely based on reputation. As such, most grant money not previously identified for a particular purpose, like the Patterson Institute, would likely come with me.*

As can be seen, while the deponent freely provides information about himself, the testimony at the same time provides a factual predicate for one of the plaintiff's potential case theories. Typically, two issues are raised within execution of the primary goal to gather information.

8. What other issues should I raise during the introductory section of the deposition?

While exploring the deponent's background, unanticipated testimony often raises topics ripe for later exploration. First, Simonson provides a version of his departure from the deanship that is different than what the plaintiff believes to be true, thereby contradicting a potential case theory for plaintiff. Simonson testifies that he left the policy school deanship to take on the Patterson Institute directorship. Professor Taylor, however, says Simonson was forced to leave deanship because of a sexual relationship with a junior faculty member at the public policy school that ended badly and resulted in her suing Simonson and the university, a suit that was later settled. Explore this disagreement at another time, however. Rather than break up the flow of information while Simonson is being so talkative, wait to question about this and other topics of disagreement until you have exhausted the flow of information Simonson is freely providing.[8]

Second, as in much litigation involving an entity such as a university, Simonson uses certain terms that are endemic to that entity—and learned by counsel through the litigation. Do not forget that the deposition's end use may involve people who are not familiar with those terms. Here, Simonson speaks about a "faculty slot," "the tenurial faculty," and a "chaired professorship." All of these terms are foreign to people unfamiliar with the workings of a university; you must define them.[9] Ask a few questions to clarify these terms. Doing so won't not stop the information flow, and the end user will know what they mean in Simonson's own words.

Taken together, this first background topic does more than just obtain information (although that information has some substantive import). It also identifies potential areas of disagreement, sets the deposition protocol of asking the witness open-ended questions and obtaining expansive answers, provides information about the deponent's communication ability and style, and—assuming video recording—reveals the witness's demeanor and whether that demeanor will enhance or detract

8. We describe the impulse to interrupt the flow of testimony as "chasing rabbits" and will discuss this topic more fully later in this chapter.

9. A "faculty slot" means that there is a budgeted position in the school that has been authorized by the university and there exists the funds to pay a slot filler. "Tenurial faculty" means those members of the faculty who have tenure (lifetime employment absent gross misconduct). And a "chaired professorship" is an honorific position on the faculty of any school made possible by a significant donation by a person who names the chair (frequently in their own name); it usually brings with it additional compensation and other financial benefits.

from his credibility in the deposition's end use. We now turn to the substantive matters at issue in the lawsuit.

9. Is there a particular manner and sequence in which I should explore the substantive issues of the lawsuit?

The lawsuit's substantive matters include all those topics that tend to prove the elements of the parties' claims and defenses, the facts that prove or disprove the potential legal theories of the case, and any other matter that has any tendency to persuade ultimate decision makers.

Identifying Appropriate Topics for Exploration

Come to the table having already identified most relevant topics for exploration. They are identified in a number of ways, the most important of which is the chronological storyline chart, which contains the topics that provide facts you have identified as necessary to prove potential legal and factual theory.

The danger is that you will limit your questioning to those topics already identified. A primary purpose of any deposition, of course, is to discover facts yet unknown and finding new relevant topics not already in the chronological storyline chart. It is not uncommon for you to have not identified all the topics for deposition until you have taken testimony. Be ready to expand your chronological storyline chart as you identify new topics.

10. How do I use the timelines, substantive elements of the claims and defenses, and the rules of evidence to expand the list of topics to be explored in the deposition?

Revisit the case timelines as they relate to the deponent and potential legal and factual theory to complete the list of appropriate topics for the deposition. New topics for consideration may be revealed by asking the witness, "What was the first thing that happened that you believe is important for us to understand to reach a fair outcome?" You can follow that answer by asking for other facts that need to be considered, using a series of "What else is important?" questions until the witness provides no further topics.[10]

Identify hidden topics by revisiting the timeline of already identified topics and matching them up with identified legal theories. Taken in conjunction with the rules of evidence, this identifies permissible areas of inquiry on relevant topics

10. Many defenders will object that these questions are either vague or overly broad. Neither objection should prevent the witness from answering the questions unless the defender claims that the questions violate Fed. R. Civ. P. 30(d)(3) as not reasonably calculated to obtain relevant evidence because their open form is unreasonably oppressive of the deponent. While these grounds will not likely be upheld in a protective order request, you must attempt to obtain the information in another way before you can legitimately seek a motion to compel answers to the question.

(admissible character evidence, refreshing documents, inconsistent statements, facts informing lay opinions, etc.).

Example: Given the nature of Williams v. Simonson, *it seems the primary timeline extends from the time that Williams was hired by the university until her tenure application was denied. After that, the only facts within the timeline relate to Williams's claimed damages. And that is true if the legal theory of the case is that she was denied tenure in retaliation for her ending her relationship with Simonson.*[11] *The retaliation, if any, was carried out by Dean Jefferson, who vetoed Williams's tenure. As a result, Jefferson's motive—which might be impacted by relationships*[12] *that existed at the time of her decision, but formed long before Williams joined the faculty—would necessarily expand the timeline to include the formation and continuation of those motivating relationships.*

Next, if the legal theory of gender discrimination is hostile work environment—based on an allegation that Simonson was a sexual predator, the university was aware of that fact, and the university condoned (at least by inaction) that activity—this expands not only the timeline, but topics within that timeline. In that case, the topic of prior sexual relations between Simonson and others—and the alleged results of the ending of those relationships—become relevant topics if known by the university or its agents. This expands the timeline both forward and back, encompassing facts that might prove that legal theory. They are admissible as Rule 404(b) prior acts that show knowledge by the university as it related to hostile work environment.

Finally, if Williams claims that the university systematically discriminated against women in tenure and promotion decisions, new topics regarding statistics on women faculty members and information about what happened to them on the tenure track become topics ripe for deposition. This will require witnesses outside those who had anything to do with the specific tenure decision regarding Williams and will stretch both backward and forward in time for facts that show that systemic discrimination.

In addition to using legal theory and evidentiary rules, identify topics for examination by asking the deponent direct questions about his knowledge of yet unidentified topics, using questioning systems (which we will discuss in full) that exhaust the witness's knowledge of the relevant topics. You can also identify new topics just by listening to what the deponent has to say.

Example: Assume that Dean Jefferson is being deposed.

---

11. The prior sexual relations of Simonson with university employees, and what occurred to their employment at the university after those relationships end, are probably inadmissible FED R. EVID. 404(b) prior acts, as they would be offered to show propensity, an inadmissible proffer.

12. With Simonson, and with the former dean of the business school about whom Williams also made a claim of sexual harassment.

Q: *You signed and verified the answer to Ms. Williams's complaint in this matter, is that correct?*
A: *Yes, I did.*
Q: *In your answer, you verified that the reasons for denying tenure were first that she was not qualified, and second that she was not collegial, is that right?*
A: *That's right.*
Q: *I'm going to ask you about both those claims, but before I do, are there other, nondiscriminatory reasons why Professor Williams was denied tenure?*
A: *In fact, there was one other reason.*
Q: *What was that reason?*
A: *I was charged by the university regulations to determine whether Professor Williams's tenure was in the long-term best interests of the university, and I determined it was not. First, because she was not qualified; second, because her destructive lack of collegiality; and third, because of the economic impact of her being tenured.*
Q: *What other reasons did you have?*
A: *None.*
Q: *Tell me about the reason that you identify as economic?*
A: *The University is constantly evaluating statistical analyses of anticipated student population, as it impacts the need for faculty and other resource allocation. With the shrinking of government positions in public policy, the university predicted a significant drop in applicants to the Public Policy School. As a result, I had been informed that although we had two approved, open faculty slots for tenured faculty, only one of those open slots was funded in the university budget. I was faced with two candidates for tenure. Professor Vasquez had received a unanimous vote by the faculty, and Ms. Williams had received a positive vote of 16-12-1. In addition, Professor Vasquez is our only faculty member focusing on healthcare issues, and Professor Williams's work replicates the focus of both Professor Binder's and Professor Simonson's academic and scholarly focus—public education. With these facts in mind, I chose Professor Vasquez, completely on the merits.*
Q: *But this claim was not in your answer, was it?*
A: *That was the lawyers' decision; they knew about the university directives.*
Q: *I'd like to follow up on this university directive after lunch, but just a few questions before we break. You mentioned that Professor Williams's tenure vote was close?*
A: *Yes, 16–12–1 in favor of tenure.*
Q: *In fact Dean, your tenure vote was closer wasn't it—12–11 in favor, and Dean Taylor recommended your tenure, correct?*
A: *That's true, but that was fifteen years ago—those were different times.*

Counsel can expand the deposition topics merely by offering the deponent the opportunity to identify a topic—here, by asking about reasons for denying the tenure of Williams not identified in the Defendant's Answer to the Plaintiff's Complaint. Deposing counsel did not limit herself to the answer that had been filed; she asked one necessary follow-up question, assuming there was information: "What other nondiscriminatory bases for denying tenure were there?" Jefferson's answered that university policy on economics was a driver of her tenure veto. She then volunteered how she made her choices among candidates, and why Williams was not informed of Jefferson's newly identified reason for denying tenure. Jefferson's deposition is expanded, and additional documents and deposition testimony on this previously unidentified topic will ensue.

Second, Jefferson's last response before the break raises yet another topic. She offhandedly says that when she was tenured, "those were different times." Explore how the nature of the "different times" relate to systematic and long-standing gender discrimination—this comment opens many new topics for consideration in this and other depositions, as well as discovery in other forms on another legal theory of gender discrimination.

The takeaway from this example is that no matter how complete your predeposition preparation, your job is not done. Actively listen during the deposition to uncover additional topics that you need to explore.

11. Once the list of topics is expanded, how do I determine the categories of facts that are contained within the topics?

Once you have completed the list of potentially relevant topics, you must then exhaust the facts within each topic. Each deposition presents unique challenges, but the one constant challenge is insuring the information you glean is complete. Accomplish this with questioning systems, or methodologies, both generally and in particular situations. Any lawyer who is having the proverbial good day can rely on talent and experience to meet the deposition's goals. Questioning systems help you on your bad days. Once they become routine and habitual, these systems can help ensure that you are meeting the fact-gathering goal of obtaining complete information.

12. Are there questioning systems that I can use to get complete factual information from a deponent?

Effective questioning systems obtain full and complete testimony by exhausting the deponent's information on every topic. They follow a pattern:

a) provide the opportunity for the deponent to tell what he knows;

b) identify all the relevant topics about which the deponent has knowledge;

c) for each topic, systematically drill down and exhaust the deponent's knowledge of the facts in that topic;

d) confront the deponent with facts about the topic you have identified as relevant that have not yet been discussed—or intentionally avoided—and give the witness the opportunity to answer expansively;

e) offer the witness one last opportunity to provide information and get his assurance that he knows nothing further about the topic;

f) move on to the next topic.

Example: Consider the following exchange between defense counsel and Professor Williams about her job duties as an assistant professor.

Q: *You have told me that your first appointment at Nita University was in YR-7 as an assistant professor. Tell us about your job duties as an assistant professor.*
A: *I was assigned to teach four classes, two in each semester, and, of course, I spent a good deal of time preparing for those classes. I had posted office hours for four hours each week. And I was required to begin exploring my scholarly interests with the goal of publishing an article within my first two years.*
Q: *What other duties did you have?*
A: *Well, I had to grade exams and papers in my courses, and I was assigned to three Public Policy School committees—two student-faculty committees and one faculty-only committee.*
Q: *What other duties did you have?*
A: *That's all of them.*
Q: *Did you also have to serve on university committees?*
A: *That's right. I was assigned to a university fundraising committee.*
Q: *Were you also required to attend faculty meetings?*
A: *I was. In addition to the committee meeting I told you about, there was a meeting of the entire faculty the first Wednesday of each month.*
Q: *What other duties did you have as an assistant professor?*
A: *As part of our service requirement, we were expected to try to obtain grant money to support our research. When I began in YR-7, my scholarship wasn't well enough defined to seek grant money; that came later.*
Q: *What other duties did you have?*
A: *This time that really is it.*
Q: *Nothing more?*
A: *Nothing more.*
Q: *All right, Professor, we have reached the ninety-minute mark, and as I promised, we will break for fifteen minutes. Is that sufficient time for you?*
A: *Yes, it is.*
Q: *OK. If over the break you remember any further information about any topics we have discussed or believe that any of your responses may have left an inaccurate misconception of what happened, will you tell your counsel so we get a fair and complete record of what you know about the facts that underlie this matter?*
A: *I will.*
Q: *Very well, will the court reporter and videographer note the time of our recess for the record? See you in fifteen minutes.*

This example illustrates the basic questioning system for information gathering. The first level of questioning uses open-ended questions (e.g., "Tell us . . . " "What other . . . "), where you encourage the witness to tell all she knows. Second, you ask those questions in a form that assumes there is information. Questions seeking expansion of the deponent's previous answer ask "what else," assuming there is something else—as opposed to "are there," or "have you told us everything," which suggests that there is no further information.[13]

Once the witness professes an end to the information flow, you will often have a "laundry list" of facts you believe are within the scope of the question.[14] At this point, use more suggestive questions to test the accuracy of your laundry list. Once the witness responds affirmatively (or negatively) to the laundry list, return to the open, information-assuming question form of "what else"—it is not uncommon to get even more information. When that flow ends, ask a question that requires the witness to say that he has no further information.

In light of later potential use of the deposition for impeachment by omission, it is important that the witness, and not counsel, states that his testimony is complete on any given topic. If the deponent's later testimony expands on the answers provided in the deposition, the omission becomes more valuable when the deponent—not deposing counsel—has stated on the record that he provided everything he knows that is responsive to the question being explored.

Many lawyers suggest one further question in this standard litany: "So have you told us every one of your duties as an assistant professor as they existed when you joined the Public Policy School in YR-6?" They are hoping for an affirmative response and another level of certainty to the completeness of the testimony on that topic. In the authors' experience, however, this question's challenging nature may meet with equivocation.[15] An answer such as, "That's the best of my recollection," leaves open the possibility of later memories. Although there are ways to minimize such equivocations, which we will discuss later in chapter eight, we suggest that a clear and unencumbered answer from the deponent a better resolution to the exhaustion process.

The example above is just the first step in asking questions about Williams's duties in her first year on the Public Policy School faculty—this topic has introduced a plethora of subtopics, including: 1) *teaching*—the courses she taught; what mate-

---

13. The form of the question used to exhaust information is important. The ground-breaking work of Elizabeth Loftus on memory, well represented in her book, Witness for the Defense: The Accused, The Eyewitness, and The Expert Who Puts Memory on Trial, Loftus & Ketchum (1991) suggests, with empirical support, that the question "What else happened?" is much more likely to engender memories that "Did anything else happen?"

14. These facts would have been identified and contained the chronological timeline chart described in chapters six and eight.

15. The question also sounds like something a lawyer would ask. When you remind the deponent that you are the opponent of the deponent or someone with whom the deponent is associated, the witness is put on edge. In all likelihood, she will become more reticent and her answers less responsive, at least for the near future in the deposition.

rials and methods she used; whether she was evaluated, assisted, had any mentors; 2) *academic service*—the names of Public Policy School and university committees, activities therein, other people on the committee, role and function as a committee member; 3) *research*—the scholarly topics she chose to pursue, progress made in research and writing, any student assistants she used; and 4) *other service*—efforts made toward fundraising. Put another way, cover each of these duties as another topic in the deposition—explore the who, what, where, when, why, and how of each topic. In your preparation, you will have anticipated many of them on the chronological storylines chart, but be sure to leave space to add unanticipated topics to the chart.

Finally, counsel makes a statement for the record about taking a break, asks the court reporter and videographer to note the time, and reminds the deponent of his agreement to make any additions or corrections that occur to her during breaks in the deposition. Noting the time is important because Civil Procedure Rule 30 limits the deposition to one seven-hour day of *testimony*. The reminder about adding to or correcting testimony is a matter of personal preference.

13. Are there good ways to conceptualize questioning systems for gathering complete information?

There are many conceptualizations of questioning systems. Scholars and practitioners client interviewing have articulated a methodology they call the "T–Funnel."[16] Others interested in fact gathering in professional settings, like psychologists, choose a chronological overview, which uses active listening techniques that follow up on the chronology provided by a client or witness.[17] Most specific to taking and defending depositions is the classic methodology described as the "funnel" approach.[18] The authors are conversant with, grateful for, and have included in this volume, the teachings of all three of the above-noted methodologies, all of which share a common core, and despite different descriptions, a same or similar methodology.

14. What characteristics do the various questioning techniques share?

The three methods have the following in common:

16. The "T-Funnel" is referred to by many scholars who explore information gathering using interviews. An excellent example of a description of this methodology is contained in Binder, Bergman & Price, Lawyers As Counselors, A Client Centered Approach (1991).

17. Zwier & Bocchino, Fact Investigation: A Practical Guide to Interviewing, Counseling and Case Theory Development (NITA 2nd Ed. 2015).

18. Malone, Hoffman & Bocchino (Contributing Author) The Effective Deposition (4th Ed. NITA 2012). The Effective Deposition is generally considered to be the best collection of the teachings of the National Institute for Trial Advocacy and contains the "best practices" of what we have described as the classic deposition.

a) systematically preparing for information gathering, using internet and other digital sources and producing a legal and factual case theory that provides a focus for the deposition;[19]

b) information gathering guided by, but not limited to, counsel's preparation;

c) information gathering that begins by identifying all potential relevant topics;

d) using simple (nonlegalistic) language for questions;

e) using a conversational style, tone, and manner;

f) encouraging narrative answers, allowing the witness to dominate the conversation;

g) using thorough witness-dominated, open-ended questions as the first source of information gathering;

h) using active listening (focusing on the witness and the information he provides) and following up on any possible incompleteness of information;[20]

i) using and embracing the classic questions of the journalism profession: who, what, when, where, why, and how;

j) exploring the deponent's relationship with other people and entities;

k) using other sources of information—other witnesses, documents, etc.;

l) progressing through a form and scope of questioning that begins with open, nondirective questions; narrows slightly to open, topic-specific questions; narrows to the journalist's questions; proceeds with directive (topic specific) questions; and concludes with leading questions, or some other system of closing off each area of inquiry to later modification;[21] and

---

19. Our suggested preparation is contained in the chronological storylines charts described in chapters five and eight.

20. Active listeners identify information provided by the deponent that either suggests further inquiry or requires clarification. When this happens we call the follow-up process "chasing rabbits." We will discuss when and how to chase later in this chapter.

21. Fact Investigation applies a combination of the T-Funnel and funnel approach and prescribes for friendly witnesses a funnel that proceeds from open-ended questions, to active listening follow-up, to eliciting details, and then theory verification. For hostile witnesses, Professor Zwier reverses the funnel, beginning with confirming that the witness has information about the topic, obtaining a conclusion (i.e., it was the plaintiff's fault), followed by memory flood (suggesting categories of facts that may support the conclusion), followed by specific details, and then open-ended questions at the end of the reverse funnel. The methodology applies to deposition practice as well.

m) producing a deposition that meets the needs of all forms of dispute resolution, including motion practice, negotiation, ADR, and trial.

Example: Consider how these information-gathering system characteristics are used in the following continuation Professor Williams's deposition from above, limited to the narrow topic of teaching.

Q: *All right, we are back on the record. I'm pleased to report that our fifteen-minute break only lasted twenty minutes and that it is 10:50 a.m., and our agreement to turn off all cell phones is in effect. Are you ready to start up again, Ms. Williams?*

A: *Yes.*

Q: *I want to talk to you about your teaching duties in your first year of teaching at the Public Policy School, but first let me ask you whether there are any of your answers from this morning that you would like to expand on?*

A: *No.*

Q: *Are there any answers you would like to change?*

A: *No, there aren't.*

Q: *And finally, did anything happen over the break that might interfere with your ability to provide full and complete information in response to my questions?*

A: *No, I'm fine to go ahead.*

Q: *Thank you. I want to focus on your course assignments at the time of your appointment to the Public Policy School as an assistant professor in YR-6. Tell me about the courses you were assigned to teach.*

A: *I was assigned to teach Introduction to Public Policy, a three-credit course, in both semesters. In addition, in the first semester, I was assigned to teach an upper-level four-credit course called Municipal Government Administration, and in the second semester, I taught my four-credit seminar, Public School Funding.*

Q: *How was your course load decided?*

A: *Dean Simonson told me that I would have a fourteen-credit course load before I accepted the offer from Nita University and that I would teach one course in both semesters. We never got beyond that. By the time I arrived on campus, Dean Jefferson had been appointed, and David had taken over as the Director of the Patterson Institute for Public Policy. It was Dean Jefferson who gave me my course load.*

Q: *How did she do that?*

A: *I got an email from Dean Jefferson about the teaching load for the academic year in June of YR-6 when I arrived on campus. The email said I would teach the Introduction to Public Policy course both semesters, then provided a list of upperclass courses that needed coverage and offered to allow me to teach a writing seminar of my own creation as my fourth course. I replied by email that of the upper-level courses needing coverage, I would prefer the Municipal Government Administration course and requested that I be able to teach a seminar in Public School Funding, which was my thesis topic and my main scholarly interest.*

Q: *And then?*
A: *She emailed me that I was assigned to the courses I told you about: the Introduction to Public Policy three-credit survey course in both semesters, Municipal Government Administration, a four-credit upperclass course in the fall semester, and my Public School Funding seminar, a four-credit seminar in the spring semester. I replied thanking her.*
Q: *I am showing you what we have premarked as Exhibit 12, which appears to be a printout of an email from Dean Jefferson to you, dated June 18, YR-6. Do you recognize Exhibit 12?*
A: *Yes, that's the email I just told you about confirming my course assignments. As I said, I responded on the same day.*
Q: *I'm showing you what we have premarked as Exhibit 13, which appears to be a printout of an email from you to Dean Jefferson dated June 19, YR-6. Do you recognize Exhibit 13?*
A: *Yes, that's my email that I told you about. I must have read her email . . . .*
Q: *Excuse me, Exhibit 12?*
A: *Yes, Exhibit 12—I must have read it on the nineteenth, because I know I immediately replied after reading Exhibit 12 to thank her, and I see on Exhibit 13 that it's dated the next day.*
Q: *What other communication did you have with Dean Jefferson about your course assignments?*
A: *That was all with her on course assignment; we had other conversations before the first semester started, but not on course assignment.*
Q: *Who else did you communicate with about course assignments?*
A: *I spoke with the Registrar, Barbara Bennett-Yates. We agreed to class meeting times and that I would have Wednesdays free to prepare. And she asked for a course description for my seminar, which I provided to her.*
Q: *What other communication did you have with the registrar?*
A: *None.*
Q: *Who else did you speak to about class assignments?*
A: *Dean Taylor stopped by my office in mid-June to greet me, and we talked about my teaching assignments—we talked about possible books, and he volunteered to send the syllabus that he had created when he taught both the Introduction and Municipal Government Administration courses. We also talked about my seminar, and he seemed very interested. As it turned out, Professor Taylor became a mentor to me.*
Q: *What else about course assignments did you and Dean Taylor talk about?*
A: *That was it about class assignments. We talked about other things, but nothing more about course assignments.*
Q: *Who else did you speak with about your course assignments?*
A: *No one else.*
Q: *Did you speak with Professor Simonson about your course assignments, other than at the time he offered you your appointment to the Public Policy School faculty?*

A: *No.*
Q: *Did you ever invite him to visit your class?*
A: *Yes, but that was halfway through the second semester, and we talked only about my teaching in the class he watched, not about course assignments.*
Q: *How many credits were you assigned?*
A: *Fourteen.*
Q: *Was that a normal course load for an entering teacher?*
A: *I thought so at the time, but I later learned that Professor Vasquez, who started the year before me, was only assigned three classes and eleven credits.*
Q: *How did you learn about his course load?*
A: *My lawyer told me.*
Q: *All right Professor, before we move to another topic, is there anything else about course assignments that you can tell me about?*
A: *No, that's everything.*
Q: *Then let's move on to the teaching of those courses. First, let me ask you about the Introduction to Public Policy course. Tell me about that course.*

Begin with some preliminary housekeeping matters before you resume questioning.[22] When coming back after a break, offer the deponent an opportunity to expand on or change earlier testimony.[23] If, as in this case, the witness assures you that there that he has no changes and that nothing happened during the break that interfered with his ability to give full and complete testimony, continue the deposition.[24]

Identify the first topic of inquiry—in this case, first-year course assignments—and begin with an open-ended question, "Tell me about. . . ." After the witness answers generally, ask a series of journalism questions that identify the "who," "what," and "how" of the topic. Ask questions in simple, nonlegalese, conversational language.[25]

---

22. The three questions demonstrated here are the only preliminary matters demonstrated in chapter seven that the authors suggest repeating on each return from a break.

23. These two questions show the fairness of the process by providing the witness with an opportunity to verify the reliability of previous testimony.

24. This question accounts for the situation where something has happened over the break (most typically a longer break, like for lunch) that compromises the completeness and accuracy of the deposition. In response to this question, the authors have discovered: a deponent who slipped, fell, and reinjured a back injury; a deponent who slipped and fell injuring her back and took a narcotic muscle relaxant; a deponent who developed a migraine; and deponents receiving all matter of bad news (the hospitalization of a loved one, damage to a house from fire, a break-in at their apartment, etc.) When this occurs, consider recessing the deposition to return on another day. Ask for the deponent's preference, but do not be ruled by that preference. If the witness wants to postpone, he can't later complain about needing to return to complete the deposition; if he continues, he can't complain that he was emotionally compromised. At the same time, you may not believe that in light of what happened, the witness can ably testify. If that is the case, it serves you both to postpone the deposition.

25. The only "lawyer sounding" questions were those regarding the use of exhibits. This is unavoidable—a goal of dealing with documents is to show their admissibility or inadmissibility, which is a legal question. The topic of dealing with exhibits will be discussed more fully in chapter nine.

After the first answer about the "who" of the topic of course assignments, the information flow on the topic is followed on with a series of "who else . . ." questions. This assumes that the deponent has more information about that topic and can identify other people involved. Do not end the "who" questions until the witness testifies that he has no more information in that topic. This protects you from a later surprise expansion of that testimony.

Once the deponent states that no one else was involved, turn to people you believe might have been involved in the topic. This is where your preparation pays off. In the example of the course assignment process, counsel specifically asked whether Simonson was involved. She followed the deponent's negative response by asking if Simonson visited her class in the first year. This received a positive answer, but confirmed that the topic of course assignment was not part of that visit.

The series of questions about how the course assignments were made was also exhausted. When Williams ended an answer about "how" assignments were made, counsel sought further information through an open-ended question (really an encouragement to talk more)—"And then?"—that revealed still further information until the topic was exhausted and closed off by the witness's testimony.

When asking a deponent to testify about corresponding documents, mark the documents, identify the document for the record, and show it to the witness. In this example, Williams corroborated that premarked Exhibits 12 and 13 are the documents referred in her testimony.

Counsel then asked another specific question about the normalcy of Williams's course load and found out that Williams has reason to believe that she was treated differently than Professor Vasquez (a man) by being assigned a more onerous course load. Deposing counsel must have been aware of the potential problem, but inquired nonetheless, confirming that plaintiff was aware of information potentially damaging to the defendants.

Finally, give the witness a final opportunity to provide information about the topic and obtain affirmation that the area of inquiry is complete and closed. Then identify the next topic and an area of inquiry, which begins with an open-ended question. Whether it's called the T-Funnel, The Chronological Overview with Active Listening, or the NITA Funnel approach, the approach yields the above results—a fairly obtained, complete, accurate, and reliable document.

Having described the basics of information gathering, we now turn to specific issues in gathering information in chapter eight and form and process issues in chapter nine.

Chapter Eight

Information Gathering Depositions—Particular Substantive Issues

In chapter seven, we discussed the basics of information gathering and effective questioning systems. However, you will encounter particular issues in the process that require special attention. These issues are both substantive and matters of form and process, and both are significant to developing the necessary skills required for the modern deposition. We turn first to typical substantive issues that we, and many other lawyers, have observed.

1. Should I take the deposition of a favorable witness if the opponent fails to notice that witness for testimony?

Traditionally, depositions were limited to witnesses likely to provide information unfavorable to deposing counsel's client, (i.e., opposing parties; witnesses identified in Rule 26 disclosures as potential sources for testimony favorable to the opposing party's claims or defenses; and people who potentially had information otherwise unavailable about the subject matter of the lawsuit). Lawyers avoided deposing witnesses known or expected to possess favorable information for their party, unless such witnesses were expected to be unavailable to testify at the time of trial. Other favorable witnesses were left to be deposed by the opposing party; if they were not, so much the better—the opposing party would be unprepared to answer the testimony of those witnesses at trial.

In light of today's case disposition mechanisms—motion practice or some form of ADR—this thinking must change. In all but a small percentage of cases, there will be no trial, and the question of whether to depose a favorable witness becomes significant. Any information that a party wants the ultimate decision maker to know needs to be preserved in its most persuasive form, usually by deposition. Without deposition, you lose the sworn information of these favorable witnesses for the entirety of the litigation, unless there is a trial.

This problem is often seen with "damage" witnesses in personal injury litigation. These witnesses describe what a plaintiff has lost—activities, relationships, freedom from pain, psychological suffering, etc. Counsel for the defendant has no desire to depose these witnesses;[1] it is to no advantage to the defendant to have this testi-

1. Most judges require that Rule 26 witness disclosures identify, in basic terms, the subject matter of the designated witness's potential testimony. The most typical basic designation split is as "liability" and "damage" witnesses. Witnesses designated as damage witness are frequently not deposed by defendants in personal injury cases.

mony available for negotiation, motion practice, or ADR, and counsel can assume that a trial is unlikely. Traditionally, plaintiff's lawyers relied on the knowledge that without the defendant taking their deposition, these witnesses would be all but impossible to contest at a trial. That tactic is no longer effective.

Deposing favorable witnesses is akin to direct examination at trial—you will use all of the persuasive skills and presentation modalities available at a trial. As we suggested in chapter five, prepare the witness to address communication problems, including issues of demeanor, and to present a concise and clear recitation of his information about the case. This type of deposition is—in style, tone, and content—a trial direct examination. Whenever possible, video record the deposition—that way, when you introduce exhibits and display them to the witness (the recording showing what the witness sees) and use all the persuasive visual aids (digital and otherwise) you would use at trial, you make your end game that much more powerful. Opposing counsel will cross-examine the witness at whatever level of content, style, tone, tactics, and completeness she came prepared to present. This can be to your advantage, because opposing counsel is unlikely to have fully developed her case theory or have a complete understanding of what this witness adds to it, so cross-examining the witness at this juncture will not be as effective as it would be at trial.

In the end, by deposing favorable witnesses, you make all positive information available from every witness available for the ultimate decision maker to see, hear, evaluate, and consider.

2. How do I make the best use of documents in a deposition?

Modern litigation is document intensive. "Documents" include word processing, document creation, document communication, and delivery devices including email, text messaging, Facebook, Twitter, and other social media. Law firms of even modest size have an IT department or person, and in large firms, there are entire sections devoted to electronic discovery issues. While you need to understand the source of relevant documents, the law, tactics, and science of electronic discovery is beyond the scope of this volume. We begin our discussion assuming that documents have been made available is some reliable way, either in paper or—more likely—digital form.

a. Marking/Identifying the Document for Record Purposes

As we discussed in chapter four, prepare for the deposition by premarking documents you plan to use and provide copies to the court reporter. Avoid the necessity of "concordance charts"[2] by marking exhibits involved in the case with the same

2. Concordance charts are necessary if each attorney marks the exhibits in the order she uses them. This leads to the same document being identified with different numbers, and thus the need for a concordance, usually kept on a spreadsheet, that identifies the document in its many appearances throughout the case: Exhibit 1 in the Simonson Deposition is the same as Exhibit 7 in the William

number sequence for all witnesses. Do this either before the deposition or in the sequence of use in the depositions—the numbers on exhibits in the first deposition are carried over to the second deposition, and the sequence of numbered exhibits in succeeding deposition(s) picks up where the exhibits numbers in the previous deposition(s) ended. In document-intensive litigation, exhibits are normally stored on a hard drive, provided in a thumb drive to all parties, and displayed to the witness and all counsel at the deposition on computer monitors.

Once exhibits are marked with a number (e.g., Exhibit 1), adopt a standard litany for dealing with the exhibits. The litany must identify the document by exhibit number, describe the document in neutral terms, and then ask the witness to identify the exhibit.

The court reporter maintains the original of a hard copy exhibit as part of the record, and the witness and all counsel are provided copies. If the witness marks on the copy provided to him, make the marked copy part of the record. For example, if the witness marks on his copy of Exhibit 1, he alters what is revealed by Exhibit 1; at the close of his testimony about Exhibit 1, his altered form of the Exhibit 1 is identified and made part of the record as Exhibit 1A.

If exhibits are maintained digitally, the digital copy of the exhibit is provided to the witness on a computer screen on which markings can be made. It is identified by its premarked number, e.g., Exhibit 1. A digital copy of the exhibit is incorporated as part of the digital record of the deposition and imposed electronically on the video recording of the deposition. If the witness wants to mark or make notes on the exhibit, she will do so on the digital monitor, and when the witness is done with the exhibit, the altered digital document is made part of the record, again as Exhibit 1A.

Example: Defendant's counsel wishes to use an exhibit in the deposition of Professor Williams.

Q: *Professor Williams, I am showing you what we have premarked as Exhibit 1. It appears to be a letter to you from then Dean Simonson of the Nita University Public Policy School to you dated June 1, YR-6. Do you recognized Exhibit 1?*
A: *Yes, I do.*
Q: *When did you first see Exhibit 1?*
A: *I received my appointment letter—*
Q: *Excuse me, by appointment letter do you mean Exhibit 1?*
A: *Yes, I received Exhibit 1 in early June of YR-6 and read it at that time.*
Q: *Let me ask you some questions about your understanding of the terms referenced in Exhibit 1.*

---

deposition, which is the same as Exhibit 14 for Taylor and Exhibit 75 for Jefferson. It is a headache for a legal assistant to maintain, a headache for the associate drafting motions, a headache for lead counsel reading and preparing to respond to motion practice, and a headache for the decision maker.

Counsel then asks further questions about the exhibit, at a minimum learning the answers to the journalist's questions (who, what, where, why, when, and how). Throughout the deposition, whenever the appointment letter is referred to, it must be referred to as Exhibit 1 to avoid confusion and to make optimal use of the digital recording of the deposition. When counsel needs to find information about what any and all deposition witnesses have to say about the appointment letter, she need only search for Exhibit 1, and all references will be collected and returned.

b. Tactics for Avoiding Confusion about References to Exhibits

Confusion often occurs when a witness is dealing with multiple exhibits of the same nature, such as four years of Dean Jefferson's evaluations of Williams. If, during Williams's examination, they are referred to as "this evaluation" or "that evaluation" or merely as "this"—although everyone at the table will know what Williams's testimony is referring to—the record is hopelessly confused. Likewise, the digital recording is less useful.

Example: Assume Williams has been shown, and has in front of her, Exhibits 7A, 7B, 7C, and 7D, evaluations of her performance by Dean Jefferson for her first four years on the Public Policy School Faculty. The following might occur.

Q: *Now Professor Williams, you have Exhibits 7A–7D. Let me refer you to those evaluations with regard to teaching, and please compare the evaluations of your teaching with the evaluations by students.*
A: *The evaluation here was 6.5, in this one 7.3, in this one 7.8, and in the last 8.4.*
Q: *You went from 7.8 here, then back to 7.3 in this other evaluation?*
A: *Right. I think that evaluation was an outlier.*

This exchange seems silly, but in fact could be the transcript from many depositions. Failing to use exhibit numbers is especially problematic when the exhibit in question is one of many of the same thing, like demonstrated above. Imagine the problem when dealing with "letters" in a commercial litigation. Although it is possible to discern the letter under consideration by factual references and testimony given by a witness, that exercise is wasted time in the digital age when identification is merely a keystroke away. The solution is a matter of developing the habit of always referring to an exhibit by its designation (e.g., Exhibit 17 rather than "this letter").

c. When to Show the Witness an Exhibit

i. Documents with Favorable Information

In most cases, you will show documents to the witness in the order in which they appear on the chronological storyline chart. That being said, the question remains whether to show the witness an exhibit before or after the witness has testified about the facts the exhibit contains. For each exhibit you use, analyze how the exhibit is characterized on the chronological storyline chart. If the facts contained in the exhibit are characterized as *believed* to be true (that is, it is not agreed on by a witness or document for the opposing party), a goal of deposing the witness is to get agreement with the exhibit's content.

If the deponent is a principal to the exhibit (author/sender), the task is straightforward. Agreement with the exhibit's content is likely assured. If, however, the deponent either received the exhibit or is merely a witness who should know about the facts covered in the exhibit, agreement with the believed facts contained in the exhibit is less certain. The deponent could either have no or incomplete knowledge about the facts revealed in the exhibit or will dispute them in whole or in part.

When seeking agreement with the facts contained in the exhibit, let the exhibit drive the witness's testimony. That is, show the exhibit to the witness before seeking his independent recollection of the facts contained in the exhibit. The theory is that when provided with an exhibit that recites particular facts, the witness is more likely to provide testimony consistent with the document. Consider the following example from the deposition of Professor Simonson.

Example: Assume that plaintiff's counsel has an evaluation of Professor Williams's performance in YR-3 (the year before her tenure vote). The evaluation states that Simonson offered a very positive recommendation of Williams's abilities—as did Dean Jefferson—using language taken directly from university regulations. University regulations set the standards for tenure regarding teaching, scholarship, and service, requiring an "outstanding" evaluation in two of the three and "excellent" in the third. The suggested deposition of Simonson is as follows.

Q: As Professor Williams's supervisor at the Patterson Institute in Academic Year YR-4–YR-3, did you have information about her teaching, scholarship, and service?

A: She did not teach at the Institute—we offer no classes—but I visited her classes and was familiar with her teaching. Her work at the Patterson Institute did directly involve both scholarship and service.

Q: In the spring of YR-3, did Dean Jefferson ask for your opinion of Professor Williams's work at the Patterson Institute?

A: She did, and I provided my evaluation to her.

Q: Did you understand that your assessment was part of the yearly evaluation of Professor Williams that the dean is required to provide annually for every nontenured faculty member.

A: I did. I performed such evaluations in my tenure as dean.

Q: Professor Simonson, let me show you what we have previously marked as Exhibit 7D on your computer screen, which appears to be entitled "YR-4–YR-3 Evaluation—Professor Mary Anne Williams" dated May 15, YR-3, with a signature that appears to be that of Dean Jefferson. Do you recognize Exhibit 7D?

A: *I recognize the form. I filled out such forms when I was the dean, and I have seen this evaluation during the course of this litigation. I did not author this evaluation nor receive it in the normal course.*
Q: *Just as a housekeeping matter, when you said "this evaluation," you were referring to Exhibit 7D, correct?*
A: *Yes.*
Q: *Is the signature on Exhibit 7D that of Dean Jefferson?*
A: *It is. I have seen her signature many, many times.*
Q: *Please read Exhibit 7D to yourself, and then I have some questions.*
Q: *Have you read Exhibit 7D?*
A: *I have.*
Q: *The fourth paragraph references your evaluation. You've said you provided an evaluation of Professor Williams's abilities to Dean Jefferson, correct?*
A: *I did, in a meeting we had in her office—the evaluation was part of a larger conversation we had about a number of matters.*
Q: *Referring to Exhibit 7D and the fourth paragraph, do you agree to what Dean Jefferson reports, that in academic year YR-4–YR-3, Professor Williams was an outstanding teacher and scholar and that she provided excellent service to the Institute.*
A: *That was the evaluation I provided, and I stand by it as of spring YR-3.*
Q: *You have also read how Dean Jefferson evaluated Professor Williams. What was Dean Jefferson's evaluation?*
A: *The same as mine.*
Q: *Which was?*
A: *Outstanding as a teacher and scholar, excellent in providing service to the institute.*
Q: *Do you know what the evaluations a candidate for tenure must receive to be qualified for tenure?*
A: *I do*
Q: *And they are?*
A: *In scholarship, teaching, and service, outstanding in two and at least excellent in the third.*
Q: *And does Exhibit 7D accurately reflect both your and Dean Jefferson's evaluation of Professor Williams in the tenure categories of teaching, scholarship, and service as of the date of Exhibit 7D.*
A: *Yes.*
Q: *Let's talk then, Professor, about the facts that you had that provided the basis for your evaluation of Professor Williams.*

By placing Exhibit 7D in front of Simonson, with the tenure category requirements contained in that exhibit as attributed to him and consistent with that of Dean Jefferson, counsel curtailed Simonson's ability to qualify or otherwise diminish the force of his tenure qualifying opinions without attacking the credibility of Dean Jefferson. The ultimate issue of whether Williams was qualified for tenure in

YR-2 is still an open one, but Simonson's testimony, driven as it was by Jefferson's exhibit, makes the task for deposing counsel less difficult. Counsel can then explore the basis for the evaluation, already agreed on, with some confidence that the information is consistent with the evaluation as shown in the exhibit and agreed on by Simonson. If Simonson was just asked about his evaluation of Williams as of YR-3, his testimony would less likely be as conclusive as that gleaned as above. Note, however, that counsel must still examine Simonson about his evaluation of Williams's abilities, using the basic fact investigation questioning systems to investigate the bases for his opinions and how, if at all, and why they changed in YR-2.

ii. Documents Containing Unfavorable Information

When a document contains facts that are not favorable to your client, question the deponent about those facts before showing the exhibit to the witness. This is especially true when the deponent is not the document's author, but was either referred to in the document or should have knowledge of the facts reflected in the document.

Example: Assume that former Dean Taylor wrote a letter to Professor Williams in May of YR-2 discussing both her lower than usual class evaluations in the Spring YR-2 semester (7.5 (on a ten-point scale) down from 8.6) and the fact that she had missed a publication deadline on an article. In light of these issues, he suggested that she delay her tenure vote until YR-1, which was her right. Professor Williams declined the offer, and it is a theory of the defendant that her failure to do so explains why she did not receive tenure. Assume further that the plaintiff is taking Taylor's deposition.[3]

Q: *Directing your attention to early May of YR-2, did you make a recommendation to Professor Williams that she delay her tenure vote until YR-1?*

A: *I wouldn't call it a recommendation. As the Chair of the Tenurial Faculty, I gave her the option to do so, since the YR-2 consideration of her tenure application was actually a year before the norm. I did believe, however, that it was in her interest to do so.*

Q: *Why did you think delaying her tenure vote until YR-1 was a good idea?*

A: *Well, Professor Williams was very upset by the ending of her relationship with Simonson, even though it was her decision to do so. She felt betrayed by him, and she was distracted by her pain over the whole ordeal. As a result, her teaching evaluations dropped significantly from the high eights to the mid sevens. Though these were still well within the acceptable evaluation for tenure, she also missed a deadline on a significant article. By May, she was feeling much better, and she assured me she would complete the article by the fall of YR-2, which she did, and that her teaching evaluations would return to her norm, thereby erasing the doubts raised by several of her colleagues regarding her teaching and scholarship—and that I believe were unfairly raised.*

---

3. The deposition of Taylor by the plaintiff's counsel is an example of a party taking the deposition of a witness who is favorable to that party.

Q: *Why else did you believe it was in her interest to delay her tenure vote?*

A: *As I said, Mary Anne was very upset about her breakup with Simonson. He had lied to her, promising that he would divorce his wife when he had no intention of doing so. He also adopted, without any form of attribution, Professor Williams's authored renewal application for a Department of Education grant that was awarded to the Patterson Institute. Unfortunately, Mary Anne complained about both of those matters to many people, and Simonson was not happy about the truth being told about him. He, of course, is a valuable asset to the school and university, and Jefferson and many of my colleagues wanted to keep him happy. By May, Mary Anne was feeling much better about herself. She had put her relationship with Simonson behind her and was no longer making any negative comments about Simonson. I thought with the passage of a year, all of that unpleasantness would be a distant memory and that civility would return between and among the faculty.*

Q: *Why did you think that would make a difference in the evaluation of Professor Williams for tenure?*

A: *In a conversation with Dean Jefferson before the Williams tenure vote, she said to me that she was very concerned that Williams's lack of collegiality was contrary to the tenure standards of "long-term interests of the faculty." Although I thought there was plenty of blame to go around, especially landing on Simonson, Jefferson's concerns made me worry about Mary Anne's tenure decision. Once things calmed down and the breakup between Mary Anne and Simonson was old news, I hoped that Jefferson's criticism of Professor Williams's supposed lack of collegiality would no longer be an issue.*

Q: *What other reasons did you have to believe a year's delay of Williams's tenure vote was in her interest?*

A: *That was all.*

Q: *You said that in your status as chair of the Tenurial Faculty Committee, you gave Professor Williams the option to delay her tenure vote for a year. How did you provide that option to her?*

A: *It was in a letter.*

Q: *Let me show you what has been marked as Exhibit 17, which appears to be a letter from you as the Tenurial Faculty Committee Chair to Professor Williams, dated May 13, YR-2. Do you recognize Exhibit 17?*

A: *Yes, that is the letter I just told you about informing Professor Williams she had the option to delay her tenure vote for a year.*

Q: *Please read Exhibit 17 to yourself. [Pause.] Have you read Exhibit 17?*

A: *I have.*

Q: *Does Exhibit 17 note benefits to Professor Williams of delaying her tenure vote?*

A: *It does.*

Q: *Does Exhibit 17 mention the opportunity to return teaching evaluations to Professor Williams's norm?*

A: *It does.*

Q: *Does Exhibit 17 mention the opportunity to complete and submit her article for publication?*
A: *It does.*
Q: *Does Exhibit 17 mention, in any way, the issue of statements made by Professor Williams being viewed as lack of collegiality and the value to her, in that regard, to delay her tenure vote?*
A: *It does not.*
Q: *Why not?*
A: *I did not believe that Professor Williams's truthful statements about Simonson demonstrated lack of collegiality, and neither did the majority of my colleagues who voted for her tenure. I saw no need to air the school's dirty laundry about Simonson in an official document that could follow the school and Professor Williams.*
Q: *Any other reason for not mentioning this issue in Exhibit 17?*
A: *No, Professor Williams was well aware of my opinion on delay and all the reasons that I thought delay was in her interest—we spoke several times on this issue—so I saw no reason to memorialize the entire matter in an official university document.*

Most of Taylor's testimony is favorable to Williams; counsel prepared Taylor for his testimony and knew his reasons for omitting the facts regarding "collegiality" from his letter. Letting Taylor affirmatively state his reasons for recommending a delay of Williams's tenure vote blunts the impact of his letter omitting facts that tended to show an atmosphere for retaliation. Therefore, it makes strategic sense to allow Taylor to testify before referring to the exhibit.

The point is the same for opposition witnesses. By examining an opposing witness about facts that underlie a presumed negative exhibit, you can blunt the document's force by exposing potential infirmities before showing the witness the exhibit on the record.

3. How do I examine the deponent about an exhibit?

Whether you show the exhibit to the deponent before or after initial testimony about it, use questions that glean the journalist's who, what, why, why, when, and how about the exhibit.

1) When did the witness first see the exhibit?
2) Who created the exhibit?
3) When was the exhibit created?
4) What was the reason for creating the exhibit?
5) Who was the intended recipient of the exhibit?
6) What other audience was intended for the exhibit?
7) Was a response required or expected?
8) Was a response received?

9) Were copies made of the exhibit?
10) What happened to the copies of the exhibit?
11) Why were copies made?
12) Where were the copies kept?
13) Why were the copies kept?
14) Were other documents of the same sort as the exhibit normally created?
15) Who created them?
16) When were they created in relation to events reflected in the exhibit?
17) Why were such documents created?
18) Were copies of these documents maintained?
19) Why were they maintained?
20) Where were they maintained?
21) How were the maintained? etc.

The journalist's questions about an exhibit, as with any event, will reveal (with follow-up) everything there is to know about how the exhibit was created. The other benefit of answers to the journalist's questions is that they will, in all likelihood, lay the foundation for the document's admissibility—or inadmissibility. These questions are about the exhibit itself. You should follow with questions about the facts reflected in the document (either before or after showing the exhibit); use the basic questioning techniques of fact gathering explored in chapter eight.

4. How can I use the deposition to lay legal and persuasive foundations?

The foundation for introducing a document requires proof of relevance, authentication, compliance with the original documents rule, accounting for hearsay—and in limited situations compliance with rules regarding privilege. Even if there is a trial, no judge wants to spend valuable court and juror time with foundational matters; the admissibility of documents is a matter for stipulations, admissions, and as a last resort, deposition practice.

a) Relevance, for deposition practice, is broadly stated as any evidence that is reasonably calculated to lead to the discovery of admissible evidence. The admissibility standard for trial or any other legal proceeding regarding relevance is whether the exhibit has any tendency to make a fact in issue more or less likely (Rules 401, 402).

b) Authentication, governed by Article 9 of the Federal Rules of Evidence, is merely a process of showing that a thing is what it purports to be and may be proved by direct or circumstantial evidence.

c) Article 10's Original Documents Rule applies in limited circumstances—the document itself must be related to the case outcome.[4] Even then, it is just a rule

4. Typically, in cases about a document, such as litigation about a written contract, a deed, or a will.

of preference, allowing copies unless there is a genuine issue of authenticity and other secondary evidence when the production of the document is excused.[5]

d) Hearsay is governed by Article 8; it is at issue when the document is offered for the truth of its contents—as opposed to for some other purpose, typically notice or knowledge. If the document is hearsay, there are twenty-two exceptions in Rule 803, five exceptions in Rule 804, and a catch-all exception in Rule 807. In most litigation, most exhibits will overcome any hearsay objection because they are a nonhearsay: an opposing party's statement (Rule 801(d)(2)(A–E)); a statement made for the purposes of medical diagnosis or treatment (Rule 803(4)); a past recollection recorded (Rule 803(5)); a record of regularly conducted activity (Rule 803(6));[6] or an official government report (Rule 803(8)).

e) Privilege is governed in the main by common law. The most typical privilege is for attorney-client statements. In addition, attorney work product is also protected from disclosure. Those and other privileges are narrowly construed, and exceptions to privileges are broadly construed. Claims of privilege to requested discovery should be identified in a "privilege log." The log describes, without divulging the privileged information, the nature of the privileged material and the privilege claimed, together with other identifying data such as date, people involved as makers, sender, and receivers of claimed privileged material.

As noted above, the journalist's questions answer any controversy about the legal admissibility of a document. Even hearsay—the most technical of the hurdles to admissibility—has thirty exceptions, including a catch-all exception, all of which are based on the facts surrounding how the written or oral statement was made. If there is a legitimate question regarding admissibility, and you believe that in the morass of fact gathering there is a sufficient foundation, distill the foundational facts for admissibility into a series of short, leading questions that track the implicated rules of evidence. These answers will provide your basis if admissibility is still at issue at a pretrial conference or in argument regarding a motion in limine.

We do not mean to suggest that the only necessary foundation for an important document is accomplished through a set of permissible leading questions.[7] When the modern deposition is most often the last opportunity for a witness to persuade a factfinder, what we call the "persuasive" foundation for the exhibit must be had in the deposition. The legal foundation shows why the exhibit is admissible; the persuasive foundation shows why the exhibit is believable, reliable, and valuable when deciding the case. Because the law of evidence itself is based on the two pillars—the

5. For example, when the original has been lost or destroyed (not at the behest of the proffering party) or the opposing party has a duplicate original and has been put on notice by the nature of the lawsuit that the document is in issue.

6. Typically referred to as a business record.

7. Questions asked solely for the purpose of showing the admissibility of evidence are considered preliminary questions, which may be asked in leading form.

reliability and the **necessity** of the evidence to a fair determination of a case—the persuasive foundation usually consists of the legal foundation expressed in ordinary language.

Example: Consider the examination of Dean Jefferson about the admissibility of a memorandum in Williams's personnel file that reflects the evaluation of Williams's performance as an Assistant Professor in YR-4. This memo contains some negative commentary.

Defense Counsel: During the examination, plaintiff's lawyer asked you about a number of written evaluations of Professor Williams that were contained in her personnel file. I'd like to ask you some questions about the keeping of such records. First, why are such records kept?

Jefferson: I am required, as the dean of the school, to evaluate each nontenured faculty member's performance during the previous academic year to provide feedback on the faculty member's progress towards tenure and to set their salary for the next academic year.

Q: And this is done for every nontenured faculty member?

A: Yes.

Q: Are these evaluations reduced to writing?

A: Yes, and they become part of the faculty member's permanent personnel file.

Q: What form does the written evaluation take?

A: It identifies the faculty member, their year academic rank, and their years of employment. I then consider the three categories of performance that are part of the tenure evaluation by university regulations.

Q: What are those categories?

A: Teaching, scholarship, and service.

Q: How do you perform the evaluation, starting with teaching?

A: Every faculty member is evaluated by their students in every class they teach. We use a ten-point scale, with ten being the highest evaluation. I receive those evaluations from the Associate Dean for Students, who collects the evaluations (they are done electronically). In addition, in their second, fourth, and tenure year (which can be either their fifth or sixth year), the faculty members are evaluated by a faculty committee of three senior faculty members, who use the same ten-point scale. The committee also provides written comments. In addition, we ask all faculty with relevant information to provide written input about the demonstrated teaching abilities of the faculty member under evaluation. All of that information is reflected in the report. The dean then draws conclusions about the faculty member's teaching, as compared to teaching evaluation norms. The faculty member is expected to improve as they gain more experience. For example, the normal evaluation of teaching in a faculty member's second year is 5–6.5. A faculty member rated at 6.5 in teaching evaluations is considered on track for tenure, assuming continued improvement. A faculty member rated at 5.0 is advised by the dean to put in extra effort on their teaching for the next academic year and is offered the assistance of senior faculty members, who will work with them on their teaching.

Q: *Does that cover the evaluation of teaching?*
A: *Yes.*
Q: *Let's then turn to scholarship. How is scholarship evaluated?*
A: *There is no way to quantify the evaluation of scholarship except by counting the number of publications, which is of course important. Beyond that, the question is much more subjective, but I should say that there is a good deal of agreement on the quality of scholarship. The faculty recognizes that diversity of opinion is important in academics, so it is not the conclusions reached by the faculty member, but the articulated intellectual process that is most important.*
Q: *Are there norms?*
A: *Yes, there are. Early scholarship is descriptive. That is, the article will collect data, report on previous scholarship in the area, and describe and identify an important issue in public policy. More mature scholarship will be more theoretical and, in addition to collecting data and reviewing scholarship, provide insight into existing scholarship and suggest new ways of resolving particular issues. At its best, scholarship reviews existing data and academic thought, critiques the old scholarship, and presents a unique view of a topic that is of significant import to the public policy academic community. These articles are often described as "seminal." They are commented on by other academics and considered important in any review of the topic about which they are written.*
Q: *Given these norms, how is the evaluation performed?*
A: *We look at whether the faculty member's scholarship is being cited by other scholars and how frequently. Most articles are available electronically; the number of downloads indicates the article's impact in the profession. In addition, I collect evaluations from all tenured faculty, and in years where there is a faculty committee (second, fourth, and tenure year), the committee will provide a written evaluation. I provide all this information to the faculty member and advise, typically, on the need to advance toward that seminal article. For tenure, we look for that seminal article or at least a number of articles that have gained general acceptance (as shown by citations and downloads).*
Q: *And this information is contained in this evaluation memo you create?*
A: *Yes.*
Q: *Let's turn then to service—how is service evaluated, and is the evaluation in your memo?*
A: *All evaluative information is referred to in the memo. What we look for in the service category is activity of two sorts. Faculty members participate in the administration of the school through committee work. I assign them to committees, and each faculty member serves on a range of committees from those requiring relatively little effort to those that are at the heart of the school's life and most important, like the Curriculum Committee. In addition, faculty members advise student groups; that is counted toward the service category. An important part of service is attracting funding to the university. Tuition only covers part of the costs*

of running the university. We need to attract grant money and donations. Faculty members are encouraged to attract funding for their scholarship, and we assist them in the art of grant writing. For tenure, we look at a mix of academic and fundraising service, but at least some fundraising effort and success is required for tenure.

Q: *And an evaluation of service is provided to the faculty member?*

A: *Yes.*

Q: *What else is contained in the evaluation memo?*

A: *Any other information that I've received that is relevant to the ultimate tenure decision.*

Q: *Where is this information maintained?*

A: *The evaluation memo is part of the permanent personnel record of each faculty member.*

Q: *Is the memo provided to the faculty member?*

A: *No, but I go over all of it in my yearly review meeting with the faculty member when we set salary for the next year.*

Q: *What if the faculty member does not agree with the evaluation?*

A: *They are invited to provide a written response, which also becomes part of their permanent file.*

Q: *How are these memoranda used, other than to communicate progress to the faculty member towards tenure?*

A: *The tenure review committee for each faculty member has access to these evaluations when writing their recommendation to the full tenurial faculty.*

Q: *Let me ask you a series of questions about these evaluation memos. Are the memos made in the ordinary course of the educational enterprise of the university?*

A: *They are.*

Q: *Are they kept in the ordinary course of the educational enterprise of the university?*

A: *They are.*

Q: *Are they created using information from people who have firsthand knowledge of the facts reported in the evaluation memo?*

A: *They are.*

Q: *Do these people have a duty to the university to provide such information?*

A: *They do.*

Q: *Are the evaluation memos made at the time the evaluation is performed?*

A: *Yes.*

Q: *And do you know the process of creating and maintaining these memos from your own firsthand knowledge?*

A: *I do.*

Q: *Now, Dean, you were shown a number of Professor Williams's evaluation memos, but let me show you what we have premarked as Exhibit 7C. This appears to be an evaluation memo for Professor Williams for YR-4, which counsel for the plaintiff did not show you.*

The final six questions establish the legal foundation to admit this document at a later proceeding over a hearsay objection. This allows the defendants to introduce the evaluation memo as a Rule 803(6) record of regularly conducted activity.[8] The previous dialogue establishes the reliability of the written evaluations.[9] Given the variety of sources, quality of sources, amount of information, and the existence and application of norms universally applied, a factfinder would be hard pressed to find a more fairly conducted and created foundation.

d. How can I use the deposition to lay negative foundations?

Another goal of deposition practice is to show that damaging documents are inadmissible. Much as with showing the legal admissibility of a document, use leading questions to show the converse; while showing inadmissibility, you can also show that the document is unreliable.

Example: Assume that the EEOC sent the university a Notice of Complaint of Discrimination regarding Williams. The university's response denied the allegation and set out, with precision, the nondiscriminatory reasons why Williams was denied tenure. The university would like to admit the reply letter as an Evidence Rule 803(6) record of regularly conducted activity, providing a factfinder with a written encapsulation of their legal case theory. Consider the following as an attempt to show that the document should be excluded by the terms of Rule 803(6). The witness is Dean Jefferson, who requested a response to the EEOC from the university counsel.

Plaintiff's Counsel: Dean Jefferson, let me show you an exhibit we have premarked as Exhibit 20. This appears to be a letter from you to Ms. Terri Mattoon, an attorney with the EEOC. Do you recognize Exhibit 20?

A: I do. It's a letter I sent in response to a Notice of Complaint regarding a claim of discrimination on our part regarding Professor Williams's negative tenure decision.

Q: You signed Exhibit 20?

A: I did.

Q: But in fact, it was written, at least in part, by university counsel Helen Jacobs, who is copied on Exhibit 20, correct?

A: That's right. The EEOC letter asked for a legal response.

Q: That's right, and you are not a lawyer?

A: I'm not.

Q: Nor are you trained in the law?

A: Correct.

8. If offered by the plaintiff, this foundation would not be necessary, because the memo is a statement of a party opponent pursuant to Rule 801(d)(2)(a).

9. Relevance is obvious. Authentication is made by the testimony of Jefferson, who created the document. The Original Documents Rule is not applicable. Any statutory protection of Williams's personnel records is waived by her bringing this lawsuit against her employment.

Q: *As a result, you are not qualified to provide legal positions on the part of the university?*
A: *Of course not.*
Q: *It is not normal in your job as the Dean of the Public Policy School to sign letters prepared in part by university counsel, is it?*
A: *Well, they did provide input for our appointment letters.*
Q: *But Exhibit 20 was not an appointment letter, was it?*
A: *No, it wasn't.*
Q: *Exhibit 20 related to potential litigation, correct?*
A: *Yes.*
Q: *Professor Williams had made a legal claim against the university?*
A: *She had.*
Q: *And you sent that claim to university counsel so they could state the strongest legal defense they could create, right?*
A: *That's their job.*
Q: *And you wanted them to do their job, true?*
A: *I did.*
Q: *You hoped they could make Professor Williams's claim go away?*
A: *Of course.*
Q: *Just a few more questions regarding Exhibit 20, Dean. Exhibit 20 would not have been prepared but for Professor Williams's claim of discrimination, true?*
A: *Yes.*
Q: *So Exhibit 20 was prepared solely for the purposes of potential litigation or forestalling that potential litigation?*
Defense Counsel: Objection. Calls for conjecture.
Plaintiff's Counsel: Dean—let me be fair—do you know of any reason, other than in response to potential litigation, for the preparation and sending of Exhibit 20?
A: *No.*
Q: *So, as far as you know, Exhibit 20 was prepared solely for the purposes of potential litigation or forestalling litigation?*
Defense Counsel: Objection. Compound.
Plaintiff's Counsel: All right. Dean Jefferson, one reason you know for the preparation and sending of Exhibit 20 was in preparation for potential litigation by Professor Williams?
A: *Yes.*
Q: *A second reason for the preparation and sending of Exhibit 20 was to forestall litigation by Professor Williams?*
A: *Yes.*
Q: *And you know of no other purposes for the preparation of and sending of Exhibit 20, right?*
A: *That's right.*

Rule 803(6)'s exception for records of regularly conducted activity excludes otherwise qualifying documents that are suspect on their face. Case law has determined that documents prepared for litigation is one such exclusion. The above examination lays the foundation for that exclusion, which would be argued in either a motion in limine or at a pretrial conference. Note the persistence of the examination, much akin to a trial; counsel follows up with a demand for a "yes" or "no" answer whenever deponent attempts to explain away an accusatory question. Even if the court overruled the motion, the questioning demonstrates the obvious bias reflected in the document and will impact the weight a factfinder will give it.

5. How should I question a deponent about conversations?

Conversations are a typical topic for exploration at a deposition. There are two categories of conversation about which a deponent might have information: conversations in which the deponent participated, and conversations that the deponent overheard.

a. Deponent Participation Conversations

When the deponent was a participant in any conversation, your questioning should identify the topic, other participants, time, location, and purpose of the conversation. Essentially, you are pursuing the journalist's questions about the conversation: who was involved; what was the topic; what was the purpose; where did it occur; how long did it last; and by inference, was it possible to have been overheard. Information about a conversation exists on three levels: transcript (all actual words exchanged); partial transcript (what actual words are known); and conversation content (all topics without quotations).

Once you have gathered all the information about the content of the conversation, ask what thoughts the witness had about the conversation, whether he related the conversation to anyone else, and whether any actions were taken as a result of the conversation.

Example: Assume that the Tenurial Committee made an initial written report, which was 2–1 in favor of tenure. Afterward, Taylor transmitted the report to Williams and then met with her privately to talk about her options. The conversation occurred on May 17, YR-2, in Taylor's office at 2:00 p.m. Taylor has testified that they spent an hour talking about the content of the report.

Defense Counsel: What was the next thing that you and Professor Williams spoke about?
Taylor: I told Professor Williams that the tenurial faculty had authorized me to suggest that she delay her tenure vote. Mary Anne was in the fifth year of her appointment to the faculty, which is the earliest time when tenure is considered; the norm is in the sixth year, which she knew.
Q: Beginning at the point that you raised the issue of delay, I would like to know exactly what you said to Professor Williams and what she said to you.
A: Verbatim?

Q: *To the extent you can.*

A: *I don't remember my precise words, but I said something to the effect that she knew that she could delay her tenure vote until YR-1.*

Q: *How did she respond—verbatim, preferably?*

A: *I remember exactly what she said. She seemed upset that I even raised the issue, looked me straight in the eye, and said: "No way, my appointment as Associate Director of the Patterson Institute requires tenure this year. I've worked too hard. I'm not going to let David screw me out of that appointment just because he may be uncomfortable around me. We can be civil at the institute; we already have been."*

Q: *How did you respond?*

A: *I agreed with that downside, but I said to her, "You have to consider the benefits versus the risk of going forward."*

Q: *How did she react to your advice?*

A: *She said, "There are no benefits. I'm qualified. The vote was only close on the report because the dissenter, Binder, was the other finalist for the AD job at Patterson. He knows if I don't get tenure this year, he'll get the job. That's why he didn't vote no on the recommendation on tenure on the merits, only suggested the delay. That was his enlightened self-interest speaking."*

Q: *Where those her exact words?*

A: *Well, that was the content. I do remember precisely her "enlightened self-interest" comment about Professor Binder; very clever; very Mary Anne.*

Q: *Thank you for that quotation, Professor; as we go through this conversation, please tell me any time you are quoting yourself or Professor Williams. What did you say to her?*

A: *I said, and this is a quote, "Funny, but not helpful; your gift of repartee can get you in trouble, you know."*

Q: *What did you mean by that comment?*

A: *Mary Anne is quick-witted; so much so that she can raise a chuckle about the target of her barbs—no one likes to be laughed at or about, even in jest.*

Q: *Was Professor Williams quick-witted in her comments about Professor Simonson?*

A: *To be sure.*

Q: *What did she say about Professor Simonson that was, as you say, "quick-witted"?*

A: *I have no quotes, but I have to say her barbs were sharp, albeit deserved, about Simonson—I have already told you about his history.*

Q: *All right. What else did you say to Professor Williams about risk-benefit on the delay decision?*

A: *I reminded her that there was a dip in her class evaluations and that she missed a publication deadline—not fatal problems, but facts that someone opposing her could use. I also said that her comments about Simonson did not go over well with some of my colleagues, and that while she had stopped making them as she got perspective about their relationship, the feelings in the faculty were a little raw. We, in academics, prefer quiet back-biting to full-blown war.*

Q: *How did Williams respond to your comments?*
A: *She said she was willing to take the risk.*
Q: *What else did she say?*
A: *Nothing. She just stopped.*
Q: *What happened next?*
A: *She seemed determined, so I didn't try to change her mind. I did tell her that she had my full support, but that if I was her, I would take the delay just to be safe. I said I knew if she chose to delay, her class evaluations would go back up off the charts where they typically were and that she would finish her article; also her spat with Simonson would be replaced by some other issue on the minds of the faculty, especially assuming, as she said, that she and David remained civil toward each other.*
Q: *How did she respond?*
A: *She said—and I'm sure about this—"I wish I had your wisdom, my mentor; I just can't do it and live with myself. I'm going forward."*
Q: *How did you respond?*
A: *I reminded her that if she chose to go forward, there were no second chances. Her tenure was up or down that spring. The decision would be final and could not be revisited. She said she understood, that she had read the regulations.*
Q: *What else was said by either of you regarding Professor Williams's decision to go forward on her tenure decision in YR-2?*
A: *Nothing else.*

b. Overheard Conversations

The information you'll seek about overheard conversations is the same as if the deponent were a participant. You will want to know if there is a transcript of the conversation—that is the simplest way to confirm that you get all the information. If there is no full transcript, is there a partial transcript or notes that the deponent made? If not, you will need to discover the conversation's substance through questions alone. For the most part, your questions will mirror the style of any deposition. However, there are some key additional questions: how the conversation was overheard (the position, including whether it was in person or through some sort of electronic device); was the conversation intended to be overheard; was it held in a place where it was obvious the conversation could be overheard; and was the conversation overheard with either the direct or tacit permission of the parties.[10] With those differences, you would proceed with the examination of a person who overheard a conversation about its contents in the same manner as one overheard by a then-present deponent.

10. If the conversation was overheard using some sort of electronic device, you must show that you complied with the state or federal law that governs the use of listening devices. In addition, you must meet all evidentiary requirements to use such a conversation.

6. What are some pitfalls I should watch out for at depositions?

a. Avoiding Perceived Bad Information for Case Theory

We have identified and argued for the importance of developing all positive information, on the record, in every deposition for the uses of the modern deposition in dispute resolution. This does not mean that you should not gather the facts that undermine your legal and factual theories and support the legal and factual theories of the opposing parties. For your legal and factual theory to be persuasive, you must identify, anticipate, and explode the legal and factual theories of the opposing party.

To that end, there is no such thing as bad information; there is only "information." Find out everything that challenges your client's legal and factual theories and bolsters the legal and factual theories of the opposing party. Too often, when a deposition witness volunteers unanticipated information that is helpful to the opposing party, deposing counsel ignores or avoids following up on the volunteered information. That is a mistake.

First, if opposing counsel is defending a modern deposition, assume she prepared the deponent to volunteer the information helpful to her client, as outlined in chapter five; she will take her opportunity to question the deponent and develop that testimony. Even if trial is anticipated, and opposing counsel takes the traditional approach and saves the information for later disclosure at trial or otherwise, the lesson is the same. Bad information does not go away when you ignore it—it just remains a hidden weapon for the opposing party to deploy at a later time. If that information remains unknown until some case dispositive event (e.g., in an affidavit attached to a summary judgment motion, trial testimony, limited testimony in arbitration, etc.), all you have achieved is the inability to prepare for what is to come.

Example: In the "conversations" transcript above, deposing counsel failed twice to follow up on hints that Taylor had further information in need of examination. In his testimony about Williams's reaction to Taylor suggesting that she delay her tenure vote, Taylor testified, "I remember exactly what she said. She seemed upset that I even raised the issue, looked me straight in the eye, and said: 'No way, my appointment as Associate Director of the Patterson Institute requires tenure this year. I've worked too hard. ***I'm not going to let David screw me out of that appointment just because he may be uncomfortable*** *around me. We can be civil at the Institute, we already have been.'" The highlighted section Taylor's answer states Williams's point of view—that Simonson was trying to damage her tenure prospects. Deposing counsel may not like what she hears, but she must follow up and ask Taylor about his understanding of the facts underlying Williams's statement. It could wait until later, but follow-up is demanded.*

Later in the deposition, deposing counsel asked what specific remarks Williams made about Simonson after their break-up. Taylor testified, "I have no quotes, but I have to say ***her barbs were sharp, albeit deserved, about Simonson*** *. . . ." Here, Taylor* *offers his own opinion of Simonson's character—or at least prior acts. Deposing counsel, again, may not like the response, but she must ask why Taylor believes that Simonson deserved Williams's barbs and at least learn about the nature of the barbs, if not what was specifically said.*

b. Instructions Not to Answer

Federal Rule of Civil Procedure 30(c)(2) provides in part:

> A person may instruct a deponent not to answer **only** when necessary to **preserve a privilege**, to **enforce a limitation** ordered by the court or to **present a motion** under Rule 30(d)(3). [emphasis added][11]

The rule is used mainly for claims of attorney-client privilege[12] and matters within the scope of "protective orders" issued pursuant to Rule 26(2)(C) or a claim by defending counsel that she will be seeking such a protective order.

Included within the ambit of "privilege" is what in reality is protection of trial preparation materials (attorney work product), as described in Rule 26(b)(3). These trial preparation materials are of two sorts. First, there is what is known as "pure work-product material," which is never discoverable. Pure work product includes "mental impressions, conclusions, opinions, or legal theories of a party's attorney."[13] Other information collected by counsel, or counsel's agents, in preparation for litigation is protected unless the opposing party can show that the information is otherwise discoverable, that there is a substantial need for the materials that will not cause undue hardship, and that their substantial substitute is also unavailable.[14]

When defending counsel instructs the deponent not to answer, deposing counsel has the right to know the legal basis for the instruction. Once this is identified, deposing counsel may ask the witness about information that is relevant to whether the instruction not to answer is valid (e.g., within the ambit of a protective order; in the case of privilege, the validity of the privilege based on the same information).

In the typical circumstance where the objection and instruction not to answer is based on attorney-client privilege, deposing counsel should ask about the nature of the communication, who the client was, who the lawyer was, the subject matter

11. Unfortunately, there are many lawyers who either have not read this rule or have decided not to be restricted by it. Those lawyers, and their tactics, will be addressed in the next section on dealing with obstreperous defending counsel.

12. Other common-law and statutory privileges, such as doctor-patient, spousal, religious advisor conversations, patient-psychotherapist (including sexual assault, child and spousal abuse counselors, etc.) are also the predicate for an instruction not to answer.

13. Fed. R. Civ. P. 26(b)(3)(B).

14. Fed. R. Civ. P. 26(b)(3)(A)(i), (ii).

of the communication (without disclosing its contents), when it was made, where it was made, who was present, whether the contents of the communication was provided to other people—and if so, how it was provided. In some jurisdictions, the privilege only covers statements made by the client and not those of the lawyer, unless the lawyer's statements reveal the content of those of the client. In other jurisdictions, the privilege extends to the statements of all parties to the communication within the scope of the privilege (including agents of the lawyer). The communication must have been intended to be confidential (e.g., made in a private place—not in a crowded restaurant, for example). The communication must be about facts within the scope of the attorney-client relationship, made during the existence of the relationship. Past criminality and fraud are covered by the privilege; the intent to future criminality or fraud is not. At the end of the day, if deposing counsel believes the statements are not privileged or meet some exception to the privilege, the deposition continues on other topics, and she will need to bring a motion to compel testimony.

Likewise, when deposing counsel makes the instruction based on a court-ordered protective order, she is allowed to ask any questions that might show she seeks information not within the order.

Finally, if defending counsel's instructions are based on an intent to seek a protective order, deposing counsel must make an effort to resolve the basis for the protective order before seeking the court's intervention. Consider the limitation of discovery itemized in Rule 26—this suggests methods for balancing the interests of the parties.[15] It is the instructing counsel's duty to seek a protective order preventing or limiting discovery; counsel can also make the request for a protective order in response to a motion to compel discovery. If the trial judge is persuaded that denying the requested discovery is necessary to protect the seeking party from annoyance, embarrassment, oppression, or undue burden or expense, she has wide discretion in crafting the protective order.

Example: Assume that Simonson is being deposed and has testified to a number of sexual relationships he had with members of the university community.

Plaintiff's Counsel: Have you testified about all the extramarital sexual relationships with members of the university community?
Simonson: All but one.
Q: And with whom was that sexual relationship?
A: I prefer not to answer.

15. Fed. R. Civ. P. 26(c)(1)(A)–(H). The rule suggests limiting the terms of discovery by time and place; providing a particular methodology; allowing inquiry into some matters, but not others, within scope of request; limiting who may be present during the deposition on certain topics; sealing the deposition and providing limited terms for opening; providing protection for trade secrets, which can be revealed only under specified circumstances; and requiring simultaneous filing of certain discovery items.

Q: Why is that?
A: I prefer not to say.
Q: Nonetheless, Professor, I must insist. Who else from the university community have you had a sexual relationship with?
A: May I consult with my lawyer?
Q: Please answer my question, and then you can consult.
Defense Counsel: Counsel, Professor Simonson and I have discussed the possibility of this question being asked, and he is adamant about not answering your question.
Plaintiff's Counsel: Are you instructing Professor Simonson not to answer my question?
Defense Counsel: I am.
Plaintiff's Counsel: On what basis?
Defense Counsel: I will be seeking a protective order to prevent this questioning.
Plaintiff's Counsel: As you know, the rules require that we attempt to resolve our differences on this discovery. Can we go off the record for that purpose?
Defense Counsel: Fine, let's take a break, and why don't we go to your office and discuss this matter; maybe we can reach some consensus.

In their conversation, defendant's counsel reveals that the relationship was with a current member of the faculty, it occurred after the relationship with Williams, the faculty member was married, and the relationship was not known by anyone other than the participants. It lasted a few days, while the participants were out of town, and was mutually ended. Plaintiff's counsel admits that based on the representations made, the evidence was of slight value. She maintains that she is nonetheless entitled to the information, but offers to ask the questions, elicit whatever information was available, and then seal the deposition. Defense counsel asks if opposing counsel will agree that the testimony in question only be recorded by stenographic means and opposing counsel agree not to divulge the information received to her client or anyone else. Plaintiff's counsel agrees to only stenographic recording, but will not agree to keep a secret from her client. Counsel then agree to disagree, but agree that their conversation will remain confidential. Defense counsel agrees to have his client respond to written interrogatories, the answers to which will be sealed (even from the plaintiff) and attached to defendant's motion for a protective order together with a stipulated writing reflecting the content of counsels' conversation attempting to resolve their differences.

The manner in which counsel handled the instruction not to answer was civil. They were both creative in suggesting a resolution of the problem, and in the end, they had a complete package of information to present to the court with the motion for a protective order.

c. Dealing with Obstreperous Defending Counsel

There is a long history of war stories about attorneys acting as literal combatants in conducting discovery, especially with regard to the behavior of defending counsel in a deposition. These lawyers believed that litigation was war and that it was their job to prevent discovery to the greatest extent possible. Fistfights, thrown furniture, and both subtle and outrageous behavior in the making of objections—and illegitimate instructions not to answer in many, if not all, jurisdictions—were common. Rule 30(d)(1) addresses the issue of the obstreperous lawyer and provides:

> Any objection during a deposition shall be stated **concisely** and in a **nonargumentative** and **nonsuggestive** manner. A party may instruct a deponent not to answer only when necessary to preserve a **privilege**, to **enforce a limitation on evidence** directed by the court, or to **present a motion under paragraph (3).** [emphasis added]

Nonetheless, the behavior became so obstructive to the goals of discovery that commissions were formed and local rules crafted to curb the behavior. They have been successful; things are better.

Such behavior is inconsistent with the modern deposition. In fact, many modern depositions are video recorded, which is the best inhibitor to obstreperous behavior. Nonetheless, the obstreperous defending counsel at depositions is not gone from litigation.

We identify obstreperous behavior in four categories: the interfering lawyer; the conferring lawyer; the testifying lawyer; and the instructing lawyer.

i. The Interfering Lawyer

Depositions should be witness-dominated conversations—that style and tone is most conducive to information gathering. The interfering lawyer inserts herself into the conversation and attempts to obstruct it.

Example: Consider the following from the deposition of Williams by defendant's counsel.

Defense Counsel: When was the first time, after joining the Public Policy School faculty, that you had any professional interaction with Professor Simonson?
Plaintiff's Counsel: Object to form; you may answer.
Williams: I believe it was in the spring semester. We had exchanged pleasantries in halls and at faculty meetings. I was teaching the survey course, and I asked Professor Simonson, on the recommendation of Professor Taylor, to sit in on my class and give advice on how to improve.
Defense Counsel: Did he do so on more than one occasion?
Plaintiff's Counsel: Objection to form; you may answer.
A: He came to several classes.
Q: How much time did he spend with you?

Plaintiff's Counsel: Objection as to form, you may answer; but counselor, do we really need to count minutes. It was seven years ago, and at this rate, we are going to go way beyond our seven hours. Go ahead; tell him how much time you spent with Simonson.

A: The classes were an hour long. He came to three classes I believe, and we met for about fifteen minutes after each class.

Q: So we're talking about just less than four hours; did he give you all the time you wanted?

Plaintiff's Counsel: Are we down to adding now?

Defense Counsel: I'll ask whatever I like. Obviously your client's relationship with Professor Simonson is at the heart of her claim, no matter how frivolous, and how their relationship developed is important. I ask you again, were his comments helpful to you?

Plaintiff's Counsel: That's another question. Objection to form, but go ahead and answer.

A: He was very helpful.

Plaintiff's Counsel: All right, can we get on to something that's relevant. I have a 5:30 flight to catch.

Defense Counsel: We'll finish when we finish. If you keep interrupting, you're going to miss your flight. Let's move on to something else.

Plaintiff's Counsel: I only object when your questions warrant it. Go ahead,

This vignette is abbreviated from actual practice; the interfering conduct would go on at least thirty minutes before the end was in sight. The goal of plaintiff's counsel was to interfere with the conversation and the free flow of information—not just by objecting, but also by attracting deposing counsel's attention to her, as opposed to the witness. With the interfering lawyer, most ubiquitous objections to form are not well founded. A possible way to stop the behavior is to ask, "What's wrong with the form? I need to know the specific problem with the form of the question so I can cure the objection." Because objecting counsel lacks a legitimate ground for objecting to the form of the question, this tactic might stop the behavior—but likely not.

The real problem is that defendant's counsel rose to the bait and fulfilled the objecting lawyer's goal of breaking deposing counsel's focus—she rewarded the behavior, and it will continue. The best strategy is to ignore the objections and continue questions unfettered. Opposing counsel will tire in time (usually thirty minutes), and in fact, the deponent—especially one who values his time—will become more forthcoming, if only to end the tedium.

ii. The Conferring Lawyer

A second way in which defending counsel may seek to interrupt the free and easy flow of information is by conferring with the deponent about either questions or exhibits that are shown to the deponent during the course of the deposition. In one way, conferring with the deponent during the deposition is just another way to slow down and make obtaining information cumbersome. There exists, however, a more nefarious purpose for the consultation: defending counsel, through consultation, can shape and limit the deponent's testimony.

For that reason, some discovery orders prohibit any consultation between the deponent and his counsel once the deposition has convened, except as required to invoke a privilege by the deponent.

Example: Consider the following from the deposition of Professor Williams.

Defense Counsel: How frequently was your performance as a professor at the Public Policy School evaluated?
Williams: I'm not sure what you mean.
Plaintiff's Counsel: Excuse me counsel, we need a moment. [About thirty seconds pass.] *Go ahead, I apologize for the interruption.*
Q: What didn't you understand about my last question?
A: Well, I received feedback on my performance on an informal basis all the time. Faculty members—some senior, some peers—would visit my class, and we would talk about teaching techniques. And it was also common to seek advice from senior faculty about scholarly projects. But there was only one formal evaluation every year, at the end of the spring semester in a meeting with Dean Jefferson.
Q: Let me show you what has been premarked as Exhibit 7A. This appears to be a Memo to Mary Ann Williams's Evaluation File, from Dean Jefferson, dated May 12, YR-5. Do you recognize Exhibit 7A?
Plaintiff's Counsel: Just a moment please. We need to look at the exhibit together. [Approximately one minute of whispered conversation.]
A: I have seen Exhibit 7A before, but only as part of this lawsuit. What I see written here, and the content of the memo, is familiar to me. As far as I remember, what she told me was consistent with what's written here. I know the salary is right. Honestly, I remember Dean Jefferson being more positive, complimentary than what is written here.
Q: What else can you tell me about the evaluation itself, apart from what's written in Exhibit 7A?
Plaintiff's Counsel: Excuse me again, counsel. [Approximately one minute of whispered conversation.]
A: That's all. I can't be sure that she said everything that's written on Exhibit 7A. I don't know why she didn't give me a copy of it during the meeting. And again, I remember her being more complimentary of my performance in my first year, especially in comparison to what she said was typical for first-year faculty members.

The above vignette raises several issues. First, even in jurisdictions where is permitted, consultation between defending counsel and the deponent should not occur while there is a pending question. The danger of consultation before answering is, as it appears above, that counsel may help the deponent formulate his answers.

Second, a paper transcript will not reflect the pauses shown in our example. To create a proper record, make a statement to the effect of, "Let the record reflect that before providing her answer to the last question, Ms. Williams and her lawyer had an approximately one-minute whispered conversation." This statement will become increasingly necessary if defending counsel continues her frequent consultations about pending questions, particularly if you believe the behavior is impacting the deposition content and want to seek relief from the court. Of course, if there is a video recording, there is a record of the consultation's fact, form, and duration.

Third, some conferring counsel will say before the consultation, "Let's go off the record." Deposing counsel controls the videographer and court reporter, and they should know not stop recording or transcribing unless deposing counsel tells them to do so. If defending counsel does instruct the videographer and court reporter to go off the record, you may have to resist and not allow this to occur.

Fourth, as a substantive matter, defending counsel's consultation with a client/deponent may be privileged. However, a strict reading of the law of privilege does not protect a lawyer instructing a witness how to testify because the purpose of the instruction is to interfere with fair discovery. As such, deposing counsel should have a right to inquire about the consultation. In reality, defending counsel will claim privilege; unless you clearly demonstrate that the consultation adulterated the testimony, the court will enforce the privilege claim.

Finally, although court orders cure consultation for inappropriate purposes, those that forbid any contact between attorney and client once the deposition convenes have critics. There are legitimate reasons why a defending lawyer might need to confer with her client during a deposition. Not infrequently, the deponent misunderstands deposing counsel's questions and needs counsel to identify the confusion, which left unresolved would result in a confused transcript. Without such a consultation, the deposition would proceed with faulty assumptions that could have been cleared up. Instead, defending counsel has to clear up the misunderstanding by examining the deponent or have substantive corrections to the deposition made at the reading and signing.

In other circumstances, the deponent may make a basic error and provide inaccurate testimony. In that situation, defending counsel has an ethical duty to correct the deposition testimony; that correction is better done at the time it occurs (after consultation) when deposing counsel can then follow up on the corrected testimony. In still other circumstances, the deponent may fail to understand the nature of either questions or their answers, and those answers will need to be corrected for a fair determination of the case.

For that reason—discovery orders to the contrary—ethical lawyers agree not to object to the defending counsel's interruption that is necessary to fairly litigate the case. The authors believe that such an agreement is appropriate as a matter of professionalism and within the ambit of permissible alteration of the rules of discovery as contemplated in Rule 29.

iii. The Testifying Lawyer

The testifying lawyer, in addition to obstructing the flow of testimony, not only violates Civil Procedure Rule 30(d)(1), but also violates the law of ethics. The tactic exists solely for the testifying lawyer to substitute her testimony for that of the witness, thereby subverting any pretention to legitimate discovery.

Example: Defense counsel is deposing Professor Williams.

Defense Counsel: Professor Williams, you've told us that Professor Simonson visited your class and offered his comments in your first year at the Public Policy School. What other professional interaction did you have with Professor Simonson?
Plaintiff's Counsel: Excuse me, counsel. Do you mean one-on-one, in faculty meetings, in committee meetings? Your question is ambiguous, but go ahead Professor, if you understand what she's asking for.
A: I'm not sure what you want me to answer.
Q: What don't you understand?
Plaintiff's Counsel: I've explained the ambiguity.
Q: Answer my question, Professor. What don't you understand?
A: I had a lot of professional interaction with Professor Simonson in groups—faculty meetings, and there was a student-faculty committee that we were both assigned to. After he visited my classes, he would stop by my office from time to time to chat.
Q: When was the first faculty meeting that the two of you attended?
Plaintiff's Counsel: If you can recall at this time.
A: I can't say for sure. We had regular meetings each month, and several special meetings, and I know he was there at least some of the time—we didn't sit together or anything.
Q: Of the fall semester meetings, how many did you both attend?
Plaintiff's Counsel: She said she doesn't remember. Answer if you can.
A: I don't remember.
Q: Was it more than five?
Plaintiff's Counsel: Counselor, she doesn't remember. How can she answer the question? But go ahead if you can.
A: I don't know for sure, but probably . . . .
Plaintiff's Counsel: Don't guess; only if you know. You're not required to guess.
Q: Please answer my question.
A: I'd prefer not to guess.

This vignette demonstrates a typical behavior of testifying lawyers. Statements that recharacterize questions—"what they are asking is . . ." are telling the witness how to answer. If counsel gives a list of potential information, discourage that behavior by asking for all of what she suggests—one question at a time. So in response to the first objection, ask, "First tell me about one-on-one meetings you had with Professor Simonson." Follow up on any loose ends in the answer and exhaust the topic. Ask next about committee meetings, then faculty meetings, and exhaust the information for both, following up with an open-ended question: "What other professional contacts did you have with Professor Simonson?"

The statement, "if you recall" is not an objection, but signals that it is just fine for the deponent to answer with a failure of recollection. Although we usually counsel ignoring obstreperous counsel, it may be worth responding to the "if you recall" instruction by telling the witness: "Professor, I want to be clear with you about our purpose here. I am interested in everything you know about this case. Obviously, you can't know what you don't recall. I apologize if I was unclear. Can we agree that you only tell me about facts that you recall?" and get the witness to agree.

You can handle the "I've explained the ambiguity" comment by asking the witness to answer the question. Just don't transfer your frustration or anger with opposing counsel to the witness. The rule is, ignore the obstructionist behavior. It's difficult, but necessary.

We then turn to the series of interjections by defending counsel about memory, estimates, opinions, and guesses. In reality, you are entitled to guesses if that's what you want. Such testimony is relevant because a guess or opinion can reasonably lead to admissible evidence. Even if an answer is speculative, you are entitled to the answer. Counsel tried to get a range of the number of meetings that both the witness and Simonson attended, but when opposing counsel intervened, she dropped the matter. Persist instead, saying, "I understand that you are giving me an estimate, and if you're off by a few that's okay. Was it more than five?"

This sort of behavior is hard for a defender to keep up; it will often end under its own weight. You can speed that process by asking clear questions that have no room for objection. That is not to say that questions must be directed to a single fact. The typical open-ended question, such as, "What professional interactions did you have with Professor Simonson in your first year at the Public Policy School?" is legitimate as an evidentiary matter. It may be useful from time to time to revert to some short, fact-based directive questions with no room for ambiguity—e.g., "What was your interaction with Professor Simonson on the committees you were on together?" After a series of such questions, return to the broader, open-ended questions that are best for information gathering.

iv. The Instructing Lawyer

The instructing lawyer makes no pretense to legitimate objections. Her purpose is not just to interfere with questioning and provide answers for the deponent, but to act so aggressively and outrageously that deposing counsel is forced to abandon her information-gathering task. These actions are unprofessional and unethical and will, if persistent, draw sanctions from a growing majority of judges. Although a dying breed, we offer the following in requiem as there are still a few who persist in the behavior we demonstrate below.

Example: Consider the following from the deposition of Simonson.

Plaintiff's Counsel: Professor, we are now back on the record after our hour-long lunch break. Is there any reason, Professor, why you cannot continue to give full and complete testimony?

Simonson: No.

Q: Would you like to change or expand on any of your previous answers?

Defense Counsel: We'll tell you if he wants to change any of his answers. There's no reason to ask that question after very break. The answer is no, but go ahead, Professor.

A: No.

Q: All right, sir. When was the first time you had a sexual relationship with a member of the Nita University community?

A: Well, my wife is the granddaughter of the former president of university, the daughter of the former dean of the dental school, and a member of the faculty of the medical school and on staff a Nita University Memorial Hospital. I met her when we were both graduate students at Harvard.

Q: When was the first time that you had a sexual relationship with a student, faculty member, administrator, or employee of Nita University, other than your wife, after you joined the Nita University faculty?

A: I don't remember.

Q: Was it more than ten years ago?

Defense Counsel: The witness said he doesn't remember. Don't speculate, Professor.

Plaintiff's Counsel: I need to get a timeframe, counsel. Was it over ten years ago that you first had a sexual relationship with any student, faculty member, administrator, or employee of Nita University?

Defense Counsel: Other than his wife?

Q: Answer the question, sir.

A: Other than my wife?

Q: Yes, other than your wife. You know what I'm asking.

Defense Counsel: That's not a question. Your comment on my client's knowledge is argumentative and inappropriate. Don't answer the question. On second thought, never mind. There's no question pending for you to answer. Don't say anything until a proper question is put to you.

Plaintiff's Counsel: All right. When was the first sexual relationship with a person, other than your wife, who was at the time of that relationship a student, faculty member, administrator, or employee of Nita University that you remember?

Defense Counsel: If you recall a date.

A: I can't recall the date. I just don't recall.

Q: Can you recall a name?

Defense Counsel: Objection. That's too vague. Don't answer, Professor.

Q: Given that you can't recall the names of students, faculty members, administrators, or employees of Nita University with whom you have had a sexual relationship, other than your wife, are you denying any such relationships existed?

Defense Counsel: Objection. Assumes a fact not in evidence.
Q: *Answer the question, sir.*
Defense Counsel: No, don't answer the question in that form. The question assumes a fact not in evidence. He can't answer the question in that form consistent with his oath.
A: *Are you instructing the witness not to answer?*
Defense Counsel: I'm instructing the witness not to answer a question that assumes a fact not in evidence and therefore any answer he could give would create an unclear and inaccurate answer. Just rephrase, and he'll be happy to answer.
Plaintiff's Counsel: Are you refusing to answer the question, Professor Simonson, based on the instruction of counsel?
Defense Counsel: I'll not allow the witness to answer any question that will create a mistaken impression, on the record, of the facts of this case.
Q: *Professor Simonson, have you ever had a sexual relationship with anyone, other than your wife, whose name you can recall?*
Defense Counsel: Don't answer that question. It's outrageous and way beyond the scope of discovery. Witch hunts aren't allowed. We will seek a protective order regarding that question. Move on counsel.

The above transcript demonstrates the unsettling effect of such behavior on deposing counsel. Putting aside, for a moment, the conduct of defending counsel, deposing counsel backed off legitimate questions and attempting precision, asked questions that were so precise and so long that it was impossible to avoid something objectionable about them. She failed to listen to the witness, and in fact did, in the end, ask a question that assumed a fact not in evidence. That was the goal of defending counsel.

The prescription for dealing with this behavior is simply stated, but hard to accomplish. First, the video deposition serves as a deterrent. All of this is worse in sound and pictures than in words. Second, do not rise to the bait. Don't look at, engage with, acknowledge, respond to, or fight defending counsel. Most important, don't fight with the witness, not matter how provocative. And listen. Remember that as long as you continue to ask short questions in simple language, the record is your friend. Any judge reading a transcript—or better, watching video—of this behavior for more than twenty minutes will sanction the obstreperous lawyer and order a new deposition at the defending counsel's cost.

7. When can I obtain information that refreshed the memory of the deponent for testimony?

Evidence Rule 612 gives an opposing party the right to receive and review any document or other source used to refresh the recollection of a deponent, because that item will have had an impact on the facts of the case. Obtaining this information is important—you may find undisclosed documents or other potential exhibits, and you may also identify people who have relevant information who you might need to depose.

Refreshing material can be in the form of privileged attorney-client communications or attorney work product. Although the case law is a bit uneven—and courts do not like to invade privilege or mental impression work product—in the end, if counsel chooses to show such material to a deponent and that information refreshes memory for testimony, it is discoverable. This analysis of the interplay between the Federal Rules of Evidence, the Federal Rules of Civil Procedure, and the law of privilege makes good sense. The process of reconstructing memory continues while preparing for deposition testimony; a document prepared by the deponent's lawyer can influence that reconstruction.

That hierarchy of legal doctrine being decided, the question of when you have the right to the refreshing material remains. Many lawyers request all documents the deponent reviewed before a deposition. When defending counsel produces no documents, motions to compel discovery are filed. Rulings on such motions are inconsistent between courts. Some courts have decided that they cannot make any meaningful distinction between documents used to refresh memory and documents used to reinforce or confirm memory.

A second group of judges, when faced with the same question, determined that moving counsel only had the right to documents identified as having refreshed the memory of the deponent. Therefore, the right to production attached as soon as a deponent testified that he had reviewed material before the deposition and some of that material refreshed memory. The deponent, together with counsel, must cull through the documents and other material reviewed before the deposition, and then provide that information to opposing counsel. If the court granted a motion to compel before testimony was taken, defending counsel would need to provide the refreshing material before the deposition begins. If the motion was made post-deposition, and the deposition was reopened at the expense of defending counsel, deposing counsel could ask further questions based on the refreshing documents.

The last group of judges, whose position is now the overwhelming majority view, referred to the plain language of Rule 612. The rule provides for production of material that "refreshed testimony." There is no way to determine whether that triggering phenomena (the refreshing of testimony) happened until the testimony of the deponent was elicited. Of course, counsel could wait until the close of the deposition and then ask whether there was any material provided to the deponent that refreshed his testimony. This task, a difficult one to be sure—especially after hours of testimony about a myriad of facts—is unlikely to produce fruitful information. Instead, ask about refreshing documents at natural junctures within the deposition. When a witness has completed testimony about one of many events, demand production of any information the witness reviewed or that was provided to him that refreshed his memory about that event. This limits the request to a particular topic just discussed in full and is better situated to produce information.

Example: During the deposition of Jefferson the following might occur.

Plaintiff's Counsel: What else did you consider in reaching your evaluation of Professor Williams's performance during her first year on the Public Policy School faculty?

Jefferson: Nothing else. I have told you everything about my evaluation.

Q: Dean Jefferson, is there anything you reviewed or any person with whom you spoke that refreshed your memory about your evaluation of Professor Williams's performance during her first year on the Nita University faculty?

Defense Counsel: You have received in discovery everything that Dean Jefferson reviewed in preparation for her deposition. My conversation with Dean Jefferson is privileged.

Q: I appreciate that information, but let me ask you two questions: first, is there anything that you reviewed that refreshed your memory for the testimony you just provided regarding Professor Williams's YR-6 evaluation?

Defense Counsel: You have everything.

Plaintiff's Counsel: Nonetheless, Dean, did you review anything that refreshed your memory of Professor Williams's YR-6 evaluation?

Defense Counsel: Answer the question about whether anything you reviewed and anyone with whom you spoke refreshed your memory about the testimony you just provided, without disclosing the identity of anything that refreshed your memory.

A: There were several documents that you provided that did jog my memory about that evaluation. I did talk to my lawyer, but she didn't provide any new information. We just went over possible questions, including what we've just gone over.

Plaintiff's Counsel: Counsel, please provide the documents you provided to Dean Jefferson that refreshed her memory for her testimony today about her YR-6 evaluation of Professor Williams.

Defense Counsel: My culling of exhibits is mental impression work product. As such they will not be produced without a court order.

Plaintiff's Counsel: OK. But work product or not, we are entitled to whatever refreshed Dean Jefferson's memory as to her testimony.

Defense Counsel: File your motion.

This exchange demonstrates a proper request for refreshing documents. The witness has testified, and the request for refreshing documents is narrowed to that testimony. It also highlights the crossover between refreshing documents and attorney work product. The predominant view is that counsel's culling of exhibits, is, in fact, mental impression work product. It is also the prevailing view that work product protection claims for anything that refreshes memory regarding testimony fail. The issue is clouded here because, as we suggested in chapter six, counsel only showed the deponent information that had already been produced. While we believe this situation presents a close question, the rule in favor of disclosure would prevail, because counsel culled more documents than were discussed in deponent's testimony; the broader production can disclose mental impressions about the case, but only those that actually refreshed testimony.

8. Should I impeach the deponent during the deposition?

For practitioners of the traditional deposition, the question of whether to impeach a deponent—especially with information opposing counsel does not know deposing counsel possesses—is a close one. For advocates of the modern deposition, the question is not a close one. First, because the modern deposition assumes no trial, the factfinder will not have the impeaching material when considering the deponent's credibility. Second, modern deposition's video recording allows viewers to see the demeanor of a deponent while his credibility is attacked and preserves that impeachment for later viewing by a factfinder. Third, in all forms of case disposition (except summary judgment), the credibility of a witness is considered. Dispositive motion practice;[16] negotiations; all forms of ADR; and, of course trials, (judge or jury) are credibility driven. Finally, for certain forms of impeachment,[17] extrinsic evidence requires, as a foundational matter, that you confront the witness with the impeaching matter and obtain a denial (or attempt to explain away) before the document can be entered into evidence.[18]

The permissible areas of impeachment are only partially codified in the evidence rules.[19] They are character evidence under Rule 608 (witnesses and traits of honesty,[20] limited bad acts relating to truthfulness[21]); convictions under Rule 609 (felonies, any crime relating to honesty, within ten years of testimony[22]); and inconsistent

16. While judges are not ordinarily supposed consider credibility of a witness on a motion for summary judgment, the requirements of the law—and the reality of human nature—sometimes suggest the contrary. Rojas v. Roman Cathoilic Dioecese of Rochester, 660 F.3d 98 (2nd Cir 2011); Gill v. Teva Respiratory,LLC., 2017 WL 6614228 (D.Conn, 2017). On a motion to dismiss under Rule 12(b)(6), a judge must determine whether the claims of the plaintiff are plausible. Ashcroft v. Iqbal, 556 U.S. 662 (2009). A similar standard should apply on summary judgment, particularly where a higher standard of proof is required, as in *Matsushita*. In a close case, if the plaintiff relies on deposition testimony of a particular witness, and if that witness has been soundly impeached, a judge could use the impeachment evidence to find lack of plausibility. In summary judgment, a court must use the standard of proof required to find whether there is a material issue of fact for trial (e.g., proof by clear and convincing evidence required in certain civil claims). When deciding whether a deponent provides that material issue of fact, applying that higher than normal burden of proof, credibility of a deponent may very well decide the increased burden issue. Finally, when presented a relevant portion of a video deposition, a powerful impeachment could have significant impact.

17. E.g., via a document, another witness, etc.—anything other than cross-examination.

18. To impeach by inconsistent statement, you must give the witness an opportunity to explain or deny the alleged inconsistency as a foundation for extrinsic evidence of the inconsistent statement. As a matter of common law, extrinsic evidence of a witness's bias, prejudice, interest, and improper motive requires confronting the witness with the alleged infirmity and providing an opportunity to deny or explain it away.

19. For a complete analysis of the law of evidence of impeachment and its execution in examination, *see* BOCCCHINO & SONENSHEIN, A PRACTICAL GUIDE TO FEDERAL EVIDENCE: OBJECTIONS RESPONSES AND PRACTICE COMMENTARY 12th Ed. (Nita 2018).

20. Opinion or reputation evidence of a witness's bad character trait of dishonesty.

21. Cross-examination regarding narrowly construed acts relating to honesty.

22. By cross-examination or extrinsic evidence showing date, place, name of crime, and fact of conviction.

statements under Rule 613 (written and oral with witness to be impeached provided opportunity to explain or deny[23]). In addition, Rule 607 allows a witness to be impeached by showing bias in favor of a party,[24] prejudice against a party,[25] interest in the outcome,[26] improper motive for providing testimony,[27] conduct inconsistent with testimony,[28] and any other set of facts that show why a witness should not be believed, left to the sound discretion of the court. A witness may be impeached by either party.

The tactics of impeachment are beyond the scope of this volume. We refer you to Steve Lubet's MODERN TRIAL ADVOCACY,[29] which we consider the best available volume on trial advocacy. Examples of an impeaching cross conducted for a specific other purposes are provided in the following sections on obtaining admissions and theory testing

9. How do I use the deposition to obtain evidentiary admissions?

To begin, Federal Rule of Civil Procedure 30(b)(6) requires that certain depositions be taken for the sole purpose of obtaining what are known as solemn judicial admissions that are binding on a party for the duration of the litigation. We will discuss those depositions in chapter ten. Second, any testimony made by certain deponents, and/or under certain circumstances as defined in Federal Rule of Evidence 801(d)(2)(A)–(E),[30] is admissible against a party if offered by an opponent. Third, this testimony is intended to collect facts, not suggest the existence of undiscovered facts or to pose unsupported conclusions. We will address this questioning tactic in the next section under the heading of "Theory Testing."

Our current topic is obtaining "admissions" (or agreement) from a deponent that certain facts are true. These admissions may be, and frequently are, obtained from party deponents. In a broader sense, however, these admissions can and should be obtained from all witnesses when there are facts within their testimony that, as a tactical matter, are so important that it is worth the time and effort to amalgamate them in one series of questions for later use in the litigation.

---

23. Cross-examination showing time, place, circumstances of inconsistent statement; extrinsic evidence if witness is provided opportunity to explain or deny.

24. By cross-examining about facts that show bias in favor of party for whom testimony is provided.

25. By cross-examining about facts that show prejudice against the party against whom testimony is provided.

26. By cross-examining how witness will benefit in the outcome of the case.

27. Usually by showing some illicit reason one of the parties is providing in exchange for the given testimony.

28. By showing that the witness acted in a way that was inconsistent with his conduct—e.g., he claims that defendant defrauded him, but he did not complain to police or any other responsible person.

29. LUBET, S, LORE, J.C., MODERN TRIAL ADVOCACY: ANALYSIS & PRACTICE, 5th Ed. (2015 NITA).

30. Witnesses who statements are attributable to a party include individual parties; representatives of individual or entity parties; employees of parties during the course of employment whose statements are within the scope of employment; statements adopted in some way by a party; and coconspirator statements.

Obtain admissions at the end of fact gathering. Once you subject a witness to the confrontational and off-putting questions and style by which evidentiary admissions are often obtained, he is less likely to be forthcoming with new and helpful information. You will use leading questions to obtain admissions, seeking one-word answers with nothing volunteered; this is inapposite to the efficient fact-gathering question formula (open-ended question, topic-specific open-ended questions, journalist's questions). Second, questions seeking admissions may become more aggressive and probing and suggest of lack of credibility. Use this most aggressive form of cross-examination at some point in every deposition, just to test the witness's tolerance for such questioning and how he reacts—this information will be useful if there is a trial. Also, this rougher form of examination can convince party deponents that they don't want to repeat the unpleasant experience at trial and thereby provide some incentive to settlement—which is in the interests of all parties. Finally, your questioning about these admissions, with some end-use in mind, will be very close to a cross-examination; unlike in the fact-gathering and exhausting phase of the deposition, there are "bad" answers to be had, the opportunity for which should be avoided.

When the modern deposition is video recorded, your full range of cross-examination skills are on display. The tone and pace of your questioning and your attitude toward the deponent are portrayed. Likewise, the demeanor of the witness as he responds to this mode and manner of questioning is recorded. This can be telling, when contrasted with his demeanor during the fact-gathering phase of the deposition.

Example: The defense to the discrimination allegation is two-fold: the plaintiff was not qualified for tenure, and her tenure was not in the long-term best interests of the university. To bolster those legal defenses, the defendant would like to show that the plaintiff is responsible for her own actions and therefore at fault in not receiving tenure.[31] *Deposing counsel would seek this as an admission. Consider the following.*

Defense Counsel: All right, ma'am, we are now back on the record. Any corrections or additions?
Williams: No.
Q: All right to proceed otherwise?
A: Yes, I'm fine.
Q: Very well. You began the sexual relationship with Professor Simonson voluntarily, correct?
A: Yes.
Q: No force?
A: No.

31. The authors accept and agree that no matter what the legal claim or defense in a case, juries—at least—decide cases on the bases of responsibility, fault, and fairness.

Q: No intimidation?
A: No.
Q: Nothing unwanted happen that first night, correct?
A: That's right.
Q: Completely mutual?
A: Yes.
Q: You knew he was married?
A: But unhappily so.
Q: He was and still is married, right?
A: Yes.
Q: You also knew he had children?
A: Yes, older children.
Q: He had children, correct?
A: Yes.
Q: Yet you entered into a long-term sexual relationship with him?
A: Yes.
Q: You knew he had other extramarital affairs, correct?
A: Yes.
Q: He never left his wife for any of those women, did he?
A: No.
Q: Professor Taylor, your mentor, warned you of this?
A: He did.
Q: You did not take his advice?
A: No, I'm an adult.
Q: That's right; responsible for your own actions, right?
A: Right.
Q: Nonetheless, and despite his history, you wanted Simonson to divorce his wife?
A: Yes.
Q: You wanted him to leave his family home, where one of his children still lived?
A: Yes, he could visit.
Q: Visit?
A: Yes.
Q: In fact you demanded that he do so, right?
A: Yes.
Q: He refused?
A: Yes.
Q: It made you mad?
A: Yes.
Q: You ended the relationship?
A: Yes.
Q: You complained about Professor Simonson not leaving his wife for you?
A: Yes.
Q: You called him a liar, right?

A: *I did; he was.*
Q: *So you say. You also accused him of plagiarism?*
A: *Yes.*
Q: *For signing a grant renewal that you, in part, wrote?*
A: *Yes.*
Q: *It was part of your job at the Patterson Institute to do this sort of drafting?*
A: *Yes.*
Q: *You had drafted other grant applications, correct?*
A: *Yes.*
Q: *Professor Simonson signed those as the proposed grantee, right?*
A: *Yes.*
Q: *You never complained about not having your name on these drafts before, had you?*
A: *No, but it bothered me.*
Q: *But you never complained to anyone, right?*
A: *Right.*
Q: *Professor Simonson was well known in his field, right?*
A: *Yes.*
Q: *He was known for his academic prowess?*
A: *Yes.*
Q: *For his intellect?*
A: *Yes.*
Q: *For his scholarship?*
A: *Yes.*
Q: *I reputation for professional excellence?*
A: *Right.*
Q: *That reputation helped him get grants, right?*
A: *Yes.*
Q: *Respectfully, ma'am, he was much better regarded than say, you?*
A: *Yes.*
Q: *He had attracted over $30 million to the university in grants and otherwise?*
A: *Yes.*
Q: *You had not—didn't have the time or the name recognition to do so?*
A: *Yes, I was at the beginning of my career.*
Q: *That's right. And your professional association with Professor Simonson was beneficial to you. Correct?*
A: *Yes.*
Q: *He offered you the position of Associate Director of the Patterson Institute?*
A: *I earned that position.*
Q: *Professor Simonson agreed, correct?*
A: *He made the offer.*
Q: *That's right. And you've admitted he was a source of a lot of donations to the university.*
A: *Yes.*

Q: *Yet you decided to tell all the world—anyone who would listen—that he was a liar and a plagiarizer, right?*
A: *I told people I knew, and who knew me and him.*
Q: *That included people outside the school?*
A: *Yes.*
Q: *And people outside the university?*
A: *Yes.*
Q: *At other Public Policy Schools?*
A: *Yes, people I knew.*
Q: *Did you think that was helping the university?*
A: *It was personal.*
Q: *Right, you had no concern whatsoever about the harm you were doing to the university did you?*
A: *I didn't think about the university, it was personal.*
Q: *You didn't think—. During this time that you were thinking about personal matters, your teaching performance suffered, right?*
A: *Yes, I was upset.*
Q: *You missed an important publication deadline in a prestigious journal, right?*
A: *Yes.*
Q: *After a while you and Professor Simonson were able to have a civil professional relationship, correct?*
A: *Yes.*
Q: *He never retracted his offer for you to be the Associate Director at the Patterson Institute, did he?*
A: *No.*
Q: *You got a tenure report?*
A: *Yes.*
Q: *The vote of the committee was 2–1 in favor of tenure, and Professor Binder suggested to delay your tenure for a year.*
A: *He did, but . . . .*
Q: *Professor Taylor, your mentor, agreed with him?*
A: *Yes.*
Q: *He advised the delay, right?*
A: *Yes.*
Q: *Others advised to take the delay?*
A: *Yes.*
Q: *You refused, correct?*
A: *Yes, I was qualified.*
Q: *It was your decision not to delay and yours alone, correct?*
A: *Yes.*
Q: *No one but you made that decision?*
A: *Right.*
Q: *Now, during that year's delay that you decided against, your teaching would have returned to its normal level right?*

A: *Yes.*
Q: *No reason for it not to?*
A: *Right, I'm a good teacher.*
Q: *You finished and published your article that fall, true?*
A: *Yes*
Q: *And as you told us, you had stopped accusing Professor Simonson of being a liar and plagiarizing, as well?*
A: *Yes.*
Q: *You were civil?*
A: *Yes.*
Q: *You were collegial?*
A: *Of course.*
Q: *Every negative thing that was said about you in YR-2 would not have been applicable in YR-1, right?*
A: *Yes.*
Q: *You would, in all likelihood have received tenure, correct?*
A: *I deserved to be tenured.*
Q: *And in YR-1 you would have been, that's right, isn't it?*
A: *Like I said, I deserved it.*
Q: *Like you said.*

The admission sought—Williams's responsibility for not being tenured—is facially made. She is mutually responsible for a consensual affair; she was angry when Simonson refused to divorce his wife;[32] she made open and public negative statements about Simonson while understanding his importance to the university; she did not care about the university; she was responsible for her lower teaching evaluations and for missing a publication deadline; she rejected an offer and advice to delay her tenure vote; she understands that if she had delayed that vote, she would be tenured. All of this, put together from various parts of the deposition, shows Williams how a third-party decision maker might view the facts to which she has agreed. Further, she has experienced cross-examination by a previously very nice woman. Finally, the information, packaged in the examination, is available for viewing by a decision maker (together with the demeanor of Williams), who can view facts negative to Williams given by her in her own testimony.

10. How do I use the deposition to test the strength of factual and legal theory?

In the process of information gathering, you will seek witnesses and other evidence that flesh out the factual storylines for your case theories. Contained within those storylines are facts that had not yet been discovered when you created the

32. Without saying so, counsel paints Williams as a "home-breaker," for any factfinder who wants to go there. While this argument will be offensive to many, including the authors, it will be in the mind of some factfinders. These same facts go to a conclusion that Williams, in light of Simonson's history, had unrealistic expectations of her affair and Simonson.

storyline—every deposition is a search for those missing facts. Frequently, there are no sources that prove a hoped-for fact. Without specific sources, you must abandon some storylines and the legal and factual theories they support.

One possible avenue to reviving those case theories remains, and that is by making inferences from the facts available. We refer to the process of getting witnesses to concur with our inferences as theory testing. Although it shares a similar questioning style to obtaining admissions, theory testing differs in one stark way. Obtaining admissions seeks the witness's agreement with an amalgamation of specific facts already discovered, which can be used to support a desired conclusion. Theory testing leads the witness through inferences from known evidence. In other words, theory testing seeks agreement, through inference(s), with the conclusions themselves.

Example: Plaintiff has a theory that Jefferson's decision to, essentially, veto Williams's tenure application was not for lack of qualifications and not for any general lack of collegiality. Rather, Jefferson was concerned about Simonson's reaction to Williams's tenure—whether he would be comfortable serving on a faculty that included someone who had attacked his personal and professional character in so public a way and, most importantly, whether he might consider one of the many lateral offers he has received over the years to move on to a more prestigious school. He would take with him the benefits he brought to the university, both in academic reputation and proven fundraising ability. Plaintiffs have been unable to discover any direct evidence of this theory. No one has testified that a decision was made to get rid of Williams solely to make Simonson happy. Further, there is no testimony that Simonson asked anyone to do so. Consider the following from the deposition of Jefferson after all information gathering has been completed.

Plaintiff's Counsel: I want to turn to one final topic regarding your decision to veto Professor Williams's tenure.
Jefferson: I wouldn't call it a veto. University regulations required that I determine whether Professor Williams's tenure was in the long-term best interests of the university. Unfortunately, I determined it was not. I wouldn't call it a veto.
Q: Let's be clear, Dean—but for your decision, Professor Williams would have received tenure, right?
A: Yes.
Q: You prevented her tenure.
A: Yes.
Q: And you said it was unfortunate that you did so, right?
A: I don't know . . . .
Q: Would you like the record read back to you. No more than a minute go you said, and let's get a quote here—Mr. Jones, please read back the dean's answer when I asked her about her veto.
Mr. Jones (court reporter): "I wouldn't call it a veto. I was required by university regulations to determine whether the tenure of Professor Williams was in the long-term best interests of the university. Unfortunately, I determined it was not."

Q: *You said it was unfortunate. Do you want to retract your testimony? You can if you want.*
A: *No.*
Q: *You were the senior woman on the faculty, correct?*
A: *Yes.*
Q: *The first women to be tenured, right?*
A: *Yes.*
Q: *You were not close with Professor Williams, were you?*
A: *We did not socialize with each other.*
Q: *Other than your yearly evaluations of her performance, you never met one-on-one?*
A: *No.*
Q: *Obtaining tenure was made more difficult by that fact, right?*
A: *I think that's fair.*
Q: *Yet you never reached out to Professor Williams.*
A: *No.*
Q: *You did not mentor her?*
A: *No.*
Q: *You were not her champion, were you?*
A: *I'm not sure what you mean.*
Q: *Really? You never were a strong advocate of her as a qualified professional colleague.*
A: *No.*
Q: *Now, your relationship with Professor Simonson was quite different, true?*
A: *Yes, he was senior to me.*
Q: *He was a mentor to you, wasn't he?*
A: *Yes.*
Q: *He did champion your professional advancements correct?*
A: *Yes.*
Q: *He preceded you as dean?*
A: *Yes.*
Q: *He left the deanship in YR-6, correct?*
A: *Yes, to become the director of the Patterson Institute.*
Q: *Also around the time he was sued by a former colleague of yours, Carol Martin, for gender discrimination.*
A: *I can't comment on that litigation—I have been told not to do so by university counsel who told me the litigation was sealed.*
Q: *You do know that Simonson had a sexual relationship with Professor Martin?*
A: *I understand he did.*
Q: *She was a junior faculty member, correct?*
A: *Yes.*
Q: *Simonson was her dean?*
A: *Yes.*

Q: *Simonson had the same tenure authority as you exercised on Professor Williams, right?*
A: *Yes.*
Q: *Did you think that relationship was appropriate?*
A: *University regulations don't forbid such relationships.*
Q: *I'm asking for your personal opinion. Would you think is appropriate to have a sexual relationship with a junior faculty member, whose tenure you controlled?*
Defense Counsel: Objection, calls for conjecture.
Q: *Not at all, please answer my question.*
A: *Me, personally, no.*
Q: *Now when Simonson stepped down as dean after just six months, no matter what the reason, you became dean, right?*
A: *Yes.*
Q: *Your mentor, Simonson, was there for you again, wasn't he?*
A: *He supported my candidacy.*
Q: *To the exclusion of all other candidates, right?*
A: *That's correct.*
Q: *You were grateful for his support?*
A: *I was.*
Q: *Given his position in the university, his singular support of you carried a great deal of weight, right?*
A: *I assume so.*
Q: *Well, you got the job; first woman dean of the Public Policy School. Congratulations.*
A: *Thank you.*
Q: *Let's look at Simonson's influence that was used in your favor. Simonson is the best known member of your faculty, correct?*
A: *Probably so.*
Q: *He has more publications?*
A: *Yes.*
Q: *He has served on Presidential Commissions?*
A: *Yes.*
Q: *He has testified before Congress and various state legislatures?*
A: *Yes.*
Q: *He has attracted a lot of money to the university?*
A: *Yes.*
Q: *Over $30 million, right?*
A: *I haven't added it up.*
Q: *Well, I have, and Professor Simonson has so testified—will you accept at least his calculation as accurate?*
A: *Yes, he would know.*
Q: *And without "adding it up," you also knew how important his fundraising was to the university?*

A: *Of course.*
Q: *You knew about the sexual relationship between Professor Williams and Simonson, correct?*
A: *They made no secret of it.*
Q: *Simonson was also Williams's employer at the Patterson Institute.*
A: *Yes.*
Q: *Had ultimate control of her employment there.*
A: *Yes.*
Q: *Just like your control over tenure as dean.*
A: *Yes.*
Q: *You've told us you would not think a sexual relationship between you and a junior faculty member whose tenure you controlled would be appropriate?*
A: *Right.*
Q: *Did you think Simonson's relationship with Professor Williams was appropriate?*
A: *They were consenting adults.*
Q: *True enough, but do you think it was appropriate in light of his control over her employment?*
A: *Well . . . it wasn't my place to judge.*
Q: *Did you ever talk to your friend and mentor about your opinion as to the appropriateness of his relationship with Williams?*
A: *No, it wasn't my place.*
Q: *Even as a friend?*
A: *I was also his dean.*
Q: *For whatever reason, you never told him that you thought it inappropriate to have a sexual relationship with his employee?*
A: *I did not.*
Q: *So you condoned the relationship, at least by silence, right?*
A: *I never said anything one way or the other.*
Q: *Never gave him any reason to end an inappropriate (to you, personally) relationship?*
A: *No, as I said it was not my place. He was acting within university regulations.*
Q: *Was it also not your place to criticize Simonson because you were also junior to him in prestige and sheer dollar value to the university?*
A: *I've answered your question.*
Q: *Not sure you have; let me ask it another way. Within the university, Simonson was an important figure, right?*
A: *He was.*
Q: *You became aware that Williams broke off her relationship with Simonson?*
A: *It ended.*
Q: *Professor Williams was upset?*
A: *She was.*

Q: *She called Professor Simonson a liar, claiming that he had promised to divorce his wife and reneged on that promise?*
A: *She said that.*
Q: *And if Simonson had promised to do something he had no intention to do, that would make him a liar, right?*
A: *Or he just changed his mind.*
Q: *She also complained that her authorship on grant applications was not acknowledged by Simonson when he signed the applications?*
A: *She accused David of plagiarism.*
Q: *Plagiarism is the unacknowledged adoption of someone else's words, thoughts, etc., as your own, correct?*
A: *Yes, but these were grant applications, not articles.*
Q: *Nonetheless, Simonson did adopt Professor Williams's words and thoughts as his own?*
A: *It's common and accepted practice for junior faculty to write these applications under the supervision of senior faculty, who then signs the grant application.*
Q: *Please answer my question. Did Simonson did adopt Professor Williams's words and thoughts as his own?*
A: *Well . . . yes.*
Q: *At any rate, Simonson was, of course, upset about what Williams said about him?*
A: *He was.*
Q: *You were well aware of his displeasure?*
A: *Yes.*
Q: *He had some unkind words to say about Professor Williams as well?*
A: *Only privately, and not outside of the Public Policy School community.*
Q: *You were concerned about Williams's statements about Simonson, especially outside the university.*
A: *I was.*
Q: *You were concerned about the effect this situation was having on your faculty?*
A: *I was.*
Q: *Were you also concerned that Simonson would be so unhappy with his situation at your school that he would leave to another university?*
A: *I don't think it would have come to that, but it was a possibility.*
Q: *Simonson could have done so if he chose?*
A: *Yes, he would be a desirable addition to any Public Policy School faculty.*
Q: *Partially because of the money he would bring?*
A: *Yes.*
Q: *And he would take that money from what would normally go to Nita University, right?*
A: *If that occurred.*

Q: But you made sure that never happened, correct?
A: I made my best professional judgment.
Q: And in your mind, you balanced the value of a young, rising academic, Professor Williams, and the value you have told us about of Professor Simonson, and that balance was easy for you.
A: Not easy, and that wasn't my calculus.
Q: That's right, you called it lack of collegiality n Professor Williams's part.
A: It was.
Q: Let me show you the very first exhibit shown to anyone in the depositions in this case. Let's display Exhibit 1 on Dean Jefferson's monitor (and everyone else's).
Q: Dean, you recognize Exhibit 1 as the Nita University Regulations Regarding Tenure and Promotion, correct? I am handing you a telestrator marker. I want you to read Exhibit 1 to yourself. Each time you see the word "collegiality" in Exhibit 1, please circle it with the telestrator marker.
Defense Counsel: Let's go off the video record while Dean Jefferson reads the exhibit.
Plaintiff's Counsel: No, just let is run, this won't take long.
Q: Go ahead, Dean, read and circle.
[After ninety seconds]
A: I'm done
Q: No circles on Exhibit 1, right?
A: Right, it's envisioned in—
Q: Yes, I know; the "long-term interests of the university." So you claim.
A: Yes.
Q: So in Nita University, true statements by a junior faculty member that upset an influential senior faculty member gets you fired?
A: That's not fair.
Q: You're right; fairness had no place in this episode.

The above vignette demonstrates the process of building a factual theory based on an inference. As a generic matter, however, here are some words of warning regarding theory testing. All of the facts that lead to a theory-verifying inference must already be in the record. You are attempting to get an opposing witness—either a party or someone associated with a party—to acknowledge those facts and agree with an inference based on the persuasive force of the presentation of the amalgamation of those facts. During that process, you provide the witness with the opportunity to modify or qualify that factual predicate, with the potential of weakening the theory. It may be best to stop at the cross-examination phase, confirming the facts that lead to your theory and arguing for the inference either in writing or orally in the process of dispute resolution. But if you are confident enough in your theory, take the advantage and crystalize it—this is most useful if the decision makers of the opposing party might not appreciate the strength of your case theory, if they base it solely on the factual record. Also, arguing in favor of disclosing the inference you seek from the collection of admissions is that the deponent has been prepared by counsel for the oncoming onslaught; what you are eliciting are unfiltered conclusions from an unprepared witness who, at the time, it likely just a bit off balance.

The inference in our example is that ultimately, the dean chose Simonson over Williams. He was valuable; she less so. He had influence; she had none. The facts that lead to the inference are covered—closing off other inferences where possible, confronting the inequities of the situation, and suggesting that "collegiality" was just a convenient excuse to fire Williams.

Counsel would seek this inference in conjunction with an examination showing that Williams met all the university's requirements in terms of her teaching, scholarship, and service, thereby narrowing the inquiry to the legitimacy of the "collegiality" requirement. This is where the danger we spoke of above exists. All of the facts elicited in this examination are already available in the case discovery. The legendary Professor Younger counsels saving the ultimate point until closing argument.[33] We violate that commandment—and intentionally so. During this examination, Jefferson can change her testimony—or expand on it—and explode the theory by persuading a factfinder that her decision on tenure was not one she relished, but rather one that was mandated by the economics of higher education. This is the ultimate danger of theory-testing depositions. And at the bottom line, choosing Simonson over Williams on economic grounds is not discrimination. To be sure, it's unfair, but not discrimination. Plaintiff's counsel is betting that the defendants will not want to make this argument—it requires the factfinder to ratify an unfair process for their client to prevail.

The practice of law becomes more specialized every day. As such, every specialty practice will have other substantive deposition issues beyond what we have identified. Counsel in those specialty practices must solve the problem of how to deal with those specialty issues. Use practice group (public and private) resources—other attorneys will have identified and solved most substantive deposition issues arising in that specialty practice. They will share their own issues and solutions with others in the group. Make wise use of this bank of deposition-specific issues and solutions, whether you are a young lawyer or more senior practitioner.

33. Irving Younger, The Art of Cross-Examination 23 (Am. Bar Assoc. Section of Litigation 1976). This is also discussed in Irving Younger, The Ten Commandments of Cross Examination (NITA, 1975).

Chapter Nine

Information Gathering Depositions—Particular Form and Process Issues

We have been offering deposition skills training in law schools and law firm programs for their early practice junior lawyers for over thirty years. From this, we have seen the typical form and process issues that we have been called on to critique. They are endemic to taking depositions, and they deserve attention. There is nothing fatal about any of these typical form and process problems, but the goal is to streamline the deposition process by identifying issues we have both faced many times, along with the rest of the lawyers in the world.

1. You have described a goal of the information-gathering deposition being a conversation and not an interrogation. Can you explain how the language I would use enhances that goal?

We suggest the following, which flows from the concept of deposition as a conversation.

Use simple, every day, conversational language.

People converse; lawyers interrogate. When lawyers talk like lawyers, their language is stilted and often cumbersome. It reminds deponents that they're not having a conversation at all—they are being asked questions by a "hired gun," who is in search of information favorable to her client, information opposed to the interests of the deponent. Mixed into this is a curious phenomenon: ask any other person on this earth to clarify what they are saying, and they will respond with a short, specific statement; ask a lawyer to do the same thing, and she will construct a long interrogatory built on a dependent clause resting on another dependent clause. We will leave our hypothetical case to offer up the classic example from an automobile collision resulting in personal injury litigation.

Example: The deponent has testified that he was standing at the corner of Fifth Avenue and Main Street in Nita City at 2:30 p.m. on June 1, YR-2 (the scene of the accident).

Plaintiff's Counsel: Mr. Johnson, directing your attention then to on or about June 1 of YR-2, at or about 2:30 p.m., as you stood at or near the intersection of Fifth Avenue and Main Street in Nita City, what, if anything, unusual happened with regard to the flow of traffic as you observed it on that date, time, and place that brings you to court today?

AS OPPOSED TO

Plaintiff's Counsel: What happened?

In an apparent attempt to create a crystal clear record, deposing counsel unnecessarily conditions the witness's next answer with convoluted, conditional language. First, the "on or about" construction adds nothing but encumbering the record—it makes the simple complex and equivocal.

The same is true for the "if anything" tag on the end of a perfectly good question. There is no functional difference between "what happened" and "what, if anything, happened." If nothing happened, the witness can say "nothing happened." If something happened, the simple question will get an informative answer while helping achieve the conversational tone you want.[1]

The first version of the question asks for only the "unusual." What if car accidents are frequent at this intersection, and the witness is a crossing guard who has seen lots of accidents? It wouldn't be unusual for him, but deposing counsel would still want to hear the crossing guard's answer. The point is, the insertion of the word "unusual" into the "what happened" question is just an encumbrance, just a lawyer trying to be more specific by being more complicated.

The "with regard to the flow of traffic" is just so many extra words that would never appear in a conversation. The witness is there to testify about an accident he saw. The witness won't need deposing counsel's direction to talk about the accident. If he strays off topic, then—and only then—should he be directed to the "flow of traffic."

And finally there is that verbiage, "that you observed at that date, time, and place." The witness can't testify to something he did not "observe"—but let's consider that word "observe." In real life, "observations" are only made by scientists and some law enforcement officers. Real people "see" things, and they will testify about what they "saw." By using the word "observe"—a word rarely used in conversation—instead of "see," the deposing lawyer drives communication wedge between herself and the deponent.

2. What is the harm in using introductory phrases for questions—it seems more conversational.

Many lawyers introduce their questions. They ask:

1) "Could you tell me?"
2) "Can you tell me?"

1. We have had former district attorneys tell us in both trial and deposition programs that they were trained that the "if anything" formula converted a leading question to a nonleading question. Not so. First the question "what happened" is not leading; it may assume a fact not in evidence that something happened (that was unusual), but really, something happened—we are in a later point in time. Finally, as evidence teachers with a combined eighty years in evidence classrooms who always had research assistants for such tasks, there is no reported case in American jurisprudence that says that attaching "if anything" to a leading question makes the question nonleading.

3) "Will you tell me?"

and our personal favorite

4) "Can you tell me a little bit about?"—which may actually have some substantive effect.

None of these introductions adds anything to a question. The real answer to a question "Could you tell me?" is "yes," "no," or "I could." What deposing counsel wants to know about is what comes after the introduction. The question is not "Could you tell me about your job duties in YR-6?", but "What were your job duties in YR-6?" The real question is superior in two ways. First, as a minor point, the "could you" question is inaccurate and imprecise, although it frequently produces the desired answer. The real problem is that these introductions ("could," "can," "will," etc.) make it acceptable—and, in fact, more likely—for the deponent to not dig into his memory to find the answer to the question. A question that suggests that information exists produces that information—"Who was there?" "What did he say?" "How did he react?") A question that suggests that information does not exist can produce less or no information. In other words, the question's form can become a self-fulfilling prophesy.[2]

The question introduction "Tell me a little bit about" contains all of the negatives described above, plus one more big problem. Deposing counsel doesn't want to know "a little bit about" anything. She wants to know everything. If a witness answered this question in a deposition and in later testimony provides additional information about the same topic, he cannot be impeached because the question asked for "a little bit." Counsel should cure this problem in the normal course of the modern deposition, where her questions should exhaust the topic and the deponent ends the information flow. Nonetheless, the phrase is just an introduction that we use because it sounds good, but adds nothing to information flow and detracts from the goal of the conversational deposition.

A final question introduction—"Do you recall?"—is most damaging to information gathering. The question, at best, is of no use—a witness will not provide information the he does not recall. More importantly, studies[3] confirm what many lawyers, including the authors, have always believed—it is much easier for a witness to testify that he does not recall when the question suggests that answer as an option.[4] That, of course, is contrary to your information-gathering goal.

2. Again we refer to groundbreaking work of ELIZABETH LOFTUS AND KATHERINE KETCHAM, WITNESS FOR THE DEFENSE; THE ACCUSED, THE EYEWITNESS; AND THE EXPERT WHO PUTS MEMORY ON TRIAL, 1991, reporting empirical research proving that word choices in formulating question matter and substantively impact resulting answers.

3. *Id.*

4. As Charles Becton, a great lawyer, then judge, then lawyer likes to say, "It is easier to avoid the truth, than to speak a lie."

3. Is there a particular form of question that encourages a deponent to search their memory for an answer?

Ask questions that assume the witness has information—such a question will extract that information. The question "Do you recall talking with anyone about Professor Williams's tenure in the spring of YR-2?" makes the answer "No, I don't" an acceptable one. The same question, rephrased to encourage recollection—"In the spring of YR-2, who did you talk to about Professor Williams's tenure?"—will yield available information, as will follow-up, information-exhausting questions on the topic—"Who else did you talk to about Professor Williams's tenure?"—repeated until the witness says "No one else." The "who else" questions are will yield information than "was there anyone else?"

4. Are there verbal habits that interfere with obtaining complete information?

There are. Every lawyer uses connectors between the last answer and the next question. That might be the source of the questions commented on in question 2, above. Other connectors take the form of unintended comments on testimony. "I see," "very good," "thank you" are the most common, along with the ubiquitous "OK." These unintended comments become habitual. "OK" before every question becomes monotonous and distracting to everyone but the lawyer using the connector.

In addition, because the connector takes the form of an affirmative comment, it is objectionable and inappropriate—again, unrecognized by deposing counsel. The classic example is from a personal injury action involving catastrophic heart-rending injuries:

Witness: I saw the semi-tractor trailer truck bearing down on a child pushing her own carriage across the street in a walkway. I yelled at him to stop; he never did. As he got closer, I shouted at the child to look out. She looked at me, saw the truck, but the truck never stopped. The truck smashed into the little girl and the carriage and sent both flying across the intersection into a row of parked cars. The little girl screamed, then went silent. She was dead.

Deposing Counsel: OK.

Really?

5. Is repeating part of the deponent's answer to the preceding answer a good tactic?

Often, it is tactically advisable at a trial or hearing to ask a question that begins with a portion of the previous answer. This technique is referred to as looping back, and you use it to emphasize important information in an answer by repeating that information. Repeating favorable testimony doesn't hurt, of course. It is also true that the technique might help you advance a chronology and continue the conversation through active listening. If you loop back in an incredulous manner, however, it might invite the witness to correct with overstated answer.

Despite these appropriate uses of the looping back form, be wary of falling in love with a question form. If you loop every question back to every previous answer, the formula loses its impact.

Example: Counsel is examining Professor Williams about his conversation with Professor Taylor when he advised Williams regarding delaying her tenure vote.

Defense Counsel: Did you provide any advice to Professor Taylor about the option of delaying her tenure vote until YR-1?

Taylor: Yes. I advised her I thought it was in her interest to delay the vote until YR-1.

Q: *After you advised her to delay her tenure vote until YR-1, what did she say?*
A: *She said that she did not want to put off her tenure.*
Q: *After she said she did not want to put off tenure, what else did she say?*
A: *She said that David was trying to screw her out of her position as the Associate Director at the Patterson Institute.*
Q: *After she said that Professor Simonson was trying to prevent her from obtaining the Associate Director's position at the Patterson Institute, how did you respond?*
A: *To be clear, before I said anything to her, she said that she didn't want to give up an opportunity just to assuage David's enormous ego.*

The first loop back was profitable, but the second led to unfavorable evidence for the plaintiff. The third, however, aggravated the deponent and engendered the worst of all answers. Of course, deposing counsel needs to know all of this negative evidence, but he does not need to enhance it by a habitual question form, which may have a net negative effect on building a persuasive version of the facts of the case.

6. What nonverbal cues do lawyers use in depositions that either help or hurt information flow?

Because depositions are formalized conversations, or interviews under oath, there are a number of things interviewing techniques can teach us about nonverbal cues.

a) Eye Contact—One of the best ways to inhibit or stop a conversation is by looking away from the person with whom you're speaking. Breaking eye contact communicates disinterest, boredom, or a desire to move onto something other than the current topic. Stated positively, maintain eye contact to encourage the deponent's flow of information in the deponent-dominated, conversational deposition. While doing so, use the best nonverbal facilitators: nod your head as the deponent answers, thereby encouraging the deponent to keep on talking.

When the deponent comes to an apparent end of an information flow on a particular topic, maintain eye contact—and silence—to encourage him to continue. Your silence conveys that you believe there is more information, and the deponent will dig deeper and frequently find more information.

b) Note Taking—Taking notes inhibits your ability to make eye contact. Generally, when you drop your eyes to take notes, you lose eye contact. And although some lawyers can take notes without losing eye contact with the deponent, the process is odd and often disquieting. This is a foolish way to disrupt the flow of information, especially since there has never been the need for extensive note taking at a deposition.

Even in the classic deposition using nondigital stenographic recording, the court reporter transcribes every word. Notes are only necessary to remind you to follow up on a new, uncontemplated line of questioning raised in the deponent's answer; to refer to some specific testimony provided by the deponent in another planned line of questioning on another topic; or to create a list of numerous items to which counsel wishes to return one by one.

In the modern deposition, with digital real-time transcription, note taking is obsolete.[5] Electronically tag testimony for later follow-up on the real-time transcript appearing on your monitor, with a note about what that testimony suggested to you at the time. Before moving from one topic to another (while requesting the court reporter to refresh the documents about the completed topic), review the real-time transcript to determine whether you need to follow up on answers provided in the just-completed topic.

One more comment on note taking. Scholars of interviewing techniques say that breaking eye contact during testimony to take a note causes one or more of three things occur. First, most witnesses will stop talking. Second, the witness will be encouraged to provide more information of the same sort about the topic under consideration when the note taking began. Third—contradictory to the second possibility—the witness will believe that he has provided damaging information and "clam up," resisting further questions on the topic. Whatever the takeaway by the witness, be aware that taking notes will have an unintended impact on the deponent's testimony.

Of course, you can take advantage of the modern deposition tools only if you are familiar with the equipment and can use it smoothly. Learn to use electronic

5. Questions and answers are transcribed and displayed on your computer monitor as they are obtained. Many lawyers find this distracting, much like multiple crawls on the bottom of the TV screen while the news is being reported in the main screen area. In the opinion of the authors, distraction is almost inevitable, and except for the necessary marking of areas that need follow-up questions, we suggest angling the monitor away from your line of sight to avoid distraction. In the ideal situation, a legal assistant can observe the transcript as it is produced and note where questioning needs to be expanded or narrowed.

tagging in the real-time transcription before taking depositions with this equipment—nothing will stop the pace of information faster than a lawyer mucking about with the computer system.

7. **Is there good way to deal with a witness who professes a lack of memory about the topic of a question?**

Some attorneys prepare deponents to say they cannot remember a matter inquired about if they have any doubt about the fact. In addition, defending counsel cautions them not to guess, speculate, or give an opinion when the question requires first-hand knowledge. Defending counsel tells the deponent that the deposing lawyer will make it seem that he should know the answer to a question, but if the truth is that the deponent does not remember the facts the question seeks, he should continue to say, "I can't remember." And that preparation is accurate and appropriate.

The fact remains, however, that from time to time, some witnesses will answer, "I don't remember," when the honest answer is, "I don't want to talk about it." It is true that if a witness persists in the refuge of lack of memory, counsel will have to be satisfied with that answer. Of course, if you, as defending counsel, know or have reasonable grounds to believe that your deponent's professed lack of memory is inaccurate, you have a duty to advise your deponent about the need to answer accurately—immediately, if the question is about a matter that will impact future testimony, or at least at the next break. If the deponent continues to claim lack of memory and you know the testimony is false, you have a duty to correct the record yourself. Before doing so, the authors suggest that you get the advice of the ethics partner or committee (if your practice group has one) or the advice of a lawyer you respect (former judge, law professor, etc.) before reporting lying under oath.[6]

Assuming, however, that the deponent accurately testifies that he does not have a current memory about the facts sought, deposing counsel should explore the professed lack of memory.

Example: The plaintiff is taking Simonson's deposition and asking about the circumstances surrounding his replacing then Dean Taylor as the dean of the Public Policy School.

Plaintiff's Counsel: Tell me about the process that occurred in YR-7 that resulted in your being appointed the dean of the Public Policy School.

Simonson: Dean Taylor's third five-year term as dean was coming to the end as of December 31 of YR-7, and the Board of Trustees advertised that the position was open. Dean Taylor had made known that he was willing and interested

6. We further suggest that if the advice is to divulge the false testimony, get that advice in a letter to protect your professional status.

in serving for another five-year term. The faculty, at that point, had a large cadre of faculty members who were fifty years old and older and an equally large cadre who were under the age of forty. I was considered a leader among my colleagues in the under-forty group. We pushed for expanding the curriculum and recruiting new colleagues who were interested in scholarship and teaching about modern governmental institutions. The over-fifties were satisfied with the classic curriculum we taught—and taught well—and which were the topics of their scholarship. A group of the under-forty group approached me and asked me to apply for the deanship. After some consideration, I determined that I could help expand the academic enterprise of the school by serving a five-year term as the dean, so I made my application.

Q: *How many other candidates were there?*

A: *There were two outside candidates from other universities, but they withdrew, and it came down to Marvin—Dean Taylor—and myself.*

Q: *Did you speak with Dean Taylor about your candidacy?*

A: *Of course. Marvin had mentored me, and while we had academic disagreements, our relationship was a cordial one. He was a frequent guest at events at my home, and me at his. He was not surprised that I was interested in the deanship and encouraged me to apply. He thought the decanal selection process would provide an excellent forum about the future direction of the school.*

Q: *How would you describe the tone of the process?*

A: *Aggressive, but professional and collegial.*

Q: *Were you aware that Dean Taylor was gay?*

A: *I was. He did not hide his sexuality—he has a long-time partner, Jeffrey, who is the curator of the Nita Art Museum—but he also did not flaunt it. To my knowledge, he was not active in the Gay Rights movement. People were less tolerant of alternative life styles as Marvin was coming up, but he felt his sexuality was a nonissue in his profession. I agree.*

Q: *Were there any of those intolerant people on the Board of Trustees?*

A: *I know of one notorious member from then, Geraldine Powers. She was vocally and persistently anti-gay; she is no longer on the Board of Trustees.*

Q: *Did you make sure that she knew of Dean Taylor's sexuality?*

A: *Of course not.*

Q: *Did any of your supporters do so?*

A: *I don't know. I hope not.*

Q: *Did you meet with your supporters about tactics to use to aid your appointment as dean?*

A: *Yes, individually, not in a group.*

Q: *Was informing Trustee Powers of Dean Taylor's sexuality discussed at one of those meetings?*

A: *Lots of tactics were suggested, many of which were not acceptable to me.*

Q: *Was informing Trustee Powers of Dean Taylor's sexuality one of the suggested tactics?*

A: *I don't remember.*

Q: *Are you testifying that you once knew whether you and one of your supporters discussed using Dean Taylor's sexuality against him and you just can't remember the event, or that you don't know whether the topic came up?*

A: *There were people among my supporters who were anti-gay, and they were opposed to Dean Taylor's continued deanship, in part based on his sexuality, so I don't want to say that no one ever discussed the topic with me; I just don't remember such a meeting.*

Q: *Is there any document or record of any kind that you could look at to refresh your memory about such a meeting?*

A: *No. I made no notes about those meetings.*

Q: *Is there anyone with whom you could speak who could refresh your memory of a conversation you had about using Dean Taylor's sexuality against his decanal candidacy?*

A: *I suppose someone might remember, but several of those anti-gay faculty members have left the faculty. Those prejudices are not part of either the school's or university's culture.*

Q: *Can you provide a list of the faculty members who supported your candidacy for the deanship?*

A: *Yes.*

Q: *Please tell me their names.*

[Assume that the witness provides a list and his recollection regarding identification of those people is exhausted.]

Q: *Let me show you a document that one of your administrators here at the Patterson Institute was kind enough to provide to my colleague while we have been talking, and I ask the court reporter mark it as the next exhibit.*

Court Reporter: Exhibit 94.

Q: *All right, showing what has been marked as Exhibit 94, which purports to be a printout of a portion of the Public Policy School's web page listing current faculty members. Would you read Exhibit 94 to yourself?*

Q: *Have you read Exhibit 94?*

A: *Yes.*

Q: *Does Exhibit 94 refresh your memory about other members of the faculty who you counted as your supporters in your decanal candidacy in YR-7.*

A: *Yes. Professors Czarnecki and Morella.*

Q: *Did either Professor Czarnecki or Morella suggest to you in YR-7 that you should try to exploit prejudice against gay people by trustees or otherwise to obtain the appointment of dean instead of Dean Taylor?*

A: *Definitely not.*

Q: *Were there supporters of your decanal application on the faculty in YR-7 whose names do not appear on Exhibit 94?*

A: *I'm sure there are. There has been a good deal of lateral movement by members of our faculty.*

Q: *Will you create a list of those faculty members who supported your decanal candidacy that you have not already identified and provide it to counsel over the lunch break—we can take an extra thirty minutes.*

Defense Counsel: We'll take your request under advisement. We can't guarantee production of such a list over the lunch break. If you want one, please send an interrogatory, and we will respond in a timely way.

Plaintiff' Counsel: I need production of the list after the lunch break, but if it is not possible, we will recess the deposition at the end of today and reconvene after receiving the list we've requested for any necessary follow-up questions.

Q: *Was Professor Andrews one of your supporters who was anti-gay?*

A: *Yes. He is out of teaching. I know he ran for Congress and lost. I think he is working with a DC think tank.*

Q: *Did Professor Andrews suggest that you tell Trustee Powers about Dean Taylor's sexuality?*

A: *I really don't remember.*

Q: *You knew he headed an anti-gay demonstration, focusing on Dean Taylor, outside a meeting of the Board of Trustees.*

A: *I did, but I did not condone it. In fact, I made several public statements that in my opinion, Dean Taylor's sexuality was not relevant to who was appointed dean.*

Q: *How many is several?*

A: *At least three.*

Q: *So you made at least three public statements that Dean Taylor's sexuality was not relevant to his seeking a fourth term as dean.*

A: *That's right.*

The above vignette presents a formula for responding to a claim of failure of memory. Ask about potential sources for refreshing memory. Produce any documents so identified—if possible, in time to examine the deponent in the current sitting. We suggested earlier that you depose parties who are used to being in control or giving direction at their offices where they will be comfortable providing information. If you've done so, documents that are identified for the first time can often be retrieved over a break. You should identify, interview, and depose—if necessary—people who may refresh memory. In this vignette, counsel requested a list from the deponent. The list may be incomplete, but the witness should be asked for the list during the deposition.

Once you have identified and retrieved those sources, show the deponent the refreshing documents as demonstrated above and confront him with circumstance or the names of people that you believe might or should be in the deponent's memory, despite his protestation of lack of memory. Frequently these suggestions will jog the deponent's memory. In this example, a person with vocal prejudice against Dean

Taylor based on his sexuality was identified, as were his actions. Finally, explore the topic about which the deponent claims he can't remember. Here we found out that Simonson made sure not to trade on Dean Taylor's sexuality by making at least three public statements that the fact that Taylor was gay was irrelevant—thus broadcasting the fact three times.

8. How should I deal with a witness who claims that he doesn't understand my question?

When trying to avoid testifying about a topic, deponents will often claim they do not understand your question. Sometimes the deponent understands the question and has information at multiple levels within the scope of the question, at least one of which he would like to avoid. Often the witness will claim ambiguity after defending counsel objects to an excellent open-ended question about an important topic that might be a problem for the witness.

Frequently, deposing counsel will attempt to clear up the ambiguity and make it "understandable" by narrowing the focus of the questioning and asking fact-specific questions contained within the penumbra of the initial open-ended question. By taking this approach, however, counsel has abandoned discovery of all of the potential information contained within the excellent open-ended question. If she does not ask a specific question about the information the deponent would prefer not to discuss, it may go forever undisclosed. To avoid that pitfall, we suggest the following routine response to a claim of ambiguity.

Example: Assume that Jefferson is being deposed about her decision to veto Williams's tenure.

Plaintiff's Counsel: I would now like to focus on how you decided not to recommend tenure for Professor Williams. What process did you use to reach your decision not to recommend tenure?
Defense Counsel: Objection, ambiguous. Answer, if you can.
Jefferson: I don't understand your question.
Q: What don't you understand about the question?
A: I don't know what you mean by process.
Q: You know the word, of course?
A: Of course.
Q: Well, what is your understanding of process?
A: In this context, the factors I considered in reaching my decision.
Q: Any other understanding of the word "process"?
A: No, that's what it means to me.
Q: OK. Let's use your definition of process. Tell me the factors you considered in deciding not recommend tenure for Professor Williams.

[Assume that, using the questioning techniques we have discussed, counsel exhausts Jefferson's list of factors she considered in her decision regarding Professor Williams's tenure.]

Q: *While considering the factors that you described in the Williams tenure decision, who did you talk to or communicate with in any way?*

[Assume all of the people communicated with in any form are identified, together with the content of those communications and their effect on the tenure decision.]

Q: *In addition to speaking to people about the factors you used in the Williams tenure decision, did you refer to any documents?*

[Assume all of the documents considered, and their effect on the Williams tenure decision are identified and explored.]

Q: *Have you testified to all the topics you considered, the people with whom you communicated, and the documents you review reaching your decision regarding Professor Williams's tenure?*
A: *Yes.*
Q: *What else did you consider in making your decision not to recommend tenure for Williams?*
A: *My own experience, of course, both generally and my experience with Professor Williams.*
Q: *What, of your own experience, did you consider in the Williams tenure decision?*

[Assume all experiences and their impact have been explored.]

Q: *In addition to the factors considered, people with whom you communicated, documents you have reviewed, and experience you have applied, what else did you consider in any way in deciding to veto Professor Williams's tenure?*
A: *That's about it.*
Q: *Is it about it, or it?*
A: *That's it.*
Q: *Nothing more?*
A: *Nothing more.*
Q: *So you have testified about the entire process you used in denying tenure to Professor Williams.*
A: *I have.*

As shown above, defeat the witness who claims ambiguity by:

a) making the witness identify the ambiguity, rather than guessing;
b) making the witness define a word she claims is ambiguous;
c) using, exploring, and exhausting information within that definition;
d) inquiring about your definitions and exhausting information within those definitions;

e) asking, again, an open-ended question about other matters that are within the definition and exhausting information about any definition(s) provided; and
f) obtaining agreement that the information about the "ambiguous" topic is complete.

This process provides reliable information and minimizes self-inflicted failure to identify a complete list of topics. It also helps train the deponent that attempts at subterfuge by professing a lack of understanding will not succeed—discouraging such future behavior.

9. Frequently when a deponent is answering a question about one topic he will raise an issue that I had not anticipated. How should I handle that situation?

The methods we have described in this volume are designed to explore all pertinent information that any witness can provide concerning a litigation. Despite having identified the legal and factual theory and prepared for the deposition, by employing the questioning techniques described in chapters seven, eight and nine, you will find that in most depositions, with most witnesses, unknown information will crop up. In most situations, the new information fits into the order that you has chosen for questioning the witness. Not infrequently, though, a witness will provide information that suggests an unanticipated line of questioning. We call that new, unanticipated information the "rabbit," and the required exploration of that information, "chasing rabbits." The chase, of course, must occur—the question is *when* the chase occurs.

Most lawyers are inclined to chase the rabbit as soon as it pops up. Partly because the rabbit was unforeseen, your curiosity may beg for an immediate chase. And frequently, the immediate chase is the best tactic. The rabbit just jumped up, it jumped up in a particular context, and the immediate chase strikes while the iron is hot. In addition, defending counsel may not have known about the rabbit either, and so did not prepare the witness to answer questions about it. The immediate chase avoids a break that would give defending counsel an opportunity to do so.[7]

The other tactic is to postpone the chase. Record the identity of the rabbit and the need for the chase for later reference. Use a written note or, preferably, mark your real-time transcript so that you have the exact context in which the rabbit popped up—ideally, a paralegal who is conversant with all aspects of the case will handle the marking. If you are subtle enough, defending counsel may not even notice that you've flushed a rabbit and the break-time preparation may never happen.

Postponing the chase gives you time to prepare. Compare the topic with other information available and determine how the rabbit fits in chronological storyline

7. Assuming the discovery order allows counsel and the deponent to communicate during the deposition about topics other than whether to claim privilege.

charts—does it support or harm your potential legal and factual theories? Pay particular attention to whether the chase will reveal one of those hoped-for facts that fills in factual gaps in your legal and factual theory.

On balance, we advise postponing the chase; you will have a greater opportunity to exhaust the topic, thus getting maximum value for the chase. In all candor, we confess that we have been drawn into the immediate chase, too tempting to postpone, more than once.

10. Is there one overarching piece of advice that will improve the results of taking deposition?

Actually two: listen, listen, listen—and follow up. We have independently experienced, when reading our own deposition transcripts,[8] failures to listen and follow up on the information provided in the deponent's answers. That is why this volume compiles technique after technique to use when preparing and executing depositions that make careful listening necessary and possible as well as preparing you to recognize the need to follow up on the deponent's answers. With complete preparation, you won't need to be looking for the next topic or question; formulaic questioning systems rely on using the deponent's answers to inform further information gathering. To execute all of the tactics and address all typical substantive issues, listening is key. The form and process issues in this chapter depend on those two directives—listen and follow-up.

Modern, technology-assisted depositions give you the chance to repair failures in listening by following up immediately, rather than weeks later when the transcript was finally available. With real-time deposition transcripts, you can review ninety minutes of deposition during a twenty-minute break. This gives you the opportunity to remedy the failures in listening and follow up on topics that you missed during the deposition, but are blatant in the instant review.

In the end, listening is a skill. Unlike other skills, experience may be an impediment to its performance. Typically, lawyers specialize in cases of a certain sort. The facts of one case blend with another, and the inherent assumptions that the current case is "just another one of those" makes listening harder—the assumption of redundancy lowers the likelihood of hearing something new when it comes. So what's the solution? Be on guard. Be happy. Our profession could be routine and redundant. Being a litigator allows us to experience new events with each case—as long as we listen.

8. Yes, we read rather than watch the digital video that we counsel. Unless called on to review the deposition taken by a colleague, we already have most of the information from the video, and reading depositions works better, at least for us, to critically analyze the facts.

Chapter Ten

Defending Depositions

1. What is the most effective overarching practice for defending depositions?

Most of what you can do to defend the deponent you can do while preparing the deponent for the deposition, as we discussed in chapter five. That process is one of the most important for producing a transcript document well suited to the deposition's functions, as described in chapter two. Prepare the deponent to give responsive answers, but not expand beyond the scope of the deposing counsel's questions. If you do not anticipate going to trial, you may have used a mock deposition so your witness could practice and prepare answers with ultimate uses of the deposition in mind.

Because most of today's depositions will be recorded, using digital technology, in both real-time printed form and by video recording, work with recording equipment so that your deponent becomes comfortable with testifying while looking directly at deposing counsel. The position of the videographer's camera will then have your deponent looking into the lens. Conduct mock depositions with a camera present and in the position the videographer will use so the deponent will become comfortable with a camera pointed at him—this is probably a new experience for the deponent, and needs it to be practiced to avoid camera-produced anxiety that translates into testimony-induced anxiety on the video transcript. In addition, identify demeanor issues that are reflected on the recording to cure them to the extent possible.

Deponent preparation is critical; once the deposition is convened, there is very little that you can do to impact the resulting discovery device, the deposition transcript. After all, you may use the ultimate tool to control deponent testimony—an instruction not to answer—only in highly limited situations. Moreover, it is unavailable when the deponent is not your client, even if you prepared him. Although many lawyers representing a party claim to represent a nonparty favorable witness "for the purpose of the deposition," we believe this claim represents a bizarre and fictional extension of the attorney-client relationship, even if most opposing lawyers are prepared to accept it. That said, as defending counsel, you have several functions to perform to help create a document designed for all of the uses of deposition described in chapter one.

2. What is the best room set up to defend a deposition?

Most depositions occur in a conference room in the office of deposing counsel.[1] The room is set up before defending counsel and her client arrive, but you can control some matters of set up to help keep the witness from being distracted from the task at hand.

First, even if a videographer is making a digital video record, a court reporter will be creating a real-time digital stenographic recording. The court reporter (deposition officer) sits at the end of the conference table. The deponent sits on one side of the table, closest to the court reporter and next to defending counsel and any support staff. Deposing counsel sits across from the deponent, along with any party representative[2] and any support staff. In multiparty cases, additional counsel will sit on the same side as the party with whom they are associated.

The videographer's camera is set up in back of and over the shoulder of questioning counsel, recording the deponent's head and shoulders. In that way, as the deponent answers the questions, he is also looking at the camera. All opposing counsel are microphoned, but whoever is questioning the deponent, be it defending counsel or a lawyer for another party, moves to the position across from the deponent, with her back to the videographer, thereby maintaining a recording where the deponent testifies looking at the camera.[3]

Take every possible step to avoid distractions for your client. A panoramic view of the city from the deponent's chair may be beautiful, but it's a distraction. Shades should be closed. Ask that distracting art work in the direct view of the deponent be removed; if this is not possible, switch sides of the table with deposing counsel to achieve the same effect. Finally, insure that water, coffee, or other refreshments are provided[4] so that the deponent will be comfortable while testifying. Consult with deposing counsel's office before the deposition to assure that the place where the deposition occurs has sufficient space for all participants (party representatives, support staff, other counsel) and is as distraction free as possible.

1. We have discussed other possible settings, including the office or premises of a witness, usually for a party who is a "boss," used to giving directions and being in control of the business setting. As we have posited, this environment makes information gathering easier because the deponent is in a place where he is comfortable.

2. It is an unusual case where a party representative actually comes to the deposition, despite the right to do so.

3. If there is no local rule about video recording a deposition (very unusual), insure that your deponent is positioned so that he is looking into the camera as he is answering questions. Averted eyes, in person or on video recording, communicates lack of credibility.

4. Normally deposing counsel will provide these; if not, send out.

3. What should my mindset be as defending counsel?

Although a step up from library research, in terms of intrinsic attorney interest, defending a deposition is not an exciting event. The process of taking depositions is repetitive and persistent, and it can be tedious. Nevertheless, you must be fully engaged in the process. Defending depositions is much more difficult than taking them because you must maintain extraordinary concentration while doing almost nothing, for up to seven hours. You must be alert for any unfair, objectionable, or forbidden questions in the midst of hundreds of appropriate ones. Football coaches are fond of admonishing their players to "play the whole sixty minutes." The same is true when you defend a deposition—you must "play" the whole seven hours, aware that opposing counsel may well try to slip in the very damaging questions near the end of the deposition when you and your deponent have started to relax and are already thinking about post-deposition activities and getting home.

Pay careful attention to deposing counsel's preliminary directives about the "rules of the deposition," especially with regard to taking breaks. Whatever those directives, make sure the deponent understands that he is free to ask for breaks in the deposition whenever necessary, as long as a question is not pending and you have not asked for a conference to discuss the possible assertion of a privilege.

4. Can my position at the deposition table impact my ability to best defend the deponent?

As already noted, you will be seated next to the deponent. Too frequently, the routine of the deposition encourages you to sit back in your chair during questioning. Although depositions are routine to defending counsel, for most deponents this is not a routine occurrence; despite your preparation, most will be anxious. Though there is little you can do to protect the witness in an evidentiary sense,[5] the deponent will consider you his protector. To provide physical assurances of protection, sit forward in your seat and in close proximity to the deponent, keeping yourself in the deponent's peripheral vision.

In addition to providing a modicum of comfort to the deponent, the position makes it easy to hold out your hand like a traffic police officer in front of your client when stating an objections or instructing the witness not to answer. The gesture is universally recognized, and the deponent will stop speaking while you make the objection or instruction before testimony to the offending question is provided.

5. Be sure to tell the deponent that objections are made at a deposition to preserve the matter for later ruling by the judge and that except in the unusual case where the witness is instructed not to answer, once an objection is interposed, the witness will be required to answer the question. Also remind the witness that the scope of the questions is very broad and might delve into matters that the witness might view as not pertinent to the lawsuit in which he is involved.

5. Can I consult with the witness during the deposition?[6]

Consulting with your deponent is governed by local rules or the case's discovery order, both of which may be modified pursuant to Rule 29. The discovery order typically controls the degree of consultation allowed between a party deponent and defending counsel during a deposition. It is common, but not universal, for a judge's discovery order to include a proscription preventing any consultation between defending counsel and the deponent once the deposition has commenced, with the exception of privilege issues. These orders are a hangover from an era when many lawyers intruded themselves into deposition testimony.[7]

The rules preventing consultation assume that defending counsel, and litigators generally, will create or limit testimony inappropriately if allowed to do so. We believe that most lawyers do not engage in such conduct, that most lawyers are ethical. We also believe that lawyers who trust in the ethical conduct of their opposing counsel, as should be the norm, are free stipulate that consultation with a client during the pendency of a deposition is permissible as allowed by Rule 29. Alternatively, an oral in-the-record agreement can accomplish the same result.

Even a discovery order limiting consultation does not prevent you from consulting with your client about whether to assert a privilege, whether the question invades a protective order, or whether to seek a protective order for the information deposing counsel seeks. The law and process of claiming privilege, seeking protective orders, and instructing the witness not to answer will be covered later in this chapter.

You have an ethical duty to ensure that your client's testimony is not false or misleading, and orders limiting consultation do not prevent you from consulting as necessary to avoid false or misleading testimony.[8] If your witness has—inadvertently or otherwise—provided false or misleading information, it is your duty to correct the record. Do this during scheduled breaks; doing so is easier when real-time digital transcription is available. If, after you review the transcript and consult with your client, you determine that a previous answer must be clarified or corrected, have your client do so; when the deposition resumes, state for the record that you consulted with the deponent and have determined that he misspoke (or misunderstood a question, provided incomplete testimony, or provided information that may be unclear). Identify the testimony that needs correcting and ask the deponent the necessary questions to clarify or correct the previous testimony.

6. We have previously discussed this issue in chapter nine, but it is so particular to defending depositions that we repeat it, at least in part, here as we contemplate readers will reference this part independently of other portions of this volume.

7. We have discussed obstreperous defending counsel in chapter nine.

8. Correcting testimony is discussed in chapter six.

6. What stipulations should defending counsel make for the deposition?

At most depositions, the following exchange occurs before the taking of testimony.

Defending Counsel: Before we get started, Lynn, can we agree to the usual stipulations?
Deposing Counsel: That will be fine, Mary. I agree to the usual stipulations.

What has just happened? What are the stipulations? The answer lies not in the practice of either lawyer, but in what court reporter understands "usual" to mean. The court reporter will list in the deposition transcript that he believes to be the usual stipulations. Most lawyers believe the usual stipulations regarding making and meeting objections to be that all objections except to the form of the question or responsiveness of the answers of the witness are reserved until the deposition is offered in evidence at trial or other proceeding.[9] This may be a wise stipulation, but the default position contained in the Federal Rules of Civil Procedure is slightly different. Rule 32(d)(3)(A) provides:

> A(3) As to Taking of Deposition
>
> (A) Objections to the competency of a witness or to the competency, relevancy, or materiality of testimony are not waived by failure to make them before or taking the deposition, **unless the ground for it might have been corrected at that time**. [emphasis added]

The rule bears some careful analysis and consideration. You will normally call on a judge to decide the admissibility of portions of deposition testimony just before trial—when discovery is closed and when a witness is unavailable for trial testimony. As a matter of fairness and economy, if the objection could have been cured if made at the deposition, a judge may rule that it should have been made and find that the objections was waived because counsel failed to comply with the Rule 32(d)(3)(A). It won't matter what stipulations counsel entered into if the judge rules that their "waiver" was beyond the scope of modifying the rules of civil procedure allowed by Rule 29.

We have therefore taken a broad view of the objections that you and opposing counsel should consider during a deposition. Consideration of these potential objections is a guideline for an effective deposition. Frame the evidentiary issues to be decided by pretrial motion practice during the deposition. Demonstrate the admissibility of your evidence during depositions. This will establish the factual predicate for opposing in limine motions by showing the foundational requirements for

9. Modern practitioners general agree that one should not agree to a stipulation that absolves the deponent of the obligation to read, sign, and correct the deposition transcript after it is printed and submitted to the witness. To the contrary, federal practice requires counsel to reserve that right and obligation.

admissibility. If you oppose testimony or exhibits, use the same practice to establish that the testimony or exhibit in question is not admissible. Sometimes called "laying a negative foundation" (as discussed in chapter nine), this process sets out the factual predicate for pretrial in limine motions against evidence you want to exclude from consideration in motion practice, trial, or otherwise.

7. What objections must I make at the deposition to preserve them for later consideration by a judge?

What follows is a collection of the objections that are within the definition of Rule 32(d)(3)(A) and the method by which the objection can be "corrected" if the objection is made at the time of the deposition. For purposes of our discussion, we will describe the process of correcting an objection as curing the objection.[10]

Normally, counsel need only make those objections that can be corrected by further questioning of the deponent at the deposition. This is so even though strict adherence to Rule 32 would require defending counsel at a discovery deposition to object when she believes the witness lacks personal knowledge; though further questioning at the deposition could correct the problem by establishing the source of the witness's personal knowledge, this objection is not waived if you do not make it.

There is no questioning at a deposition that can correct a potential trial objection pertaining to relevance issues pursuant to Federal Rules of Evidence 401–411. These rules make various offers of evidence inadmissible if they are offered at trial for a particular purpose. For example, evidence of liability insurance is inadmissible if offered at trial to prove liability or damages. Such evidence is admissible, however, if offered for impeachment or some other admissible purpose. The admissibility of such evidence cannot be established by any amount of deposition questioning; therefore, such objections need not and should not be made at the deposition. Likewise, there is no point to objecting to an out-of-court statement on hearsay grounds where counsel's concern is that the statement may be offered for a non-truth purpose—there is no questioning at the deposition that would necessarily demonstrate the purpose of the offer at trial.[11]

Therefore, the objections, other than form-of-question objections, that should be made at an *evidence* deposition are the following:

a) lack of authentication (Rules 901–903);

b) lack of personal knowledge (Rule 602);

---

10. The authors have written another volume in which the statement of objections and the questions necessary to cure those objections are set out with particularity. *See* Bocchino & Sonenshein, Deposition Evidence, 2nd Ed. (NITA 2005).

11. The exception being the *de bene esse* or "evidence" or "trial" deposition. Thus, for example, at a *de bene esse* deposition, defending counsel who believes the deponent does not have personal knowledge of the subject of his testimony should object on that ground; deposing counsel then has the opportunity to ask the witness the basis of his knowledge.

c) lack of competency to testify (Rules 601 and 702);

d) lack of foundation for character evidence (Rule 608);

e) lack of foundation for habit or routine practice (Rule 406);

f) lack of foundation for lay opinion (Rule 701);

g) lack of foundation for expert opinion (Rule 702);

h) hearsay (where the deponent can establish a foundation that would bring the hearsay statement within one of the exceptions to the hearsay rule) (Rules 803, 804, and 807);

i) original document rule (Rules 1001–1008); and

j) privilege and work product.

At a *discovery* deposition, few if any courts expect counsel to object to any of the above evidentiary offers except for privilege and work product, which must be asserted. However, because the Federal Rules of Civil Procedure, strictly construed, require an objection where the deponent is able to provide the necessary foundation, be aware of the appropriate objections and be prepared to make them, at least in the absence of the traditional stipulation that relieves counsel of the need to object to anything other than the form of the question, assuming such a stipulation will later be held to be permissible pursuant to Rule 29.

Remember, however, that the trial judge is the ultimate arbiter of whether a question can be cured by a contemporaneous objection—he controls the admission of evidence at trial. Therefore, despite the usual stipulation that preserves all substantive objections until trial, a trial judge might find fault with opposing counsel for failing to object to a curable (by laying a foundation) substantive matter. This ruling happens when the deponent who could have laid the foundation has become unavailable at the time of trial and the proffer of his deposition. In such event, the trial judge could find a waiver of an objection to such testimony where the absent deponent was the only person who could lay the foundation for admissibility and defending counsel did not call the lack of foundation to deposing counsel's attention with a contemporaneous deposition objection. Thus, even if you have stipulated to objections only to form, the safe approach is to object to curable questions—even if on substantive grounds—when the answer is important. The better practice is to make objections to form and lack of foundation—or at least as to a lack of personal knowledge—unless you object when a witness answers a question for which he lacks personal knowledge, any later consumer of the transcript and the answer may assume that he testified from personal knowledge—to the detriment of the deponent.

8. What objections can be made to the competency of a witness at an evidence deposition?

The Federal Rules of Evidence cover a wide range of witness competency issues. The following issues fall within the rubric of witness competence.

1. Testimonial Capacity—Before a witness can give testimony in a trial, deposition, or other proceeding, counsel must show that the witness has testimonial capacity—as prerequisites to proving testimony, the witness must not only appreciate the necessity to tell the truth, but also have the ability to recall events and relate them.[12] If defending counsel objects to the general competence of the witness to provide testimony, questioning counsel can show as a matter of preliminary inquiry that the witness knows what the truth is and appreciates the necessity to tell the truth. Absent the objection, the witness is presumed to be competent. Object if you have reason to believe that a witness does not have the ability to recall events or to provide testimony about them; silence would waive later objection, as the competence of the witness is presumed. Object at the beginning of the deposition if you believe the deponent lacks testimonial capacity. If the lack of testimonial capacity becomes apparent during the course of the deposition, make an immediate motion to strike the witness's testimony on that basis. This gives opposing counsel the opportunity to develop testimony from the witness that cures the objection.

2. First-hand Knowledge—Before witnesses can testify, they must demonstrate that they have first-hand knowledge about the event or topic of their proposed testimony. If an objection is made that a witness lacks first-hand knowledge of the matters of proposed testimony, questioning counsel can ask the witness about the time, place, and circumstances where the witness attained the required first-hand knowledge, thus establishing that the testimonial prerequisite is met.

3. Character Witnesses on Substantive Matters (Reputation or Opinion)—A character witness may testify about the character of a party for substantive purposes by providing reputation or opinion evidence regarding the character of the witness—or specific instances of conduct evidence regarding a party, in the rare situation when the character of a party is an essential element of a civil claim or defense.[13] Cure an objection to the competence of such a witness by showing that the witness has sufficient familiarity with the party about whom the character evidence is offered to form an opinion; sufficient familiarity with other people who know the party to be able to provide reputation evidence regarding the character of the party; or first-hand knowledge of the specific instance(s) of conduct.

4. Character Witnesses on Credibility (Reputation or Opinion Evidence)—A character witness may provide opinion or reputation evidence regarding another

12. Fed. R. Evid. 601, 603.

13. Fed. R. Evid. 405.

witness's character for truthfulness or untruthfulness.[14] Counsel can cure an objection to the competence of such a witness by showing that the witness has sufficient familiarity with the other witness about whom the character evidence is offered to give an opinion; or sufficient familiarity with other people, who also know the witness about whom character evidence is offered, to be able to give reputation evidence on the issue of honesty.

5. Lay Opinion Testimony—A lay witness may provide an opinion only if it is rationally based on his perception in a way that is helpful to the jurors, but is not an expert opinion.[15] If a lay opinion is objected to, lay a factual predicate to show that the lay opinion is in fact rationally based on perception and provide sufficient foundation to show that it is helpful to a fair determination of the case. If the proposed lay opinion is objected to as being an expert opinion, that objection too can be answered by taking further testimony from the witness that either demonstrates that the opinion is not outside the ken of the lay witness or, in the alternative, that the witness possesses the attributes that qualify him or her as an expert witness.

6. Expert Opinions—An expert witness may only provide an opinion if it requires special knowledge, the witness has that special knowledge (is an expert), the opinion will help the trier of fact, and the opinion is based on reliable and verifiable data of the sort normally relied on by such an expert, and the expert used reliable principles and methods to arrive at the opinion.[16] Objections to an expert witness's qualifications can be cured by eliciting further testimony about them. Likewise, you can show whether a principle or method meets the *Daubert/Kumho Tire* standards for reliability with testimony that meets the requirement of those cases and Rule 702. Many judges, when considering motions to exclude expert testimony on Rule 702 or *Daubert/Kumho Tire* grounds, will want counsel to have explored all matters relevant to such a motion during expert depositions, thereby saving the time and expense of having an evidentiary hearing with the testimony of the very same witnesses who have already been deposed.

9. What objections to relevance and materiality are available at an evidence deposition?

Within this collection of issues, there exists a myriad of potential evidentiary objections, as follows.

1. Character Evidence for Substantive Purposes (Conformity)—Character evidence offered to show that a party acted consistently with a character trait is admissible only when character is an essential element of a claim or defense,

14. Fed. R. Evid. 608(a).

15. Fed. R. Evid. 701.

16. Fed R. Evid. 702, 703; Daubert v. Merrill Dow, 509 U.S. 579 (1993); Kumho Tire Co. v. Carmichael, 526 U.S.137 (1999).

such as in defamation cases.[17] As such, character evidence for conformity purposes is severely limited in civil cases. It may be, however, that the proposed character evidence is about prior acts that are performed so consistently and so regularly that in the face of objection, counsel could show that it is admissible as habit or routine practice evidence.[18]

2. Character Evidence for a Substantive Purpose Other Than Conformity—Character evidence showing specific instances of conduct may be offered to prove such matters—when relevant—as identity, intent, motive, opportunity, preparation, plan, knowledge, or absence of mistake or accident.[19] If an objection is made that a question regarding specific instances of conduct calls for improper character evidence, look to the nature of the claim or defense involved to see if any of the permissible uses for character evidence in Rule 404(b) are material. Alternatively, develop the evidence to show that it meets the quantum of proof requirements of Rule 104 and is not otherwise excluded by Rule 403.

3. Habit/Routine Practice—Evidence of instances of conduct that are shown to amount to a regular response to a repeated situation is competent to show that a party acted in conformity with that habit or routine practice.[20] A timely objection to prior act evidence will allow questioning counsel to develop the facts of the prior acts to show that they have occurred in the same way with such frequency, in response to repeated situations, to meet the requirements of habit (for individuals) and routine practice evidence (for institutions).

4. Subsequent Remedial Measures—Evidence of a subsequent remedial measure may not be admitted to show negligence, culpable conduct, a defect in a product or its design, or the need for a warning, but it may be admissible for other purposes.[21] If counsel lodges an objection, questioning counsel can ask whether the party who performed the subsequent remedial measure is contesting ownership, control, or feasibility of precautionary measures, thereby curing the objection.

5. Offers of Compromise—Offers or acceptances of compromise are not admissible to prove liability, or the validity of a claim, or the amount claimed.[22] The objection will allow deposing counsel the chance to cure by showing that there was not a controversy at the time of the offer (a precursor to invoking an objection to an offer of compromise) or that the objected-to evidence is admissible to contest the credibility of the persons involved or to negate a relevant contention of delay.

---

17. Fed. R. Evid. 405(b).
18. Fed. R. Evid. 406.
19. Fed. R. Evid. 404(b).
20. Fed. R. Evid. 406.
21. Fed. R. Evid. 407.
22. Fed. R. Evid. 408.

6. Payment of Medical or Similar Expenses—Evidence of furnishing or offering to furnish payment for medical expenses is not admissible to prove liability.[23] In response to an objection, counsel can demonstrate that the offer has another admissible purpose, such as bearing on the credibility of the party offering to make such a payment in light of the circumstances surrounding and occurring before and after the offer.

7. Liability Insurance—Evidence of liability insurance is not admissible to prove the liability of the insured or the proper amount of damages, if any, that are due in a cause of action.[24] To help cure this objection, ask whether the holder of the insurance is contesting agency, ownership, or control, or whether the fact of insurance creates some sort of credibility issue for the witness (e.g., the witness is an agent for the insurer of the defendant for whom the witness testifies favorably).

8. Privileges and Trial Preparation Materials—If a question calls for information that is privileged, object before the witness provides testimony that contains privileged information or the privilege is waived. Once counsel had made that objection, together with an instruction not to answer, and specified the privilege and its applicability as required by the Rule 26(b)(5), questioning counsel can cure the objection by demonstrating that either the privilege does not apply, that there has been a waiver of the privilege by some action of the holder of the privilege either individually or by an agent, or there exists some exception to the application of the privilege.[25]

If the question calls for protected trial preparation materials, Rule 26(b)(3) employs a similar process. Make the objection, follow up with an instruction not to answer. At that point, opposing counsel has the opportunity to show that the material in question does not fall within the trial-preparation protection of Rule 26 or a sound reason exists for invading that protection, such as the evidence not being available to deposing counsel by other reasonable means.

9. Expert Opinions (Reliability of Theory/Methodology)—A qualified expert witness may only give opinion testimony if it is based on sufficient data and the scientific principles relied on and the methodology used are reliable.[26] Cure an objection to the competence of an expert opinion by showing compliance with these Rule 702 and the *Daubert/Kumho Tire* requirements—a) the theory or methodology has been tested; b) the theory applied or the methodology used has been published and subject to peer review; c) the known error rate for the methodology;

23. Fed. R. Evid. 409.

24. Fed. R. Evid. 411.

25. For example, if there is a claim of physician-patient privilege and the plaintiff/patient has put his medical condition in issue, that privilege will be waived. In the case of a claim of attorney-client privilege, questioning could show that the communication is excepted from the claimed privilege because the communication was made for the purpose or in furtherance of a crime or fraud.

26. Fed. R. Evid. 702.

d) the standards and controls for using the methodology; e) the theory or methodology is generally accepted; or f) any other indicia of the reliability of the theory or methodology.

10. Expert Opinions (Bases)—An expert opinion can be based on information and data of a type that is reasonably relied on by experts in a particular field, but that data or information may only be made known to a factfinder if the data or information is otherwise admissible.[27] An objection to the competence of bases evidence relied on by an expert will allow questioning counsel to explore whether the data or information is considered reliable within the expert's field. The objection can be further cured by showing that the relied on data or information is otherwise admissible and may be revealed to jurors.

11. Hearsay—The hearsay rule precludes admission of out-of-court statements offered for the truth of their content.[28] Cure an objection to the admissibility of such a statement by showing that a) the statement is not offered for the truth of the content of the statement, but for some other admissible purpose; and b) the statement meets the requirements of nonhearsay statement, admissible for the truth of the content of the statement;[29] or meets an exception to the hearsay rule.[30]

12. Authentication (Voices)—A witness may testify about admissible oral statement of another person, once it is established that the witness can authenticate the voice of the other person.[31] An objection to authentication will allow the questioning counsel to demonstrate that the witness is familiar with the voice of the other person or that there is sufficient circumstantial evidence to identify the voice of the person. Such familiarity may be obtained either before or after the communication in issue and may be acquired solely for the purposes of litigation.

13. Authentication (Instruments)—An instrument such as a writing, document, photograph, or audio or video recording is admissible only if its identity and authorship can be established.[32] An objection to the authentication of an instrument can be cured by showing sufficient evidence to prove that the instrument is what it purports to establish its identity and authorship. If authentication of the instrument depends on familiarity of handwriting, that familiarity cannot have been acquired for the purpose of litigation.

27. Fed. R. Evid. 703.

28. Fed. R. Evid. 801, 802.

29. Fed. R. Evid. 801(d).

30. Fed. R. Evid. 803, 804, 807.

31. Fed. R. Evid. 901.

32. Fed R. Evid. 901. In addition to being authentic, an instrument must be relevant and comply with the hearsay and original document rules to be admissible at trial. In some instances, an instrument will also present issues of privilege.

14. Original Documents Rule—To prove the contents of a document (including writings, recordings, or photographs) where the contents of that document are directly in issue, the proponent must produce an original of the document, unless its production is excused.[33] An original documents rule objection can be cured by showing a) the rule does not apply to the document in question; b) the document is an admissible duplicate; or c) the production of the original document is excused.

10. What are the objections to the form of questions or answer?

By the clear terms of Rule 32(d)(3)(A), objections to the form of questions or answers at a deposition are waived unless made at the time of deposition. These objections are made appropriate at a deposition by the terms of the Rule 30(c), which provide that the examination of witnesses may proceed as if at trial. The following are the generally recognized objections as to the form of the question or answer. It should be noted that except for Federal Rule of Evidence 611(c) regarding leading questions, there is no federal rule that governs these objections except Rule 611(a), which gives courts the general authority to regulate the mode of witness questioning. Procedurally, counsel must make objections to the form of a question before the deponent answers; once the objection is made, the deponent answers the question. Deposing counsel has the opportunity to rephrase, but need not do so to obtain an answer to a potentially form-impaired question.

It is important to emphasize that objecting to the form of a question is a two-edged sword. As we discussed in chapter five on witness preparation, you prepared your deponent to listen carefully to your objections to the form of the question, because these questions present some danger of resulting in unclear, imprecise answers—or answers that leave a false impression or inference of the deponent's testimony. A properly prepared deponent should think about the question, as asked, and be sure that he clarifies any potential misimpression that might arise in his response to the form-objectionable question.

At the same time, deposing counsel faces danger from questions that are faulty in their form—faulty questions result in unclear and otherwise faulty information from the witness. In other words, objections to the form of a question provide a road map to make deposing counsel a better gatherer of information.[34] If when deposing you are confronted with a form objection, pay attention and decide whether you can ask a better question that enhances the value of the deponent's answer.

---

33. Fed R. Evid. 1000—In addition to being the original, a document must be relevant, authentic, and comply with the hearsay rule to be admissible. In some instances a document will also present issues of privilege.

34. Not necessarily the goal of defending counsel. We suggest, however, that the modern deposition gets its value from providing accurate information in the most usable form for case disposition, so objections that further that goal by showing questioning counsel a better way of inquiring, although counterintuitive, may actually be of long-term benefit.

1. Leading—Although deposing counsel can ask an adverse party witness leading questions in a deposition, they can suggest the desired answer to the deponent in such a way that it would be unclear whether the lawyer or the witness is testifying. Leading questions are generally not allowed on direct examination, but are allowed on cross-examination.[35] The party who is taking a deposition is generally considered to be conducting a direct examination, thus with a witness other than an opposing party or a person associated with the opposing party, questions should be nonleading. To preserve the objection, make it at the deposition. Leading questions on direct examination are permitted when examining adverse parties, witnesses associated with the adverse party, and hostile witnesses. In addition, leading questions are permitted for preliminary matters, such as laying the foundation for introduction of an exhibit or where they are necessary to develop the witness's testimony. Leading questions are generally permitted on cross-examination, except where the witness is a party, or associated with a party, and is being examined by that party's counsel. For that reason, if you are defending the deposition of a party you represent and choose to ask questions at the end of the testimony taken by deposing counsel, be sure to ask nonleading questions. Cure an objection to a leading question by rephrasing the question or demonstrating that the leading question is necessary to adequately develop the testimony of the witness.

2. Ambiguous/Vague—An ambiguous or vague question is one that is susceptible to at least two interpretations or is so vague or unintelligible that it either confuses the deponent or that a response to the question will create an unclear record. The objection can be cured by rephrasing the question or by demonstrating that the witness understands the question.

3. Argumentative—An argumentative question does not seek information from the witness, but rather makes an argument regarding the facts of the case in the guise of a question, hoping the witness agrees. Counsel will ask argumentative question to get the witness to agree to inferences drawn from the facts. For that reason, the objection is frequently accompanied by an objection that the question calls for inadmissible lay opinion or conjecture. Counsel can cure the objection by rephrasing the question to seek facts versus inferences. Of course, counsel may ask for inferences in search of admissible evidence—the objection merely precludes later admissibility of the conjectured response.

4. Asked and Answered—Object to a question as asked and answered when it calls for the deponent to repeat testimony previously provided to the same question by deposing counsel. This objection can also be stated as calling for cumulative evidence. The objection is cured by making it clear that the thrust of the question is different from what has already been asked during the deposition. Some counsel will ask an already asked question in a different way to test the credibility of the witness

35. Fed. R. Evid. 611(c).

and the information he has provided. Because it is often used to move the deponent off his story, make this objection to remind the witness that he has already answered the question fully and accurately. Be aware, however, some district courts hold that the "asked and answered" objection is inappropriate at a deposition.

5. Assuming Facts Not in Evidence—Object if the question assumes, in the asking, facts that have not already been proved through the testimony of the deponent or by other competent evidence. Counsel can cure the objection by asking the witness about the fact that was assumed in the objected-to question and verifying that the witness knows the fact, then follow up with the main body of the objected-to question. This objection can also be stated as "objection, misleading."

6. Compound Questions—Object if the question asks for two or more items of information at the same time. The problem here is that either it is impossible to understand the meaning of the answer to the question or the answer will create a misleading or confusing record of the deponent's testimony. Cure the objection by breaking the component parts of the question into single fact inquiries.

7. Misquoting the Witness—Object if the question misstates the previous testimony of the deponent. Counsel can cure the objection by having the witness repeat earlier testimony or by having previous testimony of the witness read back to clarify what was said.

8. Narratives (Questions and Responses)—Object if a question is overbroad. A question that calls for a narrative creates a danger that a deponent will fail to include all of the information within the broad scope of the question, making it difficult to be sure that the answer is complete. You can also object to the narrative form of the answer, which makes it difficult to interpose timely substantive objections to the broad and often-times rambling testimony of the deponent. In depositions, questions that call for narrative responses are good starting points for discovery about a particular topic. The danger of the objection is that more specific questions will not elicit all relevant information about a topic. If the responses fail to elicit everything you want opposing counsel to know about those facts, you can question the witness at the end of the deposition to exhaust the topic.

9. Nonresponsive Answers—Object if a deponent's answer exceeds the scope of the question or fails to respond to the question, and be sure to follow up with a motion to strike. If, however, the answer was nonresponsive, but provided relevant information, defending counsel can follow up those matters at the end of the deposition. Unless deposing counsel intends to use the deposition testimony of a witness who responds outside the question for a particular, narrow purpose, and the volunteered response is otherwise inadmissible, the motion to strike has no legal or tactical effect.

There is a key distinction between the objections that must be made at a discovery deposition and those that must be made at an evidence, or *de bene esse* (to preserve trial testimony), deposition. This distinction does not appear in the Federal Rules of

Civil Procedure, but becomes critical at the time of trial. If the deponent becomes unavailable (within the meaning of Rule 32) at the time of trial, that deponent's deposition may be offered in lieu of the deponent's live testimony.[36] Thus, if you anticipate that the deponent will not be available at the time of trial, make all curable objections—those objections cannot be obviated or cured when the deposition is proffered, because the curing witness, the deponent, is now unavailable Because of the expense of an expert's appearance, many lawyers stipulate to *de bene esse* depositions of expert testimony, which proceed much the same as expert witness examination at trial (*see* chapter twelve).

If, however, you expect the witness to be available at trial, you need only make those objections that can be cured by questioning the deponent further at the deposition. Thus, for example, at a *de bene esse* deposition, object if you believe the deponent does not have personal knowledge of the subject of his testimony so deposing counsel can ask the witness about the basis of his knowledge.

11. Do the Federal Rules of Civil Procedure require that objections and instructions not to answer be made in a particular form?

a. Form of Objections

Since the landmark case of *Hall v. Clifton Precision Tools* in 1993,[37] the manner and form of objecting at depositions has received increased scrutiny from judges, commentators, and rule makers. Litigators listened, and there has been a general return to a higher standard of professionalism. Judges, legal scholars, and the organized bar have criticized lawyers who make objections—and instruct the witness not to answer legitimate questions—as a means to coach witnesses and interfere with the right of deposing counsel to ask for and discover relevant testimony. The result has been changes to the Federal Rules of Civil Procedure, restrictive local rules in the district courts, and individual judges fashioning discovery orders that govern the conduct of counsel during depositions.

The civil procedure rules make clear the proper manner for making objections and the limited circumstances in which a lawyer defending a deposition can instruct a witness not to answer. Rule 30(c)(2) provides that an objection during a deposition "must be stated concisely and in a non-argumentative and non-suggestive manner." Taken together with Rule 32(d)(1)(3),[38] the rule envisions that an attorney would say, "Objection," followed by a brief statement of the specific legal grounds for the objection. In this way, objecting counsel makes clear the basis for objection without coaching the deponent, and questioning counsel has a fair opportunity to cure the

36. Fed. R. Evid. 804(b)(1).

37. Hall v. Clifton Precision Tools, 150 F.R.D. 525 (E.D. Pa. 1993).

38. Fed. R. Civ. P. 32(d)(3)(A) suggests the purpose of an objection at deposition is to obviate or remove the objectionable nature of a question or response.

objection. At the same time, Rule 30(c)(1) states that deposition examination must be made "as at trial"—use the word "objection" and concisely state the ground. For example, "Objection, leading." Local rules in many jurisdictions, however, preclude defending counsel at the deposition from stating the ground and limit the word(s) of the objection to "Objection" or "Objection, form."

1. Making Objections to the Form of the Question—An example of a proper objection to a question that assumes a fact not in evidence is:

Objection. Assumes a fact not in evidence.

The same objection might be stated:

> *Objection. That question assumes that my client has testified to* (insert fact), *which he has not. It further assumes that he knows* (insert fact), *which he does not and further assumes that the fact exists, which is plainly not true.*

While this objection makes clear the grounds of the objection, it is argumentative and suggests several answers to the witness. It's a classic example of what are called "speaking objections." This objection is designed to interfere with taking discovery by being argumentative, and to instruct the deponent, in the form of an objection, about how she should answer the question.

On the other end of the spectrum, the objection could be made by stating:

Objection.

or

Objection to the form.

These objections are neither argumentative nor suggestive, but do not provide sufficient legal grounds to allow opposing counsel a fair opportunity to cure the objection.

2. Substantive Objections—An example of a substantive objection that is in compliance with the letter and the spirit of the civil procedure rules is:

Objection, calls for a lay opinion.

Faced with this objection, deposing counsel can instruct the witness to answer, as even inadmissible opinions can lead to relevant evidence. In the alternative, counsel can ask the witness questions sufficient to show that the lay opinion was rationally based on the witness's perception and helpful to a trier of fact, and thus admissible as a lay opinion.[39]

---

39. FED. R. EVID. 701.

Alternatively, counsel could make this objection by stating:

> *Objection. You're asking my client to guess the meaning of what he saw, and that's asking for an inadmissible opinion—not much more than a guess that he doesn't have to give if he is uncomfortable in doing so. But if you want him to guess, go ahead and let him guess, but I don't see any value in it.*

This objection states the grounds for the objection so it could be cured, but it is both argumentative, suggesting the witness should either say that he would prefer not to guess or make clear that what he's doing is guessing. Alternatively, the objection could be made by stating:

> *Objection, foundation.*
>
> or
>
> *Objection.*

These objections are neither argumentative nor suggestive. However, they provide no clear guidance to deposing counsel about what needs to be done to cure the objection.

Note, however, that there are some local rules that limit counsel to stating the word "objection" or "objection, form." Most local rules don't address whether questioning counsel has the right to be informed of the specific grounds for the objection so she can cure the objection. Courts uniformly require, however, that objecting counsel answer a request for further information with the specific grounds for her objection. In addition, judges routinely issue individual discovery orders that do not overly restrict the form of objections at deposition.

b. Instructions Not to Answer a Question

Historically, obstreperous lawyers interfered with fair discovery at depositions by both interposing suggestive and argumentative objections and by instructing deponents not to answer questions without legitimate grounds to do so. The only legitimate grounds for instructing deponents not to answer a question that seeks information likely to lead to relevant evidence are contained in Rule 30(c)(2), which provides:

> A person may instruct a deponent not to answer only when necessary to preserve a privilege, to enforce a limitation ordered by the court, or to present a motion under Rule 30(c)(2).

Rule 30(d)(3)(A) provides:

> At any time during a deposition, the deponent or a party may move to terminate or limit it on the ground that it is being conducted in bad faith or in a manner that unreasonably annoys, embarrasses, or oppress the deponent or party. The motion may be filed in the court where the action is pending or the deposition is being taken. If the objecting deponent or party so demands, the deposition must be suspended for the time necessary to obtain an order.

As stated, the civil procedure rules envision limited opportunity for counsel to instruct a deponent not to answer a question that seeks information that can lead to admissible evidence. A witness may be instructed not to answer a question:

1) to preserve a privilege or protect trial preparation material;
2) to enforce a protective order limiting discovery; or
3) to allow a party or deponent the opportunity to seek a protective order.

If questioning counsel seeks privileged information, object *and* instruct the deponent not to answer—otherwise the privilege will be waived. When counsel asks a question that calls for privileged information, immediately interpose an objection, instruct the deponent not to answer, and seek a recess to discuss the propriety of claiming a privilege. Most questioning counsel will honor such a request, but even if questioning counsel protests, a recess must be taken. Although the privilege belongs to the client and can be waived by the client, always assume that the deponent wants to invoke the privilege and act accordingly. Follow the same procedure to protect trial preparation materials from discovery during the course of the deposition.[40]

Once the client decides to invoke a privilege, provide information to questioning counsel sufficient to let her determine whether the assertion of the privilege is proper, This information should also be sufficient to for a to rule on either a protective order to enforce the claim of privilege or a motion to compel that seeks to overcome the claim of privilege.

Federal Rule of Civil Procedure 26(b)(5)(A) provides:

> When a party withholds information otherwise discoverable by claiming that the information is

40. *See* Fed. R. Civ. P. 26(b)(3), limiting discovery documents and other tangible things prepared by or for a party in anticipation of trial, and Fed. R. Civ. P. 26(b)(4)(B), limiting discovery relating to consulting expert witnesses.

> privileged or subject to protection as trial preparation material, the party must:
>
> > (i) expressly make the claim; and
> >
> > (ii) describe the nature of the documents, communications, or tangible things not produced or disclosed—and do so in a manner that, without revealing information itself privileged or protected, will enable other parties to assess the claim.

For example, suppose you are defending the client's deposition in a case in which the plaintiff claims that the defendant defrauded him when he entered into a contract for the sale of goods. Plaintiff's counsel asks whether your client spoke to anyone before he decided to enter into the contract that underlies the cause of action, and the defendant responds that he spoke with a lawyer. You must object to any attempt to determine the content of that conversation and instruct the deponent not to answer such questions, following up with a private consultation. If, after conferring with your client, you assert the attorney-client privilege on behalf of the client-deponent, be prepared to provide the information numbered below. Note that in most circumstances, you will provide items 1, 2, and 7—deposing counsel will ask about the other areas.

1) The name of the client.
2) The name of the person spoken to.[41]
3) The date of the communication.[42]
4) The place of the communication.[43]
5) People present during the communication.[44]
6) Any person to whom the subject matter of the communication was given either orally or in writing.[45]

---

41. This information will insure that the person spoken to was either a licensed lawyer or an agent of a licensed lawyer.

42. This information will help determine whether the attorney-client relationship existed at the time of the communication.

43. This information will help determine whether the communication occurred in a place where there was a reasonable expectation that it would be confidential (i.e., in the lawyer's office, as opposed to a crowded restaurant).

44. This information will help determine whether there were people present during the communication, whose presence might obviate the privilege.

45. This information will help determine whether the privilege was destroyed because the alleged privileged information was communicated to someone not also protected by the privilege.

7) The general nature and purpose of the communication (e.g., oral or written communication the purpose of obtaining legal advice).[46]
8) Whether the communication was recorded, and, if so, to whom the record was shown and where it exists.[47]

Once deposing counsel receives this information, she can ask questions about any of the factors listed above to try to show that the communication does not meet the attorney-client privilege because of waiver or because it meets an exception to the privilege. Armed with that information, she can seek a motion to compel disclosure of the communication as not privileged or seek in camera inspection by the judge to determine whether the privilege is properly claimed, if there has been waiver, or if it an exception to the privilege exists.

Use the same process for a claim that the information deposing counsel seeks is trial preparation material protected by Rule 26. After objecting and instructing the witness not to answer, provide sufficient information to outline the trial preparation material protection claim so that deposing counsel can ask questions about the validity of the claim. If there is a motion to either protect the material in question or to compel its production, provide sufficient information for a judge to make an appropriate ruling.

In addition to attacking the validity of counsel's claim that the material or information sought are indeed trial preparation materials, questioning counsel may also attempt to show that valid reasons exist for invading the claimed trial preparation materials protection. The protection of these materials from discovery can be invaded on a showing of 1) substantial need for the material and 2) the inability, without undue hardship, to obtain the substantial equivalent of the materials by some other means.[48] Typical of such a situation is when one party has obtained a statement from a witness with unique information, who has since become unavailable by death or whose location cannot be found after a diligent search.

12. Should I, as defending counsel, ever ask questions of the deponent?

When trials were common, defending counsel would minimize or avoid putting any questions to her own witness at the conclusion of the deposition, absent the obligation to clear up misleading testimony from her witness. The theory behind this decision was simple the less information the deponent reveals to the opponent, the better. The modern deposition, however, assumes the extreme statistical

46. The communication must have been one that seeks legal advice and may not be for a purpose that destroys the privilege, such as the preparation for or furtherance of a crime or fraud.

47. Communicating the record of the communication to a nonprivileged entity, or the failure to keep it safely, may be evidence that the communication was not intended to remain confidential.

48. Fed. R. Civ. P. 26(b)(3)(A)(ii).

unlikelihood of trial and considers the option of defending counsel questioning the deponent once deposing counsel has completed her questioning.

In the modern deposition of your own clients and associated witnesses, you will have prepared party and party-associated deponents to testify, as if on direct examination, about information that you want an end user of the deposition to know. These deposition are the last/best opportunity to provide personal testimony under oath about important matters in the lawsuit. For example, in personal injury cases, deposing counsel for the defendant asks very few questions about the damages the plaintiff claims. You must elicit any information solely in the possession of the plaintiff, like the psychological effect on them of the injuries which they claim are the responsibility of the defendant, or lose that persuasive evidence for end use. This, in our ongoing example, would be an issue to explore with Professor Williams at her deposition.

And the testimony you elicit from your client is not limited to those topics about which deposing counsel failed to inquire. In a well-done deposition, deposing counsel will have discovered information damaging to her client, but will not emphasize it and not cast it in a persuasive light. To the contrary, deposing counsel's goal is to seek information that weakens your case theory and diminishes any damage to hers. But you can and should recast that very same information in its most persuasive light. Use the opportunity to question your client as you would at trial—present your case. Thinking of it as case presentation will put you in the proper mindset—you may not ask leading questions, and deposing counsel will object to narrative answers. But do not squander this opportunity to make your case.

You will have also prepared nonparty and party-associated deponents to testify about the favorable information they possess for your client, if they have agreed to be prepared. For these deponents as well, elicit favorable information not discovered by deposing counsel, and recast favorable testimony in the most persuasive way, just like a trial direct examination. Pay particular attention to information that can fill in the factual gaps necessary to prove your legal and factual theory.

Chapter Eleven

30(b)(6) Depositions Fact Gathering and Admissions

1. How can I use the Rule 30(b)(6) deposition?

The Rule 30(b)(6) deposition is one of the most efficient discovery devices in the litigator's arsenal.[1] There are two sorts. In one iteration, the Rule 30(b)(6) deposition serves as a roadmap for the entire litigation—it occurs as the first deposition in a case and perhaps the first discovery device after receiving Rule 26 voluntary disclosures. In its other iteration, the 30(b)(6) deposition is used near the end of a discovery to seek admissions that will speed the litigation to its conclusion—either supporting motion practice that ends or limits the scope of the litigation or deciding factual disputes to clear the way to a fair and speedy resolution by negotiation, mediation, arbitration, or some other means of dispute resolution. We categorize the first form on these depositions as "fact-gathering groundwork" and the second as "admissions seeking." We will explore these uses in some detail, suggesting efficient ways of noticing, opposing, preparing witnesses, and taking and defending the deposition. But first we provide a brief tutorial on the law.

2. What are the articulated purposes of the Rule 30(b)(6) deposition?

Rule 30(b)(6) provides, in relevant part, that a notice of subpoena may name as the deponent a public or private corporation, a partnership, an association, a governmental agency, or other entity. The notice must describe with reasonable particularity the matters for examination. The named organization must designate one or more representatives to testify on its behalf; it may also designate on which matters each designated person will testify. If a subpoena is served on a nonparty organization, it must advise that organization of its duty to designate a representative. The persons designated must testify about information known or reasonably available to the organization.

1. Federal Rule of Civil Procedure 30(b)(6) states: "Notice or Subpoena Directed to an Organization. In its notice or subpoena, a party may name as the deponent a public or private corporation, a partnership, an association, a governmental agency, or other entity and must describe with reasonable particularity the matters for examination. The named organization must then designate one or more officers, directors, or managing agents, or designate other persons who consent to testify on its behalf; and it may set out the matters on which each person designated will testify. A subpoena must advise a nonparty organization of its duty to make this designation. The persons designated must testify about information known or reasonably available to the organization. This paragraph (6) does not preclude a deposition by any other procedure allowed by these rules."

The purposes of the rule, as made clear in its legislative history, are

1) reducing the difficulty in determining whether a person deposed is a managing agent;
2) curbing the "bandying" by which various officers of a corporation are deposed, in turn, but each disclaims knowledge of facts that are known by someone in the organization;
3) protecting the corporation or agency by eliminating unnecessary and unproductive depositions; and
4) giving entity parties notice of the areas of inquiry to ease identifying appropriate deponents and insuring they are prepared for the deposition.[2]

The rule recognizes the difficulty in finding the right person to provide testimony about the activity of entities who are litigants. As such, the rule provides an efficient vehicle for information to be obtained from entities and makes clear the responsibilities of the parties in reaching that stated goal. It's not up to the deposing counsel to search for the "right" witness for certain information from an entity; the entity must choose and provide one.

3. What legal issues must I consider when seeking a Rule 30(b)(6) deposition?

The rule requires that matters for examination be stated with reasonable particularity so the proper witness can be provided. Meet this requirement by referring to the law underlying the litigation in question. Use the elements of claim or defense to outline the facts that make those elements appropriate matters for entity designee testimony. When considering the elements of a claim or defense, you need only identify the sort of information required to prove those items and list them as a "matter" for designee testimony.

There is no limit to the number of entity designee depositions you can take. As the litigation proceeds, the list of matters for designee testimony can become more precise and sophisticated than at the litigation's outset. Initiate information gathering in the same way that we advise gathering all information via deposition. Begin with a known, reasonably broad, but easily cabined list of matters for examination—broad enough to help expand the information base for the litigation, but narrow enough to meet the particularity requirement. Find out what there is to find out, including other people within the entity with other information. Then take the fact depositions of people identified in the first Rule 30(b)(6) deposition in addition to witnesses identified by Rule 26 voluntary disclosures who have information within the topics identified in the first round of Rule 30(b)(6) depositions. Finally,

2. *See generally*, Crouse, *An Unreasonable Scope: The Need for Clarity in Federal Rule (30)(b)(6) Depositions*, 49 U. Louisville L. Rev. 133 (2010); Schenkier, *Deposing Corporations and Other Fictive Persons: Some Thoughts on Rule 30(b)(6),* Litigation, Winter 2003.

depose other potential witnesses identified by other means. If and when you reach an information roadblock, consider a second round of Rule 30(b)(6) depositions to clear the way for future discovery.

Entities often produce a designee who is not the best possible witness for the information sought by the deposition notice, and that can be frustrating. Entities often have a designated person within its organization to respond to broadly stated matters.[3] The designated witness, with limited information, may forestall, for the moment, your exploration of certain issues. But that witness should be able to identify the appropriate people to speak for the entity on particular issues and, just as important, the fact witnesses within the entity who have specific information about the matters involved in the litigation.

One last suggestion for the notice. When noticing party designee depositions, be sure to include, whenever possible, that the deposition is to be video recorded. In most instances, the camera has an even more sobering effect on entity designees than on the regular lay witness and encourages full and fair answers. An entity designee is the face of the entity, and the impression left, especially if it is one of avoiding providing information to fair questions, will have an impact on case resolution, no matter how the case is resolved.

4. What legal issues must I consider when responding to the Rule 30(b)(6) deposition?

a. The Notice

The first issue for responding parties is to respond to the notice itself. The most typical objection lodged is a claim or claims that the notice is burdensome. These arguments maintain that the matters specified are too numerous; the expense involved is too onerous; and/or the notice requires multiple designees. And in fairness, all of these responses are valid in many cases where the notice takes a shotgun approach to identifying matters for inquiry and runs dozens of pages. Do not use the shotgun notice. These objections are less viable if you follow our suggestion to use the Rule 30(b)(6) deposition incrementally. That approach will, in most cases, obviate the typical objections made to the notice. At the same time, the authors are not in favor of form objections that merely claim that the deposition overburdens the entity. Rather, you should state with specificity what about the notice is overly burdensome.

3. Professor Bocchino has had the privilege of representing a number of individuals in Pennsylvania insurance "bad-faith" litigations. In those lawsuits, in response to entity designee deposition requests, we found that each insurance company had one person who—no matter what area of insurance or type of claim—was designated to respond to the Rule 30(b)(6) notice. While having imprecise information regarding any particular area of their company's business, they were very good at identifying the specific people involved in the claim on which bad-faith causes of action were based, and we just proceeded apace, learning the identity of the people who had issue specific control and information.

i. Pre-Notice Conference

Given the centrality of Rule 30(b)(6) depositions to litigation involving entities (on one or both sides of a litigation), we suggest that the trial judge, as part of the Rule 16 discovery conference, require— before any Rule 30(b)(6) notice be served on an opposing party—that the parties confer to see if they can agree what matters will be designated and who will serve as designees. Doing so avoids wrangling over the notice and protracted litigation about it, allowing the Rule 30(b)(6) depositions to fulfill their stated purpose.

Even if the judge does not make such an order, nothing prevents counsel from conferring about the Rule 30(b)(6) notice and designates to save time and litigation costs. There are categories of lawsuits where Rule 30(b)(6) are inevitable, and the lawyers opposing each other do so with some regularity.[4] In those cases, once there has been one such litigation where, after protracted litigation, both parties achieved an equitable result and the appropriate deposition(s) occurred, the likelihood of such an agreement is possible. No entity wants to increase costs unnecessarily, and if a phone call and an exchange of correspondence or a meeting can achieve an agreement acceptable to all parties at a savings of time and expense, the process has the potential for success.[5]

b. Whom to Designate and How to Prepare

The person to be designated is, of course, controlled in part by the content of the notice. Efficiency in terms of number of depositions suggests designating a witness with the broadest information about the matters to be discussed—or at least a witness who can come up to snuff on the matters in the notice. As we have noted, for entities frequently involved in litigation of a certain sort, there will be a person within this entity whose job description includes designation as a Rule 30(b)(6) representative. Normally, the designee is neither the CEO or high-level manager, nor an employee who works at the operational level, but rather a midlevel manager who has risen to his current managerial status by working through the operational ranks of the entity.

Responding counsel must often navigate the tension between the number of designees—or the quality of the designee in terms of knowledge of the subject matter involved—and the preparation time needed for each designee to perform well

4. Entities use the same practice group to defend these actions, and lawyers who bring them tend to do so frequently

5. As noted earlier, Professor Bocchino was faced with the prospect of Rule 30(b)(6) deposition litigation in a fair number of insurance bad-faith claims. Not only did designees repeat, but so did counsel. After several go-rounds on notice issues, he and counsel for several insurance companies were able to agree—before the Rule 30(b)(6) notices were issued—on the content of the notice, the person designated, and the time and place of the deposition, saving the time of all counsel, and pleasing the insurance company internal litigation managers.

at the deposition. The more the witness knows, the easier the preparation and the better the quality of the information provided. A designee who is not prepared to answer the matters contained in the notice will neither speed the process nor limit the information provided. Failing to provide information about the matters in the notice only leads to further litigation and, at the best for the entity, more designees to identify, prepare, and defend at depositions—and at the worst, sanctions up to and including preclusion of evidence on matters within the notice for the rest of the litigation, together with some sort of fine and awarding of costs.

Counsel should prepare the chosen designee to be as forthcoming at the deposition as other witnesses, as we discuss in chapter six. Prepare the designee to provide all the information within his ken that is both *responsive* to questions and *favorable* to the entity's position (avoiding answers will only lead to more questions and an assumption that the entity has something to hide).

Finally, if the deposition is noticed, as we suggest, for video recording, work on the designee's demeanor and presentation skills so that he presents as an honest, forthright, and willing witness. Entities, at the dispute resolution phase of litigation, are often at a tactical disadvantage when suing or being sued by an individual, especially one who has been injured in any way. As we noted above, this witness is the face of the entity for the entirety of the litigation; whoever views this deposition needs to be impressed with the honesty of the designee, overcoming any built-in prejudice against large entities, to help reach a fair resolution of the case.

5. What tactical and practical issues does the party noticing the Rule 30(b)(6) deposition face?

a. The Purpose of the Deposition

The Fact-Gathering Groundwork Deposition—Take this variation of the Rule 30(b)(6) deposition very early in the discovery process. This is most necessary when you are unfamiliar with the entity, its organization, and the manner in which it does business. You will often start with only your client, perhaps some friendly witnesses, and the internet as background information sources as the deposition begins. In that case, the fact-gathering groundwork deposition is essential.

This may not be your best tactic, however, in cases involving complex transactions and where the potential amount in play is great. It is not unusual, at some point, to hire a consulting expert, preferably someone with actual knowledge about the entity, to help you prepare. In that circumstance, this variation of the Rule 30(b)(6) deposition may not be necessary.[6] Normal interrogatories and document production can proceed based on the information the consultant provides.

6. You will still need to verify the organization information provided by the consulting expert with a Rule 30(b)(6) deposition. But in that case, the purpose would be to obtain party statements and

That being said, the typical goal of this deposition is to obtain the same information that could be provided by a well-informed consulting expert. If you have only client-based and internet sources, assume that you know nothing of litigation value about the entity.[7] Initially, get the "lay of the land" regarding the entity—use a series of the journalist's questions we have referenced to find out about the entity and how it performs the function that underlies the claims of the lawsuit. Who is this entity (in all its iterations); what functions does it undertake; how long has it been performing the function involved in the suit; how important is that function to the entity's financial (or other) well-being? Who is responsible for the functions; what are their qualifications; how are they trained; is there a training manual and how often does it change; is there an employee manual regarding how the function involved is performed, how is it maintained, by whom, does it change, how often does it change? How is the function executed; by whom; are they evaluated, by whom? How are records made regarding the function, what are they called, where are they stored, who makes them, who keeps them? And so on.

b. Preparation

You are unlikely to have any more information as you prepare for the deposition than you had when preparing the Rule 30(b)(6) notice. Your specific sources for preparation will have been provided by the client and client-produced witnesses who have been interviewed. In addition, you will have whatever documents and records the client has and information about documents or records lost, destroyed, or not maintained. General internet research about the company will be helpful, but the first place visited should be the entity's website. It is always helpful to learn what an entity says about itself. If the lawsuit involves a transaction, search the website to see what digital documents are produced in similar transactions—and just as important, what they are called.[8] The website will also provide names of people and places involved in similar transactions. Also search public records for other lawsuits similar to yours. Further, there are internet services that gather information about litigation of the type involved (e.g., product liability, patents and copyright, construction, etc.) that you can search (for a fee) by the name of the involved entity and the type of litigation. Do not let this internet knowledge make you complacent about what will be divulged in the deposition; while helpful, the internet should never be the only source for anything—sometimes it's wrong; often it's out of date.

It is too early to create legal and factual theory charts; in fact, if prepared, they would be counterproductive as narrowing the scope of questioning too early. You

admissions that verify that what you have been told by the consulting expert is accurate and was operational at the time of the events underlying the lawsuit.

7. One should never believe, as gospel, what they read on the internet.

8. Making for efficient interrogatories and document requests.

should assemble, group, and compile available documents in the order you expect to use them. Finally, remember that the deposition notice itself is a critical exhibit.

6. What are the most effective techniques I can use to take and defend the fact-gathering version of the Rule 30(b)(6) deposition?

Taking the designee's Rule 30(b)(6) deposition has the same information-gathering goals as taking the deposition of any other witness—obtaining complete, comprehensive, and reliable information from the designee regarding the matters within the notice. The beginning of the deposition, however, requires preliminary questioning to determine whether the designated witness who has appeared at the deposition is qualified for the task. This questioning is designed to address, from the beginning of the deposition, the most important legal issues in the Rule 30(b)(6) deposition: the designee's competence to provide information on behalf of the entity. We have provided a Rule 30(b)(6) deposition notice in our hypothetical case to use for the rest of this chapter.

This notice, although much shorter than many of its breed, raises what we consider the key issues for Rule 30(b)(6) deposition practice. It has been our experience that entities lose in a litigation for one of two basic reasons—1) the entity had faulty policies, procedures, and practices (as defined in the hypothetical) or it failed to train their administrators, managers, employees, or agents, which caused the problem in litigation; or 2) their policies, procedures, and practices were violated by the administrators, managers, employees or agents of the entity. The motion follows.

IN THE UNITED STATES DISTRICT COURT
FOR THE EASTERN DISTRICT OF NITA

Mary Anne Williams,	:	
Plaintiff	:	Civ. No. YR-1-106
v.	:	
	:	
Nita University, et al,	:	
Defendants	:	

PLAINTIFF'S NOTICE TO PRODUCE ENTITY DESIGNEE OF THE DEFENDANT NITA UNIVERSITY PURSUANT TO FED. R. CIV. PRO. 30(B)(6)

Comes now the plaintiff, by and through her counsel, Morella & Desjardins, LLC, to demand that a representative be sent to testify on behalf of the defendant at deposition to be recorded by audiovisual means on September 12, YR-1, at plaintiff's offices at 214 Stowe Blvd., Nita City, Nita, 10:30 a.m., with regard to the following matters:

1. The policies, procedures, and practices of Nita University with regard to tenure and promotion of faculty members at Nita University and the Nita University School of Public Policy as they existed from January 1, YR-7, through December 31, YR-2;

2. Written and/or oral directives, instructions, or statements of any kind and in any form made by the defendant, its officers, employees, or agents, regarding the tenure and promotion policies, procedures, and practices of Nita University and the Nita University School of Public Policy as they existed from January 1, YR-7, through December 31, YR-6, made to its officers, employees, and/or agents;

3. The policies, procedures, and practices of Nita University or any of its schools regarding sexual relationships of administrators and tenured faculty members with students, nontenured faculty members, or employees at Nita University as they existed from January 1, YR-7, to the present.

4. The policies, procedures, and practices of the Nita University or any of its schools regarding sexual harassment allegations made against the university, any of its schools, administrators, deans, faculty members, or employees by any dean, administrator, faculty member, student, or employee.

5. The policies, practices, and procedures with regard to decision making in circumstances where a complaint has been made as to an alleged violation of those policies, procedures, and practices referred to in Paragraph 3.

6. The reasons for the adoption and maintenance of the policies, procedures, and practices referred to in Paragraphs 1 and 3.

7. The confirmed violations of the policies, practices, and procedures referred to in Paragraph 3 that occurred from January 1, YR-7, through the present, and the punishment, if any, for those violations.

8. Any lawsuit brought against Nita University or any of its schools, deans, administrators, or faculty members by any student, faculty member, or employees claiming gender discrimination from January 1, YR- 9, through the present.

9. The policies, procedures, and practices of Nita University or any of its schools, but in particular, the Nita University School of Public Policy, designed to insure a workplace that is not hostile to women.

10. The gender of faculty members, stated in terms of the percentage of men versus the percentage of women, in every school of Nita University, as existed for each academic year, for the period of January 1, YR-7, to the present.

11. The gender of faculty members, stated by academic rank, and in terms of the percentage of men and the percentage of women in each rank in all schools of Nita University, as existed for each academic year, for the period of January 1, YR-7, through the present.

DOCUMENT PRODUCTION PURSUANT FRCP R. 30(B)(2); AND R. 34

12. Plaintiff requests that defendant produce any and all documents or electronically/digitally stored information, in any form, written, electronic, digital, or recorded in any way that communicate, notify, memorialize, codify, reflect, refer to, or record any of the policy or policies, practice or practices, and/or procedure or procedures referred to in Paragraphs 1, 3, 4, 5, and 9 above, regarding the subject matter referred to in Paragraphs 1–11, above, within thirty days of the receipt of this notice to counsel for the plaintiff at 214 Stowe Blvd. Nita City, Nita.

DEFINITIONS

13. For the purposes of this notice, the words policy or policies are intended to communicate their common dictionary definitions and to include any mandatory or suggested manner, mental processing, decision making, procedures, practices, presumptions or conduct which governs or guides Nita University's educational mission, as conducted by its officers, agents, employees, or attorneys.

14. For the purpose of this notice, the words procedure or procedures are intended to communicate their common dictionary definition and to include any mandatory or suggested methodology used and/or intended to implement the policy or policies of Nita University identified in Paragraphs 1, 3, 4, 5, and 9.

15. For the purpose of this notice, the words practice or practices are intended to communicate their common dictionary definition and to include any method or manner used by the defendant, its officers, agents, employees, or attorneys to implement the policy or policies and procedure or procedures of Nita University as identified in Paragraphs 1, 3, 4, 5, and 9.

Diane C. Desjardins

Diane C. Desjardins, Esq.
Counsel for the Plaintiff

Example: The Rule 30(b)(6) deposition, as noticed above, is now beginning. The witness has been sworn in and identified himself as Robert Wells.

Plaintiff's Counsel: Good morning, sir. My name is Mary Gibson, and I represent the plaintiff, Mary Anne Williams, in the Case of Williams v. Nita University, et al. Are you employed by Nita University?

Wells: I am. I am the Assistant Provost for Academic Personnel at the university.

Q: Do you have an ultimate degree?

A: Yes—I have a PhD in Biochemistry.

Q: Are you comfortable with my addressing you as Dr. Wells?

A: That's fine.

Q: Dr. Wells, you have been designated by Nita University as its representative to answer questions identified with particularity in a notice to the university. Is that your understanding?

A: Yes.

Q: Have you ever testified as a designee of the university for the same purpose in other litigation?

A: I have.

Q: Before we get into the substance of your testimony, I'd like to go over some preliminary matters regarding this deposition, and to the extent they are "old-hat" to you as an experienced witness, I apologize.

[At this point, counsel covers the same preliminary matters as accomplished with any other witness, as described in chapter seven.]

Q: Let me show you what has been premarked for this deposition as Exhibit 1, which appears to be a four-page document entitled "Plaintiff's Notice to Produce an Entity Designee of the Defendant Nita University Pursuant to Fed. R. Civ. P. 30(b)(6)." Have you ever seen Exhibit 1 before?

A: I have not.

Q: All right, Dr. Wells. I need to ask you a number of questions about Exhibit 1 before we get to your designee testimony. I ask you to read Exhibit 1, and of course you have the availability of Ms. Stein, the university's counsel, if you have question. Will a break of thirty minutes be sufficient to review Exhibit 1, Ms. Stein?

Defense Counsel: Yes, we have prepared Dr. Wells to testify regarding the subject matter of the Notice, Exhibit 1, so I'm not sure why this is necessary, but it's your deposition; thirty minutes will be fine.

Plaintiff's Counsel: Fine, let's break for thirty minutes until 11:10 a.m.

Rule 30(b)(6) does not require the designee to review the notice; only to be prepared to testify about the matters set out in the notice. But because asking the designee if he has read the notice is standard, take time for its review before proceeding with the deposition. Make clear that the time to review does not count toward the deposition's time limit—seven hours of testimony absent stipulation to the contrary (Rule 30(d)(1)).

One last small, but typical issue is raised in the second question in the deposition. Plaintiff's counsel asks about whether the witness has received an "ultimate degree," a term of art in academics counsel learned during this litigation. When litigators become involved in a complex case, they learn the "lingo" of the litigants. Keep in mind the end-user of the deposition; assume they won't know this specialized language, and avoid the temptation to speak the tribal dialect of the deponent. This is especially true in Rule 30(b)(6) depositions and when dealing with experts—do not lose your factfinder in bewildering language.

Example: The deposition continues.

Plaintiff's Counsel: Back on the record at 11:15 a.m. Dr. Wells, is there anything that occurred over the break that would prevent you from providing full and complete testimony today?

A: *No.*
Q: *Have you reviewed Exhibit 1 with Ms. Stein?*
A: *I have.*
Q: *Are you prepared to testify about all of the matters contained in the notice—Exhibit 1?*
A: *I believe so. In regard to Paragraph 9, I do not have any specific information about the steps taken in the Public Policy School to insure a nonhostile work environment. I know what policies the university follows, and I assume that they are followed in the Public Policy School, but I do not have what you call "particular" information about Paragraph 9 with regard to that school.*
Q: *Are there any other items in the notice—Exhibit 1—about which you not prepared to provide designee testimony?*
A: *I do not have personal knowledge about many of the items in Exhibit 1, but I have been prepared to testify about them.*
Q: *All right. We will keep that in mind. Have you brought the documents requested in Paragraph 12?*

Defense Counsel: I tried to reach you this morning, and we came right into this deposition. Of the documents you requested, I have all that we have been able to collect. Your request was quite broad. We are going to need another thirty days for the rest of the information. It is all statistical and related to Paragraphs 10 and 11. We considered requesting a protective order, given the volume of information you seek, but the University informs us that their IT people can cull the information from various sources. We just need more time.

Plaintiff's Counsel: I wish you would have raised this before today. Would you like to put off this deposition? In the alternative, I assume you will agree to recessing this deposition when we finish, and reconvening, at your client's expense, once we have received the missing documents.

Defense Counsel: Let's see how far we get today. If we need to reconvene to review the documents and testimony they engender regarding Paragraph's 10 and 11, we will pay the appearance fees for the court reporter and videographer.

Plaintiff's Counsel: Sorry for that interruption, Dr. Wells. You have told us that you have a PhD in chemistry; did you serve on the Nita University faculty before becoming the Assistant Provost for Academic Personnel?

A: I did not.

Q: Have you ever served on a university faculty?

A: Yes. I was a member of the faculty of the Harrison University Medical School for ten years before I became Associate Provost at Harrison University. My primary responsibilities were in biochemical research. I was offered my current position at Nita University four years ago and have been there ever since. I have tenure at the Nita University Medical School, but I do not teach there. My current job is full time.

Q: Have you had any other faculty appointments at any college or university?

A: No.

Q: Have you ever participated in the tenure review of a university faculty member?

A: No, I have not.

Plaintiff's Counsel: Counsel, given Dr. Wells background, I am not confident we will be able to get the full information that Rule 30(b)(6) entitles us to receive. Perhaps we should come back another day with a better witness for this case.

Defense Counsel: Dr. Wells is our designee, and he has been prepared.

This portion of the deposition raises several issues, the most important of which deals with designee selection. First, Rule 30(b)(6) does not require that the designee be the best possible witness for the particular case. Here, Dr. Wells is peculiarly unqualified. He has never been an arts and sciences academic. His experience is as a research biochemist at a medical school. His idea of scholarship is the report on clinical experimentation. He has never participated in a tenure decision, though he knows all about the need to attract outside funding to further the academic mission of the university. He is, however, the designee; if he is prepared, he can serve the designee function for this deposition.

Second, the designee need not have first-hand knowledge about anything in the notice. Preparation is all that's necessary. For example, even though he has no knowledge about the particular steps taken at the Public Policy School to avoid a hostile work environment, he can be educated and prepared about them. Here, however, he has not been—and this is not the sort of information that can be obtained over a lunch break. The university may have to designate another witness to testify about the Public Policy School's standards and practices.

Third, entity counsel has brought the typical midlevel management witness entities often designate. Unlike most designees, however, his current position is not based on experience similar to the issues in this lawsuit. In all likelihood, preparing him will be difficult and time consuming. If faced with such a witness, be vigilant and probing about areas where the designee can't answer questions within the notice.

Fourth, this deposition should have been postponed until all of the requested documents were received. In fact, a better practice is to request responsive documents within the time limits provided for in Rule 34 and then schedule the deposition on the designee. As it stands, the documents provided may be voluminous—too many to address in the deposition without time to review.[9] While those documents would later be available to use in fact witnesses depositions, the 30(b)(6) deposition is much more useful when you are already familiar with the documents and can ask substantive questions about them, rather than questions based on a quick skim while the clock is ticking.

Finally, if you suspect that the witness is not prepared to provide information designated in the notice, especially if the information sought is more lawsuit-specific, it makes sense to question whether the designee is prepared to answer questions about each paragraph in the notice.

Example: Assume the deposition has continued and the next topic for discussion is Paragraph 9, regarding the university's actions to prevent the occurrence of a hostile work environment for women faculty members.

Plaintiff's Counsel: Dr. Wells, you have told us that the university's policy is to provide a workplace friendly to all ages, genders, and races. Does the university provide any training to its administrators and faculty members about, in particular, how to maintain a workplace friendly to women—that is, nonhostile?

A: Yes. All administrators and faculty members are provided with a video about avoiding gender discrimination and work-environment issues.

Q: I have seen that video—and we will talk about it in a moment—but in addition, do you provide deans and other school administrators with any written materials, whether electronic, physical, or any other medium, about avoiding a hostile work environment for women?

A: I don't know.

Q: When you say that you don't know, do you mean that there are no such materials or that there are such materials and you just haven't seen them or been made aware of them?

A: My answer to that question is I don't know.

Q: Do you think there are written materials?

A: I'm sorry, I don't know.

Q: Do you think there should be some written materials on avoiding a hostile work environment for women?

9. If, in this vignette, the documents provided are voluminous, defendant counsel's failure to be fully responsive offers an opportunity to postpone the entirety of the deposition. The statistical information not yet available will most certainly be relevant to matters contained in the notice, and postponing the deposition is in the client's best interest.

Defense Counsel: Objection. Asked and answered.

Plaintiff's Counsel: It's a different question. (Reading from real time transcript.) I asked, "Do you think there should be some written materials on avoiding a hostile work environment for women?"

Q: Please answer my question.

Defense Counsel. Objection. The question is outside the scope of the notice. You're asking Dr. Wells for an opinion.

Plaintiff's Counsel: I would like his answer, if not as a designee, then personally. Are you instructing the witness not to answer?

Defense Counsel: Yes. We can take up this matter, along with the other disputes we have had today. I will file a motion for a protective order.

Plaintiff's Counsel: Can we get Dr. Wells's answer to my question? It's a matter within his employment at the university. We can stipulate that based on the judge's ruling, it will either be his personal opinion or his opinion as a designee. It goes to the policies of the university on hostile work environments.

Defense Counsel: That does make some sense. With that stipulation—and I will draft it for our signatures—go ahead and answer the question, Dr. Wells.

Plaintiff's Counsel: I agree. Would you like the question again, Doctor?

A: Yes.

Q: "Do you think there should be some written materials on avoiding a hostile work environment for women?"

A: Yes, I do. It is much easier to refer to a written document when a policy question arises.

Q: Including hostile work environments for women?

A: Of course. All policies that effect the day-to-day operation of the university's educational mission.

This portion of the deposition raises several typical issues with Rule 30(b)(6) witnesses. First, when a designee states that he does not know the answer to a question within the designation, you have several options. You can accept the answer as the answer of the entity and move on. In that case, defending counsel has the responsibility to correct the answer. She will need to find the actual answer at the earliest possible time (perhaps over a break), prepare the witness, produce the document (if any), and thereby correct the record. Otherwise, she tacitly accepts the answer. If the necessary information is found after the close of the deposition, defending counsel can prepare the witness to correct the record[10] of the deposition. Depending on the seriousness and volume of correcting material, counsel can volunteer to respond to written deposition questions to be put to the designee and thus avoid reconvening the 30(b)(6) deposition.

Second, the example raises the issue of questioning outside the scope of the notice, albeit on a minor issue. The scope of the notice is perhaps the most litigated issue at a Rule 30(b)(6) deposition. There are cases offering a wide variety of resolutions, but the majority rule disfavors instructions not to answer, preferring the resolution

10. At least the written record.

reached here by counsel. The witness answers the question(s) defending counsel objected to as "outside the scope;" a protective order is filed; and then the testimony is treated in accordance with the ruling. If the information is outside the scope, but relevant and within the ken of the designee, it becomes admissible as the statement of designee in his individual capacity. If, however, the information is outside the scope of the notice *and* irrelevant, it is stricken from the record and deleted from the official video record.

It is not unusual for counsel to ask the designee questions that are outside the scope of the notice, but within the actual first-hand knowledge of the designee and relevant to the case. In our example, the issue of whether there is, or should be, a written manual about maintaining a hostility free workplace is not just relevant, but directly within the job of the designee as the Assistant Provost for Academic Personnel. Although his statement may not be admissible as the statement of the university per Rule 30(b)(6)[11] it would be attributable to the university under Evidence Rule 801(d)(2)(C) as an opposing party statement made by an employee about matters within the scope of his employment.

7. What issues must I consider when taking an admissions-seeking Rule 30(b)(6) deposition?

The questions in this variation of the Rule 30(b)(6) deposition ask the opposing party to state or admit to facts that inform a particular legal or factual theory of the case. We have already discussed this function and how you should perform it incrementally at the end of, and during, a fact-gathering deposition.[12] Near the end of the discovery process, when factual discovery has been completed, either party can notice this form of Rule 30(b)(6) deposition to tie down legal and factual theory as well as prepare for case dispositive motion practice and/or ADR.[13] Prepare the questions as you would a well-constructed cross-examination, using both substantive and persuasive exhibits, enhance with computer-generated (and otherwise) visual aids.

Example: Assume that Dr. Wells's deposition was completed five months ago. Litigation ensued, and the plaintiff had focused on hostile work environment as one of the discrimination claims to pursue to disposition. Plaintiff modified paragraph 9 from the original notice (Exhibit 1) to make clear that she seeks a designee's testimony about the existence of a hostile work environment at the Public Policy School from January 1, YR-7, through December 31, YR-2, as it applied to Professor Williams. Dr. Wells is once again the witness. He has been sworn in.

11. And arguably binding on the University.

12. *See* chapter eight.

13. We maintain our position that in all likelihood there will be no trial. Rule 30(b)(6) motions in either of the iterations we have discussed are appropriate to use in cases going to trial as well.

Plaintiff's Counsel: Good afternoon, Dr. Wells. Good to see you. Have you read the notice for this deposition, which is modified from Paragraph 9 of the original Rule 30(b)(6) deposition you gave five months ago?

A: *Yes, I have.*

Q: *To be sure, I'm showing you what we have marked as next-in-line Exhibit 438 (it's been quite the litigation). Is that the notice you just told us about?*

A: *Yes.*

Q: *Are you prepared to provide the information covered by that notice?*

A: *I am.*

Q: *It is true, as you testified, that Nita University's policy forbids the maintenance of a hostile work environment for its faculty members?*

A: *And other employees as well.*

Q: *Thank you. And that policy is then implemented in every work setting, correct?*

A: *Yes.*

Q: *And that would include the Public Policy School, true?*

A: *Yes, of course.*

Q: *It was left to the Public Policy School to implement the university's policy that forbids maintenance of a hostile work environment for women, correct?*

A: *Yes.*

Q: *And, of course, the policy has to be flexible?*

A: *I'm not sure what you mean.*

Q: *Not every faculty member has the same experiences, so the work environment for a particular woman faculty member can be hostile to her, even if not to other women.*

A: *Only if known by the university.*

Q: *Through the dean, correct.*

A: *Yes, that would be true.*

Q: *If the dean knew about a work environment hostile to a particular faculty member and allowed it to continue, that would violate university policy, would it not?*

A: *You lawyers and your questions. Yes, that would be a violation of our policy.*

Q: *Now, Dr. Wells, I want to focus on the Public Policy School and in particular, the period of January 1, YR-1, through December 31, YR-2. The dean of the Public Policy School as of January 1, YR-7, was David Simonson, correct?*

A: *Yes, newly minted.*

Q: *I want to show you some portions of Dr. Simonson's deposition.*

[Whereupon counsel shows the witness Simonson's deposition, in which he admitted to attempting to have sexual relations with: a member of the Business School, who declined and left the university that spring; an administrator of the university IT department in YR-8, who also declined and left the university the next spring; a junior faculty member of the Public Policy School, Carol Merritt, who accepted his advances and began a relationship with Simonson that continued from October of YR-8 until March of YR-7, when it ended, with Professor Merritt leaving the university in the spring of YR-7.]

Q: *Was the university aware of Professor Simonson's history of attempted or actual sexual relations with members of the university community?*

A: *I don't know.*

Q: *You said that the dean of the school was the representative of university, correct?*

A: *Yes.*

Q: *So if the dean knew, the university knew, right?*

Defense Counsel: Objection. Beyond the scope of the notice.

Q: *You may answer.*

A: *Yes, that's correct.*

Q: *The dean of the Public Policy School from YR-22 to YR-7 was Marvin Taylor, correct?*

[Assume that counsel shows the witness the deposition of Taylor, who corroborated that he knew of all of the relationships about which Simonson testified, as shown to Dean Wells.]

Q: *So the university, through Dean Taylor, knew of Dr. Simonson's sexual conduct up to and including the time the university appointed Simonson as the dean?*

A: *Apparently so.*

Q: *Nothing was done about it?*

A: *At the time, university policy did not preclude sexual relations among members of the faculty and staff, even when there was a supervisory relationship coexisting.*

Q: *That's right. University policy did not. The dean has control over the hiring and tenure process at the Public Policy School, correct?*

A: *Ultimately, yes, but with faculty consultation.*

Q: *So when Professor Williams was hired by Dean Simonson, he was fresh off a sexual relationship with Professor Merritt, over whom he had ultimate control?*

A: *That, too, was consistent with university policy.*

Q: *OK by the university. The person in charge of hiring and tenure of faculty had two attempted sexual relations in the two years before the appointment of Professor Williams?*

A: *True.*

Q: *And an ongoing sexual relationship with a member of his faculty that ended just before he appointed Professor Williams?*

A: *Yes.*

Q: *This is the person sent out to hire Professor Williams and other young women?*

A: *That was his job.*

Q: *Good for the work environment of women?*

A: *There was nothing untoward about that hiring.*

Q: *Professor Williams became a member of the faculty?*

A: *Yes.*

Q: *A requirement, correct?*

A: *Yes.*

Q: *In the early spring semester of YR-4, Professor Williams made a sexual harassment claim against a member of one of those committees, Dean Dressler of the business school, who allegedly fondled her several times and made inappropriate sexual proposals, correct?*
A: *Yes. I read her complaint.*
Q: *The university never responded to Professor Williams, did it?*
A: *She was allowed to leave the committee.*
Q: *That was her remedy from the university?*
A: *That's what happened.*
Q: *She did hear from her dean, Dean Jefferson, the voice of the university, correct?*
A: *I don't know.*

[The witness is shown the Williams YR-4 evaluation memo that states "serious question of lack of collegiality in university committee with regard to senior administrator." She is also shown Jefferson's deposition, which states that she was unaware of Williams's complaint and that Dressler was a friend of hers and had said that Williams was standoffish to other members of the fund-raising committee and alums. She responded in the evaluation. She also testified that Williams did not protest the comment during their yearly review, which was otherwise very positive.]

Q: *You're also aware of the relationship between Professors Williams and Simonson, correct?*
A: *Yes.*
Q: *He was her employer and direct supervisor at the Patterson Institute?*
A: *Yes.*
Q: *OK with university policy?*
A: *Yes.*
Q: *And also had a vote on her tenure?*
A: *About which he abstained.*
Q: *Professor Williams and Simonson broke up when he refused to divorce his wife—you know that from the depositions, right?*
A: *True.*
Q: *You also know Professor Williams complained about Simonson's behavior?*
A: *Yes, long and loud.*
Q: *She was denied tenure?*
A: *Yes.*
Q: *Based in the main, as Dean Jefferson admitted in her deposition, because of lack of "collegiality."*
A: *That's true. It was her discretionary call, and she made it professionally.*
Q: *So a woman who declines or ends a sexual relationship with a senior man in the university or at her own school is not "collegial?"*
A: *There was more.*

Q: *Yes, but looking at the entirety of the circumstances of her employment, and as known by the university through two of its deans, did Professor Williams experience a hostile work environment under university policy?*
A: *Not according to our policy at that time.*
Q: *That's some policy, doctor. Nothing further.*

This Rule 30(b)(6) deposition doesn't achieve an ultimate admission from the designee, but it does create a record—and a video recording of the closing argument of the plaintiff on the issue of hostile work environment for a decision maker in the case, whether that be the responsible university agent (probably university counsel together with the chancellor and provost) for settlement, a mediator, or a panel of arbitrators. The deposition also sends a strong message about how the case will look to jurors, should the trial option even be on the table.

Chapter Twelve

Expert Witness Depositions

We live in a world dominated by innovation. Economies rest on the ability to create, develop, and apply the newest technology. New organizations, private and governmental, come into existence at a rapid pace. Old organizations, both private and governmental, add new aspects to their entity portfolios to meet the demands of the modern world. Professionals who create, manage, and operate these new and old organizations acquire information and form specialty areas of knowledge and the implementation of that knowledge at a rate that matches the innovations they oversee. All of this change and innovation means that lawyers are litigating about increasingly complex matters. To do so, lawyers rely more and more on the help of expert witnesses.

As simple a case as one involving serious injuries from an automobile collision often uses multiple expert witnesses. These can include civil engineers to create accident reconstructions, computer experts to animate those reconstructions, and a variety medical professionals to testify about the diagnosis, treatment, cause of condition and prognosis for recovery.[1] Further, life-care planners determine the cost of future medical care, vocational experts determine the employment available to the plaintiff given his current condition, and economists determine economic losses reduced to present cash value. In many such cases, both the plaintiff and the defendant will retain experts on these topics (or at least some of them) to testify on their behalf. Of course, this single automobile case does not even approach the complexity of an antitrust claim, an intellectual property dispute, or a products liability claim. Litigation about modern commerce introduces another level of expertise—the factfinder must be educated about the device or business setting involved as well as the science, accounting, and economics of it all.

1. When in the litigation will I take expert witness depositions?

Expert testimony must be based on the broadest range of facts that underlie the lawsuit. Most discovery orders and the rules of civil procedure contemplate that expert witnesses will provide the last piece of discovery, operating after a full factual discovery of the matter at hand. The civil procedure rules provide that parties must disclose

1. For example, in a case in which a plaintiff claims to have suffered a brain injury, the plaintiff will be tested and perhaps treated by a PhD neuropsychologist in tandem with medical neurologists and physiatrists.

expert witnesses at least ninety days before trial[2] and that experts must provide a report (hereinafter the Rule 26 expert report) if they have been retained or employed to provide expert testimony. Party employees providing expert testimony whose duties regularly include such testimony must also produce a Rule 26 expert report.[3]

In our hypothetical gender discrimination case, both parties retained expert forensic economists to testify about the economic damage the plaintiff suffered, assuming for the purposes of their opinions that she was the victim of either defamation or gender discrimination. In addition, the university may call an expert witness from its human resources department. This should be the person who maintains and provides statistical analyses of the university's compliance with its own anti-discrimination policies and provides evidence of the same whenever the university is sued for alleged discrimination. All these witnesses must serve their Rule 26 expert reports on the opponent in a timely manner.

If the expert is not required to provide a full report, the expert witness must provide a written disclosure that includes a statement of the subject matter for which the witness will provide expert testimony and a summary of the facts and opinions that the witness will provide (hereinafter the Rule 26 expert disclosures).[4] In our hypothetical discrimination case, Williams may call a colleague from the Public Policy School who has served as the Chair of the Tenurial Faculty. This witness will provide an expert opinion of the plaintiff's strong teaching and scholarship as criteria for tenure. Such a witness would be required to provide the abbreviated Rule 26 expert disclosures.

A party in a federal court has the right to take the deposition of an expert witness who has been identified as someone who may testify as such at trial.[5] If a Rule 26(b)(1) or (b)(2) expert report is required under the rules, the deposition must be scheduled after the report has been provided.[6] For those expert witnesses who need not file an exhaustive report, their deposition would not occur until after the subject matter of their testimony and a summary of facts and opinions of that testimony are reported as Rule 26 expert disclosures.

---

2. Fed. R. Civ. P. 26(a)(2)(A).

3. Fed. R. Civ. P. 26(a)(2)(B).

4. Fed. R. Civ. P. 26(a)(2)(C). These experts are typically party employees who, for example, may have participated in the creation of a product now claimed to be defective or an employee such as an accountant who is called to explain and provide opinions about the way in which the books and records of an entity are maintained.

5. Fed. R. Civ. P. 26(b)(4). Many state courts do not permit the deposition of a person who may provide expert testimony as a matter of right. In those states, the parties will frequently stipulate to the depositions of opposing experts. Otherwise, the deposition of an expert witness can only be had by court order with the usual standard being for "good cause shown." Suffice it to say that expert witness depositions are less common in state than federal courts.

6. Fed. R. Civ. P. 26(b)(4)(A).

2. What information about an expert must be provided before his deposition is taken?

An expert must provide a Rule 26 expert report. Scrutinize the report required of specially retained experts and employees whose duties regularly require providing expert testimony—it will help you decide whether to depose an opposing expert. The report must contain the following:

(i) a complete statement of all of the opinions the witness will express and the basis and reasons for them;

(ii) the facts or data considered by the witness in forming the opinions;[7]

(iii) any exhibits that will be used to summarize or support the opinions;

(iv) the witness's qualifications, including a list of all publications authored in the previous ten years;

(v) a list of all other cases in which, during the previous four years, the witness testified as an expert at trial or by deposition;[8] and

(vi) a statement of compensation to be paid for the study and the testimony in the case.[9]

This report, which the drafters clearly intended to expand the factual disclosure required beyond "bases and reasons" to "facts or data considered" by the expert witness in forming opinions, should contain facts, data, and theories that were rejected by the expert witness. Assuming opposing counsel chooses to depose the expert, the information provided in the Rule 26 report will provide the outline for much of that deposition.

3. Should I take the deposition of every expert who provides a Rule 26 report?

When deciding whether to depose an opposing expert witness, you must consider both the practical and tactical as aspects.

---

7. The Federal Rules of Civil Procedure protect the following from disclosure: draft reports (regardless of their form) and communications between the party's attorney and the expert during the report preparation (regardless of form) unless they relate to compensation for the expert's study or testimony; facts provided by the attorney that were considered (even if rejected) by the expert; and assumptions provided to the expert by the attorney on which the expert relied. FED. R. CIV. P. 26(b)(4)(B) and (C).

8. Some district judges' discovery orders require the witness to provide the name of the party and lawyer on whose behalf expert testimony was given. If not, the same information can be had through written interrogatory, as well as during the deposition.

9. FED. R. CIV. P. 26(a)(2)(B).

a. The Practical—Costs

Will the case economically support the taking of expert depositions? In contingency fee cases, the costs of litigation, including those associated with taking expert depositions, are—after a successful verdict—the responsibility of the client.[10] There are cases where a substantial percentage of any award will be eaten up by the extra cost of taking expert witness depositions—in addition to the normal costs of taking a deposition, experts are entitled to reasonable fees for the time spent in deposition. The court will determine the reasonableness of an expert's fee by reviewing the fee arrangement between the expert and the lawyer who engaged the expert and applying that hourly rate to the time spent providing deposition testimony. In addition, a court might include travel and expense reimbursement, if in the agreement between the expert and engaging counsel.[11] Before undertaking expert depositions in a contingency case, also consider the possibility that your client will lose. Experts still have to be paid, and unless your client has deep pockets, you may find yourself entangled in another lawsuit over costs.

Cost is also an issue when you bill at an hourly rate. Expert witness costs are part of the ongoing expense of litigation, billed with attorney's fees on a monthly basis or drawn against a retainer.

Always consider the amount in controversy and/or the importance of the issue in litigation—irrespective of expense—before incurring any expense; the costs associated with deposing an expert witness may exceed the value, in dollar terms or otherwise, of its worth to your client.

In any event, if you choose to depose an opposing expert, ordinary good practice suggests that you consult with your own retained expert to prepare for deposing the opposing expert. This consultation has attendant costs.

Finally, taking an expert deposition may provide a cost incentive to an opposing party to settle a case, given the time and expense it imposes on the opposing party. The noticing of an expert deposition to increase the costs of an opponent as an inducement to settlement, however, may be considered "frivolous"[12] and as

10. The Model Rules of Professional Conduct allow a contingent fee lawyer to advance the costs of the litigation, the payment of which may be contingent on the outcome of the case. MRPC 1.8(e). This rule made legitimate the practice of most contingent fee lawyers not to seek payment of advanced costs (although the legal responsibility of the client) unless the case is won.

11. Fed. R. Civ. P. 26(b)(4)(C). Most courts will not grant fees to the expert for preparation time before the deposition. The expert is assumed to know the subject matter of his testimony, and obviously preparation time with retaining and defending counsel for the deposition is excluded. In addition, the rule excuses the payment of fees for expert depositions if "manifest injustice would result." Such circumstances are rare and usually involve indigent clients in cases involving issues of public importance where substantial financial recovery is unlikely, such as in cases where the primary goal of the litigation is injunctive or other equitable relief.

12. MRPC Rule 3.1, 3.4(d).

such be barred ethically, but such tactics do exist. They are, in fact, defended by many lawyers as effective advocacy—or even required in the zealous representation of a client.[13]

b. The Tactical

i. The Existence of a Rule 26 Expert Report

As noted above, Rule 26 expert reports are required of expert witnesses who have been specifically retained to provide expert testimony in the case as well as by those employees of the party who, as part of their regular job duties, provide expert testimony for a party.[14]

The rules also contemplate cases in which a party calls an expert witness who is not specifically retained to provide expert testimony and is not an employee whose regular duties require the providing of expert testimony.[15] As noted earlier, for these latter experts, written discovery is limited to the Rule 26 expert disclosures.[16] Because of this limited discovery, you would be well advised to depose such a witness.

In our hypothetical case, for example, defending counsel should depose the chair of the tenurial faculty, who the plaintiff has identified as an expert who will present an opinion about Ms. Williams's teaching and scholarly qualifications. His deposition will reveal the sources of information on which he relied, the scope of his opinions, his credibility as a witness, his professional relationship with the plaintiff, and any other fact or circumstance relevant to his opinions.

ii. Potential Limiting Effect of the Rule 26 Expert Report

Rule 26 requires the expert report to be complete.[17] Based on this, many federal judges are treating the report as having the same effect as "four corners" statutes. This means that any opinion, fact, or basis not contained within the four corners of the expert's report cannot be referenced.[18] These are rules of fairness because they require an expert witness to state the factual bases for an opinion, the facts relied on for that opinion, and the methodological bases for that opinion. Opposing counsel can then fashion a proper response in the form of an opposing expert or cross-examination.

---

13. The ancillary effect on settlement of noticing an expert deposition on settlement is not advocated by the authors—merely noted as a tactic that does exist.

14. *Supra* at note 3.

15. *Supra* note 4.

16. The subject matter of the expert testimony and a summary of the facts and opinions about which the witness is expected to testify must be provided.

17. Fed. R. Civ. P. 26(b)(4)(A).

18. These "four corners" rule statutes typically exist in those jurisdictions where the ability to depose expert witnesses is limited by the rules of discovery.

If you are before a court inclined to enforce a four-corners approach to the Rule 26 expert report, and you can live with the report and its contents,[19] you might not want to depose the expert witness disclosed during discovery. The four-corners report interpretation is limited to the report, and so does not affect any information you obtain while deposing the expert, which would become fair game for trial testimony. If, however, an expert's testimony will not be limited by the report's content, consider deposing the expert to obtain further information—additional opinions, factual bases, theories or methodologies, or reasons for the expert's opinion—so you can be prepared for opposing expert testimony and cross-examination at trial.

iii. The Opportunity to Show Demeanor and Explain Expert Opinions

If experts will not be called as witnesses at a trial or an ADR proceeding, the sole expert input for the eventual decision makers will be the expert witness reports and depositions. Mediators, arbitrators, and party decision makers will consider the important technical information in these reports to decide what occurred in the events underlying the lawsuit; how they occurred; their causation; and the damages, if any, caused to the parties. In most forms of ADR, the decision maker will not hear live expert testimony. They will be able to peruse deposition testimony, and of course we assume the modern deposition of any variety will be recorded using video digital technology.[20]

An expert witness deposition, especially a video-recorded one, can put a face to the testimony, giving it life and persuasiveness. While deposing counsel elicits information about the expert witness's opinions and the bases for those opinions, she is, at the same time, providing an opportunity for the expert witness to explain and clarify the meaning of his opinions. An expert with a good demeanor will further persuade the decision maker. Digital video recorded testimony, will, in most cases, out-persuade a written report.[21]

A deposition gives opposing counsel as well as deposing counsel a chance to question the witness. Counsel can explore and expand the meaning and nuance of the expert's opinion, which in the end may enhance the expert testimony's credibility and evidentiary worth.

19. This is especially so when the report omits important facts about how the expert formed such opinions or relies on a methodology or theory that is subject to a *Daubert*/Rule 702 challenge.

20. For this reason, a party might conduct a Rule 32(a)(4) deposition of an expert witness after discovery has been completed to preserve trial testimony. In that deposition, the expert will be examined on direct and cross-examination as if at trial. Thus, even if the case will be disposed through a variety of ADR techniques, the factfinder will have the benefit of the demeanor and persuasiveness of presentation available from such an examination, as opposed to the less focused and coherent typical discovery deposition.

21. It is possible, of course, that any given expert may be well known for poor presentation skills. Obviously, in those cases, putting a face on the opinion might very well serve the deposing party.

These two factors—the ability to display demeanor and the ability to explain and clarify information contained in written discovery—will normally mitigate against deposing an expert witness. Don't count on the poor demeanor of an expert and an opposing counsel who will not take the opportunity to clarify and explain testimony that may be confusing or misleading.

iv. Impeaching Information

When the litigation end game is a trial, counsel often withholds information available to impeach the credibility of an expert witness until trial cross-examination—this is so the expert cannot shore up weaknesses in his testimony revealed at the deposition. Given the modern assumption that trial is unlikely and the fact that there are often few unexpected lines of cross-examination available, consider deposing an expert witness to explore the credibility of his opinions, including presenting impeaching information at the deposition. If you cannot impeach an opposing expert witness extrinsically,[22] the availability of impeaching evidence about an opposing expert witness mitigates in favor of conducting that deposition. The downside, of course, is that opposing counsel can rebut that impeachment at the deposition (albeit without the same length of time for consideration) or present other rehabilitating evidence.

Do not take an expert's deposition only to present impeaching evidence. If there is another advisable reason for taking the expert deposition, however, be sure to include impeachment in the topics you explore and thereby make available to the ultimate ADR decision maker.

4. How do I best prepare for the expert witness deposition?

Begin by reviewing the information already provided by the opposing party.[23] Before you receive the Rule 26 expert report or the Rule 26 expert disclosures, you will have developed information about the party's position on any particular matter where expert testimony is required. At the outset, unless you or your client is familiar with the particular area of expertise, retain a consulting expert to help you understand the basics of the science, technology or other area of expertise. The consulting expert is not subject to discovery by the opposing party except under the following extraordinary circumstances.[24] First, trial preparation materials protection can be overcome if the consulting expert possesses information, or its equivalent, that is

22. The report of a party's own expert, a document, or the testimony of another witness are examples of extrinsic impeachment.

23. Counsel will have made at least a form of this review by the time she needs to decide whether to conduct the deposition.

24. Fed. R. Civ. P. 26((b)(4)(D).

otherwise discoverable and cannot be obtained without undue hardship.[25] In that case, the consulting expert may be deposed, although limited by the above-stated exception.[26] Second, if the consulting expert's work product is later provided to the testifying expert, it becomes material considered by the testifying expert and is discoverable, as required by Rule 26.[27]

With or without the help of a consulting expert, once other discovery is completed you will likely have retained your own expert, had preliminary discussions about the scope and content of the expert's opinions, exchanged factual information developed during informal and formal discovery, and at least have spoken about the theories or methodologies the expert will use—you might even have received draft reports from the retained expert.

Rules 26(b)(4)(B) and (C) provide work-product protection to communications between you and an expert witness that are required to prepare a Rule 26 expert report.[28] This includes drafts of such reports as well as the impressions, conclusions, opinions, or legal theories about which you and the expert communicated while the report was being prepared. Excluded from this protection is information provided by the lawyer to the expert and, of course, information about expert compensation.

Note that the rules are silent about work-product protections for expert witnesses who need only supply Rule 26 expert disclosures.[29] This will, of course, be relevant to the preparation of such experts. The best opinions arise from an expert who is informed of all the facts and relevant information. But if you have sensitive information that you do not want disclosed, share it on a strict need-to-know basis. And be careful about discussing legal and factual theories with such experts.

Most discovery orders require the plaintiff's Rule 26 expert reports and/or disclosures to be made first, with the defendants having a certain time (usually thirty days) to respond with their own Rule 26 expert reports and/or disclosures. This

25. FED. R. CIV. P. 26(b)(3)(A). For example, in a collision case where serious injury is involved, an entity (e.g., UPS) may, as a matter of routine, send a team of investigators who are employee consulting experts to investigate the scene of the collision. Unless there is equivalent information—e.g., an accident reconstruction performed at the scene by law enforcement—the plaintiff (or his estate) may not be able to replicate the information obtained in that private investigation when the lawsuit is filed several years after the incident.

26. A party may discover from the opposing consulting expert only the work-product information that the witness possesses, is otherwise discoverable, and is not available without undue hardship to the discovering party.

27. FED. R. CIV. P. 26(a)(2)(B).

28. As set out in Rule 26(b)(3)(A) and (B).

29. Traditional rules of statutory construction would suggest that the drafters of the Federal Rules of Civil Procedure intended that all communications between a lawyer and a Rule 26(a)(2)(C) expert witness, as well as all draft reports— whatever their form—be discoverable by the opposing party by way of deposition, document production request pursuant to Rule 34, or otherwise. If draft reports are discoverable, there is an arguable duty to preserve them as potential evidence in the case.

exchange of reports/disclosures must be completed ninety days before trial, unless the court discovery order sets a different timeframe.[30] This leaves time to conduct expert depositions. The plaintiff's expert may then respond to the defense expert reports, and those submissions are then subjected to a short turnaround response by the plaintiff.[31]

Once you have the Rule 26 expert report or disclosure—and earlier, if you know the identity of opposing counsel's expert—undertake the following.

1) Subject the identified expert witness to a Google or similar search to check for a full statement of professional qualifications, affiliations, accomplishments, etc. In addition, an electronic search of court filings can identify expert witness testimony, etc., as can various subject-matter related services.
2) Send the Rule 26 expert report or disclosure report to your own testifying expert (and/or consulting expert) for analysis and critique.
3) Make an electronic search for previous testimony by the witness (four years of which will be provided in a Rule 26 expert report).[32] Have a paralegal—or in a case involving sufficient importance to warrant the expense, a consulting expert—review that former testimony for inconsistencies, such as use of a methodology or theory in a previous case that is rejected in the current case.[33]
4) Assign the publications listed in a Rule 26 expert report to a paralegal or consulting expert for analysis; have them prepare a synopsis of each publication to determine whether the expert has writings that are inconsistent with the opinions provided.
5) Determine the factual basis for the opinions expressed and the source of that factual basis. Identify the particular exhibit(s) or testimony that provides the factual basis for the opinions stated by the expert in her report. This information should be available in the Rule 26 report, but often, the report is far from specific source the source of any particular fact. Most Rule 26 reports do not cite to an exhibit or a deposition for a particular fact, but begin with a list of the information considered

30. Fed. R. Civ. P. 26(a)(2)(D)(i).

31. Rule 26(a)(2)(D)(ii) provides that if the response is intended solely as rebuttal or contradiction by either party of subject matter contained in either the Rule 26 expert report or disclosure, the response time is thirty days.

32. Qualifications, publications, previous testimony, and exhibits used to summarize or support experts who must provide Rule 26 Expert Disclosures are not required to be made in the disclosure. You should obtain that information through alternative sources, such as expert interrogatories pursuant to Rule 33 or informal fact investigation, and you should apply the same scrutiny to an expert providing a Rule 26 expert report as you would to those experts for whom Rule 26 expert disclosures need only be provided.

33. For the purposes of this review, a graduate student in the area of expertise involved can conduct the review as a consulting expert.

when preparing the report (e.g., in our hypothetical case, party depositions, Professor Taylor's deposition, employment records, etc.). The process of identifying particular sources for facts underlying the testimony of experts who provide only Rule 26 disclosures is more difficult given the lack of information required by the rules for such witnesses.

6) Determine the methodology or theory employed by the expert.
7) Determine and review the authoritative sources or other technical support for the opinion mentioned in the report.
8) Compare the points of similarity, agreement, and disagreement between the qualifications, opinions, and bases of the opposing experts and your experts.[34]

5. What are the typical topics for the expert deposition?

The above information, once gathered, should provide the basis for a discussion between you and your client's expert to prepare for the topics that you should consider for the opposing expert's deposition. The best sources for the basic topics to be covered in an expert deposition are the Rule 26 expert reports or disclosures about his testimony that the identified expert witness is required to divulge, the *Daubert/Kumho Tire*[35] factors for admissibility of opinions, and the Federal Rules of Evidence requirements governing expert testimony.[36]

Federal Rule of Evidence 702 provides that an expert witness can be qualified by "knowledge, skill, experience, training, or education."[37] The Rule 26 expert report[38] must include the witness's qualifications, including a listing of publications within ten years of the report, as well as trial and deposition expert testimony in the four years before the report.[39] The evidence rule, then, is not comprehensive, in that the acquiring of expertise is not limited to the factors mentioned in the rule, and the Rule 26 procedure leaves the extent of qualifications to be listed in the report (with the exception of publications and previous expert testimony) to its drafter.

Those two sets of rules leave open a great deal of potential inquiry about the qualifications and potential impeachment of an expert witness. The expert wit-

34. You should have the same comparison made between the draft reports available from those experts for whom Rule 26 expert disclosures are required.

35. Daubert v. Merrill Dow Pharmaceuticals, Inc., 509 U.S. 579 (1973); Kumho Tire v. Carmichael, 526 U.S. 127 (1999)

36. FED R. EVID. 702–706.

37. FED R. EVID. 702.

38. Assume that all those factors of qualification contained in the Rule 26 expert report should be obtained and are areas of inquiry in the deposition of an expert witness for whom only Rule 26 expert disclosures are required.

39. This requirement can serve as qualifying factors as it shows that the witness has been accepted as an expert witness. It also opens the door to potential impeachment of that the witness on a number of bases.

ness may be asked about the following matters of qualification, which may lead to matters of impeachment.

1) His qualifications—Rule 26 requires the expert witness to provide some qualifications in his report. For witnesses required to make such reports, résumés may be created for the case. Review the complete recitation of sources of knowledge, skill, experience, training or education. While interesting and informative in and of itself, this recitation may reveal that although the opinion in question is within the ambit of the witness's expertise sufficient for qualification as an expert under the rules of evidence, the particular matter about which testimony is given may be a sidelight in his day-to-day practice of his profession.[40] It may also reveal a bias in terms of a school of thought to which the witness subscribes, which may have an impact on the persuasiveness of an opinion.

   If the expert uses a website to advertise his availability for litigation support, this is a good source for qualifications information. Because the website is a marketing device, it is designed to cast a large net for potential clients. As such, there is a tendency to inflate the advertiser's expertise and the types of cases and testimony on which the expert can provide an opinion. The broader the claim of expertise, the more likely it is that the special expertise required for any given case will be lacking, at least to some degree.

2) The number of times the witness has testified for the law firm (or the law firm's clients law firm) and/or the particular party on whose behalf they have been retained to testify in the present matter.[41] As a result, in our hypothetical case, deposing counsel should ask how many times the expert has been retained for the purpose of providing advice, a report, or testimony for Nita University (or any other defendants) or similar parties (e.g., another defendant sued for gender discrimination), or for the lawyer or law firm responsible for retaining the expert in the hypothetical case.

40. In a case where the plaintiff claims a traumatic brain injury as the result of a car collision, any neurologist would be qualified to provide a diagnosis of the plaintiff's condition, opine on its cause, opine on the necessary treatment, and opine on the prognosis for a plaintiff who claims such an injury. But the neurologist who spends most of his professional life dealing with organic brain conditions (such as those presented by a stroke)—as opposed to a neurologist who works with traumatic brain injured patients—may not be as credible on the subject. Fully exploring the expert's qualifications would reveal such a weakness, which might not be so apparent in the qualifications provided in the Rule 26 report.

41. Lawyers and law firms tend to return to experts with whom they have had good experiences, both in terms of interaction and ease in dealing with them, and in the results obtained for their clients when retaining the expert. The same is so of parties that are sued with some frequency over matters of a certain sort. For example, a large entity will frequently be sued for allegations of discrimination of all sorts (race, gender, age, national origin, etc.), and need expert economic testimony about the economic loss of the particular plaintiff, assuming there was discrimination. In such cases, the paid expert has a potential economic interest in reaching a favorable opinion for a returning client. This sometimes referred to as a personal bias.

3) The percentage of cases in which an expert testifies for one position or another. For example, in our hypothetical case, the defense expert may testify on a regular basis for institutional defendants in discrimination cases;[42]

4) Rule 26 requires the report to list testimony in trial or deposition in the four years previous to the report, but does not require a listing of testimony outside the four year parameter; nor does it require a list of times when the expert was retained to provide advice or opinions that did not result in testimony, but for which he provided a report or other written analysis. Previous testimony provides fertile ground for contradictions between methodology or judgments made in previous cases and the present case.

5) Rule 26 requires the report to state the compensation that an expert has received or will receive for services to a party, presumably as a potential source of inferred bias or improper motive.[43] The rule does not require the expert to disclose the total amount of annual compensation he receives from providing expert witness services. Experts are all paid, but for some, acting as an expert witness is a one-time event. For others, such retention is occasional. For yet others, delivering expert witness services provides a significant portion of their annual compensation, although they may retain another occupation (e.g., university professor or physician). Finally, there are those expert witnesses who do nothing but provide expert witness services (sometimes called litigation support).[44] This information is valuable is assessing the reliability and weight to be given the opinions of such experts, no matter who acts as the final decision maker.

6) Rule 26 requires the report to list the expert's publications within ten years of filing the report. The report does not require him to disclose the topic (other than by title) of the publication. Although in most cases a lawyer or paralegal will be tasked to read and provide a synopsis of such publications in search of inconsistent statements regarding topics relevant to the current

42. This is sometimes referred to as a positional bias. This is not unusual, especially in the field of economics, accounting, and other financial matters, where assumptions legitimately made in the field of expertise can be favorable to plaintiffs or to defendants. If an expert testifies for both plaintiffs and defendants, he will easily be impeached because the assumptions made when testifying for a plaintiff in one case would be inapposite to assumptions made when testifying for a defendant in another. Most experts would prefer to be consistent in their assumptions and be open to an attack for positional bias (which can be explained in an intellectually honest way (e.g., the assumption is appropriate for the following reasons . . . .)), than inconsistent based on the party who hired the expert.

43. This issue, at least with regard to the compensation for expert witness services in any given case, is usually a nonstarter for impeachment, because what is true for the defendant's expert is usually true for the plaintiff's expert.

44. For example, there are physicians who do nothing but conduct Rule 35 physical or mental examinations on behalf of parties to litigation (usually defendants because plaintiffs with claimed injuries normally rely on treating medical professionals for their expert opinions). In addition, there are businesses that do nothing but provide expert testimony, typical of which are consulting engineers and economists.

lawsuit, some cases warrant enlisting the services of a consulting expert.[45] In either case, the expert's publications may reveal changes in philosophy or expert point of view from written scholarship to retained testimony.

7) Most Rule 26 expert reports provide the expert's qualification in résumé form. That résumé will demonstrate the expertise (in addition to those methods discussed above) using Rule 702 as a guideline. Given that, you should examine the expert's qualifications with regard to his "knowledge, skill, experience, training, or education." A well-qualified expert's resume will show the requisite knowledge and skill, demonstrated through education and formal training, but especially through experience. Again, when looking at qualifications, consider whether the expert merely has intellectual or educational expertise or whether he has demonstrated the ability to use that knowledge in a real-world setting.

   For example, in our hypothetical case, an economist whose sole qualifications are academic (degrees and teaching) will likely be outmatched by an economist with comparable education and experience applying that education (in the form of governmental or private economic forecasting experience or advice on the economics of hiring decisions). An expert for the defendant in our discrimination case can support an opinion that the plaintiff's tenure was not "in the long-term interests of the university" (a requirement for tenure) because the forecast of students entering the public policy school was declining; he is qualified to so opine, having performed such analyses for real-world decisions in the private sector on the size of a labor force, even if (and perhaps because) that analysis was unrelated to any litigation.

8) Be sure to ask about the amount of actual work performed by the designated testifying expert in the preparation of his report. It is not unusual for testifying experts to delegate some or most research and other work involved in the creation of reports to less qualified colleagues, graduate students, or others. Obtaining this information and the qualifications of the person(s) who contributed to the report can impact the report's credibility and the opinions expressed therein.

6. How do I test the reliability of the methodology or theory used by the expert?

The Federal Rules of Evidence require that expert testimony, to be admissible, must be "the product of reliable principles and methods."[46] In so doing, the rule

45. In a case involving a potentially substantial amount of damages, the task of reading and critiquing scholarship may fall to an expert witness—either the witness who will also provide a report and potential testimony or a consulting expert who is usually younger and less experienced in the area of expertise and therefore less expensive.

46. Fed. R. Evid. 702(2).

makers incorporated the *Daubert* and *Kumho Tire*[47] rulings and their progeny as a matter of federal evidentiary law. *Daubert* set out nonexclusive factors to be considered when determining whether a matter was a proper one for expert testimony, all of which are appropriate matters for expert depositions. Those factors were:

a) whether the expert's methodology (or theory)[48] has been tested;

b) whether the methodology or theory in question has been published and subject to peer review;

c) what is the error rate when applying the methodology or theory;

d) are there standards or controls for the use of the methodology or theory; and

e) whether the methodology or theory has been generally accepted in the field to which it belongs.[49]

In addition to the list of *Daubert* factors, many courts include in their reliability calculation whether the methodology has "nonjudicial uses"—is there any real-world application,[50] as opposed to being used solely for litigation purposes; they also look at whether the theory or methodology is part of the normal curriculum within a particular area of academic study.

You should first consider the methodology or theory applied by your own expert. If opposing counsel's expert uses a different methodology or theory, be prepared to rebut that the opposing expert's choices as less reliable. (Also expect that opposing counsel will try to do the same with your expert's methodologies—make sure your results are defensible.)

---

47. Daubert v. Merrill Dow Pharmaceuticals, Inc., 509 U.S. 579 (1973); Kumho Tire v. Carmichael, 526 U.S. 127 (1999).

48. *Daubert* dealt with a methodology used by proposed expert witnesses to determine whether a causative link existed between the use of a particular pharmaceutical product and birth defects, which in the view of the court was a matter science. In *Kumho Tire*, the court made clear that the holding of *Daubert* applied to technology as well. Finally, the analysis applies whether the expert witness relies on either a "methodology" or a "theory."

49. This factor is taken from *Frye v. United States*, 293 F. 1013 (D.C. Cir. 1923), and was the predominant test for the admissibility of expert testimony as applied in both the state and federal courts. In fact, some states (including New York, Pennsylvania, Illinois, and California) still follow the *Frye* rule, although the trend is toward the more flexible reliability test of the federal evidence rules. That being said, the authors have not found any case where a federal court has found that a methodology or theory meets the *Frye* test and the opinion has been declined on that basis. If a methodology or theory an expert witness uses meets *Frye*, a court would look to the application or a sufficient factual or database deficiency to disallow the proposed opinion.

50. This is an excellent logical place to begin an inquiry into a methodology or theory. If the methodology or theory is accepted for real-world decisions (e.g., a doctor's medical treatment decisions about a patient or an economist's decisions on the value of a business for the purpose of sale or financing), then a court would be hard pressed to find the theory or methodology unreliable (although application and factual predicate issues might remain).

In addition, explore the bases for the methodology or theory in authoritative writings. The well-crafted Rule 26 expert report will identify the authoritative writings that provide the reliability basis for the methodology or theory that the expert used. You and your client's expert should review those sources. Compare them with the sources your expert relied on to determine why different sources were used by each expert. The answer may be as easy as the theory or methodology is so well accepted that it can be found in any authoritative source. It might be that the opposing authoritative source represents one school of thought, different from that relied on by your expert. This is not uncommon in matters of economics where, unlike accounting for example, there are not generally accepted published principles. If the schools of thought are different—and, of course, if they yield different results—then you must explore reasons for the different schools of thought and their implications. Finally, it might be that the authoritative text used by the opposing expert (or by your expert) is out of date and presents serious admissibility issues.

When analyzing the theory or methodology employed by an opposing expert, as noted earlier, consider whether to hold an expert deposition. If you are left with substantial questions about the reliability of the methodology, theory, its basis or applications after analyzing the opposing expert's Rule 26 expert report, you may be wise to not take the expert's deposition and just go forward, with an in limine motion objecting to the admissibility of expert testimony based on the opposing expert's Rule 26 report.[51]

7. How do I test the reliability of the application of the expert of theories and methodologies?

For an expert opinion to be admissible pursuant to Rule 702, the expert must not only use a reliable methodology or theory, but also must execute that methodology or theory in a reliable way. In other words, a reliable methodology, performed in an unreliable way, is inadmissible. It is to this issue that several *Daubert* factors were addressed. Using the teaching of *Daubert*, place a premium on whether the expert's methodology has standardized procedures that can be replicated, has been tested, and has an error rate that is known.

Those standards will inform your preparation for the expert's deposition. Although you and your expert will stake out a position regarding the accepted methodology, there is some profit in determining whether the opposing expert knows the standardized procedures for a particular methodology and whether he actually followed them. It is not uncommon for expert witnesses to modify a methodology to produce what they consider more accurate results. Even assuming that he had a legitimate reason for varying with the standard (or the expert's standard) methodology, make the expert defend and validate his variances. To explore the issue of variance, request the expert's working papers under Civil Procedure Rule 34 when noticing the opposing expert for deposition.

---

51. Based on *Daubert/Kumho Tire* and FED. R. EVID. 702.

8. How do I test the sufficiency of data or other information the expert relied on?

The factual predicate for the expert's opinion must be set out in the Rule 26 expert report or disclosures. When preparing for the opposing expert's deposition, consider those factual bases and their sources.

Rule 26 requires the expert report or disclosure to state (in list or prose form) the facts that underlie the stated opinions. Sometimes, however, the report does not attribute the facts or data to a particular opinion with any specificity. For example, the typical expert report or disclosure will contain a section entitled Materials Reviewed and include such items as the pleadings, the depositions of (list deponents), certain exhibits, official reports (police, etc.), authoritative sources, interviews with (list witnesses), etc. You must ferret out which fact or set of facts have been provided from which source. The less reliable the source, the less reliable the opinion will be—and if you show that, the less persuasion it will carry with a factfinder.

Consider in our hypothetical case Professor Taylor's expert testimony for the plaintiff about plaintiff's scholarship and teaching. If Professor Taylor relies on student-class evaluations taken by the plaintiff herself and gives them greater weight than those done as a matter of course by the university, his opinion is marginalized. In preparation then, try to determine where the expert obtained the information he used to determine the appropriate weight of the evaluations. If the source is unclear, use the deposition to pinpoint the factual predicate for the expert's opinion to help determine its weight.

When the expert witness seeks to draw inferences from statistical studies, pay attention to the facts or data on which he relies. The expert's opinion is only as good as the factual sample on which the statistical analysis is performed. In our hypothetical case, Ms. Williams wants to show institutional prejudice against granting tenure to women by Nita University or the School of Public Policy. For that inference, she would retain a statistician to examine the tenure-granting tendencies of those institutions. In that circumstance, the sample size chosen and the time period used will affect the inferences that can be drawn from the statistical analysis. If the plaintiff's statistician examines the granting of tenure to professors at the university or public policy school of women over a twenty-five-year period and concludes that there is a prejudice against women, defendants will argue that the basis is unreliable—decisions made several decades before plaintiff's tenure decision may be stale and not reflect the institutional position on tenure and gender at the time the plaintiff was considered.

9. What are the characteristics of an effective expert deposition?

a. Use Your Expert to Be Ready

You do not possess the opposing expert's knowledge; consult with your own experts when preparing and executing depositions of opposing experts. Only a foolish lawyer would not ask her paid expert to criticize the tasks undertaken by the opposing expert, the methodology used, and opinions that result. Work in partnership—the expert's world is about medical treatments, engineering theories, econometric models, or other matters about which we know little; your world is about persuasion and understanding the importance of any piece of evidence to a factfinder. Combining topic expertise with persuasive ability leads to the optimal outcome for your client. Learn what your expert can teach you about deposing the opposing expert. But keep in mind that it is a mistake to follow up on every criticism one expert makes of another. Experts are interested in their field of expertise, and what interests them may be arcane and irrelevant to the business of representing a client in litigation. After hearing what the expert says, use your judgment to decide what is helpful and discard what is of small or no relevance.

b. Limit the Topics of Inquiry

The lawyer's role in litigation is to represent her client's interests and obtain a good result for that client.[52] A good result does not require every fact to be resolved in your client's favor at the deposition. It does mean that the facts necessary for the good result must be proved at the deposition. To be clear, it is not necessary to win every point to provide a good result. But we, as lawyers, are aggressive by nature and want to win. When dealing with experts, don't get side tracked trying to win every point with the opposing expert—it's not necessary to get a good result, and may be detrimental.

Let's consider our hypothetical case. The plaintiff has claimed institutional gender discrimination in tenure decisions; a hostile work environment towards women; and gender discrimination via retaliation for her ending a sexual relationship with one of her employers, Professor Simonson. Assume that the statistical evidence from the plaintiff's point of view supports the claim of systemic gender discrimination, but only in a long view (twenty-five years). The statistics are weaker on that issue in the shorter (seven-year) view, and the opposing statistician uses this data for his opinion. While the plaintiff's expert has some questions about the defense expert's methodology, he generally agrees with the opposing conclusions.

Plaintiff's counsel has multiple options: drop the claim of institutional gender discrimination; argue that the twenty-five-year view is the appropriate one; argue that the opposing expert's methodology is faulty; or accept the view and make the claim based on the less forceful statistics of the seven-year view. Assume that

52. We define a good result as one in which the client's rights have been zealously represented and that the law has provided the relief to which a client is entitled. We do not believe that means that to get a good result every plaintiff must receive every nickel available, no matter what tactic is necessary. Nor does it mean that for every defendant the only good result is to pay nothing. That philosophizing done, we claim no moral or ethical superiority, but we are of the opinion that a good result requires a well-prepared, thoughtful, and persistent lawyer in pursuit of the client's legitimate goals. We also believe that most lawyers do precisely that in representing their clients.

a focus group gave the twenty-five-year statistic less weight than the seven-year statistic when considering whether systemic gender discrimination affected the plaintiff's tenure. In that case, there is no need to challenge the opposing expert in deposition about the twenty-five-year view. Instead, establish that there is some (albeit not conclusive) statistical evidence of institutional gender discrimination given a seven-year view. Then obtain the facts of the methodology used by defendant's expert and figure out why, if it does, the methodology departs from the accepted methodology. Any information obtained can be used for trial and as the basis for an *in limine* motion—that is enough for this witness.

c. Facts v. Conclusions

It is an unusual case where the lawyer knows more about the relevant area of expertise than the expert, can demonstrate that during the expert's deposition, and win the case. The lawyer may know what her experts have told her, and she may believe she has sufficient acquired knowledge about the area of expertise to determine that her experts are "better" or "correct" and the opposing party's experts are "not so good" and "wrong." But it's a rare opposing expert who recants or changes his mind. If you mount a substantive challenge, you may make the other side aware of weaknesses in the opposing expert's opinion that they can analyze and refine or explain away at trial. In cases where the opposing expert relied on inaccurate facts or misapplied facts, spend your deposition time locking the opposing expert down on the facts on which he relied. Then later argue that the facts are insufficient or unreliable as a basis for the opinion provided—both in motion practice and presenting affirmative expert testimony that considers all relevant facts.[53]

d. Simple Language

After consulting with experts, reading about the area of expertise involved, and participating in expert discovery, you will acquire new vocabulary from the area of expertise involved. We have learned about econometric models, subdural hematomas, coefficients of friction, and the like—and when communicating with our experts, we use this new vocabulary regularly. To do so is efficient and appropriate as it tests our knowledge and assures that we understand what the expert has to offer.

The expert's deposition is another matter. Now you are obtaining information that a finder of fact (arbitrator, party decision maker, maybe even jurors) can use in making a finding that benefits your client. This ultimate audience won't understand the new vocabulary you learned in the litigation process. Thus, for the purposes of

53. We are mindful that the expert, after having received notice of the facts he was missing, can modify hs opinion or attempt to explain the facts away. That risk is one to be weighed, but usually such modification or explanation will ring hollow with a factfinder.

deposition—and all of litigation—simple language is important. This is not an easy task when dealing with an expert. It is incumbent on you to have the expert deponent translate the technical and complex into plain language.

If the case is to be arbitrated by a professional arbitrator in a particular industry, the simple language is not a problem; the arbitrator will know more about the area of expertise than you. The problem here might be your lack of sophistication, not too much. If, however, trial or an ADR option that involves lay people is possible, then use language to describe the complex and technical that reflects the level understood by the intelligent, high-school educated person—the typical juror. If an expert's trial testimony is inconsistent with his deposition testimony, the deposition testimony must be in language that the factfinder understands; otherwise the impeachment's force is lost.

This plain language proscription does not mean the expert language may never be used when deposing an expert—sometimes it is inevitable that the factfinder must be taught some new vocabulary to decide the case. For example, in a civil case involving goods lost in transit, the phrase "risk of loss" will be critical to the case, and jurors must know what that phrase means. During deposition, the defense expert should describe "risk of loss" as "who has to pay for lost shipments—the buyer, seller, or shipper." But you won't have to insert that definition each and every time this key phrase is used. If, however, a doctor describes a plaintiff as having sustained "contusions and abrasions," coach him to use "bruises and scratches" instead.[54]

10. Can you provide direction for effective examination techniques in expert depositions?

With the above guidance in mind, here are some examples of questioning techniques that you may find helpful to illustrate these points. We will consider typical topics of deposition inquiry, provide examples, and briefly describe their import.

a. Qualifications

Example: Discovery has provided the expert's résumé and other qualifications. With that information as a base, consider the following from our hypothetical case, with the defendant taking the plaintiff expert's deposition. We know from his résumé that he is a distinguished academic who testifies infrequently (once in the past four years).

Q: *I am showing you Exhibit 41, Dr. Morris, which appears to be a report authored by you in this matter. Do you recognize Exhibit 41?*

A: *I do—it's my report that I prepared in this case about the potential lost earnings of Professor Williams.*

54. The plaintiff might want to use "contusions" and "abrasions" under the theory that they sound worse and are therefore worth more. If you have a focus group, you can use it to judge the reactions to the phrase.

Q: *Please describe what your task was in preparing this report.*
A: *I was to assume that Professor Williams was the victim of gender discrimination and determine the loss of past and future income on account of that discrimination.*
Q: *I look at your list of classes taught in Exhibit 41. Do any of them cover, in depth, the issue about which you are providing testimony?*
A: *I cover the basic way in which future income can be calculated in my Forensic Economics Seminar, which I teach every three years or so.*
Q: *What other courses cover the topic?*
A: *None.*
Q: *So none of the other ten courses you have taught have anything to do with your task in this matter?*
A: *Well, prediction of future economic events is covered in many of these courses listed here.*
Q: *I'm sorry, Dr. Morris, my question was limited to the particular task you undertook in this case.*
A: *So limited, the answer is no.*
Q: *To be clear, the only course you teach that involves the task undertaken by you in this case is a seminar that you offer every three years?*
A: *Yes.*
Q: *Dr. Morris, during the past ten years you have, according to Exhibit 1, authored almost a hundred books, book chapters, or articles, is that accurate?*
A: *I haven't counted, but that sounds right.*
Q: *Would you like to take the time to count?*
A: *No, that won't be necessary, the number sounds right.*
Q: *Of those approximate hundred writings, how many of them have dealt with the task that you undertook in this case?*
A: *There is a chapter on the topic in my book,* Forensic Economics, *Third and Fourth editions.*
Q: *With the exception of that chapter, what other publications do you have dealing with the topic about which you are testifying today?*
A: *The function I performed here is a simple one; it does not require the kind of scholarly inquiry that is typical of academic writing.*
Q: *So your answer is one chapter, out of one book out of about a hundred publications in the past ten years, covers the topic about which you are here to testify?*
A: *Technically, that's true.*
Q: *That's true in every sense. Right, Doctor?*
A: *Yes,*

The previous vignette demonstrates how to minimize a very impressive résumé: while Dr. Morris is overqualified for the task he undertakes, the prediction of lost future income is not an interest or area of specialized expertise for him. It will be true with many experts that a lot of their CV qualifications, as listed in a Rule 26 report or résumé, will be irrelevant to the opinion to be rendered, diminishing a factfinder's view of the witness's qualifications or lessen the value of his opinion when a university decision maker makes an offer of settlement. The vignette also offers attempts by counsel to rein in the professor by insisting on direct answer. If you tug the bridle often enough, many witnesses will just tire of qualifying answers and give direct responses. Then, when a witness does explain or quarrel about a topic, he signals that he might perceive some vulnerability in the area.

b. All Opinions Reached or Rejected, Assumptions Made or Rejected, Bases Relied On or Considered and Rejected, Theories Used or Considered but Rejected, Methodologies Used or Considered but Rejected.

The primary purpose in taking an expert witness's deposition is to determine the opinions reached or considered and rejected, assumptions made or considered rejected, bases relied on or considered and rejected; theories used or considered and rejected, and methodologies employed or considered and rejected by the expert witness. To get this information, use the basic techniques of discovery depositions. Begin with a topic, such as the opinions reached, and exhaust those considered by the expert.

Example: The questioning of Dr. Morris, the expert economist for the plaintiff, continues.

Q: *What ultimate opinion have you reached regarding the plaintiff's past and future lost income, assuming that she was discriminated against or defamed by the defendants?*

A: *$3,125,787 to $5,788,602.*

Q: *Do you hold that opinion to a reasonable degree of economic certainty?*

A: *I do.*

Q: *In reaching that ultimate opinion, was it necessary for you to reach any other opinions?*

A: *Yes.*

Q: *Were those opinions formulated to a reasonable degree of professional certainty?*

A: *Yes, they were.*

Q: *What are those opinions?*

A: *That her work life would be an additional twenty-five years from the date of dismissal from the university; that she would be compensated for productivity, in addition to time in the profession; and that inflation would continue at 2.5 percent per year. I also had to make some assumptions.*

Q: *We'll get into assumptions later, Doctor, but let's explore further opinions you have reached.*

A: *All right . . . .*

[Counsel asks the question "what other opinions did you reach" until the expert says there were no more. If counsel thinks there are other opinions, she would inquire about

those, concluding with the question, "Have you told me every opinion you have reached in this case?" She would only go on after obtaining a "yes" answer from the deponent.]

Q: *While we are on the topic of opinions, are there any opinions that you considered or tentatively reached, but ultimately rejected?*

[Counsel uses the same technique of inquiry regarding opinions reached (above) when drilling down on opinions rejected.]

Q: *Thank you, Doctor. Let's now talk about assumptions you made.*
A: *I assumed that the plaintiff would not be able to find another position in academia at the university level, but I assumed she would be able to find a position in the public or private sector in the field of public policy.*
Q: *What other assumptions did you make?*
A: *I also assumed . . . .*

[Counsel asks the question "what other assumptions did you make" until the expert has agreed that were no more. If counsel thinks the expert made other assumptions, she would ask about those, concluding with the question, "Have you told me every assumption you have made in this case?" She would only go on after obtaining a "yes" answer from the deponent.]

Q: *Are there any assumptions that you considered, but ultimately did not apply?*

[Counsel would use the same technique of inquiry regarding assumptions made when exhausting assumptions that were rejected.]

Apply the same questioning system to the bases for the expert's opinions.

Assume that our hypothetical plaintiff has called an expert witness in the field of statistics to testify that based on his examination of tenure decisions at the university, there is a de facto policy to discriminate against women. As assumed earlier, defense counsel knows that the statistical case is a strong one when viewed from a history of twenty-five years at the university, but not if viewed in a seven-year history, which is the basis used by the university's expert statistician.

Example: Defense Counsel examines plaintiff's expert on a portion of this issue.

Q: *Dr. Charleston, your opinion is that the university's history in granting tenure to women candidates demonstrates that women have a 40 percent less chance of obtaining tenure than men candidates, is that right?*
A: *Yes.*
Q: *In reaching that opinion, you studied the past twenty-five years of tenure decisions made by the university, is that right?*
A: *Yes, I believe that it would take at least that amount of information to reach a statistically valid conclusion.*
Q: *Did you include in your analysis the qualifications of the tenure candidates in their particular fields of study?*

A: *No, I made no effort to do so. I have no expertise in most academic areas at the university. I couldn't begin to evaluate the teaching or scholarship of an English professor, nor would any statistician.*
Q: *Did you include the "long-term interest of the university" tenure factor in your study?*
A: *I did not.*
Q: *Did you consider the changing population of women in the professional teaching ranks in your study?*
A: *Not in particular, but the number of candidates—which has increased—should not impact my statistical analysis of the percentage of candidates granted tenure.*
Q: *Did you consider using a shorter number of years?*
A: *I considered it, but concluded that twenty-five years was the appropriate time.*
Q: *Did you consider using twenty years or fifteen years?*
A: *Again, I considered using shorter time periods, but Nita University is a large institution, and it takes a significant period of information over a considerable period of time to reach valid statistical conclusions.*
Q: *In the past twenty years, there is less imbalance in tenure for men and women than you found in twenty-five years, correct?*
A: *Yes, and somewhat less over fifteen years, but statistically significant difference in treatment of men and women on tenure decisions still existed, albeit at a lower rate.*
Q: *The plaintiff was denied tenure two years ago and was employed at the university for seven years; why not use that time frame for your analysis?*
A: *Although that sounds appealing, as a matter of statistics, your implication that newer information is better information when making a statistical analysis is not supported by the literature.*
Q: *We will get to that later, sir. Are you aware of the statistical study done by Dr. Warshnov and submitted by the university in this litigation?*
A: *I am.*
Q: *He used seven years of information, correct?*
A: *Yes.*
Q: *And he came to a different conclusion about whether there was statistical evidence of gender discrimination at the university during Ms. Williams time there, finding there was a statistically insignificant difference in the granting of tenure for men and women?*
A: *It's different, but in my opinion not valid.*
Q: *Why?*

The vignette illustrates several points. First, counsel is satisfied to get the expert to agree that a study over a different time frame results in a different conclusion and that the statistics are more favorable to the university within a shorter (and more relevant, the university would argue) time period. Counsel does not rise to the expert's bait about either the literature he claims exists or the statistical significance of certain data. That inquiry, if it occurs at all, will happen when deposing counsel consults her own expert or be delayed until deposing counsel's expert testifies and challenges the literature and/or the statistical significance of data.

Use the same questioning system to gather a list of the methodologies the expert employed or considered and rejected. Also get a list of the theories the expert either used or considered and rejected. Having listed all of the above, explore the actual process the expert said he used to reach his opinions. For each opinion, find out the following: 1) facts used and facts rejected and why; 2) assumptions made and assumption rejected and why; 3) bases used and bases rejected and why; 4) methodologies used and rejected and why; and 5) theories used and rejected and why.

Finally, ask the expert, in light of all of the above, to describe the process he used to reach the opinions he expressed in this case.

c. Disagreement with Other Experts

Earlier in the examination, there were several instances where the plaintiff's expert chose a different authoritative source than the one the defendant's expert used and disagreed further about the statistical significance of other information. As mentioned earlier, counsel could leave those issues for defendant's expert to explain. Nonetheless, it is useful to explore this disagreement.

Example: What follows is a vignette demonstrating the form which that examination could take.

Q: *You told us that you disagree with the number of years of data the university's expert statistician used. Why do you disagree with that number of years?*
A: *Because [response].*
Q: *What else do you disagree with about his choice of number of years considered?*
A: *I disagree with [response].*
Q: *What else?*
A: *Nothing else.*
Q: *You have told us all the reasons you disagree with the choice of years considered by the university's expert statistician?*
A: *Yes, I have.*
Q: *What other disagreements do you have with the methodology used by the university's expert statistician?*
A: *The rest of his methodology is fine; I do disagree with some of his conclusions.*
Q: *Let's talk about them. What are those disagreements?*

In the typical expert witness deposition designed to gather information, this questioning would continue until the witness had an opportunity to provide all criticisms of opposing expert's report. Alternatively, it is possible that the expert is being deposed for another reason, such as to limit the scope of matters considered by him; lock him in to those matters, and then proceed to the next level of litigation, whether it be motion practice or disposition by other methods.[55]

55. Depositions of an expert for so limited purposes are unusual because of the Rule 26 report requirement and the potential use of expert witness interrogatories to accomplish the same result.

d. Impeaching the Expert at Deposition

Earlier, we discussed the issue of impeaching an expert witness during deposition. What follows are a number of ways that you can discover impeachment information for later use—or if the deposition is the final word for the witness, to challenge the expert's credibility.[56] When deciding whether to impeach an expert witness during deposition—or save the matter for potential later testimony—a key question is whether there is time for the expert to rebut impeachment between the deposition and any future testimony. If the impeachment is one that cannot be effectively rebutted, then conduct the impeachment during the deposition. Positional/party/lawyer/economic bias is one such area.

i. Positional/Party/Lawyer/Economic Bias

As we discussed earlier, it is not unusual for an expert who testifies frequently to almost always testify for one position or another—e.g., plaintiff's economist in personal injury; for the manufacturer in products cases; for defendant doctors in medical negligence cases.[57] Secondly, lawyers are creatures of experience; if a defendant's lawyer in a personal injury case obtained a good result using a particular expert as an economist (or people in her firm have had such success), she will retain the same economists in future cases. The same is true for entity parties. Experts in cases with successful outcomes for the entity (or similar entities) are often retained again by an entity faced with a similar legal problem. Sometimes, the Rule 26 report makes these apparent biases clear. For example, in our hypothetical case, if the expert economist's Rule 26 report showed that he appeared on behalf of Nita University seven times in the last four years, the party bias is apparent. In other cases and other circumstances, such positional, party, or lawyer bias is not so apparent, and you must elicit it during the deposition.

Example: Plaintiff's counsel is questioning defendant's expert economist.

Q: *Dr. Sullivan, I would like to direct you to your report in this matter, Exhibit 72. Refer if you will to the instances of testimony you have provided as an expert witness in the past four years. If I've counted correctly, over the past four years you have provided expert testimony in twenty depositions and three trials, is that correct?*

A: *I trust your counting. That sounds right.*

Q: *And in each of those occasions you have testified as an expert economist?*

---

56. As has been made clear, the authors believe that the deposition is likely the last testimony to be taken from most witnesses, which mitigates in favor of impeachment. In cases where trial is likely or a form of ADR is used where there is limited testimony (some of which may be from an expert, especially on the issue of damages), if you know of impeachment material, you may save it for that later predictable event.

57. This is so because in cases involving similar issues there are likely methodologies that achieve better results for one position or the other. If an expert were to use methodology A and reject methodology B when testifying on behalf of a plaintiff in a personal injury case, and use methodology B and reject methodology A when testifying for a defendant in another personal injury case, their credibility is easily attacked. Most experts, then, essentially pick a side so that their testimony regarding choice of methodology is intellectually supportable in every case.

A: *That's right.*
Q: *In how many of those occasions were you providing an opinion about lost past and future income of an individual?*
A: *At least 60 percent.*
Q: *And in how many of those occasions did you testify on behalf of an entity, a business?*
A: *All but one.*
Q: *And when you testified as an expert witness in cases about past and future lost income of an individual, how often did you testify on behalf parties against whom a claim had been made?*
A: *All of them.*
Q: *How many of those occasions involved claims of discrimination?*
A: *Of any sort?*
Q: *Yes, let's start there.*
A: *About 50 to 60 percent.*
Q: *And how many of those occasions involved allegations of gender discrimination?*
A: *I'd say about 80 percent.*
Q: *And on each of those occasions you understood that it was in your client's interest that the lost income figure be low as opposed to higher, correct?*
A: *Yes, but that has nothing to do with my opinion.*
Q: *But on each occasion when you provided expert testimony about the claimed amount of past and future lost income, your opinion was for a lower dollar amount than the expert for the party making the claim.*
A: *Of course.*
Q: *In addition to providing testimony on behalf of parties against which claims for past and future lost income have been made, have you been engaged to provide reports concerning the proper amount of those claims and not been called to give testimony?*
A: *I have.*
Q: *How often has that occurred in the past four years?*
A: *I am guessing here, but I'd say about fifteen times a year.*
Q: *You have records that would show an accurate number of those occasions, don't you?*
A: *I do.*
Q: *Can you get that information from your office over a break?*
A: *I can try.*
Q: *[To Defending Counsel] In case Dr. Sullivan cannot get that information from his office, will you provide the information about Dr. Sullivan's engagements when he prepared a report regarding past and future lost income, but did not provide testimony?*
Defending Counsel: We'll take your request under advisement.
Q: *Dr. Sullivan, you have ever been engaged by a party against which a claim of past and future lost income has been made and you provided advice that was not reduced to a report?*

A: *That has happened, but I can't tell you how many times in the past four years, and for sure I can't get that information in a phone call.*

Q: *[To Defending Counsel] Will you provide that information, Mary?*

Defending Counsel: Again Jean, we'll look, but I can't promise will find the information you are looking for.

Q: *Dr. Sullivan, has Ms. Smith's law firm retained by you in the past to provide the sort of expert economic testimony you are providing in this case in the past?*

A: *Yes.*

Q: *How many times?*

A: *Looking at this list, in the past four years, on five occasions.*

Q: *And are there other times when you prepared a report, but not testimony?*

A: *I'm sure there have. When I'm looking for the information you requested, I'll find that out, too.*

Q: *I appreciate that, Dr. Sullivan; and will you also check your records for the past four years for times you provided advice to Ms. Smith or her law firm, but did not write a report?*

A: *I will.*

Q: *Dr. Sullivan, if a client comes to you and asks for your advice on a lost income claim that does not result in a report, what is your fee?*

A: *$350 per hour.*

Q: *And how about if your study results in a report?*

A: *The same, $350 per hour.*

Q: *What is your rate for providing testimony at deposition?*

A. *$7,000 per seven-hour day, with a minimum charge of $3,500 for preparation time with counsel and testimony.*

Q: *What is your fee for providing trial testimony?*

A: *$7,000 per day or any portion of a day.*

Q: *Do you charge for travel time?*

A: *Yes, $250.00 per hour*

Q: *Have you told me about all the potential fees you charge in a matter such as this one in which you are retained?*

A: *I have, but those are gross, not net figures. I have costs of doing business, support people to pay, rent to pay, utilities, just like any business.*

Q: *How long does it take to provide an opinion, not reduced to a report, in a case such as this one?*

A: *It varies—somewhere between four and ten hours.*

Q: *And to write a report?*

A: *About another five hours.*

Q: *And has your testimony at deposition and trial over the past four years as reflected in your report been typical for you?*

A: *Yes, as time goes on, deposition testimony has become more frequent and trial testimony less frequent.*

You can do the math on all of the above later to show the range of income Dr. Sullivan earned by providing favorable testimony for defendants. The examination could be more specific, going through each engagement listed on the report and determining the position taken, the law firm involved, the fee charged; you could do the same regarding engagements not resulting in testimony. Given, however, that deposing counsel's client is paying the expert's rates for deposition testimony and the fact that in many cases the positional and lawyer bias, with financial incentive, will be similar for deposing counsel's own expert, the above is probably the extent of most such inquiry.

In our hypothetical case, however, Sullivan's financial bias is important because he is in contrast with the plaintiff's expert who testifies infrequently. Sullivan is in the litigation support business, which provides him a lot of experience and makes him an effective witness, but comes with economic bias baggage. So for him, this portion of the deposition takes on some significance.

The above vignette demonstrates the importance of getting beyond the disclosure requirements of Rule 26, in which the expert need only provide occasions of testimony, not retention. Further, the expert must divulge fees charged in the instant case, but not generally, nor the amount earned by providing litigation support services. That sort of inquiry is vital with a witness like a medical doctor who both practices medicine and provides expert testimony (not related to his own patients). Some such witnesses earn a surprising percentage of their total income from litigation support, it being a lucrative sideline for many professionals.

Finally, the vignette illustrates the typical response for requests for information outside the questioning at deposition. On two occasions, deposing counsel asked that information be provided from the records of Dr. Sullivan and received the stock reply, "We'll take that under advisement." The phrase is code for "if you want this information, you better file a motion."

As discussed earlier, when a deponent refers to a document in a deposition that was not produced in discovery, ask for production before the deposition record is closed. Where the document is one that either 1) was the subject of a Rule 34 request or subpoena duces tecum or 2) should have been produced as a matter of mandatory disclosure, demand that the document be produced immediately during the deposition, mentioning sanctions for failure to comply. If such a document is demanded from you, however, do not produce the document until you have determined that it is within the scope of discovery or mandatory disclosure and is not privileged.

ii. Prior Inconsistent Methodology

Review previous deposition or trial testimony of opposing counsel's expert. You may identify cases in which the expert made assumptions or used methodology that is inconsistent with the assumptions and the methodology used in the current litigation. This inconsistency is not one that is easily rebutted, so impeach during the deposition.

Example: Consider the plaintiff expert's deposition in our hypothetical case:

Q: *Dr. Morris, when you provided your opinion on the plaintiff's past and future lost income, you needed to make some assumptions, correct?*
A: *That is true in virtually all economic analyses.*
Q: *That's right Doctor; and you made some assumptions in this case, didn't you?*
A: *I did.*
Q: *One assumption you made is that there would be a productivity increase in plaintiff's income over her lifetime employment.*
A: *That's right. I used a modest productivity increase figure of 2 percent.*
Q: *In other words, in addition to increases in income accounted for by inflation, and by promotions within the university pay scale, that she would also receive additional income because her productivity would increase?*
A: *That's right; in our faculty contract with the university, we have merit increases that are negotiated each year.*
Q: *That assumes, of course, that there are productivity or merit raises available at the university in the future, doesn't it?*
A: *Yes, it does.*
Q: *Dr. Morris, your report states that you've testified in only one other case in the past four years and that was on behalf of Techno-Associates, defendant in a claim that they had wrongfully fired an individual because of his ethnicity, is that right?*
A: *Yes.*
Q: *Techno-Associates was a consulting business run by a member of the Nita University Electrical Engineering Department—Dr. Dorothy Ellis, wasn't it?*
A: *Yes, I had known Dorothy for many years. She asked for my assistance in a nuisance litigation, and I helped her out.*
Q: *Nuisance litigation is your characterization, isn't it, Doctor?*
A: *Yes, but the man she fired was an incompetent.*
Q: *Nonetheless, your task was to assume discrimination and opine regarding the plaintiff's past and future income in that case, wasn't it?*
A: *Yes, it was.*
Q: *And in doing so, you had to make an assumption about whether the plaintiff's future income would increase due to an increase in productivity?*
A: *I did, and I assumed there would not be productivity increases.*
Q: *Why was that?*
A: *Because the plaintiff's work record, as I understood it after reading his deposition, was one in which he could not keep a job. He moved almost yearly, so I thought the assumption a fair one.*

This vignette demonstrates several issues. First, it is possible to search previous testimony and determine that the expert used a different set of assumptions about the same topic, in different litigations. This tends to show a positional bias on the expert's part. Second, and just as important, the vignette demonstrates that impeachment is not always effective. Here, the expert admits to different assumptions. That impeaches his testimony. However, he had a good reason for the difference in assumption and was able to rebut the impeachment.

Students of trial advocacy would say that the lawyer here asked the "one question too many," the "why" question. While deposing counsel got more information than she wanted, the fact is that even at trial, opposing counsel will inevitably ask the "why" question. The information does not go away, but as trial lawyers, we prefer it not come out during our examination—and perhaps we can overcome the problem with an effective cross. In a deposition, however, as has been discussed previously, you should virtually always ask the "why" question. At least we now know that if the witness testifies at trial, this impeachment won't work, and the few questions asked were worth the risk of bad answers. For the moment, Dr. Morris is not diminished as a witness, but there may be other matters in which his impact on the outcome of the case can be blunted. Just from this vignette, for example, Dr. Morris seems to be available for expert testimony only for friends and colleagues.

iii. Authoritative Texts

Disagreement between experts and authoritative materials are a potential source of impeachment. But this is another area of impeachment that is difficult to rehabilitate, and the party who has retained the expert will assume that you need to rebut it.[58] If you expect the case to resolve without a trial, then the deposition is a good place to point out to a later decision maker that the expert is at odds with the common wisdom on the subject. The alternative, or course, is to have your own expert discuss the discrepancy. He can testify about the proper position/methodology/theory and the ways in which the opposing expert ignored those standards. If your jurisdiction has adopted a version of Rule 803(18), you may publish the pertinent authoritative text.[59]

Assume in our hypothetical case that Dr. Sullivan, the defendant's expert, has opined that even if the plaintiff were discriminated against or defamed, the income loss is temporary. That is, that while in the short term her income will be lower than if she had received tenure at the university, her alternative income from another employer or self-employment will catch up over seven years with what she would have earned at the university. This "catch-up" theory results in a damages estimate in which lost income ends seven years after the plaintiff's being denied tenure.

58. In reviewing the opinions of an expert, always ask whether there are any controversial positions, theories, or methodologies, and if so, where the controversy has played out. Authoritative texts will be one such place where a different position, theory, or methodology than that used by an expert will exist, and the expert will have a reason why he has chosen to depart from a particular authority or orthodoxy.

59. The manner of publication is limited to reading by the witness who relied on the text. Many jurisdictions, while recognizing the common-law impeachment by authoritative text and incorporating its use in evidence codes, do not allow the affirmative use of the authoritative text to bolster the testimony of an expert witness.

The plaintiff's expert has assumed that there will be a lessening but residual loss of income for the plaintiff that will last for her normal work life of twenty-five years after her dismissal from the university.

Example: Plaintiff's attorney is examining defendant's economic expert.

Q: *Dr. Sullivan, in your estimate of Ms. Williams's future lost earnings, you assume that the effect of discrimination or defamation on her future earnings will decrease over time and disappear by seven years after her dismissal from the university.*

A: *Yes, I assume that given her talents and qualifications, she will obtain alternative employment and in a period of seven years catch up with what she would have earned at the university.*

Q: *Dr. Sullivan, in response to an interrogatory, defendant's counsel identified the seventh edition of* Forensic Economics, *by Professor Edith Howard of Nita Loyola University, as a volume that you consider to be authoritative, is that true?*

A: *It is, generally.*

[Deposing counsel then goes through the qualifications of the author of Forensic Economics *with the witness and gets the witness to agree about the author's expertise.]*

Q: *Showing you what has been marked as Exhibit 77, that is the seventh edition of Professor Howard's treatise, isn't it?*

A: *Yes.*

Q: *Directing your attention to Chapter 15, entitled Calculating Lost Income, page 247. Professor Howard discusses the issue of "catching up," correct?*

A: *Yes, she does.*

Q: *And doesn't it read: "With regard to a person who has lost income for some reason that does not compromise their actual abilities (e.g., discrimination in the work place versus a physically impairing injury), there is a dispute in the literature about the length of time it will take, if ever, for that person's income level to 'catch up' with what they would have earned, absent the interruption of income earning ability. The theory is a promising one, but needs further examination. To date, there is insufficient data to verify the theory, although published articles seem to suggest that the 'catch-up' phenomena, if it exists, takes in excess of ten to fifteen years for a person under the age of thirty." Have I read that correctly?*

A: *You have.*

Q: *And in a footnote, Professor Howard writes—please refer to Page 250, footnote 17—"There is one study, by Professor Scheiner of Corona College, of questionable methodology, that claims that in the professions, catch up can occur in as little as seven years. No other literature makes such a claim." Have I read the footnote completely?*

A: *You have, but I believe that the article by Professor Scheiner regarding catch up in the professions is persuasive, which is why I used that period in my estimate.*

Q: And that's the study that Professor Howard suggests is "of questionable methodology" and deserving of only footnote discussion?
A: According to her. I do not agree.

The vignette illustrates several things. First, when conducting the impeachment, be careful to read all portions of the treatise that are necessary for the quoted portion to be understood in context.[60] This is why deposing counsel also reads the footnote from several pages later in the treatise, allowing her to say that the expert relied on, in the terms of the treatise, "questionable methodology." The vignette also illustrates how the language of a profession can interfere with best advocacy. Economists call their studies "estimates." A lawyer recognizes that "estimate" is just a technical term with ambivalence built into it. To bolster your expert, refer to the exercise performed by the economist as a "calculation," which is much more certain and worthy of credence.

The above are just three examples of potential impeachment counsel can conduct an expert deposition. The downside, of course, of any impeachment at deposition is that it might educate the expert to be better prepared at a later testimony opportunity. None of these examples travel too far into the area of expertise. Leave quarrels with the expert's credibility based on the nuts and bolts of his opinion to your own expert witness.

11. What are the most important issues in defending the expert deposition?

Just as with a lay witness, defending the expert's deposition testimony begins with witness preparation. If the witness is well prepared, there will be precious little for deposing counsel to do but to be sure that the record of the expert's opinions, and the reasons for those opinions, is unambiguous. The well-crafted and complete Rule 26 report is a good starting place.

a. The Rule 26 Report or Disclosures

The rules for the Rule 26 report or disclosures have been discussed throughout this section. The contents of the Rule 26 report are precise and understandable. The rules for the Rule 26 disclosures for experts (usually party employees who do not provide expert testimony as a regular party of their duties) are less precise.

i. The Rule 26 Expert Report[61]

The rule, either by design or happenstance, may be less precise than might be required. It provides no guidance on information required for qualification except the ten years of publications and four years of provided testimony. Most parties provide

60. In a federal court, Rule 106, known as the Rule of Completeness, requires the context to be provided. It is better to provide the "completing information" than to have a later consumer of the deposition wonder if you were trying to hide something.
61. Fed. R. Civ. P. 26(a)(2)(B).

their expert's résumé as part of the report. That résumé typically tracks Rule 702's requirements for education, training, and experience. The rule is silent about the completeness of that information, and some lawyers err on the side of overinclusion of qualifications and make no effort to style the résumé to the testimony provided. The more effective expert report will highlight qualifications that are relevant to the opinions provided and limit qualifications that are of no matter. For example, a neurologist is going to testify about a traumatic brain injury (and there is no question that trauma caused the injury); she has a post-graduate fellowship in which the main focus was traumatic brain injury. The résumé should describe that fellowship, emphasizing the expert's experience that will be applied to the case at hand. If that same neurologist had a second post-graduate fellowship in organic causes of brain injury, that fellowship, while listed, need not be fully described in the résumé as it is of marginal relevance to the qualifications for the relevant opinion.

The same would be true for other elements of qualifications. Even with regard to the ten years of publications required by the rule, emphasize and explore the scholarship relevant to traumatic brain injury. Similarly, when addressing the neurologist's presentations to professional meetings, emphasize and bolster talks about trauma to the brain and de-emphasize or omit unrelated presentations (if they are not required by Rule 26). This résumé crafting highlights the expert's qualifications for the task at hand.

ii. The Rule 26 Disclosures[62]

The rules provide little guidance for these disclosures and fail to delineate when a party's employee crosses the line to one for whom a report, as opposed to disclosures, must be provided.[63] The content of the disclosures required by the rule is also uncertain. What is required is notice that the witness will provide an opinion within the ambit of Rules 702, 703, or 705; the subject matter of that opinion; and a summary of the facts and opinions on which the witness will base his testimony. The lack of precision in the rules has led many judges to include a clause in the case discovery order that states all expert witnesses who will be called to provide opinions at trial or in other proceedings must produce reports consistent with Rule 26(a)(2)(B). In other cases, the parties just stipulate to the same.

If no such discovery order or stipulation exists in your case, you may choose to provide a disclosure that is consistent with the full Rule 26 report. If not, you may face an expert deposition, with its attendant cost and expense, and the witness will have to be prepared to answer questions that would have been included in a full Rule 26 report—so it is far better and less expensive to prepare that report in the first place.

62. Fed. R. Civ. P. 26(a)(C).

63. It is conceivable that an employee can have an understanding with her employer that should there be litigation regarding a certain matter within the purview of her employment, it would be her duty to provide an expert opinion on such a matter, but that job requirement never became relevant in the past because there were no such litigations.

iii. The Report, Disclosures, and Witness Preparation

The first area for preparation of an expert witness, then, is the content—or lack thereof—of their report or disclosure. In addition to the following preparation for "reporting" experts, prepare "disclosure" experts to respond to questions that a report would answer. Prepare reporting experts to testify about the details of the information suggested by, but not covered in, the report, such as:

a) education, training, and experience (their content and relevance to the opinion at hand);

b) ten years of publications and older (their content and relevance to the current opinion);

c) four years of testimony and beyond (for who, its content, and its relevance to current testimony);

d) past expert engagements not leading to reports or testimony; and most importantly

e) the opinions, facts, assumptions, methodologies, and theories as well as everything considered, accepted, or rejected in reaching the conclusions about which testimony is given.

b. Manner and Style

We hope, in selecting your testifying expert, you have chosen a person who has the teaching skills to relate to ordinary folks (the jurors) and make the complex understandable. Focus on these qualities when preparing and "moot courting" your expert. Hone the witness's ability to relate in simple terms. Provide a mock audience of nonlawyers and nonexperts to whom the expert can deliver his projected testimony. Until all in the mock audience have understood the expert's testimony, the expert is not "ready for prime time."

Many experts testify for a living. As such, they have a way they like to proceed, a manner they like to adopt, and a style they feel is effective. Many of them are quite good at what they do, and we might be able to learn from them. That being said, you must take control of this witness. You make the tactical decision; you decide whether to reveal information not otherwise discovered; and you are in charge of the expert and his demeanor, at least while a fee is being paid.

Preparing the expert witness has the same basic outline as preparing a lay witness, with the addition of the following.

1) Provide the witness's previous writings (report, opposing expert report, authoritative texts relied on by both parties) before the preparation session begins.

2) Allow the witness the opportunity to express any concerns (substantive or otherwise).

3) Obtain additional information the expert gathered or received since you last communicated.

4) Find out if expert has spoken with anyone about the expert testimony (if so, who, when, what, and to what effect).

5) Review the expert's role in the litigation (the purpose of his testimony and its place in the case).

6) Go over your understanding of the witness's testimony and opinions.

7) Practice the deposition in question and answer form, discussing form of answers; length of answers; information to be provided and when; the importance of listening to the questions; the importance listening to objections and the dangers in the deposition signified by their being imposed.

8) Role-play the testimony. Video record and critique, if possible.

9) Explain that you will ask clarifying questions once opposing counsel has completed her questions. Discuss what questions you expect you will need to ask and practice answers.

10) *Daubert*-proof the expert's methodology, including discussing the nonligation uses of the methodology.

c. Defending the Deposition

Defending an expert's deposition differs from defending the lay deposition in very few, but important respects. Most parties reserve all objections except as to the form of the question until the deposition is offered as evidence in any proceeding, as in the lay deposition. In the case of an expert witness's deposition, whose opinion may be challenged as inadmissible on *Daubert/Kumho Tire/* Rule 702 grounds, the parties may also stipulate that objections to opinions or their bases are also preserved to when they are the subject of a motion in limine before the court.[64]

Therefore, be prepared to object to question forms that might lead to unclear or inaccurate deposition testimony, to instruct the witness not to answer on valid grounds of privilege,[65] and to seek a protective order.[66] There are, however, two unique matters for defending the expert deposition that deserve mention.

64. Many lawyers would argue that such a stipulation is unnecessary because an objection to the reliability of expert testimony is an objection to competence and relevance, which are not waived pursuant to Rule 32(d)(3)(A).

65. *See* FN 68 and related text.

66. In cases involving products liability or any other case involving unique processes with economic value, there is a good chance that there will have been protective orders granted or the need to seek a protective order pending the development of the deposition.

12. Are there special rules protecting information considered in preparation of the Rule 26 expert report?

Amendments to Rule 26(b) in 2010 put to rest an on-going debate on the extent to which a lawyer and an expert need disclose communications made before the preparation of the Rule 26 expert report. The issue was raised with the 1993 amendment to Rule 26(a)(2)(B)(ii) that the report must contain "the facts or data ***considered*** by the witness in forming them (opinions)." The language was read to include:

a) facts rejected by the expert;

b) theories and methodologies rejected by the expert;

c) draft reports (which has previously been routinely destroyed); and

d) conversations between the expert and counsel about the expert's opinions and the facts and theories that informed them.

Academic commentary and the virtual unanimous negative reaction of national, state, and local bar associations had experts keeping drafts of opinions intended only as working papers, and records of communications with counsel became open game for the deposition of the expert witness. The word "consulted" caused an uproar among the organized bar, and lawyers were genuinely unsure what was required of them, particularly in terms of preserving draft reports and making records of communications with their testifying expert witnesses. The 2010 amendments allow a limited attorney-expert privilege, providing some clarity on what attorney-expert communications must be disclosed.[67]

Rule 26(b)(4)(B) provides complete protection for draft reports, no matter what their form. Rule 26(b)(4)(C)(i)–(iii) limits discovery of communications between attorneys and expert witnesses to those that:

(i) relate to compensation for the expert's study or testimony;

(ii) identify facts or data that the party's attorney provided and that the expert considered in forming the opinions to be expressed; or

(iii) identify assumptions that the party's attorney provided and that the expert relied on in forming the opinions to be expressed.[68]

67. Sometimes inaccurately referred to as a privilege.

68. Consulting experts' communications retain full trial preparation materials protection with limited exceptions. It is also arguable that consulting experts are engaged to help the lawyer provide legal advice to a client, and therefore communications between the client and that consulting expert enjoy a derivative attorney-client privilege (*see* In Re Cendant Corp, Sec. Litig., 343 F.2d 658 (3rd Cir 2003) concurring opinion of Judge Garth).

Thus, communications exempted from protection are fair game for discovery; prepare the expert to respond to questions about such communications.

13. Is there one pitfall that faces all lawyers when questioning expert witnesses?

Given that the deposition may be last word from the witness in the litigation, we have urged throughout this book that you make sure that the last word of the witness contains the best words he has to offer. Once deposing counsel had completed her questions, take the opportunity to question witness. The expert witness's last best word might take the form of simplifying testimony he gave in the jargon of his profession into language a decision maker can understand—be it party, arbitrator, judge, or jurors.

We have noted that lawyers with a little bit of knowledge about a new area of learning may display that knowledge through newly learned vocabulary. The expert witness, of course, will use the vocabulary and special meaning of words[69] common to his profession. You must, therefore, act as the language police. When breaks are taken during the deposition—if discovery order allows you to speak with the expert[70]—remind him to explain his technical findings in simple language. If that communication is not allowed, the keep notes about words and phrases that need translation for the end users of the testimony. Once opposing counsel has completed the examination, ask questions that clarify the testimony, in language and otherwise, to preserve its value for the rest of the litigation.

69. For example, when a medical doctor says that he has to "rule out a heart attack," he means to communicate that he believes the patient had a heart attack and that he is going to test and treat for that condition, not the common parlance which would take those words to mean, whatever else is wrong with the patient, thank God its's not a heart attack because the doctor "had to rule it out."

70. As discussed earlier, some discovery orders prohibit a lawyer from communicating with a witness about the subject matter of the deposition once the deposition has begun, except when necessary to do so to claim a privilege or correct the record.

CONCLUSION

The one thing that we can offer in conclusion to this volume is that it will live up to its title for a relatively short time. The basic skills of taking and defending depositions will remain much the same, but the frequency of their occurrence, manner of taking, manner of recording, uses, their scope, and the ways for lawyers to best prepare for the event, and prepare their witnesses to participate, will certainly change. It is inevitable that the things that we litigate about will change, likely engendering new tactics and techniques. So too, it is a virtual certainty that technology will develop in some way to impact how lawyers can remain competent and even skilled in the use of this most important discovery device. We will be watching and mindful of things to come, and we encourage our readers to do the same.

www.ingramcontent.com/pod-product-compliance
Lightning Source LLC
LaVergne TN
LVHW080029210926
848481LV00011B/3136
9781601567918